THE COMPLETE WORKS OF ROBERT BROWNING, VOLUME IX

Photograph, by Julia Margaret Cameron, 1870

The Complete works of Robert Browning

With
Variant Readings & Annotations

EDITED BY ROMA A. KING, JR.

AND SUSAN CROWL

Volume IX

OHIO UNIVERSITY PRESS
ATHENS, OHIO
BAYLOR UNIVERSITY
WACO, TEXAS
1989

Library of Congress Cataloging-in-Publication Data

(Revised for vol. 9)

Browning, Robert, 1812-1889.
The complete works of Robert Browning, with variant
readings & annotations. Editorial board.

Vol. 7-   : general editor, Jack W. Herring.
Vol. 8-9 have imprint: Waco, Tex. : Baylor University;
Athens, Ohio : Ohio University Press.
Includes bibliographical references and indexes.
I. King, Roma A. (Roma Alvah), 1914-ed.   II. Herring,
Jack W., 1925-   .   III. Title.
PR4201.K5   1969   821'.8   68-18389
ISBN 0-8214-0381-8

CONTENTS

I CONTENTS

This edition of the works of Robert Browning is intended to be complete. It will comprise at least fourteen volumes and will contain:

1. The entire contents of the first editions of Browning's works, arranged in their chronological order of publication. (The poems included in *Dramatic Lyrics, Dramatic Romances and Lyrics*, and *Men and Women*, for example, appear in the order of their first publication rather than in the order in which Browning rearranged them for later publication.)

2. All prefaces and dedications which Browning is known to have written for his own works and for those of Elizabeth Barrett Browning.

3. The two prose essays that Browning is known to have published: the review of a book on Tasso, generally referred to as the "Essay on Chatterton," and the preface for a collection of letters supposed to have been written by Percy Bysshe Shelley, generally referred to as the "Essay on Shelley."

4. The front matter and the table of contents of each of the collected editions (1849, 1863, 1865, 1868, 1888-1889) which Browning himself saw through the press.

5. Poems published during Browning's lifetime but not collected by him.

6. Poems not published during Browning's lifetime which have come to light since his death.

7. John Forster's *Thomas Wentworth, Earl of Strafford,* to which Browning contributed significantly, though the precise extent of his contribution has not been determined.

8. Variants appearing in primary and secondary materials as defined in Section II below.

9. Textual emendations.

10. Informational and explanatory notes for each work.

II PRIMARY AND SECONDARY MATERIALS

Aside from a handful of uncollected short works, all of Browning's works but *Asolando* (1889) went through two or more editions during his lifetime. Except for *Pauline* (1833), *Strafford* (1837), and *Sordello* (1840), all the works published before 1849 were revised and corrected for the 1849 collection. *Strafford* and *Sordello* were revised and corrected for the collection of 1863, as were all the other works in that edition. Though no further poems were added in the collection of 1865, all the works were once again corrected and revised. The 1868 collection added a revised *Pauline* and *Dramatis Personae* (1864) to the other works, which were themselves again revised and corrected. The printing of the last edition of the *Poetical Works* over which Browning exercised control began in 1888, and the first eight volumes are dated thus on their title-pages. Volumes 9 through 16 of this first impression are dated 1889, and we have designated them 1889a to distinguish them from the second impression of all 16 volumes, which was begun and completed in 1889. Some of the earlier volumes of the first impression sold out almost immediately, and in preparation for a second impression, Browning revised and corrected the first ten volumes before he left for Italy in late August, 1889. The second impression, in which all sixteen volumes bear the date 1889 on their title-pages, consisted of a revised and corrected second impression of volumes 1-10, plus a second impression of volumes 11-16 altered by Browning in one instance. This impression we term 1889 (see section III below).

Existing manuscripts and editions are classified as either primary or secondary material. The primary materials include the following:

1. The manuscript of a work when such is known to exist.

2. Proof sheets, when known to exist, that contain authorial corrections and revisions.

3. The first and subsequent editions of a work that preserve evidence of Browning's intentions and were under his control.

4. The collected editions over which Browning exercised control:

1849—*Poems.* Two Volumes. London: Chapman and Hall.

1863—*The Poetical Works.* Three Volumes. London: Chapman and Hall.

1865—*The Poetical Works.* Three Volumes. London: Chapman and Hall.

1868—*The Poetical Works.* Six Volumes. London: Smith, Elder and Company. Reissued in stereotype impressions with varying title pages.

1888-1889—*The Poetical Works.* Sixteen Volumes. London: Smith, Elder and Company. Exists in numerous stereotype impressions, of which two are primary material:

1888-1889a—The first impression, in which volumes 1-8 are dated 1888 and volumes 9-16 are dated 1889.

1889—The corrected second impression of volumes 1-10 and a second impression of volumes 11-16 altered by Browning only as stated in section III below; all dated 1889 on the title pages.

5. The corrections in Browning's hand in the Dykes Campbell copy of 1888-1889a, and the manuscript list of corrections to that impression in the Brown University Library (see section III below).

Other materials (including some in the poet's handwriting) that affected the text are secondary. Examples are: the copy of the first edition of *Pauline* which contains annotations by Browning and John Stuart Mill; the copies of the first edition of *Paracelsus* which contain corrections in Browning's hand; a very early manuscript of *A Blot in the 'Scutcheon* which Browning presented to William Macready, but not the one from which the first edition was printed; informal lists of corrections that Browning included in letters to friends, such as the corrections to *Men and Women* he sent to D. G. Rossetti; Elizabeth Barrett's suggestions for revisions in *A Soul's Tragedy* and certain poems in *Dramatic Romances and Lyrics*; and the edition of *Strafford* by Emily Hickey for which Browning made suggestions.

The text and variant readings of this edition derive from collation of primary materials as defined above. Secondary materials are occasionally discussed in the notes and sometimes play a part when emendation is required.

III COPY-TEXT

The copy-text for this edition is Browning's final text: the first ten volumes of 1889 and the last six volumes of 1888-1889a, as described above. For this choice we offer the following explanation.

Manuscripts used as printer's copy for twenty of Browning's thirty-four book publications are known to exist; others may yet become available. These manuscripts, or, in their absence, the first editions of the works, might be considered as the most desirable copy-text. And this would be the case for an author who exercised little control over his text after the manuscript or first edition stage, or whose text clearly became corrupted in a succession of editions. To preserve the intention of such an author, one would have to choose an early text and emend it as evidence and judgment demanded.

With Browning, however, the situation is different, and our copy-text choice results from that difference. Throughout his life Browning continually revised his poetry. He did more than correct printer's errors and clarify previously intended meanings; his texts themselves remained fluid, subject to continuous alteration. As the manuscript which he submitted to his publisher was no doubt already a product of revision, so each subsequent edition under his control reflects the results of an ongoing process of creating, revising, and correcting. If we were to choose the manuscript (where extant) or first edition as copy-text, preserving Browning's intention would require extensive emendation to capture the additions, revisions, and alterations which Browning demonstrably made in later editions. By selecting Browning's final corrected text as our copy-text, emending it only to eliminate errors and the consequences of changing house-styling, we present his works in the form closest to that which he intended after years of revision and polishing.

But this is true only if Browning in fact exercised extensive control over the printing of his various editions. That he intended and attempted to do so is apparent in his comments and his practice. In 1855, demanding accuracy from the printers, he pointed out to his publisher Chapman, "I attach importance to the mere stops . . ." (DeVane and Knickerbocker, p. 83). There is evidence of his desire to control the details of his text as early as 1835, in the case of *Paracelsus*. The *Paracelsus* manuscript, now in the Forster and Dyce collection in the Victoria and Albert Museum Library, demonstrates a highly unconventional system of punctuation. Of particular note is Browning's unrestrained use of dashes, often in strings of two or three, instead of more precise or orthodox punctuation marks. It appears that this was done for its rhetorical effect. One sheet of Part 1 of the manuscript and all but the first and last sheets of Part 3 have had punctuation revised in pencil by someone other than Browning, perhaps J. Riggs, whose name appears three times in the margins of Part 3. In addition to these revisions, there are analogous punctuation revisions (in both pencil and ink) which appear to be in Browning's hand, and a few verbal alterations obviously in the poet's script.

A collation of the first edition (1835) with the manuscript reveals that a major restyling of punctuation was carried out before *Paracelsus* was published. However, the revisions incorporated into the first edition by no means slavishly follow the example set by the pencilled revisions of Parts 1 and 3 of the manuscript. Apparently the surviving manuscript was not used as printer's copy for the first edition. Browning may have submitted a second manuscript, or he may have revised extensively in proof. The printers may have carried out the revisions to punctuation, with or without the poet's point by point involvement. With the present evidence, we cannot be conclusive about the extent of Browning's control over the first edition of *Paracelsus*. It can be stated, however, in the light of the incompleteness of the pencilled revisions and the frequent lack of correspondence between the pencilled revisions and the lines as printed in 1835, that Browning himself may have been responsible for the punctuation of the first edition of *Paracelsus*. Certainly he was responsible for the frequent instances in the first and subsequent editions where the punctuation defies conventional rules, as in the following examples:

> What though
> It be so?—if indeed the strong desire
> Eclipse the aim in me?—if splendour break
>   (Part I, ll. 329-331)

> I surely loved them—that last night, at least,
> When we . . . gone! gone! the better: I am saved
>   (Part II, ll. 132-133)

> Of the body, even,)—what God is, what we are,
>   (Part V, l. 642, 1849 reading)

The manuscripts of *Colombe's Birthday* (1844) and *Christmas-Eve and Easter-Day* (1850) were followed very carefully in the printing of the first editions. There are slight indications of minor house-styling, such as the spellings *colour* and *honour* for the manuscripts' *color* and *honor*. But the unorthodox punctuation, used to indicate elocutionary and rhetorical subtleties as well as syntactical relationships, is carried over almost unaltered from the manuscripts to the first editions. Similar evidence of Browning's painstaking attention to the smallest details in the printing of his poems can be seen in the manuscript and proof sheets of *The Ring and the Book* (1868-69). These materials reveal an interesting and significant pattern. It appears that Browning wrote swiftly, giving primary attention to wording and less to punctuation, being satisfied to use dashes to indicate almost any break in thought, syntax, or rhythm. Later, in the proof sheets for Books 1-6 of the poem and in the manuscript itself for Books 7-12, he changed the dashes to more specific and purposeful punctuation marks. The revised punctuation is what was printed, for the most part, in the first edition of *The Ring and the Book*; what further revisions there are conform to Browning's practice, though hardly to standard rules. Clearly Browning was in control of nearly every aspect of the published form of his works, even to the "mere stops."

Of still greater importance in our choice of copy-text is the substantial evidence that Browning took similar care with his collected editions. Though he characterized his changes for later editions as trivial and few in number, collations reveal thousands of revisions and corrections in each successive text. *Paracelsus*, for example, was extensively revised for the 1849 *Poems*; it was again reworked for the *Poetical Works* of 1863. *Sordello*, omitted in 1849, reappeared in 1863 with 181 new lines and short marginal glosses; Browning admitted only that it was "corrected *throughout*" (DeVane and Knickerbocker, p. 157). The poems of *Men and Women* (1855) were altered in numerous small but meaningful ways for both the 1863 and 1865 editions of the *Poetical Works* (See Allan C. Dooley, "The Textual Significance of Robert Browning's 1865 *Poetical Works*," *PBSA* 71 [1977], 212-18). Professor Michael Hancher, editor of Browning's correspondence with his publisher, George Smith, has cited evidence of the poet's close supervision of the 1868 collected edition ("Browning and the *Poetical Works* of 1888-1889," *Browning Newsletter*, Spring, 1971, 25-27). Mrs. Orr, writing of the same period in Browning's life, reports his resentment of those who garbled his text by misplacing his stops (*Life*, pp. 357-58).

There is plentiful and irrefutable evidence that Browning controlled, in the same meticulous way, the text of his last collected edition, that which we term 1888-1889. Hancher has summarized the relevant information:

> The evidence is clear that Browning undertook the 1888-1889 edition of his *Poetical Works* intent on controlling even the smallest minutiae of the text. Though he at one time considered supplying biographical and explanatory notes to the poems, he finally decided against such a scheme, concluding, in his letter to Smith of 12 November 1887, "I am correcting them carefully, and *that* must suffice." On 13 January 1888, he wrote, regarding the six-volume edition of his collected works published in 1868 which was to serve as the printer's copy for the final edition: "I have thoroughly corrected the six volumes of the Works, and can let you have them at once." . . . Browning evidently kept a sharp eye on the production of all sixteen of the volumes, including those later volumes. . . . Browning returned proof for Volume 3 on 6 May 1888, commenting, "I have had, as usual, to congratulate myself on the scrupulous accuracy of the Printers"; on 31 December he returned proofs of Volume 11, "corrected carefully"; and he returned "the corrected Proofs of Vol. XV" on 1 May 1889.

Throughout his long career, then, Browning continuously revised and corrected his works. Furthermore, his publishers took care to follow his directions exactly, accepting his changes and incorporating them into each successive edition. This is not to say that no one else had any effect whatsoever on Browning's text: Elizabeth Barrett made suggestions for revisions to *A Soul's Tragedy* and *Dramatic Romances and Lyrics*. Browning accepted some suggestions and rejected others, and those which he accepted we regard as his own. Mrs. Orr reports that Browning sent proof sheets to Joseph Milsand, a friend in France, for corrections (*Life*, p. 265), and that Browning accepted suggestions from friends and readers for the corrections of errors in his printed works. In some of the editions, there are slight evidences of minor house-styling in capitalization and the indication of quotations. But the evidence of Browning's own careful attention to revisions and corrections in both his manuscripts and proof sheets assures us that other persons played only a very minor role in the development of his text. We conclude that the vast majority of the alterations in the texts listed above as Primary Materials are Browning's own, and that only Browning's final corrected text, the result of years of careful work by the poet himself, reflects his full intentions.

The first impression of Browning's final collected edition (i.e., 1888-1889a) is not in and of itself the poet's final corrected text. By the spring of 1889 some of the early volumes of the first impression were already sold out, and by mid-August it was evident that a new one would be required. About this time James Dykes Campbell, Honorary Secretary of the London Browning Society, was informed by Browning that he was making further corrections to be incorporated into the new impression. According to Dykes Campbell, Browning had corrected the first ten volumes and offered to transcribe the corrections into Dykes Campbell's copy of 1888-1889a before leaving for Italy. The volumes altered in Browning's hand are now in the British Library and contain on the flyleaf of Volume 1 Dykes Campbell's note explaining precisely what happened. Of course, Dykes Campbell's copy was not the one used by the printer for the second impression. Nevertheless, these changes are indisputably Browning's and are those which, according to his own statement, he proposed to make in the new impression. This set of corrections carries, therefore, great authority.

Equally authoritative is a second set of corrections, also in Browning's hand, for part of 1888-1889a. In the poet's possession at the time of his death, this handwritten list was included in lot 179 of Sotheby, Wilkinson, and Hodge's auction of Browning materials in 1913; it is today located in the Brown University Library. The list contains corrections only for Volumes 4-10 of 1888-1889a. We know that Browning, on 26 July 1889, had completed and sent to Smith "the corrections for Vol. III in readiness for whenever you need them." By the latter part of August, according to Dykes Campbell, the poet had finished corrections for Volumes 1-10. Browning left for Italy on 29 August. The condition of the Brown University list does not indicate that it was ever used by the printer. Thus we surmise that the Brown list (completing the corrections through volume 10) may be the poet's copy of another list sent to his publisher. Whatever the case, the actual documents used by the printers—a set of marked volumes or handwritten lists—are not known to exist. A possible exception is a marked copy of *Red Cotton Night-Cap Country* (now in the Berg Collection of the New York Public Library) which seems to have been used by printers. Further materials used in preparing Browning's final edition may yet appear.

The matter is complicated further because neither set of corrections of 1888-1889a corresponds exactly to each other nor to the 1889 second impression. Each set contains corrections the other omits, and in a few cases the sets present alternative corrections of the same error. Our study of the Dykes Campbell copy of 1888-1889a reveals fifteen discrepancies between its corrections and the 1889 second impression. The Brown University list, which contains far fewer corrections, varies from the second impression in thirteen instances. Though neither of these sets of corrections was used by the printers, both are authoritative; we consider them legitimate textual variants, and record them as such. The lists are, of course, useful when emendation of the copy-text is required.

The value of the Dykes Campbell copy of 1888-1889a and the Brown University list is not that they render Browning's text perfect. The corrections to 1888-1889a must have existed in at least one other, still more authoritative form: the documents which Browning sent to his publisher. That this is so is indicated by the presence of required corrections in the second impression which neither the Dykes Campbell copy nor the Brown University list calls for. The significance of the existing sets of corrections is that they clearly indicate two important points: Browning's direct and active interest in the preparation of a corrected second impression of his final collected edition; and, given the high degree of correspondence between the two sets of corrections and the affected lines of the second impression, the concern of the printers to follow the poet's directives.

The second impression of 1888-1889 incorporated most of Browning's corrections to the first ten volumes of the first impression. There is no evidence whatever that any corrections beyond those which Browning sent to his publisher in the summer of 1889 were ever made. We choose, therefore, the 1889 corrected second impression of volumes 1-10 as copy-text for the works in those volumes. Corrections to the first impression were achieved by cutting the affected letters of punctuation out of the stereotype plates and pressing or soldering in the correct pieces of type. The corrected plates were then used for many copies, without changing the date on the title pages (except, of course, in volumes 17 [*Asolando*] and 18 [*New Poems*], added to the set by the publishers in 1894 and 1914 respectively). External evidence from publishers' catalogues and the advertisements bound into some volumes of 1889 indicate that copies of this impression were produced as late as 1913, although the dates on the title pages of volumes 1-16 remained 1889. Extensive plate deterioration is characteristic of the later copies, and use of the Hinman collator on early and late examples of 1889 reveals that the inserted corrections were somewhat fragile, some of them having decayed or disappeared entirely as the plates aged. (See Allan C. Dooley, "Browning's *Poetical Works* of 1888-1889," *SBHC* 7:1 [1978], 43-69.)

We do not use as copy-text volumes 11-16 of 1889, because there is no present evidence indicating that Browning exercised substantial control over this part of the second impression of 1888-1889. We do know that he made one correction, which he requested in a letter to Smith quoted by Hancher:

I have just had pointed out to [me] that an error, I supposed corrected, still is to be found in the 13th Volume—(Aristophanes' Apology) page 143, line 9, where the word should be Opora—without an i. I should like it altered, if that may be possible.

This correction was indeed made in the second impression. Our collations of copies of volumes 11-16 of 1889a and 1889 show no other intentional changes. The later copies do show, however, extensive type batter, numerous scratches, and irregular inking. Therefore our copy-text for the works in the last six volumes of 1888-1889 is volumes 11-16 of 1888-1889a.

IV VARIANTS

In this edition we record, with a very few exceptions discussed below, all variants from the copy-text appearing in the manuscripts and in the editions under Browning's control. Our purpose in doing this is two-fold.

1. We enable the reader to reconstruct the text of a work as it stood at the various stages of its development.

2. We provide the materials necessary to an understanding of how Browning's growth and development as an artist are reflected in his successive revisions to his works.

As a consequence of this policy our variant listings inevitably contain some variants that were not created by Browning; printer's errors and readings that may result from house-styling will appear occasionally. But the evidence that Browning assumed responsibility for what was printed, and that he considered and used unorthodox punctuation as part of his meaning, is so persuasive that we must record even the smallest and oddest variants. The following examples, characteristic of Browning's revisions, illustrate the point:

Pauline, 1. 700:
    1833: I am prepared—I have made life my own—
    1868: I am prepared: I have made life my own.
"Evelyn Hope," 1. 41:
    1855: I have lived, I shall say, so much since then,
    1865: I have lived (I shall say) so much since then,
"Bishop Blougram's Apology," 1. 267:
    1855: That's the first cabin-comfort I secure—
    1865: That's the first-cabin comfort I secure:
The Ring and the Book, Book 11 ("Guido"), 1. 1064:
    1869: What if you give up boys' and girls' fools'-play
    1872: What if you give up boy and girl fools'-play
    1889a: What if you give up boy-and-girl-fools' play

We have concluded that Browning himself is nearly always responsible for such changes. But even if he only accepted these changes (rather than originating them), their effect on syntax, rhythm, and meaning is so significant that they must be recorded in our variant listings.

The only variants we do not record are those which strongly appear to result from systematic house-styling. For example, Browning nowhere indicated that he wished to use typography to influence meaning, and our inference is that any changes in line-spacing, depth of paragraph indentation, and the like, were the responsibility of the printers of the various editions, not the poet himself. House-styling was also very probably the cause of certain variants in the apparatus of Browning's plays, including variants in stage directions which involve a change only in manner of statement, such as *Enter Hampden* instead of *Hampden enters*; variants in the printing of stage directions, such as *Aside* instead of *aside*, or *[Aside.]* instead of *[Aside]*, or *[Strafford.]* instead of *[Strafford]*; variants in character designations, such as *Lady Carlisle* instead of *Car* or *Carlisle*. Browning also accepted current convention for indicating quotations (see section V below). Neither do we list changes in type face (except when used for emphasis), nor the presence or absence of a period at the end of the title of a work.

V ALTERATIONS TO THE COPY-TEXT

We have rearranged the sequence of works in the copy-text, so that they appear in the order of their first publication. This process involves the restoration to the original order of the poems included in *Dramatic Lyrics, Dramatic Romances and Lyrics*, and *Men and Women*. We realize, of course, that Browning himself was responsible for the rearrangement of these poems in the various collected editions; in his prefatory note for the 1888-1889 edition, however, he indicates that he desired a chronological presentation:

> The poems that follow are again, as before, printed in chronological order; but only so far as proves compatible with the prescribed size of each volume, which necessitates an occasional change in the distribution of its contents.

We would like both to indicate Browning's stated intentions about the placement of his poems and to present the poems in the order which suggests Browning's development as a poet. We have chosen, therefore, to present the poems in order of their first publication, with an indication in the notes as to their respective subsequent placement. We also include the tables of contents of the editions listed as Primary Materials above.

We have regularized or modernized the copy-text in the following minor ways:

1. We do not place a period at the end of the title of a work, though the copy-text does.

2. In some of Browning's editions, including the copy-text, the first word of each work is printed in capital letters. We have used the modern practice of capitalizing only the first letter.

3. The inconsistent use of both an ampersand and the word *and* has been regularized to the use of *and*.

4. We have eliminated the space between the two parts of a contraction; thus the copy-text's *it 's* is printed as *it's*, for example.

5. We uniformly place periods and commas within closing quotation marks.

6. We have employed throughout the modern practice of indicating quoted passages with quotation marks only at the beginning and end of the quotation. Throughout Browning's career, no matter which publisher or printer was handling his works, this matter was treated very inconsistently. In some of the poet's manuscripts and in most of his first editions, quotations are indicated by quotation marks only at the beginning and end. In the collected editions of 1863 and 1865, issued by Chapman and Hall, some quoted passages have quotation marks at the beginning of each line of the quotation, while others follow modern practice. In Smith, Elder's collected editions of 1868 and 1888-1889, quotation marks appear at the beginning of each line of a quotation. We have regularized and modernized what seems a matter of house-styling in both copy-text and variants.

The remaining way in which the copy-text is altered is emendation. Our policy is to emend the copy-text to eliminate apparent errors of either Browning or his printers. It is evident that Browning did make errors and overlook mistakes, as shown by the following example from "One Word More," the last poem in *Men and Women*. Stanza sixteen of the copy-text opens with the following lines:

What, there's nothing in the moon noteworthy?
Nay: for if that moon could love a mortal,
Use, to charm him (so to fit a fancy,
All her magic ('tis the old sweet mythos)
She . . .

Clearly the end punctuation in the third line is incorrect. A study of the various texts is illuminating. Following are the readings of the line in each of the editions for which Browning was responsible:

MS:	fancy)	1855:	fancy)	1865:	fancy)	1888:	fancy
P:	fancy)	1863:	fancy)	1868:	fancy)	1889:	fancy,

The omission of one parenthesis in 1888 was almost certainly a printer's error. Browning, in the Dykes Campbell copy corrections to 1888-1889a, missed or ignored the error. However, in the Brown University list of corrections, he indicated that *fancy* should be followed by a comma. This is the way the line appears in the corrected second impression of Volume 4, but the correction at best satisfies the demands of syntax only partially. Browning might have written the line:

> Use, to charm him, so to fit a fancy,

or, to maintain parallelism between the third and fourth lines:

> Use, to charm him (so to fit a fancy),

or he might simply have restored the earlier reading. Oversights of this nature demand emendation, and our choice would be to restore the punctuation of the manuscript through 1868. All of our emendations will be based, as far as possible, on the historical collation of the passage involved, the grammatical demands of the passage in context, and the poet's treatment of other similar passages. Fortunately, the multiple editions of most of the works provide the editor with ample textual evidence to make an informed and useful emendation.

All emendations to the copy-text are listed at the beginning of the Editorial Notes for each work. The variant listings for the copy-text also incorporate the emendations, which are preceded and followed there by the symbol indicating an editor's note.

VI APPARATUS

1. *Variants.* In presenting the variants from the copy-text, we list at the bottom of each page readings from the known manuscripts, proof sheets of the editions when we have located them, and the first and subsequent editions.

A variant is generally preceded and followed by a pickup and a drop word (example a). No note terminates with a punctuation mark unless the punctuation mark comes at the end of the line; if a variant drops or adds a punctuation mark, the next word is added (example b). If the normal pickup word has appeared previously in the same line, the note begins with the word preceding it. If the normal drop word appears subsequently in the line, the next word is added (example c). If a capitalized pickup word occurs within the line, it is accompanied by the preceding word (example d). No pickup or drop words, however, are used for any variant consisting of an internal change, for example a hyphen in a compounded word, an apostrophe, a tense change or a spelling change (example e). A change in capitalization within a line of poetry will be preceded by a pickup word, for which, within an entry containing other variants, the < > is suitable (example f). No drop word is used when the variant comes at the end of a line (example g). Examples from *Sordello* (all from Book 1 except c [2] which is from Book 4):

a. ^{611}| *1840:*but that appeared *1863:*but this appeared

b. variant at end of line: ^{109}| *1840:*intrigue:" *1863:* intrigue.

variant within line: ^{82}| *1840:*forests like *1863:*forests, like

c. ^{132}| *1840:*too sleeps; but 1863:too sleeps: but ^{77}| *1840:*that night by *1863:*that, night by night, *1888:*by night

d. ^{295}| *1840:*at Padua to repulse the *1863:*at Padua who repulsed the

e. ^{284}| *1840:*are *1863:*were

^{344}| *1840:*dying-day, *1863:*dying day,

f. capitalization change with no other variants: ^{741}| *1840:* retaining Will, *1863:*retaining will,

with other variants: ^{843}| *1840:*Was < > Him back! Why *1863:* Is < > back!" Why *1865:*him

g. ^{427}| *1840:*dregs; *1863:*dregs.

Each recorded variant will be assumed to be incorporated in the next edition if there is no indication otherwise. This rule applies even in cases where the only change occurs in 1888-1889, although it means that the variant note duplicates the copy-text. A variant listing, then, traces the history of a line and brings it forward to the point where it matches the copy-text.

An editor's note always refers to the single word or mark of punctuation immediately preceding or following the comment, unless otherwise specified.

In Browning's plays, all character designations which happen to occur in variant listings are standardized to the copy-text reading. In listing variants in the plays, we ignore character designations unless the designation comes within a numbered line. In such a case, the variant is treated as any other word, and can be used as a pickup or drop word. When a character designation is used as a pickup word, however, the rule excluding capitalized pickup words (except at the beginning of a line) does not apply, and we do not revert to the next earliest uncapitalized pickup word.

2. *Line numbers.* Poetic lines are numbered in the traditional manner, taking one complete poetic line as one unit of counting. In prose passages the unit of counting is the type line of this edition.

3. *Table of signs in variant listings.* We have avoided all symbols and signs used by Browning himself. The following is a table of the signs used in the variant notes:

§ . . . §	Editor's note
< >,	Words omitted
/	Line break
/ / , / / / , . . .	Line break plus one or more
	lines without internal variants

4. *Annotations.* In general principle, we have annotated proper names, phrases that function as proper names, and words or groups of words the full meaning of which requires factual, historical, or literary background. Thus we have attempted to hold interpretation to a minimum, although we realize that the act of selection itself is to some extent interpretative.

Notes, particularly on historical figures and events, tend to fullness and even to the tangential and unessential. As a result, some of the information provided may seem unnecessary to the scholar. On the other hand, it is not possible to assume that all who use this edition are fully equipped to assimilate unaided all of Browning's copious literary, historical, and mythological allusions. Thus we have directed our efforts toward a diverse audience.

TABLES

1. *Manuscripts.* We have located manuscripts for the following of Browning's works; the list is chronological.

Paracelsus
   Forster and Dyce Collection,
   Victoria and Albert Museum, London
Colombe's Birthday
   New York Public Library
Christmas-Eve and Easter-Day
   Forster and Dyce Collection,
   Victoria and Albert Museum, London
"Love Among the Ruins"
   Lowell Collection,
   Houghton Library, Harvard University
"The Twins"
   Pierpont Morgan Library, New York
"One Word More"
   Pierpont Morgan Library, New York
Dramatis Personae
   Pierpont Morgan Library, New York
The Ring and the Book
   British Library, London
Balaustion's Adventure
   Balliol College Library, Oxford

Prince Hohenstiel-Schwangau
  Balliol College Library, Oxford
Fifine at the Fair
  Balliol College Library, Oxford
Red Cotton Night-Cap Country
  Balliol College Library, Oxford
Aristophanes' Apology
  Balliol College Library, Oxford
The Inn Album
  Balliol College Library, Oxford
Of Pacchiarotto, and How He Worked in Distemper
  Balliol College Library, Oxford
The Agamemnon of Aeschylus
  Balliol College Library, Oxford
La Saisaiz and The Two Poets of Croisic
  Balliol College Library, Oxford
Dramatic Idylls
  Balliol College Library, Oxford
Dramatic Idylls, Second Series
  Balliol College Library, Oxford
Jocoseria
  Balliol College Library, Oxford
Ferishtah's Fancies
  Balliol College Library, Oxford
Parleyings With Certain People of Importance in Their Day
  Balliol College Library, Oxford
Asolando
  Pierpont Morgan Library, New York

We have been unable to locate manuscripts for the following works, and request that persons with information about any of them communicate with us.

Pauline	*The Return of the Druses*
Strafford	*A Blot in the 'Scutcheon*
Sordello	*Dramatic Romances and Lyrics*
Pippa Passes	*Luria*
King Victor and King Charles	*A Soul's Tragedy*
"Essay on Chatterton"	"Essay on Shelley"
Dramatic Lyrics	*Men and Women*

2. *Editions referred to in Volumes VII, VIII, and IX.* The following editions have been used in preparing the text and variants presented in this volume. The dates given below are used as symbols in the variant listings at the bottom of each page.

1868	*The Ring and the Book.* Volumes 1 and 2. Two Volumes. London: Smith, Elder and Company.

1868 *The Ring and the Book.* Volumes 1 and 2.
   Two Volumes. London: Smith, Elder and Company.

1869 *The Ring and the Book.* Volumes 3 and 4.
   Two Volumes, London: Smith, Elder and Company.

1872 *The Ring and the Book.*
   Four Volumes. London: Smith, Elder and Company.

1888 *The Poetical Works.*
   Volumes 1-8. London: Smith, Elder and Company.

1889a *The Poetical Works.*
   Volumes 9-16. London: Smith, Elder and Company.

1889 *The Poetical Works.*
   Sixteen Volumes. London: Smith, Elder and Company.
   (second impression of 1888-1889a)

   3. *Short titles and abbreviations.* The following short forms of reference have been used in notes for this edition:

Altick	*The Ring and the Book*, ed. Richard D. Altick. Baltimore: Penguin Books, 1971.
B	Browning
BrU	Browning's list of corrections located at Brown University
Cook	A.K. Cook. *A Commentary upon Browning's "The Ring and the Book."* Hamden, Connecticut: Archon Books, 1966 (first pub. 1920).
Corrigan	*Curious Annals: New Documents Relating to Browning's Roman Murder Story*, ed. and tr. Beatrice Corrigan. Toronto: University of Toronto Press, 1956.
DC	Browning's corrections in James Dykes Campbell's copy of 1888-1889a
DeVane, *Hbk.*	William Clyde DeVane. *A Browning Handbook.* New York: Appleton-Century Crofts, 1955.
DeVane and Knickerbocker	*New Letters of Robert Browning*, ed. William Clyde DeVane and Kenneth L. Knickerbocker. New Haven: Yale University Press, 1950.
EBB	Elizabeth Barrett Browning
Gest	*The Old Yellow Book*, ed. and tr. John Marshall Gest. Philadelphia: University of Pennsylvania Press, 1927.

Griffin and Minchin	W. H. Griffin and H. C. Minchin. *The Life of Robert Browning.* New York: Macmillan, 1910.
Heydon and Kelley	*Elizabeth Barrett Browning's Letters to Mrs. David Ogilvy,* ed. Peter N. Heydon and Philip Kelley. London: Murray, 1974.
Hodell	*The Old Yellow Book,* in facsimile, ed. and tr. Charles W. Hodell. Washington: The Carnegie Institution, 1908.
Hood, *Ltrs.*	*Letters of Robert Browning Collected by T. J. Wise,* ed. Thurman L. Hood. New Haven: Yale University Press, 1933.
Irvine and Honan	William Irvine and Park Honan. *The Book, the Ring, and the Poet.* New York: McGraw-Hill, 1974.
Landis and Freeman	*Letters of the Brownings to George Barrett,* ed. Paul Landis and Ronald E. Freeman. Urbana: University of Illinois Press, 1958.
Letters of EBB	*The Letters of Elizabeth Barrett Browning,* ed. F.G. Kenyon. 2 vols. New York: Macmillan, 1897.
New Poems	*New Poems by Robert Browning and Elizabeth Barrett Browning,* ed. F.G. Kenyon. New York: Macmillan, 1915.
Orr, *Hbk.*	Mrs. Sutherland Orr. *Handbook to the Works of Robert Browning.* New Edition. Revised and in Part Rewritten by F.G. Kenyon. New York: McMillan, 1915.
Orr, *Life*	Mrs. Sutherland Orr. *Life and Letters of Robert Browning.* Second Edition. London: Smith, Elder, 1891.
OYB	Browning's source for *The Ring and the Book,* in its original format.
OYB, E	*The Old Yellow Book,* ed. and tr. Charles W. Hodell. New York: E. P. Dutton (Everyman's Library), 1911.
P-C	*The Complete Works of Robert Browning,* ed. Charlotte Porter and Helen A. Clarke. New York: Thomas Y. Crowell, 1898.
RB-EBB, ed. Kintner	*The Letters of Robert Browning and Elizabeth Barrett Barrett,* 1845-1846, ed. Elvan Kintner. 2 vols. Cambridge, Mass.: The Belknap Press of Harvard University Press, 1969.

Story	William Wetmore Story. *Roba di Roma*. 2 vols. Boston and New York: Houghton, Mifflin and Co., 1887 (first published 1862).
Treves	Sir Frederick Treves. *The Country of The Ring and the Book*. London: Cassell and Company, 1913.
Vasari	Giorgio Vasari. *Lives of the Painters, Sculptors and Architects*, ed. and tr. A. B. Hinds. Intro. by William Gaunt. 4 vols. London: Dent (Everyman's Library), 1963.

Citations and quotations from the Bible refer to the King James Version.

Citations and quotations from Shakespeare refer to *The Riverside Shakespeare*, ed. G. B. Evans, et. al. Boston: Houghton Mifflin, 1974.

ACKNOWLEDGMENTS

For providing money and services which have made it possible for us to assemble the vast materials required for the preparation of this edition, the following institutions have our especial appreciation: the Ohio University Press, the Ohio University Library, the Ohio University English Department, the Baker Fund Awards Committee of Ohio University; Baylor University and the Armstrong Browning Library of Baylor University; the American Council of Learned Societies; the Kent State University Library and its Bibliographical and Textual Center, the Kent State University Research Council, the Kent State University English Department.

We also thank the following for making available to us materials under their care: the Armstrong Browning Library; the Balliol College Library, Oxford; the Beinecke Rare Book and Manuscript Library, Yale University, and its director Mr. H. W. Liebert; the British Library; the John Hay Library, Brown University; the Houghton Library, Harvard University; the Henry E. Huntington Library; the Department of Special Collections, Kent State University; Mr. E. V. Quinn; Mr. Philip Kelley; Mr. John Murray; the Library of the Victoria and Albert Museum.

We are also grateful to Professor Paul Murphy and Professor Bartolomeo Martello for their invaluable assistance in translation of Latin and Italian sources and passages, and to Susan E. Dooley for editorial labors on this volume.

The frontispiece is reproduced by permission of the Armstrong Browning Library of Baylor University.
Morgan Library.

THE RING AND THE BOOK
Books IX-XII

Edited by Roma A. King, Jr. and Susan Crowl

THE RING AND THE BOOK

THE RING AND THE BOOK

1868-9

IX

JURIS DOCTOR JOHANNES-BAPTISTA BOTTINIUS
FISCI ET REV. CAM. APOSTOL. ADVOCATUS

Had I God's leave, how I would alter things!
If I might read instead of print my speech,—
Ay, and enliven speech with many a flower
Refuses obstinate to blow in print,
As wildings planted in a prim parterre,—
This scurvy room were turned an immense hall;
Opposite, fifty judges in a row;
This side and that of me, for audience—Rome:
And, where yon window is, the Pope should hide—
Watch, curtained, but peep visibly enough.
A buzz of expectation! Through the crowd,
Jingling his chain and stumping with his staff,
Up comes an usher, louts him low, "The Court

₅ on line "As wildings planted in a prim parterre,—"
₁₀ on line "Watch, curtained, but peep visibly enough."

§ MS in Department of Manuscripts of the British Library. P1868, CP1868, P1869, CP1869,
Ed. 1868-69, 1872, 1888, 1889 §
1-16| MS:§ written in right hand margin, corrected, and then crossed out: copied on
separate sheet which is glued to back of MS page; referred to here as MS1 and MS2 §
2-6| MS:MS1:speech,—/ § next two lines inserted to side § Ay, and add flowers of speech
refuse in print/ To blow, like wildings in a prim parterre,—/ This little § crossed out and
replaced above by § sorry <> turned § inserted above line § MS2:speech,—/ Ay, and
enliven speech with many a flower/ Refuses obstinately blow in print/ As wildings barren §
crossed out § planted in a prim § last two words inserted above line § parterre,—/ This sorry
§ written over by § scurvy   1872:// <> print,   1889a:// Refuses obstinate to blow
7| MS1:Opposite,—fifty <> row;—   MS2:Opposite, fifty <> row;   8| MS:me
for audience,—Rome;   MS2:me, for audience—Rome   P1869:audience—Rome:
9| MS1:And where the window <> should watch   MS2:And, where yon window <>
should be—   1872:should hide—   10| MS1:Curtained—but somehow visible
the same! § last two words crossed out and replaced above by two words and period §
no less.   MS2:Watch, curtained, but yet visibly enough.   1872:but peep visibly
11-14| MS:§ inserted to right §   11| MS1:expectation:thro'
the   MS2:expectation! thro' § altered to § Thro'   CP1869:expectation!
Through   13| MS1:usher, bends him   MS2:usher, louts him

Requires the allocution of the Fisc!"
15 I rise, I bend, I look about me, pause
O'er the hushed multitude: I count—One, two—

Have ye seen, Judges, have ye, lights of law,—
When it may hap some painter, much in vogue
Throughout our city nutritive of arts,
20 Ye summon to a task shall test his worth,
To manufacture, as he knows and can,
A work may decorate a palace-wall,
Afford my lords their Holy Family,—
Hath it escaped the acumen of the Court
25 How such a painter sets himself to paint?
Suppose that Joseph, Mary and her Babe
A-journeying to Egypt, prove the piece:
Why, first he sedulously practiseth,
This painter,—girding loin and lighting lamp,—
30 On what may nourish eye, make facile hand;
Getteth him studies (styled by draughtsmen so)
From some assistant corpse of Jew or Turk
Or, haply, Molinist, he cuts and carves,—
This Luca or this Carlo or the like.
35 To him the bones their inmost secret yield,
Each notch and nodule signify their use:
On him the muscles turn, in triple tier,

---

¹⁵| MS1:rise, I bow, I § last two words inserted above line § look
around me,—calmly § written over illegible word; another word illegibly crossed
out above § pause § perhaps added in revision §   MS2:rise, I bend, I look about me, pause
¹⁶| MS1:hushed people; § word and semi-colon crossed out and replaced above by §
multitude <> two, three—   MS2:two—   ¹⁹| MS:of such § crossed out and replaced
above by word and comma § arts,   ²⁰| MS:task and § crossed out and replaced above by
§ shall   ²¹| MS:And manufacture   DC,BrU:To manufacture   1889:To manufacture
²⁶| MS:That § crossed out and replaced above by § Suppose   ²⁷| MS:to Egypt prompt
§ crossed out and replaced above by § prove   1872:to Egypt, prove   ²⁸| MS:practiseth
P1869:practiseth,   ³⁰| MS:hand,   P1869:hand;   ³¹| MS:studies, styled <> so,
P1869:studies (styled <> so)   ³²| MS:Of wh § last two words crossed out §
³⁴| MS:This Luca or this Carlo § last four words crossed out, replaced by illegibly crossed
out words above line, and then restored § <> like:—   P1869:like: 1872:like.
³⁶| MS:Their use each <> signify, § transposed to § Each <> signify their use,   1872:use:

And pleasantly entreat the entrusted man
"Familiarize thee with our play that lifts
⁴⁰ Thus, and thus lowers again, leg, arm and foot!"
—Ensuring due correctness in the nude.
Which done, is all done? Not a whit, ye know!·
He,—to art's surface rising from her depth,—
If some flax-polled soft-bearded sire be found,
⁴⁵ May simulate a Joseph, (happy chance!)—
Limneth exact each wrinkle of the brow,
Loseth no involution, cheek or chap,
Till lo, in black and white, the senior lives!
Is it a young and comely peasant-nurse
⁵⁰ That poseth? (be the phrase accorded me!)
Each feminine delight of florid lip,
Eyes brimming o'er and brow bowed down with love,
Marmoreal neck and bosom uberous,—
Glad on the paper in a trice they go
⁵⁵ To help his notion of the Mother-maid:
Methinks I see it, chalk a little stumped!
Yea and her babe—that flexure of soft limbs,
That budding face imbued with dewy sleep,
Contribute each an excellence to Christ.
⁶⁰ Nay, since he humbly lent companionship,
Even the poor ass, unpanniered and elate
Stands, perks an ear up, he a model too;
While clouted shoon, staff, scrip and water-gourd,—
Aught may betoken travel, heat and haste,—
⁶⁵ No jot nor tittle of these but in its turn
Ministers to perfection of the piece:
Till now, such piece before him, part by part,—
Such prelude ended,—pause our painter may,
Submit his fifty studies one by one,

---

^{38|} MS:§ crowded between 37-39 § man,— *1872:*man   ^{40|} MS:leg
arm *P1869:*leg, arm   ^{43|} MS:He, from § crossed out and replaced above by § to
*CP1869:*He,—to   ^{44|} MS:found *P1869:*soft-beared <> found, *CP1869:*soft-bearded
^{45|} MS:a Joseph,—happy chance!— *P1869:*a Joseph, (happy chance!) *1889a:*chance!)—
^{50|} MS:poseth,—be <> me,— *P1869:*poseth, (be <> me,) *CP1869:*poseth? (be <> me!)
^{55|} MS:the Mother-Maid— *P1869:*the Mother-Maid: *1872:*the Mother-maid:
^{65|} MS:No jot nor § last two words inserted above line § <> but ministers § crossed out § ,
in its § inserted above line § turn, *P1869:*turn   ^{66|} MS:piece,— *P1869:*piece:

⁷⁰   And in some sort boast "I have served my lords."

But what? And hath he painted once this while?
Or when ye cry "Produce the thing required,
Show us our picture shall rejoice its niche,
Thy Journey through the Desert done in oils!"—
⁷⁵   What, doth he fall to shuffling 'mid his sheets,
Fumbling for first this, then the other fact
Consigned to paper,—"studies," bear the term!—
And stretch a canvas, mix a pot of paste,
And fasten here a head and there a tail,
⁸⁰   (The ass hath one, my Judges!) so dove-tail
Or, rather, ass-tail in, piece sorrily out—
By bits of reproduction of the life—
The picture, the expected Family?
I trow not! do I miss with my conceit
⁸⁵   The mark, my lords?—not so my lords were served!
Rather your artist turns abrupt from these,
And preferably buries him and broods
(Quite away from aught vulgar and extern)
On the inner spectrum, filtered through the eye,
⁹⁰   His brain-deposit, bred of many a drop,
E pluribus unum: and the wiser he!
For in that brain,—their fancy sees at work,
Could my lords peep indulged,—results alone,
Not processes which nourish such results,
⁹⁵   Would they discover and appreciate,—life
Fed by digestion, not raw food itself,

---

⁷⁰⁻⁷¹| MS:§ marginal note that new ¶ begins §   ⁷²| MS:required— *P1869:*required,
⁷³| MS:niche *P1869:*niche,   ⁷⁵| MS:mid *1869:*'mid   ⁷⁶| MS:this then
*CP1869:*this, then   ⁷⁸| MS:§ followed by erasure, perhaps *up* §   ⁷⁹| MS:tail
*P1869:*tail,   ⁸¹| MS:in,—piece<>out *P1869:*in, piece<>out—   ⁸²| MS:life,—
*P1869:*life, *CP1869:*life—   ⁸⁴| MS:not—do *CP1869:*not! do   ⁸⁵| MS:lords?—
Not *P1869:*lords?—not   ⁸⁶| MS:turns from these, abrupt § altered to § turns abrupt
from these,   ⁸⁷| MS:broods, *CP1869:*broods   ⁸⁸| MS:Quite <> from all
§ crossed out and replaced above by § aught externe, *P1869:*extern, *CP1869:*(Quite
<> extern)   ⁹⁰| MS:The § written over by § His   ⁹²| MS:brain,
which § crossed out and replaced above by § their *P1869:*brain,—their
⁹³| MS:indulged, results *P1869:*indulged,—results   ⁹⁴| MS:nourish the result,
*1889a:*nourish such results,   ⁹⁵| MS:life, *P1869:*life   ⁹⁶| MS:digestion
not the § crossed out and replaced above by § raw *P1869:*digestion, not

No gobbets but smooth comfortable chyme
Secreted from each snapped-up crudity,—
Less distinct, part by part, but in the whole
100 Truer to the subject,—the main central truth
And soul o' the picture, would my Judges spy,—
Not those mere fragmentary studied facts
Which answer to the outward frame and flesh—
Not this nose, not that eyebrow, the other fact
105 Of man's staff, woman's stole or infant's clout,
But lo, a spirit-birth conceived of flesh,
Truth rare and real, not transcripts, fact and false.
The studies—for his pupils and himself!
The picture be for our eximious Rome
110 And—who knows?—satisfy its Governor,
Whose new wing to the villa he hath bought
(God give him joy of it) by Capena, soon
('Tis bruited) shall be glowing with the brush
Of who hath long surpassed the Florentine,
115 The Urbinate and . . . what if I dared add,
Even his master, yea the Cortonese,—
I mean the accomplished Ciro Ferri, Sirs!
(—Did not he die? I'll see before I print.)

End we exordium, Phœbus plucks my ear!
120 Thus then, just so and no whit otherwise,
Have I,—engaged as I were Ciro's self,
To paint a parallel, a Family,
The patriarch Pietro with his wise old wife
To boot (as if one introduced Saint Anne
125 By bold conjecture to complete the group)

101| MS:my Judges say,— *P1869:*my Judges spy,— 102| MS:Than
§ crossed out and replaced in margin by § Not 104| MS:eyebrow,
not the fact *P1869:*eyebrow, the other fact 106| MS:flesh— *P1869:*flesh,
107| MS:Truth § over illegible erasure § <> false § over perhaps *feat* §
115| MS:and . . what *1889a:*and . . . what 116| MS:master, him the
*P1869:*master, yea the 117| *P1869:*accomplished Ciro Ferri, sirs! *CP1869:*accomplished
Ciro Ferri, Sirs! 118| MS:§ crowded between 117-19 § —Did <> print. *P1869:*(—Did
<> print.) 118-19| MS:§ marginal note that new ¶ begins § 122| MS:a Family
*P1869:*a Family, 123| MS:patriarch Pietro—with *P1869:*patriarch Pietro with
124| MS:boot, (as *P1869:*boot (as 125| MS:group)— *P1869:*group)

9

And juvenile Pompilia with her babe,
Who, seeking safety in the wilderness,
Were all surprised by Herod, while outstretched
In sleep beneath a palm-tree by a spring,
130 And killed—the very circumstance I paint,
Moving the pity and terror of my lords—
Exactly so have I, a month at least,
Your Fiscal, made me cognizant of facts,
Searched out, pried into, pressed the meaning forth
135 Of every piece of evidence in point,
How bloody Herod slew these innocents,—
Until the glad result is gained, the group
Demonstrably presented in detail,
Their slumber and his onslaught,—like as life.
140 Yea and, availing me of help allowed
By law, discreet provision lest my lords
Be too much troubled by effrontery,—
The rack, law plies suspected crime withal—
(Law that hath listened while the lyrist sang
145 *"Lene tormentum ingenio admoves,"*
Gently thou joggest by a twinge the wit,
"Plerumque duro," else were slow to blab!)
Through this concession my full cup runs o'er:
The guilty owns his guilt without reserve.
150 Therefore by part and part I clutch my case
Which, in entirety now,—momentous task,—
My lords demand, so render them I must,
Since, one poor pleading more and I have done.
But shall I ply my papers, play my proofs,
155 Parade my studies, fifty in a row,
As though the Court were yet in pupilage,
Claimed not the artist's ultimate appeal?
Much rather let me soar the height prescribed
And, bowing low, proffer my picture's self!

126| MS:babe—   *P1869:*babe,   142| MS:effrontery,   *CP1869:*effrontery,—
143| MS:rack § followed by word illegibly crossed out and replaced above by § Law
*P1869:*rack, law   145| *P1869:*"Leno   *CP1869:*"Lene   147| MS:to budge!)—
*P1869:*to blab!)   148| MS:o'er—   *P1869:*o'er: 151| MS:Which in   *P1869:*Which,
in   152| MS:demand, and § crossed out and replaced above by § so
156| MS:pupilage   *1889a:*pupilage,   157| MS:And not   *1889a:*Claimed not

160 No more of proof, disproof,—such virtue was,
Such vice was never in Pompilia, now!
Far better say "Behold Pompilia!"—(for
I leave the family as unmanageable,
And stick to just one portrait, but life-size.)
165 Hath calumny imputed to the fair
A blemish, mole on cheek or wart on chin,
Much more, blind hidden horrors best unnamed?
Shall I descend to prove you, point by point,
Never was knock-knee known nor splay-foot found
170 In Phryne? (I must let the portrait go,
Content me with the model, I believe)—
—I prove this? An indignant sweep of hand,
Dash at and doing away with drapery,
And,—use your eyes, Athenians, smooth she smiles!
175 Or,—since my client can no longer smile,
And more appropriate instances abound,—
What is this Tale of Tarquin, how the slave
Was caught by him, preferred to Collatine?
Thou, even from thy corpse-clothes virginal,
180 Look'st the lie dead, Lucretia!
                              Thus at least
I, by the guidance of antiquity,
(Our one infallible guide) now operate,
Sure that the innocence thus shown is safe;
Sure, too, that, while I plead, the echoes cry
185 (Lend my weak voice thy trump, sonorous Fame!)
"Monstrosity the Phrynean shape shall mar,
Lucretia's soul comport with Tarquin's lie,

161| MS:Such evil § crossed out and replaced above by § vice was not § crossed out and
replaced above by § never   164| MS:life-size.)—   P1869:life-size.)   165| MS:the
Fair   P1869:the fair   170| MS:In Phryne?—(I < > go   P1869:In Phryne? (I < > go,
172| MS:I   P1869:—I   174| MS:Why § crossed out and replaced above by § And
178| MS:him preferred   P1869:him, preferred   179| MS:thy virginal corpse-clothes
§ transposed to § corpse-clothes virginal   P1869:virginal,   181| MS:antiquity
P1869:antiquity,   182| MS:(Our sole sure § last two words crossed out and replaced
above by two words § one infallible guide) forthwith would § last two words crossed out and
replaced above by § now   183| MS:innocency once § crossed out § shown is safe—
P1869:safe;   1889a:innocence thus shown   187| MS:soul with Tarquin's trick § written
over perhaps lie § comport § transposed to § soul comport with < > trick   P1869:with

When thistles grow on vines or thorns yield figs,
Or oblique sentence leave this judgment-seat!"

190   A great theme: may my strength be adequate!
For—paint Pompilia, dares my feebleness?
How did I unaware engage so much
—Find myself undertaking to produce
A faultless nature in a flawless form?

195   What's here? Oh, turn aside nor dare the blaze
Of such a crown, such constellation, say,
As jewels here thy front, Humanity!
First, infancy, pellucid as a pearl;
Then childhood—stone which, dew-drop at the first,

200   (An old conjecture) sucks, by dint of gaze,
Blue from the sky and turns to sapphire so:
Yet both these gems eclipsed by, last and best,
Womanliness and wifehood opaline,
Its milk-white pallor,—chastity,—suffused

205   With here and there a tint and hint of flame,—
Desire,—the lapidary loves to find.
Such jewels bind conspicuously thy brow,
Pompilia, infant, child, maid, woman, wife—
Crown the ideal in our earth at last!

210   What should a faculty like mine do here?
Close eyes, or else, the rashlier hurry hand!

Which is to say,—lose no time but begin!
Sermocinando ne declamem, Sirs,
Ultra clepsydram, as our preachers smile,

215   Lest I exceed my hour-glass. Whereupon,

Tarquin's lie,   189| MS:sentence leaves this Judgment-seat!"   *P1869:*sentence leave this
judgment-seat!"   189–90| MS:§ marginal note that new ¶ begins §   190| MS:theme,
—may *P1869:*theme: may   196| MS:say *P1869:*say,   198| MS:First infancy <>
pearl— *P1869:*First, infancy <> pearl;   200| MS:sucks by <> gaze *P1869:*sucks, by
<> gaze,   201| MS:the heavens and <> so,— *P1869:*the sky and <> so:
205| MS:of flame § written over *fire* § ,—   209| MS:the Ideal *P1869:*the ideal
211| MS:or else, § word and comma inserted above line §   211–12| MS:§ marginal note
that new ¶ begins § *1889a:*§ no ¶ § *1889:*§ no ¶; emended to restore ¶; see Editorial
Notes §   212| MS:no Time but begin— *P1869:*no time but begin!   213|
*P1869:*sirs, *CP1869:declamem*, Sirs,   214| MS:as the sage man § last two words
crossed out and replaced above by § preachers says § altered to § say, *P1869:*as our preachers

As Flaccus prompts, I dare the epic plunge—
Begin at once with marriage, up till when
Little or nothing would arrest your love,
In the easeful life o' the lady; lamb and lamb,
220 How do they differ? Know one, you know all
Manners of maidenhood: mere maiden she.
And since all lambs are like in more than fleece,
Prepare to find that, lamb-like, she too frisks—
O' the weaker sex, my lords, the weaker sex!
225 To whom, the Teian teaches us, for gift,
Not strength,—man's dower,—but beauty, nature gave,
"Beauty in lieu of spears, in lieu of shields!"
And what is beauty's sure concomitant,
Nay, intimate essential character,
230 But melting wiles, deliciousest deceits,
The whole redoubted armoury of love?
Therefore of vernal pranks, dishevellings
O' the hair of youth that dances April in,
And easily-imagined Hebe-slips
235 O'er sward which May makes over-smooth for foot—
These shall we pry into?—or wiselier wink,
Though numerous and dear they may have been?

For lo, advancing Hymen and his pomp!
Discedunt nunc amores, loves, farewell!
240 *Maneat amor*, let love, the sole, remain!
Farewell to dewiness and prime of life!
Remains the rough determined day: dance done,
To work, with plough and harrow! What comes next?

---

*1889a:*preachers smile,   216| MS:prompts, we § crossed out and replaced above by § I
217| MS:marriage: up   *P1869:*marriage, up   219| MS:of § altered to § o' the lady;
girl § crossed out and replaced above by § lamb and girl § crossed out § lamb,
221| MS:she—   *P1869:*she.   223| MS:that, like lamb, she § transposed to § that, lamb-
like, she   224| MS:sex—   *P1869:*sex!   235| MS:over smooth   *P1869:*over-smooth
236| MS:wink.—   *P1869:*wink,   237| MS:have proven § crossed out and replaced above
by § been.   *P1869:*been?   237-38| MS:§ marginal note that new ¶ begins §   *1889a:*§ no
¶ §   *1889:*§ no ¶; emended to restore ¶; see Editorial Notes §   239| MS:*amores*—
§ there follows an illegible erasure § Loves   *P1869:amores*, loves   240| MS:*amor*—let
P1869:amor, let   241| MS:Farewell the § crossed out and replaced above by § to

13

'Tis Guido henceforth guides Pompilia's step,
245 Cries "No more friskings o'er the foodful glebe,
Else, 'ware the whip!" Accordingly,—first crack
O' the thong,—we hear that his young wife was barred,
Cohibita fuit, from the old free life,
Vitam liberiorem ducere.
250 Demur we? Nowise: heifer brave the hind?
We seek not there should lapse the natural law,
The proper piety to lord and king
And husband: let the heifer bear the yoke!
Only, I crave he cast not patience off,
255 This hind; for deem you she endures the whip,
Nor winces at the goad, nay, restive, kicks?
What if the adversary's charge be just,
And all untowardly she pursue her way
With groan and grunt, though hind strike ne'er so hard?
260 If petulant remonstrance made appeal,
Unseasonable, o'erprotracted,—if
Importunate challenge taxed the public ear
When silence more decorously had served
For protestation,—if Pompilian plaint
265 Wrought but to aggravate Guidonian ire,—
Why, such mishaps, ungainly though they be,
Ever companion change, are incident
To altered modes and novelty of life:
The philosophic mind expects no less,
270 Smilingly knows and names the crisis, sits
Waiting till old things go and new arrive.
Therefore, I hold a husband but inept

244| MS:step— *P1869:*step, 245| MS:oer *P1869:*o'er 250| MS:Demur I
*P1869:*Demur we 251| MS:I seek not § followed by illegible erasure § to see § last
two words crossed out and replaced above by two words § there should *P1869:*We seek
252| MS:king, *P1869:*king 253| MS:The husband *P1869:*And husband
254| MS:Only I *P1869:*Only, I 255| MS:hind, for *P1869:*hind; for
256| MS:nay—restive *P1869:*nay, restive 257| MS:just *CP1869:*just,
258| MS:And, all <> ways *P1869:*way *CP1869:*And all 259| MS:grunt, though
hind § last two words inserted above line § strike husband § crossed out § <> hard?—
*P1869:*hard? 265| MS:aggravate her § crossed out; followed by word illegibly crossed
out § chagrin § crossed out; last three words replaced above by two words, comma and
dash § Guidonian ire,— 271| MS:go and § crossed out and then restored § new things
come § last two words crossed out and replaced above by § arrive. 272| MS:husband for

Who turns impatient at such transit-time,
As if this running from the rod would last!

275 Since, even while I speak, the end is reached:
Success awaits the soon-disheartened man.
The parents turn their backs and leave the house,
The wife may wail but none shall intervene:
He hath attained his object, groom and bride
280 Partake the nuptial bower no soul can see,
Old things are passed and all again is new,
Over and gone the obstacles to peace,
Novorum—tenderly the Mantuan turns
The expression, some such purpose in his eye—
285 *Nascitur ordo!* Every storm is laid,
And forth from plain each pleasant herb may peep,
Each bloom of wifehood in abeyance late:
(Confer a passage in the Canticles.)

But what if, as 'tis wont with plant and wife,
290 Flowers,—after a suppression to good end,
Still, when they do spring forth,—sprout here, spread there,
Anywhere likelier than beneath the foot
O' the lawful good-man gardener of the ground?
He dug and dibbled, sowed and watered,—still
295 'Tis a chance wayfarer shall pluck the increase.
Just so, respecting persons not too much,
The lady, foes allege, put forth each charm
And proper floweret of feminity

---

§ crossed out and replaced above by § but   273| MS:transit-time—   *P1869:*transit-time,
274-75| MS:§ marginal note that new ¶ begins §   275| *P1869:*reached   *1872:*reached:
276| MS:man, *1872:*man.   278| MS:intervene, *1872:*intervene:
279| MS:object,—groom   *P1869:*object, groom   280| MS:soul to see—   *P1869:*see,
*1872:*soul can see,   281| MS:all is new again, § transposed to § all again is new,
282| MS:peace *P1869:*peace,   284| MS:eye, *P1869:*eye—   287| MS:late—
*P1869:*late: 288-89| MS:§ marginal note that new ¶ begins § *1889a:*§ no ¶ § *1889:*§ no
¶; emended to restore ¶; see Editorial Notes §   289| MS:as the way § last two words
crossed out and replaced above by two words § 'tis wont with flower § crossed out and
replaced above by § plant   293| MS:Of § altered to § O' the lawful lord and § last two
words crossed out and replaced above by § good-man   295| MS:wayfarer will §
overwritten by § shall <> the prize § crossed out and replaced above by § increase.
297| MS:lady, 'tis § crossed out and replaced above by § foes alleged § altered to § allege

15

To whosoever had a nose to smell
300 Or breast to deck: what if the charge be true?
The fault were graver had she looked with choice,
Fastidiously appointed who should grasp,
Who, in the whole town, go without the prize!
To nobody she destined donative,
305 But, first come was first served, the accuser saith.
Put case her sort of . . . in this kind . . . escapes
Were many and oft and indiscriminate—
Impute ye as the action were prepense,
The gift particular, arguing malice so?
310 Which butterfly of the wide air shall brag
"I was preferred to Guido"—when 'tis clear
The cup, he quaffs at, lay with olent breast
Open to gnat, midge, bee and moth as well?
One chalice entertained the company;
315 And if its peevish lord object the more,
Mistake, misname such bounty in a wife,
Haste we to advertise him—charm of cheek,
Lustre of eye, allowance of the lip,
All womanly components in a spouse,
320 These are no household-bread each stranger's bite
Leaves by so much diminished for the mouth
O' the master of the house at supper-time:
But rather like a lump of spice they lie,

301| MS:The case § crossed out and replaced above by § fault were
altered § crossed out and replaced above by § graver   303| MS:the grace
§ crossed out §   304| MS:To § inserted in margin § Nobody she § inserted
above line § destined to such § last two words crossed out §   *P1869:*To
nobody   305| MS:But, § word and comma inserted in margin § First § altered
to § first <> served, saith the accuser: § transposed to § the accuser saith:
§ followed by illegibly crossed out word in margin §   *P1869:*saith
*1872:*saith.   306| MS:of . . in <> kind . . escapes *1889a:*of . . . in <>
kind . . . escapes   307| MS:often § altered to § oft   308| MS:Impute
not § crossed out and replaced above by § ye   310| MS:Which denizen §
crossed out and replaced above by § butterfly   314| MS:company,
*CP1869:*company;   315| MS:if a § altered to § its   316| MS:misname the
liberal § last two words crossed out and replaced above by § such bounty here,
§ word and comma crossed out and replaced above by three words and comma § in a
wife,   318| MS:Lustre of the § crossed out §   319| MS:a wife § crossed out §
320| MS:household bread *CP1869:*household-bread   322| MS:O' the
good man § last two words crossed out and replaced above by § master <>
supper-time,— *P1869:*supper-time: 323| MS:liken § altered to § like

16

Morsel of myrrh, which scents the neighbourhood
325   Yet greets its lord no lighter by a grain.

Nay, even so, he shall be satisfied!
Concede we there was reason in his wrong,
Grant we his grievance and content the man!
For lo, Pompilia, she submits herself;
330   Ere three revolving years have crowned their course,
Off and away she puts this same reproach
Of lavish bounty, inconsiderate gift
O' the sweets of wifehood stored to other ends:
No longer shall he blame "She none excludes,"
335   But substitute "She laudably sees all,
Searches the best out and selects the same."
For who is here, long sought and latest found,
Waiting his turn unmoved amid the whirl,
"*Constans in levitate*,"—Ha, my lords?
340   Calm in his levity,—indulge the quip!—
Since 'tis a levite bears the bell away,
Parades him henceforth as Pompilia's choice.
'Tis no ignoble object, husband! Doubt'st?
When here comes tripping Flaccus with his phrase
345   "Trust me, no miscreant singled from the mob,
Crede non illum tibi de scelesta
Plebe delectum," but a man of mark,
A priest, dost hear? Why then, submit thyself!
Priest, ay and very phœnix of such fowl,
350   Well-born, of culture, young and vigorous,
Comely too, since precise the precept points—
On the selected levite be there found
Nor mole nor scar nor blemish, lest the mind
Come all uncandid through the thwarting flesh!

325-26| MS:§ marginal note that new ¶ begins §   326| MS:so,—he *P1869*:so,
he   328| MS:man! *P1869*:man!   329| MS:lo, Pompilia—she <>
herself— *P1869*:lo, Pompilia, she <> herself;   333| MS:Of § altered to §
O' <> ends,— *P1869*:ends: 336| MS:same:"— *P1869*:same."
337| MS:is there § crossed out and replaced above by § here   339| MS:*levitate*,
—indulge a quip!— § last three words and punctuation crossed out §
340| MS:quip,— *CP1869*:quip!—   341| MS:bears away the bell § transposed to §
bears the bell away *P1869*:away,   353| MS:blemish lest *P1869*:blemish, lest
354| MS:Come out § crossed out and replaced above by § all <> flesh. *P1869*:flesh!

355 Was not the son of Jesse ruddy, sleek,
Pleasant to look on, pleasant every way?
Since well he smote the harp and sweetly sang,
And danced till Abigail came out to see,
And seeing smiled and smiling ministered
360 The raisin-cluster and the cake of figs,
With ready meal refreshed the gifted youth,
Till Nabal, who was absent shearing sheep,
Felt heart sink, took to bed (discreetly done—
They might have been beforehand with him else)
365 And died—would Guido have behaved as well!
But ah, the faith of early days is gone,
Heu prisca fides! Nothing died in him
Save courtesy, good sense and proper trust,
Which, when they ebb from souls they should o'erflow,
370 Discover stub, weed, sludge and ugliness.
(The Pope, we know, is Neapolitan
And relishes a sea-side simile.)

Deserted by each charitable wave,
Guido, left high and dry, shows jealous now!
375 Jealous avouched, paraded: tax the fool
With any peccadillo, he responds
"Truly I beat my wife through jealousy,
Imprisoned her and punished otherwise,
Being jealous: now would threaten, sword in hand,
380 Now manage to mix poison in her sight,
And so forth: jealously I dealt, in fine."
Concede thus much, and what remains to prove?

355| MS:sleek *P1869:*sleek,   356| MS:way— *P1869:*way?   357| MS:sang
*P1869:*sang,   358| MS:And deftly § crossed out §   360| MS:§ crowded between
359-61 §   361| MS:The ready meal, refreshed *P1869:*With ready meal refreshed
365| MS:would Guido but § crossed out and replaced above by § had behaved *1872:*would
Guido have behaved   368| MS:and graceful § crossed out and replaced above by §
proper trust— *P1869:*trust,   370-73| MS:ugliness./ § marginal note that new ¶ begins §
Deserted *P1869:*ugliness./ § ¶ § (The Pope, you know, is Neapolitan/ And relishes a
sea-side simile.) Deserted *CP1869:*§ ¶ replaced to beginning of line 373 § *1869:*§ ¶ omitted
both at line 371 and at line 373 § *1889a:*The Pope, we know *1889:*§ no ¶ between lines
372-73; emended to restore ¶; see Editorial Notes §   375| MS:the fool § written
over *man* §   376| MS:peccadillo he *P1869:*peccadillo, he   380| MS:Now
silently § crossed out and replaced above by two words § manage to   382| MS:Concede

Have I to teach my masters what effect
Hath jealousy, and how, befooling men,
385 It makes false true, abuses eye and ear,
Turns mere mist adamantine, loads with sound
Silence, and into void and vacancy
Crowds a whole phalanx of conspiring foes?
Therefore who owns "I watched with jealousy
390 My wife," adds "for no reason in the world!"
What need that, thus proved madman, he remark
"The thing I thought a serpent proved an eel"?—
Perchance the right Comacchian, six foot length,
And not an inch too long for that rare pie
395 (Master Arcangeli has heard of such)
Whose succulence makes fasting bearable;
Meant to regale some moody splenetic
Who, pleasing to mistake the donor's gift,
Spying I know not what Lernæan snake
400 I' the luscious Lenten creature, stamps forsooth
The dainty in the dust.

                    Enough! Prepare,
Such lunes announced, for downright lunacy!
Insanit homo, threat succeeds to threat,
And blow redoubles blow,—his wife, the block.

---

the fact and   *1872:*Concede thus much, and   384| MS:jealousy and   *1872:*jealousy,
and   386| MS:§ word illegibly crossed out and replaced above by § Turns the mist
*1872:*Turns mere mist   390| MS:wife" adds   *1872:*wife," adds   391| MS:What
§ over illegible word § need that who says "madman" should remark   *1872:*says "Madman"
*1889a:*that, thus proved madman, he remark   392| MS:thing he thought <> eel?"—
*1872:*thing I thought   *1889a:*eel"?—   393| MS:—Perchance   *P1869:*Perchance
394-96| MS:And § inserted in margin § Not an § inserted above § <> that same dainty § last
two words crossed out and replaced above by § illustrious § crossed out and replaced, still
above, by § same pie/ <> bearable,   *P1869:*And not <> / (Master Arcangeli has heard of
such)/   *1869:*bearable;   *1889a:*that rare pie   397-99| MS:regale the § crossed out and
replaced above by § some <> / Who spies—I   *P1869:*/ Who pleases to mistake the donor's
gift,/ And spies   *1872:*/Who, pleasing to <> / Spying I   401| MS:dust. § note
that new ¶ begins § Enough   402| MS:My judges § last two words crossed out §
His lunes announced, and § crossed out and replaced above by word and syllable § for
downright the § crossed out §   *1872:*Such lunes announced   403| MS:*homo,—*
threat succeeds   *P1869:homo,* threat succeeds   404| MS:blow redoubles blow: 'tis to
blow: but in § last seven words crossed out; then first two restored § his wife the § over

19

405 But, if a block, shall not she jar the hand
That buffets her? The injurious idle stone
Rebounds and hits the head of him who flung.
Causeless rage breeds, i' the wife now, rageful cause,
Tyranny wakes rebellion from its sleep.
410 Rebellion, say I?—rather, self-defence,
Laudable wish to live and see good days,
Pricks our Pompilia now to fly the fool
By any means, at any price,—nay, more,
Nay, most of all, i' the very interest
415 O' the fool that, baffled of his blind desire
At any price, were truliest victor so.
Shall he effect his crime and lose his soul?
No, dictates duty to a loving wife!
Far better that the unconsummate blow,
420 Adroitly baulked by her, should back again,
Correctively admonish his own pate!

Crime then,—the Court is with me?—she must crush:
How crush it? By all efficacious means;
And these,—why, what in woman should they be?
425 "With horns the bull, with teeth the lion fights;
To woman," quoth the lyrist quoted late,
"Nor teeth, nor horns, but beauty, Nature gave."

---

illegible word §   *P1869:*redoubles blow,—his wife, the   407| MS:and breaks § crossed
out and replaced above by § fits the <> flung: *P1869:*flung.   *1872:*and hits the
409| MS:Tyranny calls § crossed out and replaced above by § brings § crossed out and
replaced, still above, by § wakes rebellion into life § last two words crossed out § <> sleep,
*P1869:*sleep.   411| MS:Praiseworthy § crossed out and replaced above by § Laudable
412| MS:Impels § crossed out and replaced above by § Pricks our Pompilia on to fly the
foe   *1872:*our Pompilia now to fly the fool   413| MS:more,—   *P1869:*more,
414| MS:in § altered to § i' the true § crossed out and replaced above by § very
415| MS:Of the foe that   *1872:*O' the fool that   416| MS:price, is truliest <> so—
*P1869:*so.   *1872:*price, were truliest   417| MS:Let him § last two words crossed
out and replaced above by § Shall he   418| MS:Who dictates such a duty to a wife?
*P1869:*What dictates duty to a loving wife?   *CP1869:*No,—dictates <> wife.   *1869:*No,
dictates <> wife!   419| MS:blow   *CP1869:*blow,   420| MS:baulked, I say, should
<> again   *P1869:*again,   *CP1869:*baulked by her, should   421| MS:Correctively
rebound to § last two words crossed out and replaced above by § admonish
421-22| MS:§ marginal note that new ¶ begins §   422| MS:me?—we must crush;
*P1869:*me?—she must   *1889a:*crush: 425| MS:fights,   *1889a:*fights;   426| MS:To
woman" quoth   *P1869:*To woman," quoth   427| MS:nature gave!"   *P1869:*beauty,

20

Pretty i' the Pagan! Who dares blame the use
Of armoury thus allowed for natural,—
430 Exclaim against a seeming-dubious play
O' the sole permitted weapon, spear and shield
Alike, resorted to i' the circumstance
By poor Pompilia? Grant she somewhat plied
Arts that allure, the magic nod and wink,
435 The witchery of gesture, spell of word,
Whereby the likelier to enlist this friend,
Yet stranger, as a champion on her side?
Such man, being but mere man, ('twas all she knew),
Must be made sure by beauty's silken bond,
440 The weakness that subdues the strong, and bows
Wisdom alike and folly. Grant the tale
O' the husband, which is false, were proved and true
To the letter—or the letters, I should say,
Abominations he professed to find
445 And fix upon Pompilia and the priest,—
Allow them hers—for though she could not write,
In early days of Eve-like innocence
That plucked no apple from the knowledge-tree,
Yet, at the Serpent's word, Eve plucks and eats
450 And knows—especially how to read and write:
And so Pompilia,—as the move o' the maw,

Nature   *1889a:*gave. § emended to § gave." § see Editorial Notes §   428| MS:the pagan!
Who shall § crossed out and replaced above by § dares   *P1869:*the Pagan   429| MS:Of
the armoury he finds § replaced above by § owns but § last four words crossed out and
replaced above by three words § thus allowed for   *1889a:*Of armoury   430| MS:Exclaim
§ inserted in margin § Except against § last two words crossed out, *against*
restored, replaced above by § Cry out unfair § last three words crossed out § a single
§ crossed out and replaced above by § seeming-dubious   437| MS:Nay, §
crossed out and replaced above by § That stranger   *1869:*Yet stranger   *1889a:*Yea
stranger § emended to § Yet stranger § see Editorial Notes §   438| MS:Such, § word
and comma inserted in margin § Who § crossed out § being < > man, 'twas < > knew,
*P1869:*mere man, ('twas < > knew),   *1872:*Such man, being   442| MS:the Husband
< > false, were § crossed out and replaced above by § for proved   *P1869:*the husband
*1872:*false, were proved   443| MS:letter,—or   *1872:*letter—or   444| MS:The
abominations   *1872:*Abominations   446| MS:Allow them § written over illegible
word §   448| MS:plucks < > knowledge-tree,—   *P1869:*plucked < > knowledge-tree,
449| MS:the serpent's   *P1869:*the Serpent's   450| MS:write,   *P1869:*write:
451| MS:at the spur § crossed out and replaced above by § move o' the
taste § crossed out § maw   *P1869:*at < > maw   *CP1869:*as < > maw,

Quoth Persius, makes a parrot bid "Good day!"
A crow salute the concave, and a pie
Endeavour at proficiency in speech,—
455 So she, through hunger after fellowship,
May well have learned, though late, to play the scribe:
As indeed, there's one letter on the list
Explicitly declares did happen here.
"You thought my letters could be none of mine,"
460 She tells her parents—"mine, who wanted skill;
But now I have the skill, and write, you see!"
She needed write love-letters, so she learned,
"Negatas artifex sequi voces"—though
This letter nowise 'scapes the common lot,
465 But lies i' the condemnation of the rest,
Found by the husband's self who forged them all.
Yet, for the sacredness of argument,
For this once an exemption shall it plead—
Anything, anything to let the wheels
470 Of argument run glibly to their goal!
Concede she wrote (which were preposterous)
This and the other epistle,—what of it?
Where does the figment touch her candid fame?
Being in peril of her life—"my life,
475 Not an hour's purchase," as the letter runs,—
And having but one stay in this extreme,
Out of the wide world but a single friend—
What could she other than resort to him,

451| MS:at the spur § crossed out and replaced above by § move o' the taste
§ crossed out § maw   *P1869:*at <> maw   *CP1869:*as <> maw,
452| MS:§ crowded between 451-53 § Which § crossed out and replaced in margin
by § Quoth Persius, found would § last two words crossed out § makes §s apparently
added in revision § a parrot speaks § crossed out §   453| MS:§ added
in left margin § and a § inserted above line §   454| MS:§ added in left margin §
Strives to attain § last three words crossed out and replaced below by two words § Endeavor
at   454-56| MS:speech,—/ —May   *P1869:*speech,—/ May   *CP1869:*speech,—/
So she, through hunger after fellowship,/ May   458| MS:Declares explicitly to be the
case.   *CP1869:*Explicitly declares did happen here.   460| MS:skill,   *P1869:*skill;
462| MS:learned—   *P1869:*learned   *CP1869:*learned,   463| MS:*voces*"!—though
P1869:voces"—though   465| MS:Lies in <> rest   *P1869:*But lies i' <> rest,
466| MS:forged the same § last two words crossed out § <> all,—   *P1869:*all.
471| MS:wrote . . which <> preposterous . .   *P1869:*wrote (which <> preposterous)
473| MS:figment fleck her   *CP1869:*figment touch her   477| MS:And out <> world a

And how with any hope resort but thus?
480 Shall modesty dare bid a stranger brave
Danger, disgrace, nay death in her behalf—
Think to entice the sternness of the steel
Yet spare love's loadstone moving manly mind?
—Most of all, when such mind is hampered so
485 By growth of circumstance athwart the life
O' the natural man, that decency forbids
He stoop and take the common privilege,
Say frank "I love," as all the vulgar do.
A man is wedded to philosophy,
490 Married to statesmanship; a man is old;
A man is fettered by the foolishness
He took for wisdom and talked ten years since;
A man is, like our friend the Canon here,
A priest, and wicked if he break his vow:
495 Shall he dare love, who may be Pope one day?
Despite the coil of such encumbrance here,
Suppose this man could love, unhappily,
And would love, dared he only let love show!
In case the woman of his love, speaks first,
500 From what embarrassment she sets him free!
" 'Tis I who break reserve, begin appeal,
Confess that, whether you love me or no,
I love you!" What an ease to dignity,
What help of pride from the hard high-backed chair
505 Down to the carpet where the kittens bask,

---

*1872:*Out < > world but a   479| MS:but so? *1869:*but thus?   480| MS:What
modesty shall bid *P1869:*Shall modesty dare bid   483| MS:Save by this magnet moves
the manly mind— *CP1869:*mind? *1872:*Yet spare love, loadstone moving manly
*1889a:*love's loadstone   484| MS:Most of all when *1869:*—Most *1872:*all, when
490| MS:statesmanship, a < > old, *P1869:*statesmanship; a < > old;   492| MS:since,
*P1869:*since: *1869:*since;   494| MS:vow, *1869:*vow: 495-501| MS:And dare to
love—he may < > day!/ Suppose this man could love, though, all the same—/ From what
embarrassment you set him free/ Should you, a woman he could love, speak first—/ " 'Tis
CP1869:/ / < > embarrassment she sets him < > / Should one, a < > / " 'Tis *1869:*He dare
to love, who may < > day? /// " 'Tis *1872:*Shall he dare love < > / Despite the coil of such
encumbrance here,/ Suppose < > love, unhappily,/ And would love, dared he only let love
show!/ In case the woman of his love, speaks first,/ < > free!/ " 'Tis   502| MS:And
§ crossed out § confessed § altered to § Confess— § dash crossed out and replaced above
by § that, < > or not § altered to § no,   505| MS:kittens roll § crossed out §

All under the pretence of gratitude!

From all which, I deduce—the lady here
Was bound to proffer nothing short of love
To the priest whose service was to save her. What?
510   Shall she propose him lucre, dust o' the mine,
Rubbish o' the rock, some diamond, muckworms prize,
Some pearl secreted by a sickly fish?
Scarcely! She caters for a generous taste.
'Tis love shall beckon, beauty bid to breast,
515   Till all the Samson sink into the snare!
Because, permit the end—permit therewith
Means to the end!
                                    How say you, good my lords?
I hope you heard my adversary ring
The changes on this precept: now, let me
520   Reverse the peal! *Quia dato licito fine,*
Ad illum assequendum ordinata
Non sunt damnanda media,—licit end
Enough was found in mere escape from death,
To legalize our means illicit else
525   Of feigned love, false allurement, fancied fact.
Thus Venus losing Cupid on a day,
(See that *Idyllium Moschi*) seeking help,
In the anxiety of motherhood,
Allowably promised "Who shall bring report
530   Where he is wandered to, my winged babe,

---

⁵⁰⁶| MS:under cover § crossed out and replaced above by § the pretense of mere § crossed
out §   ⁵⁰⁶⁻⁰⁷| MS:§ new ¶ indicated in margin §   ⁵⁰⁷| MS:deduce the
*P1869:*deduce—the   ⁵¹²| MS:Or pearl *1872:*Some pearl   ⁵¹³| MS:taste:
*P1869:*taste.   ⁵¹⁶| MS:In fact § crossed out and replaced above by § Because
⁵¹⁷⁻²⁰| MS:end! *Quia dato licito fine,* *P1869:*end! § ¶ § How say you, good my lords?/ I
hope you heard my adversary ring/ The changes on this precept: now, let me/ Reverse
the peal! *Quia dato licito fine,*   ⁵²³| MS:Enough was the escape from death,
I hope *1872:*Enough in the *1889a:*Enough was found in mere escape from death,
⁵²⁴| MS:Which legalized the means *P1869:*To legalize *1889a:*legalize our means
⁵²⁵| MS:fact— *P1869:*fact *1869:*fact.   ⁵²⁷| MS:that *Idyllium Moschi,* masters mine!)
*CP1869:*that *Idyllium Moschi*) seeking help,   ⁵²⁸| MS:motherhood *P1869:*motherhood,
⁵²⁹| MS:promised "Who shall § inserted above line § brings § altered to § bring

I give him for reward a nectared kiss;
But who brings safely back the truant's self,
His be a super-sweet makes kiss seem cold!"
Are not these things writ for example-sake?

535 To such permitted motive, then, refer
All those professions, else were hard explain,
Of hope, fear, jealousy, and the rest of love!
He is Myrtillus, Amaryllis she,
She burns, he freezes,—all a mere device
540 To catch and keep the man, may save her life,
Whom otherwise nor catches she nor keeps!
Worst, once, turns best now: in all faith, she feigns:
Feigning,—the liker innocence to guilt,
The truer to the life in what she feigns!
545 How if Ulysses,—when, for public good
He sunk particular qualms and played the spy,
Entered Troy's hostile gate in beggar's garb—
How if he first had boggled at this clout,
Grown dainty o'er that clack-dish? Grime is grace
550 To whoso gropes amid the dung for gold.

Hence, beyond promises, we praise each proof

531| MS:Shall have § last two words crossed out and replaced above by three words § I give
him for recompense § crossed out and replaced above by § reward   532| MS:But
§ inserted in margin § Who brings safely back § last two words inserted above line § < > self,
in safety back— § last three words crossed out § P1869:But who   533| MS:An
ambrosial super-sweet P1869:His be a super-sweet   534| MS:To such § last two words
crossed out and replaced above by § Are not   534-35| MS:§ marginal note that new ¶
begins §   537| MS:jealousy and P1869:jealousy, and   539| MS:burns, she
CP1869:burns, he   540| MS:the § followed by word illegibly crossed out § man may
§ inserted above line § saved § altered to § save 1872:man, may   541| MS:Who
§ altered to § Whom   542| MS:once, is best now: for good ends, we feign: P1869:now:
in all faith, she feigns: 1872:once, turns best   544| MS:life and thing she plays
§ crossed out § P1869:life is what she 1889a:life in what   545| MS:What if
P1869:How if   546| MS:sunk his private § last two words crossed out and replaced
above by § particular   547| MS:Entered Troy's hostile § inserted above line §
548| MS:What if he eyed daintily § last two words crossed out and replaced above by two
words § first had P1869:How if   549| MS:Grown squeamish § crossed out and
replaced above by § dainty   550-51| MS:§ marginal note that new ¶ begins §
551| MS:And, more than § last three words crossed out and replaced above by two words §
Hence, beyond < > we applaud when § last two words crossed out and replaced above by

That promise was not simply made to break,
Mere moonshine-structure meant to fade at dawn:
We praise, as consequent and requisite,
555 What, enemies allege, were more than words,
Deeds—meetings at the window, twilight-trysts,
Nocturnal entertainments in the dim
Old labyrinthine palace; lies, we know—
Inventions we, long since, turned inside out.
560 Must such external semblance of intrigue
Demonstrate that intrigue there lurks perdue?
Does every hazel-sheath disclose a nut?
He were a Molinist who dared maintain
That midnight meetings in a screened alcove
565 Must argue folly in a matron—since
So would he bring a slur on Judith's self,
Commended beyond women, that she lured
The lustful to destruction through his lust.
Pompilia took not Judith's liberty,
570 No faulchion find you in her hand to smite,
No damsel to convey in dish the head
Of Holophernes,—style the Canon so—
Or is it the Count? If I entangle me
With my similitudes,—if wax wings melt,
575 And earthward down I drop, not mine the fault:

---

two words § praise each   552| MS:break,— 1872:break,   553| MS:No moon shine
§ crossed out and then restored § fabric § crossed out and replaced above by § fabrication §
crossed out and replaced above by § structure <> at day § crossed out § P1869:moonshine-
structure 1872:Mere moonshine-structure   554| MS:So call—(Proofs consequent and
requisite)— 1872:We praise, as consequent and requisite,   555| MS:What enemies
allege of—more 1872:What, enemies allege, were more   556| MS:meetings <>
twilight-tryst, P1869:meeting 1872:meetings <> twilight-trysts,   558| MS:And <>
palace,—lies P1869:Old <> palace; lies   559| MS:we have § crossed out §, long since,
§ word and   comma inserted above line §   560| MS:Does such P1869:Would
such 1872:Must such   561| MS:intrigue must lurk 1872:intrigue there lurks
562| MS:hazel-sheath contain § crossed out and replaced above by § disclose
565| MS:Shall § crossed out and replaced above by § Must   566| MS:So does
he P1869:So would he   567| MS:women that 1872:women, that
570| MS:smite,— 1872:smite,   571| MS:convey the head in dish, 1872:convey in
dish the head   574| MS:similitudes,—and § crossed out and replaced above by § if
wax-wings P1869:wax wings   575| MS:earth-ward down I drop, like Icarus § last five
words crossed out and replaced above by four words and comma § Icarus comes a-tumbled
Down, § last four words crossed out and the following three words restored § down I drop,
not mine the fault,— § last four words, comma and dash inserted below line § P1869:fault:

Blame your beneficence, O Court, O sun,
Whereof the beamy smile affects my flight!
What matter, so Pompilia's fame revive
I' the warmth that proves the bane of Icarus?

580 Yea, we have shown it lawful, necessary
Pompilia leave her husband, seek the house
O' the parents: and because 'twixt home and home
Lies a long road with many a danger rife,
Lions by the way and serpents in the path,
585 To rob and ravish,—much behoves she keep
Each shadow of suspicion from fair fame,
For her own sake much, but for his sake more,
The ingrate husband's. Evidence shall be,
Plain witness to the world how white she walks
590 I' the mire she wanders through ere Rome she reach.
And who so proper witness as a priest?
Gainsay ye? Let me hear who dares gainsay!
I hope we still can punish heretics!
"Give me the man" I say with him of Gath,
595 "That we may fight together!" None, I think:
The priest is granted me.

                    Then, if a priest,
One juvenile and potent: else, mayhap,
That dragon, our Saint George would slay, slays him.
And should fair face accompany strong hand,

576| MS:beneficence, O Court, my § crossed out § sun, *P1869:*beneficence, O Court,
O sun, 577| MS:flight— *P1869:*flight! 578| MS:—What matter, since § crossed
out and replaced above by § if Pompilia's *P1869:*What matter, so Pompilia's
579-80| MS:§ marginal note that new ¶ begins § 581| MS:Pompilia quit § crossed out
and replaced above by § leave 582| MS:Of *P1869:*O' 588| MS:husband!
Evidence must speak, § last two words crossed out and replaced above by two words § shall
be, *1872:*husband: Evidence *1889a:*husband's. Evidence 589| MS:A § crossed out
and replaced in margin by § Some witness *1889a:*Plain witness 590| MS:ere Rome be
§ crossed out and replaced above by § she reached § altered to § reach. 591| MS:who
that § crossed out and replaced above by two words § so proper but § crossed out and
replaced by § as a priest? How § crossed out § 593| MS:§ crowded between 592-94 §
595| MS:to-gether *P1869:*together 596| MS:me. § new ¶ indicated in margin §
597| MS:potent—else *P1869:*potent: else 599| MS:And if § crossed out § < >
accompany stout § crossed out and replaced above by § strong

600 The more complete equipment: nothing mars
Work, else praiseworthy, like a bodily flaw
I' the worker: as 'tis said Saint Paul himself
Deplored the check o' the puny presence, still
Cheating his fulmination of its flash,
605 Albeit the bolt therein went true to oak.

Therefore the agent, as prescribed, she takes,—
Both juvenile and potent, handsome too,—
In all obedience: "good," you grant again.
Do you? I would you were the husband, lords!
610 How prompt and facile might departure be!
How boldly would Pompilia and the priest
March out of door, spread flag at beat of drum,
But that inapprehensive Guido grants
Neither premiss nor yet conclusion here,
615 And, purblind, dreads a bear in every bush!
For his own quietude and comfort, then,
Means must be found for flight in masquerade
At hour when all things sleep.—"Save jealousy!"

601| MS:Work else § last two words written in margin § Praiseworthy §
altered to § praiseworthy work § crossed out § like *P1869:*Work, else praiseworthy,
like   602| MS:the workman § altered to § worker—as *P1869:*worker:
as   603| MS:Deplored the check o' the § last three words inserted above
line §   604| MS:fulminations of its § crossed out and replaced above by §
their flash, *P1869:*fulmination of its flash,   605-8| MS:Albeit the § crossed out and
replaced above by § each bolt therein § inserted above § <> true enough § crossed out § <> /
§ marginal note that new ¶ begins § <> takes/ In *P1869:*Albeit the bolt <> / § ¶ § <>
takes,— / A priest, juvenile, potent, handsome too,—/ In   *1869:/* § no ¶ /// *1872://* Both
juvenile and potent <> /   *1889:/* § no ¶; emended to restore ¶; see Editorial Notes § ///
609| MS:would ye *1872:*you   610| MS:and easy § crossed out and replaced above by §
facile would § crossed out and replaced above by § had departure be § altered to § been!
*P1869:*facile might departure be!   611-12| MS:§ crowded between 610-13 and divided by
slash between *Priest* and *Marched* § boldly had § written over by § would <> Priest/
Marched § altered to § March bag and baggage forth, § last four words crossed out and
replaced above by five words § out of door, spread flag *P1869:*the priest   613| MS:But
had § altered to § that the § crossed out § inapprehensive husband § crossed out and replaced
below by § Guido   615| MS:And, § word and comma added in margin § Purblind
§ altered to § purblind, he § crossed out §   617| MS:found to § altered to § for fly §
altered to § flight in privacy § crossed out and replaced above by two words § secret § crossed
out § masked § altered to § masquerade   618| MS:By night § last two words crossed out
and replaced above by two words § At hour <> sleep.—"Save Jealousy!" *P1869:*sleep.—

Right, Judges! Therefore shall the lady's wit
620   Supply the boon thwart nature baulks him of,
And do him service with the potent drug
(Helen's nepenthe, as my lords opine)
Which respites blessedly each fretted nerve
O' the much-enduring man: accordingly,
625   There lies he, duly dosed and sound asleep,
Relieved of woes or real or raved about.
While soft she leaves his side, he shall not wake;
Nor stop who steals away to join her friend,
Nor do him mischief should he catch that friend
630   Intent on more than friendly office,—nay,
Nor get himself raw head and bones laid bare
In payment of his apparition!

               Thus
Would I defend the step,—were the thing true
Which is a fable,—see my former speech,—
635   That Guido slept (who never slept a wink)
Through treachery, an opiate from his wife,

"Save jealousy!"   621| MS:And § added in margin § Do his § altered to § him work
§ uncertain; crossed out § < > drug—   *P1869:*do < > drug   622| MS:as the skilled
§ last two words crossed out and replaced above by two words § my lords opine)—
*P1869:*opine)   623| MS:Shall § added in margin § Brings § crossed out and replaced
above by § gives § crossed out § blessed § altered to § blessedly respite § transposed to read §
respite blessedly to § crossed out § each frittered nerve   *1872:*Which respites < > each fretted
nerve   624-25| MS:Accordingly, watch § reading uncertain § there lies he sound asleep,/
And keeps the frightened man would harm himself § both lines crossed out and replaced
by § O' the much-enduring man: accordingly,/ There lies he, duly dosed and sound asleep,
626| MS:of all § crossed out § woes, or real or § last three words inserted above line § < >
about, or real, § last two words crossed out §   *P1869:*about.   *1889a:*woes or real
627| MS:—While < > side; he < > wake   *P1869:*While < > side, he < > wake;
628| MS:Nor § added in margin § And § crossed out § stop her as she § last three words
crossed out and replaced by § who steals away § inserted above line § to join the priest
§ last two words crossed out and replaced above by two words, dash and comma § her
friend—, § dash crossed out §   629| MS:do a § altered to § him   631| MS:Obtain a
bloody § last three words crossed out and replaced above by four words § Nor get himself the
§ crossed out § raw head and broken § crossed out §   632| MS:his interference § crossed
out and replaced above by § apparition! No § crossed out; marginal note that new ¶ begins §
633| MS:That § crossed out § would § altered to § Would I justify § crossed out and replaced
by § defend the step   635-37| MS:That Guido got an opiate from his wife, § altered
to § That Guido slept (who never slept a wink)/ Through treachery, an opiate from
his wife, who not so much as knew what opiates mean. § line added in margin §   *P1869:*/

Who not so much as knew what opiates mean.

Now she may start: or hist,—a stoppage still!
A journey is an enterprise of cost!
640 As in campaigns, we fight but others pay,
Suis expensis, nemo militat.
'Tis Guido's self we guard from accident,
Ensuring safety to Pompilia, versed
Nowise in misadventures by the way,
645 Hard riding and rough quarters, the rude fare,
The unready host. What magic mitigates
Each plague of travel to the unpractised wife?
Money, sweet Sirs! And were the fiction fact
She helped herself thereto with liberal hand
650 From out her husband's store,—what fitter use
Was ever husband's money destined to?
With bag and baggage thus did Dido once
Decamp,—for more authority, a queen!

So is she fairly on her route at last,
655 Prepared for either fortune: nay and if
The priest, now all a-glow with enterprise,
Cool somewhat presently when fades the flush
O' the first adventure, clouded o'er belike
By doubts, misgivings how the day may die,

<> wife,/ Who   637-38| MS: § marginal note that new ¶ begins §   *1889a:*§ no ¶
§   *1889:*§ no ¶; emended to restore ¶; see Editorial Notes §   638| MS:start: but
hist   *1872:*start: or hist   639| MS:is a thing § last two words crossed out and
replaced above by two words § an enterprise which costs! which costs! § last two
words crossed out §   *1872:*Enterprise of cost!   640-41| MS:§ crowded between
639-42 § pay: *P1869:*pay,   641| MS:*militat!*   *P1869:militat.*
646| MS:host,—what   *P1869:*host. What 647| MS:Dur § uncertain; partly erased §
Each   648| MS:sweet sirs <> fact, *CP1869:*sweet Sirs   *1889a:*fact   650| MS:out a
§ written over by § the husband's   *1872:*out her husband's   652| MS:baggage
thus § crossed out and then restored § did § word inserted above line and
illegibly crossed out §   653| MS:Decamp: § colon crossed out § why we have that
queen's authority § last six words crossed out and replaced above by seven words and
exclamation point § so § crossed out § ,—for our § crossed out § more authority, a queen!
654| MS:§ marginal note that new ¶ begins § So is she § last two words written over illegible
words § <> last—   *P1869:*last,   656| MS:now ardent in the § last three words
crossed out and replaced above by four words § all a glow with   *P1869:*a-glow

660 Though born with such auroral brilliance,—if
The brow seem over-pensive and the lip
'Gin lag and lose the prattle lightsome late,—
Vanquished by tedium of a prolonged jaunt
In a close carriage o'er a jolting road,
665 With only one young female substitute
For seventeen other Canons of ripe age
Were wont to keep him company in church,—
Shall not Pompilia haste to dissipate
The silent cloud that, gathering, bodes her bale?—
670 Prop the irresoluteness may portend
Suspension of the project, check the flight,
Bring ruin on them both? Use every means,
Since means to the end are lawful! What i' the way
Of wile should have allowance like a kiss
675 Sagely and sisterly administered,
Sororia saltem oscula? We find
Such was the remedy her wit applied
To each incipient scruple of the priest,
If we believe,—as, while my wit is mine
680 I cannot,—what the driver testifies,
Borsi, called Venerino, the mere tool
Of Guido and his friend the Governor,—

660| MS:§ word illegibly written over by § Though <> brilliance—if *P1869:*brilliance,—
if   661| MS:The brow § followed by illegible erasure §   662| MS:the play was
pleasant § last three words crossed out and replaced above by two words § prattle lightsome
late— *P1869:*late,—   663| MS:Thought but through § last three words crossed out
and replaced above by § Induced by <> a lengthy § crossed out and replaced above by §
prolonged *P1869:*Vanquished by   664| MS:road *P1869:*road,   665| MS:one
companion to replace § last three words crossed out and replaced above by three words §
young female substitute   666| MS:For § added in margin § The § crossed out §
668| MS:haste by all her main § last four words crossed out and replaced above by two
words § might and § last two words crossed out § to dissipate § last two words added in
margin §   669| MS:To dissipate § last two words crossed out § the § altered to § The
silent § inserted above line § <> that, gathering, § word and comma inserted above line §
<> bale,— *P1869:*bale?—   672| MS:both?—use *1872:*both? Use   673| MS:Since
§ added in margin § Those § crossed out § means to § inserted above line § the Court allows
her, § last three words and comma crossed out and replaced above by three words and question
mark § end, are lawful? that § written over by § What *P1869:*end are *1872:*lawful! What
675| MS:administered— *P1869:*administered,   677| MS:the calm § crossed out and
replaced above by § remedy   678| MS:§ added in margin § To § word illegibly crossed
out § <> priest,— *P1869:*priest,   680| MS:I shall § crossed out and replaced above
by § cannot,—half § crossed out and replaced above by § what   681–82| MS:§ crowded

31

Avowal I proved wrung from out the wretch,
After long rotting in imprisonment,
685 As price of liberty and favour: long
They tempted, he at last succumbed, and lo
Counted them out full tale each kiss and more,
"The journey being one long embrace," quoth he.
Still, though we should believe the driver's lie,
690 Nor even admit as probable excuse,
Right reading of the riddle,—as I urged
In my first argument, with fruit perhaps—
That what the owl-like eyes (at back of head!)
O' the driver, drowsed by driving night and day,
695 Supposed a vulgar interchange of lips,
This was but innocent jog of head 'gainst head,
Cheek meeting jowl as apple may touch pear
From branch and branch contiguous in the wind,
When Autumn blusters and the orchard rocks:—
700 That rapid run and the rough road were cause
O' the casual ambiguity, no harm
I' the world to eyes awake and penetrative.
Say,—not to grasp a truth I can release
And safely fight without, yet conquer still,—
705 Say, she kissed him, say, he kissed her again!

---

between 680-83 in continuous line with slash between *tool* and *Of* §   683| MS:The
avowal *1872:*Avowal   686| MS:succumbed,—and *P1869:*succumbed, and
687| MS:kiss required,— *1872:*kiss and more,   688| MS:§ crowded between 687-89 §
The journey was one < > embrace, quoth he: *P1869:*"The < > embrace,"
*1872:*journey being one   690| MS:excuse— *P1869:*excuse,   691| MS:riddle—what
I *P1869:*riddle, as I *CP1869:*riddle,—as   693| MS:That thus § crossed out and
replaced above by § what   695| MS:a § followed by two illegible words crossed out, the
second perhaps *more* § vulgar § followed by two or more words, the first perhaps *case*;
illegibly crossed out and replaced above by three words and comma § interchange of love,
*1872:*of lips,   696| MS:was an § altered to § but   698| MS:On orchard-boughs
§ last two words crossed out and replaced above by four words § From branch and branch
699| MS:§ crowded between 698-700 § rocks. *1872:*rocks:—   700| MS:The rapid
§ followed by word, perhaps *march*, illegibly crossed out and replaced below by § run
*1872:*That rapid   701| MS:ambiguity,—no *P1869:*ambiguity, no
702| *1872:*penetrative:— *1889a:*penetrative.   703| MS:Yet, shall § crossed out and
replaced above by § —not so § altered to § to < > can forego *1872:*Say,—not < > can release
704| MS:without and conquer still? § altered to § still,— *1872:*without, yet conquer
705| MS:him, and he kissed her again § last three words transposed to *again kissed
her* and then original reading restored § ,— *P1869:*again! *1872:*him, say, he

32

Such osculation was a potent means,
A very efficacious help, no doubt:
Such with a third part of her nectar did
Venus imbue: why should Pompilia fling
710 The poet's declaration in his teeth?—
Pause to employ what—since it had success,
And kept the priest her servant to the end—
We must presume of energy enough,
No whit superfluous, so permissible?

715 The goal is gained: day, night and yet a day
Have run their round: a long and devious road
Is traversed,—many manners, various men
Passed in review, what cities did they see,
What hamlets mark, what profitable food
720 For after-meditation cull and store!
Till Rome, that Rome whereof—this voice
Would it might make our Molinists observe,
That she is built upon a rock nor shall
Their powers prevail against her!—Rome, I say,
725 Is all but reached; one stage more and they stop
Saved: pluck up heart, ye pair, and forward, then!

Ah, Nature—baffled she recurs, alas!
Nature imperiously exacts her due,

706-7| MS:§ crowded between 705-8 as a continuous line with a division indicated between
means and *A* § means—/ A *P1869:*means,/ A   708| MS:This with *1872:*Such with
709| MS:fling § over illegible word §   710| MS:teeth,— *P1869:*teeth?—
711| MS:what,—since DC,BrU:what—since *1889:*what—since   712| MS:end,—
DC,BrU:end— *1889:*end—   713| MS:energy no whit § last two words crossed out §
714| MS:No whit § last two words added in margin above line § Superfluous § altered to §
superfluous, § so permissible? Pass we on! § last three words crossed out §   714-15| MS:§
marginal note that new ¶ begins § *1889a:*§ no ¶ § *1889:*§ no ¶; emended to restore ¶;
see Editorial Notes §   715| MS:and another § uncertain; crossed out and replaced above
by two words § yet a   718| *1872:*in view, what DC,BrU:in review, what *1889:*in
review, what   720| MS:store, *P1869:*store!   721| MS:Till Rome—that
<> this voice, *CP1869:*Till Rome, that *1872:*voice   724| MS:her,—
Rome *P1869:*her!—Rome   725| MS:reached,—one *P1869:*reached; one
726| MS:Saved,—pluck up heart, ye pair, § last two words and punctuation
inserted above line § *P1869:*Saved: pluck   727| MS:§ marginal note that
new ¶ begins § Ah, nature <> alas!— *P1869:*alas! *CP1869:*Ah, Nature <>

Spirit is willing but the flesh is weak:
730　Pompilia needs must acquiesce and swoon,
Give hopes alike and fears a breathing-while.
The innocent sleep soundly: sound she sleeps,
So let her slumber, then, unguarded save
By her own chastity, a triple mail,
735　And his good hand whose stalwart arms have borne
The sweet and senseless burthen like a babe
From coach to couch,—the serviceable strength!
Nay, what and if he gazed rewardedly
On the pale beauty prisoned in embrace,
740　Stooped over, stole a balmy breath perhaps
For more assurance sleep was not decease—
"*Ut vidi*," "how I saw!" succeeded by
"*Ut perii*," "how I sudden lost my brains!"
—What harm ensued to her unconscious quite?
745　For, curiosity—how natural!
Importunateness—what a privilege
In the ardent sex! And why curb ardour here?
How can the priest but pity whom he saved?
And pity is so near to love, and love
750　So neighbourly to all unreasonableness!
As to love's object, whether love were sage
Or foolish, could Pompilia know or care,
Being still sound asleep, as I premised?

729|　MS:Pompilia's spirit is § last three words crossed out and replaced above by
two words § Spirit is willing, but <> weak, *P1869*:willing but *1872*:weak:
731|　MS:Lay § crossed out and replaced above by § Give <> breathing-while:
P1869:breathing-while.　　732|　MS:sleeps. *1872*:sleeps,　　733|　MS:There
§ crossed out and replaced above by § So　　734|　MS:triple charm § crossed
out § mail,　　737|　MS:servicable man! *1872*:to coach,—the serviceable
strength! DC,BrU: to couch,—the　*1889*:to couch,—the　　739|　MS:prisoned by §
crossed out and replaced above by § in　　740|　MS:breath perhaps § written over illegible
word §　　743|　MS:my wits, § word and comma crossed out and replaced above by word
and comma § head, § word and comma crossed out §　　744|　MS:inconscious
P1869:unconscious　　747|　MS:sex! And whence § altered to § why the § crossed out §
want § inserted above line § ardour　*P1869*:why curb ardour　　748|　MS:saved,— § altered
to § saved?—　*P1869*:saved?　　749|　MS:is how near　*1872*:is so near　　750|　MS:How
neighbourly to unreasonableness—　*P1869*:unreasonableness! *1872*:So neighbourly to all
unreasonableness!　　751|　MS:And for Pompilia § crossed out and replaced above by two
words § love's object, whether he was § last two words crossed out and replaced above by two
words § love were　　752|　MS:care *CP1869*:care,　　753|　MS:Being still § written over

Thus the philosopher absorbed by thought,
755 Even Archimedes, busy o'er a book
The while besiegers sacked his Syracuse,
Was ignorant of the imminence o' the point
O' the sword till it surprised him: let it stab,
And never knew himself was dead at all.
760 So sleep thou on, secure whate'er betide!
For thou, too, hast thy problem hard to solve—
How so much beauty is compatible
With so much innocence!

　　　　　　　Fit place, methinks,
While in this task she rosily is lost,
765 To treat of and repel objection here
Which,—frivolous, I grant,—my mind misgives,
May somehow still have flitted, gadfly-like,
And teased the Court at times—as if, all said
And done, there seemed, the Court might nearly say,
770 In a certain acceptation, somewhat more
Of what may pass for insincerity,
Falsehood, throughout the course Pompilia took,
Than befits Christian. Pagans held, we know,
Man always ought to aim at good and truth,
775 Not always put one thing in the same words:
Non idem semper dicere sed spectare
Debemus. But the Pagan yoke was light;

---

illegible word § 754| MS:philosopher immersed § crossed out and replaced above by §
absorbed by § written over *in* § 755-56| MS:§ crowded between 754-57 in continuous
line, divided between *book* and *The* § Even Archimedes busy <> book,/ <> besiegers
sacked § written over perhaps *took* § *P1869:*Even Archimedes, busy <> book/
758| MS:the § followed by word illegibly crossed out § sword till it § last two words inserted
above line § 760| MS:betide— *P1869:*betide! 763| MS:§ marginal note that new
¶ begins with § Fit 766| MS:frivolous, I know § crossed out and replaced above by §
grant,—but, why misgives *P1869:*grant,—but, still misgives *1872:*grant,—my mind
misgives, 767| MS:My mind, it § inserted above line § may still § crossed out §
have *1872:*May somehow still have 768| MS:teazed <> said and done
§ last two words crossed out § *1889a:*teased 769| MS:there still seemed, one might
nearly § inserted above line § *1872:*there seemed, the Court might 771| MS:may
§ followed by illegible erasure § 772| MS:took *P1869:*took, 773| MS:befits
Christian: Pagans *P1869:*befits Christian. Pagans 774| MS:We always <> at a
§ crossed out § good end § altered to § and, § crossed out § *1872:*Man always
775| MS:always put § inserted above § 777| MS:*Debemus*: but <> light:

"Lie not at all," the exacter precept bids:
Each least lie breaks the law,—is sin, we hold.
780 I humble me, but venture to submit—
What prevents sin, itself is sinless, sure:
And sin, which hinders sin of deeper dye,
Softens itself away by contrast so.
Conceive me! Little sin, by none at all,
785 Were properly condemned for great: but great,
By greater, dwindles into small again.
Now, what is greatest sin of womanhood?
That which unwomans it, abolishes
The nature of the woman,—impudence.
790 Who contradicts me here? Concede me, then,
Whatever friendly fault may interpose
To save the sex from self-abolishment
Is three-parts on the way to virtue's rank!
And, what is taxed here as duplicity,
795 Feint, wile and trick,—admitted for the nonce,—
What worse do one and all than interpose,
Hold, as it were, a deprecating hand,
Statuesquely, in the Medicean mode,
Before some shame which modesty would veil?
800 Who blames the gesture prettily perverse?
Thus,—lest ye miss a point illustrative,—
Admit the husband's calumny—allow

P1869:Debemus. But < > light;   779| MS:sin, ye say § crossed out § hold.   1872:sin,
we hold.   780| MS:to reply—   P1869:to submit—   783| MS:so: P1869:so.
788| MS:unwomans, and § comma and *and* crossed out and replaced above by two words §
it, which § crossed out §   789| MS:The § written over perhaps *Her* § virtue § crossed
out and replaced above by § nature < > woman,—impudence § crossed out and replaced
by illegibly crossed out word above line; original restored §.   790| MS:here?
Proceed a step § last three words crossed out and replaced above by § Concede
791| MS:friendly fault § written over illegible word §   792| MS:sex § followed by word
illegibly marked out and replaced above by § from self-abolishment,   P1869:self-abolishment
793| MS:rank: P1869:rank!   794| MS:Now, what is taxed here § inserted above § as §
next word ends in *ity* but illegibly crossed out and altered to § duplicity,   1872:And,
what   795| MS:Such § uncertain; crossed out and replaced above by word and comma
§ Feint,   796| MS:What other § crossed out and replaced above by § worse do
they § crossed out and replaced above by word illegibly crossed out and replaced by three
words § one and all than thus § crossed out §   801| MS:miss an § crossed out and
replaced above by two words § a point   802| MS:Allow § written over by § Admit the
Husband's calumny—put case § last two words crossed out §   P1869:the husband's

That the wife, having penned the epistle fraught
With horrors, charge on charge of crime she heaped
805 O' the head of Pietro and Violante—(still
Presumed her parents)—having despatched the same
To their arch-enemy Paolo, through free choice
And no sort of compulsion in the world—
Put case she next discards simplicity
810 For craft, denies the voluntary act,
Declares herself a passive instrument
I' the husband's hands; that, duped by knavery,
She traced the characters she could not write,
And took on trust the unread sense which, read,
815 And recognized were to be spurned at once:
Allow this calumny, I reiterate!
Who is so dull as wonder at the pose
Of our Pompilia in the circumstance?
Who sees not that the too-ingenuous soul,
820 Repugnant even at a duty done
Which brought beneath too scrutinizing glare
The misdemeanours,—buried in the dark,—
Of the authors of her being, as believed,—
Stung to the quick at her impulsive deed,
825 And willing to repair what harm it worked,

803| MS:§ illegibly crossed out word replaced above by three words and comma § That the
wife, having <> epistle which § crossed out § 804| MS:With § written over illegible
word § <> crime, she 1872:crime she 806| MS:parents)—and despatched the
§ inserted above § thing 1872:parents)—having dispatched the same 1889a:despatched
809| MS:Put case § last two words added in margin § that § inserted above § She,—taking
thought, § last two words crossed out § P1869:that she discards 1872:case she next
discards 812| MS:the hands of Guido; duped by the dull brain § last three words
crossed out and replaced by § knavery,— P1869:knavery, 1872:the husband's hands;
that, duped 813| MS:She § added in margin § Traced the § inserted above line §
characters, § followed by word illegibly crossed out § she P1869:She traced the
1872:characters she 814| MS:the unread § inserted above § 815| MS:Were
recognized § followed by two words illegibly crossed out and replaced above by three words §
but to be <> once. 1872:And recognized were to <> once: 816| MS:calumny, for
truth I say: § last four words and colon crossed out and replaced by two words, comma and
dash § I reiterate,— P1869:reiterate! 817-18| MS:§ crowded between 816-19 in
continuous line with break indicated between pose and Of § the § followed by two words
illegibly crossed out § <> / 821| MS:brought before § crossed out and replaced above
by § beneath too § written over a § <> glare § written over illegible word §
823| MS:being, she believed,— 1872:being, as believed,— 824| MS:her own righteous
§ last two words crossed out and replaced above by § impulsive 825| MS:§ crowded

37

She—wise in this beyond what Nero proved,
Who when folk urged the candid juvenile
To sign the warrant, doom the guilty dead,
"Would I had never learned to write," quoth he!
830 —Pompilia rose above the Roman, cried
"To read or write I never learned at all!"
O splendidly mendacious!

But time fleets:
Let us not linger: hurry to the end,
Since flight does end, and that disastrously.
835 Beware ye blame desert for unsuccess,
Disparage each expedient else to praise,
Call failure folly! Man's best effort fails.
After ten years' resistance Troy succumbed:
Could valour save a town, Troy still had stood.
840 Pompilia came off halting in no point
Of courage, conduct, her long journey through:
But nature sank exhausted at the close,
And as I said, she swooned and slept all night.
Morn breaks and brings the husband: we assist
845 At the spectacle. Discovery succeeds.
Ha, how is this? What moonstruck rage is here?
Though we confess to partial frailty now,

between 824-26 §   826| MS:what Nero proved § written over *was* § ,
827| MS:Who, in his youthful candour called one day § last seven words crossed out and
replaced above by six words § when needs were the candid juvenile   *1872:*when folks urged
the   *1889a:*folk   828| MS:To § crossed out and replaced in margin by § Should sign
<> warrant, dooming § *ing* crossed out §   *1872:*To sign   830| MS:the Roman—cried
*P1869:*the Roman, cried   832| MS:mendacious! § marginal note that new ¶ begins §
fleets,—   *P1869:*fleets: 833| MS:I linger not but hurry to the close § crossed out §
*CP1869:*Let us not linger: hurry   834| MS:Since § added in margin § End § altered to §
end does our § crossed out § flight and all disastrously.   *1872:*Since flight does end and that,
disastrously.   DC,BrU: end, and that disastrously.   *1889:*end, and that disastrously.
835| MS:unsuccess—   *P1869:*unsuccess,   836| MS:Disparage the § crossed out and
replaced above by § each expedients § altered to § expedient   838| MS:resistance Troy
fell flat—   *P1869:*flat: *1872:*resistance Troy succumbed: 839| MS:a city § crossed
out § town, Troy § written over illegible word §   840| MS:Pompilia proved deficient
§ last two words crossed out and replaced above by three words § came off halting
841| MS:conduct, the long <> through,—   *P1869:*through: *1872:*conduct, her long
843| MS:And, as <> night: *P1869:*night.   *1889a:*And as   846| MS:moonstruck rage
§ written over illegible word § have we § last two words crossed out and replaced above by
two words and question mark § is here?   847| MS:§ crowded between 846-48 § frailty

To error in a woman and a wife,
Is't by the rough way she shall be reclaimed?

850 Who bursts upon her chambered privacy?
What crowd profanes the chaste *cubiculum?*
What outcries and lewd laughter, scurril gibe
And ribald jest to scare the ministrant
Good angels that commerce with souls in sleep?

855 Why, had the worst crowned Guido to his wish,
Confirmed his most irrational surmise,
Yet there be bounds to man's emotion, checks
To an immoderate astonishment.
'Tis decent horror, regulated wrath,

860 Befit our dispensation: have we back
The old Pagan license? Shall a Vulcan clap
His net o' the sudden and expose the pair
To the unquenchable universal mirth?
A feat, antiquity saw scandal in

865 So clearly, that the nauseous tale thereof—
Demodocus his nugatory song—
Hath ever been concluded modern stuff
Impossible to the mouth of the grave Muse,
So, foisted into that Eighth Odyssey

870 By some impertinent pickthank. O thou fool,
Count Guido Franceschini, what didst gain
By publishing thy secret to the world?
Were all the precepts of the wise a waste—
Bred in thee not one touch of reverence?

---

here, *P1869:*frailty now,   848| MS:When we confess § last three words crossed out § to
§ altered to § To <> in a woman and § last three words inserted above line §
851| MS:profanes the § written over *her* § <> *cubiculum*— *P1869:cubiculum?*
853| MS:the ministry § altered to § ministrant   854| MS:O' the § last two words crossed
out § Good § inserted above line §   858| MS:astonishment,— *P1869:*astonishment.
859| MS:His § altered to § 'Tis   863| MS:the quenchless § altered to § unquenchable
<> mirth?—a feat § last two words crossed out § *P1869:*mirth?   864| MS:A feat, § last
two words and comma added in margin § Antiquity itself § crossed out § *P1869:*feat,
antiquity   868| MS:grave muse § altered to § Muse *P1869:*grave Muse,
869| MS:So foisted *P1869:*So, foisted   870| MS:pickthank. Still, despite § last two
words crossed out § <> fool *CP1869:*fool,   871| MS:what were gained *1872:*what
didst gain   872| MS:thy shame thus to *1872:*thy secrets to *1889a:*secret
873| MS:wise a § written over *in* § waste?— § question mark crossed out §

875 Admit thy wife—admonish we the fool,—
Were falseness' self, why chronicle thy shame?
Much rather should thy teeth bite out thy tongue,
Dumb lip consort with desecrated brow,
Silence become historiographer,
880 And thou—thine own Cornelius Tacitus!

But virtue, barred, still leaps the barrier, lords!
—Still, moon-like, penetrates the encroaching mist
And bursts, all broad and bare, on night, ye know!
Surprised, then, in the garb of truth, perhaps,
885 Pompilia, thus opposed, breaks obstacle,
Springs to her feet, and stands Thalassian-pure,
Confronts the foe,—nay, catches at his sword
And tries to kill the intruder, he complains.
Why, so she gave her lord his lesson back,
890 Crowned him, this time, the virtuous woman's way,
With an exact obedience; he brought sword,
She drew the same, since swords are meant to draw.
Tell not me 'tis sharp play with tools on edge!
It was the husband chose the weapon here.
895 Why did not he inaugurate the game
With some gentility of apophthegm
Still pregnant on the philosophic page,

875| MS:"Why, say my wife"—admonishes the sage, *P1869:*Why, say thy wife—admonish
we the fool, *1869:*fool,— *1872:*Admit thy 876| MS:"Were false, and I bid chronicle
the first § last two words crossed out § my shame, § last two words obviously added in
revision § *P1869:*and thou bid *1872:*Were falseness' self, why chronicle thy shame?
877| MS:should my teeth <> out my tongue, *P1869:*should thy teeth <> out thy tongue,
878| MS:And § added in margin and crossed out § Dumb my § crossed out § <> brow,—
*P1869:*brow, 879| MS:Silence were ever § last two words crossed out and uncertain;
replaced above by § become 880| MS:And I—mine own <> Tacitus!" *P1869:*And
thou—thine own <> Tacitus! 880-81| MS:§ marginal note that new ¶ begins §
1869:§ no ¶ § *1889:*§ no ¶; emended to restore ¶; see Editorial Notes § 881| MS:lords,
*P1869:*lords! 882| MS:—Still, moon-like, § last word and commas inserted above § <>
encroaching cloud § crossed out § 883| MS:And, all its § illegible word § peeps
through § last five words crossed out and replaced above by six words § bursts, all broad and
bare, on *P1869:*And bursts 884| MS:§ crowded between 883-85 § 889| MS:his
own § followed by illegible word, both crossed out § 890| MS:this time § written over
true § and § crossed out § the § inserted above line § <> way *CP1869:*way,
894| MS:weapons here— *P1869:*here. *CP1869:*weapon 897| MS:Still § over illegible
word § <> page? § question mark erased and replaced by § ,— *P1869:*page,

40

Some captivating cadence still a-lisp
O' the poet's lyre? Such spells subdue the surge,
900   Make tame the tempest, much more mitigate
The passions of the mind, and probably
Had moved Pompilia to a smiling blush.
No, he must needs prefer the argument
O' the blow: and she obeyed, in duty bound,
905   Returned him buffet ratiocinative—
Ay, in the reasoner's own interest,
For wife must follow whither husband leads,
Vindicate honour as himself prescribes,
Save him the very way himself bids save!
910   No question but who jumps into a quag
Should stretch forth hand and pray us "Pull me out
By the hand!" such were the customary cry:
But Guido pleased to bid "Leave hand alone!
Join both feet, rather, jump upon my head:
915   I extricate myself by the rebound!"
And dutifully as enjoined she jumped—
Drew his own sword and menaced his own life,
Anything to content a wilful spouse.

And so he was contented—one must do
920   Justice to the expedient which succeeds,
Strange as it seem: at flourish of the blade,
The crowd drew back, stood breathless and abashed,

898| MS:Some artful § crossed out and replaced above by § captivating   899| MS:lyre?
Such spells § inserted above line § subdue § written over illegible word § the surge § written
over *sea* § ,   900| MS:tempest—much *P1869:*tempest, much   901| MS:mind—
and most of all § last three words crossed out §   *P1869:*mind, and   902| MS:a rosy
blush. *CP1869:*a smiling blush.   903| MS:No,—he must needs § last two words inserted
above line § preferred § altered to § prefer brute force, § last two words and comma crossed
out §   *P1869:*No, he   904| MS:and she § inserted above §   905| MS:Returned the
§ crossed out and replaced above by § him   910| MS:question but § written over *that* §
who sinks § crossed out and replaced above by § jumps   911| MS:Should § added in
margin § stretches § altered to § stretch a § crossed out § hand forth
§ transposed to § forth hand and pray one § last two words inserted above line § cries §
crossed out and replaced above by § bids § crossed out § "Pull   *1889a:*pray us "Pull
912| MS:hand? § altered to § !   913| MS:to cry § crossed out and replaced above by §
bid, "Leave <> alone—   *P1869:*bid "Leave <> alone!   914| MS:head,   *1872:*head:
915| MS:myself by § written over *on* § the rebound— § crossed out and replaced by § !"
917| MS:§ crowded between 916-18 §   919| MS:§ marginal note that new ¶ begins §

Then murmured "This should be no wanton wife,
No conscience-stricken sinner, caught i' the act,
925 And patiently awaiting our first stone:
But a poor hard-pressed all-bewildered thing,
Has rushed so far, misguidedly perhaps,
Meaning no more harm than a frightened sheep.
She sought for aid; and if she made mistake
930 I' the man could aid most, why—so mortals do:
Even the blessed Magdalen mistook
Far less forgiveably: consult the place—
Supposing him to be the gardener,
'Sir,' said she, and so following." Why more words?
935 Forthwith the wife is pronounced innocent:
What would the husband more than gain his cause,
And find that honour flash in the world's eye,
His apprehension was lest soil had smirched?

So, happily the adventure comes to close
940 Whereon my fat opponent grounds his charge
Preposterous: at mid-day he groans "How dark!"
Listen to me, thou Archangelic swine!
Where is the ambiguity to blame,
The flaw to find in our Pompilia? Safe
945 She stands, see! Does thy comment follow quick
"Safe, inasmuch as at the end proposed;

923| MS:wife— *P1869:*wife,   924| MS:conscience-stricken creature, caught
*1872:*conscience-stricken sinner, caught   926| MS:thing *P1869:*thing,
927| MS:far—misguidedly perhaps— *P1869:*far, misguidedly perhaps,   929| MS:for
help § crossed out and replaced above by § aid   930| MS:could help best § last two
words crossed out and replaced above by two words § aid most, chose § crossed out § <>
mortals do § written over *are* § :   932| MS:forgiveably § altered to § forgivably
*P1869:*forgiveably   934| MS:and what § crossed out and replaced by § so follows
§ altered to § following <> words? § followed by illegible erasure §   937| MS:honour
white § crossed out and replaced above by § flash   938| MS:Which § added in margin §
His § crossed out § <> soil besmirched § altered to § had smirched? *P1869:*His
939| MS:§ marginal note that new ¶ begins §   940| MS:my great § crossed out and
replaced above by § fat   941| MS:Preposterous—at *P1869:*Preposterous:
at   942| MS:§ inserted between 941-43 § me, thou § over illegible erasure §
943| MS:blame? *P1869:*blame,   944| MS:find or Sin § uncertain § , Venus-like she
stands, § last five words crossed out and replaced above by § in our Pompilia?—Safe
*P1869:*our Pompilia? Safe   945| MS:Pompilia § crossed out § she stands, there § crossed
out and replaced above by § see! *P1869:*She   946| MS:"Safe—inasmuch <> proposed

42

But thither she picked way by devious path—
Stands dirtied, no dubiety at all!
I recognize success, yet, all the same,
950 Importunately will suggestion prompt—
Better Pompilia gained the right to boast
'No devious path, no doubtful patch was mine,
I saved my head nor sacrificed my foot!'
Why, being in a peril, show mistrust
955 Of the angels set to guard the innocent?
Why rather hold by obvious vulgar help
Of stratagem and subterfuge, excused
Somewhat, but still no less a foil, a fault,
Since low with high, and good with bad is linked?
960 Methinks I view some ancient bas-relief.
There stands Hesione thrust out by Troy,
Her father's hand has chained her to a crag,
Her mother's from the virgin plucked the vest,
At a safe distance both distressful watch,
965 While near and nearer comes the snorting orc.
I look that, white and perfect to the end,
She wait till Jove despatch some demigod;
Not that,—impatient of celestial club
Alcmena's son should brandish at the beast,—
970 She daub, disguise her dainty limbs with pitch,
And so elude the purblind monster! Ay,

P1869:"Safe, inasmuch <> proposed;   947| MS:But there § crossed out and replaced
above by § thither <> picked a path § last two words crossed out and replaced above by §
way by devious § illegible erasure §   948| MS:Is § added in margin § Dirtied, § comma
apparently added in revision § beyond § crossed out and replaced above by § without §
crossed out § no § apparently added in revision § *P1869:*Stands dirtied   949| MS:I §
written over *we* §   950| MS:Importunately the § crossed out and replaced above by §
will suggestion prick— *P1869:*prick *CP1869:*prick,— *1869:*prick— *1889a:*suggestion
prompt—   951| MS:What, had Pompilia <> boast— *P1869:*boast *1872:*Better
Pompilia   952| MS:patch were mine, *P1869:*patch was mine,   953| MS:foot?'
*1872:*foot!'   958| MS:Somewhat, but still § last two words inserted above line § <>
fault— *P1869:*fault,   959| MS:high and *CP1869:*high, and   960| MS:Methinks
we § crossed out and replaced above by § I <> bas-relief— *P1869:*bas-relief.
962| MS:crag § over illegible erasure §,   963| MS:from § followed by two words
illegibly crossed out and replaced above by § the virgin <> vest and veil § last two words
crossed out § ,— *P1869:*vest,   965| MS:and near comes *CP1869:*and nearer comes
970| MS:daubs § altered to § daub, disguises § altered to § disguise her pure § crossed out
and replaced above by § dainty   971| MS:eludes § altered to § elude

The trick succeeds, but 'tis an ugly trick,
Where needs have been no trick!"

My answer? Faugh;
Nimis incongrue! Too absurdly put!
975 *Sententiam ego teneo contrariam,*
Trick, I maintain, had no alternative.
The heavens were bound with brass,—Jove far at feast
(No feast like that thou didst not ask me to,
Arcangeli,—I heard of thy regale!)
980 With the unblamed Æthiop,—Hercules spun wool
I' the lap of Omphale, while Virtue shrieked—
The brute came paddling all the faster. You
Of Troy, who stood at distance, where's the aid
You offered in the extremity? Most and least,
985 Gentle and simple, here the Governor,
There the Archbishop, everywhere the friends,
Shook heads and waited for a miracle,
Or went their way, left Virtue to her fate.
Just this one rough and ready man leapt forth!
990 —Was found, sole anti-Fabius (dare I say)
Who restored things, with no delay at all,
Qui haud cunctando rem restituit! He,
He only, Caponsacchi 'mid a crowd,
Caught Virtue up, carried Pompilia off
995 Through gaping impotence of sympathy
In ranged Arezzo: what you take for pitch,

972| MS:tis *P1869:*'tis   973| MS:answer? Faugh! *1872:*answer? Faugh;
974| MS:absurd § altered to § absurdly a speech § last two words crossed out §
975| MS:*contrariam— P1869:contrariam,*   976| MS:,I § comma and word added in
margin § Maintain, § comma added in revision § that § crossed out § trick § transposed to
beginning of line and altered to § Trick *P1869:*I maintain   978-79| MS:§ crowded
between 977-80 in continuous line with break indicated between *to* and *Arcangeli* §
981| MS:virtue § altered to § Virtue   982| MS:And § crossed out § the § altered to § The
983| MS:Of the earth § last two words crossed out and replaced above by § Troy
985| MS:the Governor *P1869:*the Governor,   986| MS:everywhere the mob
*P1869:*mob, *CP1869:*everywhere the friends,   990| MS:Was <> anti-Fabius,—dare I
say,— *P1869:*anti-Fabius (dare I say) *CP1869:*—Was   991| MS:To restore things
with *P1869:*things, with *1872:*Who restored things   992| MS:*Qui, haud cunctando,
rem 1872:Qui haud 1889a:cunctando rem*   993| MS:mid *1869:*'mid
994| MS:Caught virtue § altered to § Virtue   995| MS:Thro' the gaping
*1872:*Through gaping   996| MS:ranged Arezzo: strains § altered to § what

Is nothing worse, belike, than black and blue,
Mere evanescent proof that hardy hands
Did yeoman's service, cared not where the gripe
1000 Was more than duly energetic: bruised,
She smarts a little, but her bones are saved
A fracture, and her skin will soon show sleek.
How it disgusts when weakness, false-refined,
Censures the honest rude effective strength,—
1005 When sickly dreamers of the impossible
Decry plain sturdiness which does the feat
With eyes wide open!
                                    Did occasion serve,
I could illustrate, if my lords allow;
Quid vetat, what forbids I aptly ask
1010 With Horace, that I give my anger vent,
While I let breathe, no less, and recreate,
The gravity of my Judges, by a tale?
A case in point—what though an apologue
Graced by tradition?—possibly a fact:
1015 Tradition must precede all scripture, words
Serve as our warrant ere our books can be:
So, to tradition back we needs must go
For any fact's authority: and this

997| MS:nothing worse, § word and comma added above line §   998| MS:An
evanescent *P1869:*Mere evanescent   1000| MS:energetic—skin § crossed out § bruised
*P1869:*energetic: bruised,   1001| MS:Might § crossed out and replaced above by § She
smart § altered to § smarts <> but the § crossed out and replaced above by § her bones were
§ altered to § are   1002| MS:A breaking § crossed out and replaced above by § fracture,
and the § crossed out and replaced above by § her skin would § crossed out and replaced
above by § will soon grow § crossed out and replaced above by § show
1003| MS:disgusts me § crossed out § when the § crossed out and replaced above by word
and comma § weakness, false-refined *P1869:*false-refined,   1004| MS:Blam § crossed
out and replaced above by § Censures   1005| MS:And sickly § over illegible erasure §
*P1869:*When sickly   1006| MS:Decry the sturdiness which did § crossed out and
replaced below by § does *CP1869:*Decry plain sturdiness   1007| MS:open! § marginal
note that new ¶ begins § Did   1008| MS:illustrate . . would § crossed out § if §
inserted above line § <> allow? *P1869:*illustrate, if <> allow;   1009| MS:forbids, I
*P1869:*forbids I *1872:*forbids, I *1889a:*forbids I   1010| MS:With Flaccus, that
*P1869:*With Horace, that   1011| MS:recreate *1872:*recreate,   1012| MS:a a
§ crossed out § tale— *1872:*tale?   1014| MS:tradition,—possibly <> fact: *P1869:*fact?
*1872:*tradition?—possibly a fact: 1016| MS:Must be § last two words crossed out and
replaced above by two words § Serve as   1018| MS:For best § crossed out and replaced

Hath lived so far (like jewel hid in muck)

¹⁰²⁰ On page of that old lying vanity
Called "Sepher Toldoth Yeschu:" God be praised,
I read no Hebrew,—take the thing on trust:
But I believe the writer meant no good
(Blind as he was to truth in some respects)

¹⁰²⁵ To our pestiferous and schismatic . . . well,
My lords' conjecture be the touchstone, show
The thing for what it is! The author lacks
Discretion, and his zeal exceeds: but zeal,—
How rare in our degenerate day! Enough!

¹⁰³⁰ Here is the story: fear not, I shall chop
And change a little, else my Jew would press
All too unmannerly before the Court.

It happened once,—begins this foolish Jew,
Pretending to write Christian history,—

¹⁰³⁵ That three, held greatest, best and worst of men,
Peter and John and Judas, spent a day
In toil and travel through the country-side
On some sufficient business—I suspect,
Suppression of some Molinism i' the bud.

¹⁰⁴⁰ Foot-sore and hungry, dropping with fatigue,
They reached by nightfall a poor lonely grange,
Hostel or inn: so, knocked and entered there.

---

above by two words § any fact's authority,—and this I cite § last two words crossed out §
*P1869:*authority: and   ¹⁰²⁰| MS:O' the page *1872:*On page   ¹⁰²¹| MS:Called
"Sephir Toldos Jeschu": God   *P1869:*Called "Sephir Toldos Jeschu:" God
*CP1869:*Called "Sepher Toldoth Yeschu:" God   ¹⁰²⁴| MS:§ line squeezed between lines
1023-25 § Blind <> respects,   *P1869:*(Blind <> respects)   ¹⁰²⁵| MS:schismatic . .
well, *1889a:*schismatic . . . well,   ¹⁰²⁹| MS:How all § crossed out §
¹⁰³⁰| MS:story; fear § written over illegible word § not me, who § last two words crossed out
and replaced above by two words § I shall   *P1869:*story,—fear *1872:*story: fear
¹⁰³¹| MS:little, spare § crossed out §   ^{1032–33}| MS:§ marginal note that new ¶ begins §
¹⁰³⁴| MS:§ line squeezed between lines 1033-35 §   ¹⁰³⁷| MS:thro' *CP1869:*through
¹⁰³⁸| MS:suspect *P1869:*suspect,   ¹⁰³⁹| MS:some heresy § crossed out and replaced
above by § Molinism in § altered to § i' the egg § crossed out and replaced by § bud:
*P1869:*bud.   ¹⁰⁴⁰| MS:§ line squeezed between lines 1039-41 § Foot-sore, and
*1869:*Foot-sore and   ¹⁰⁴¹| MS:They § inserted in margin § And § crossed out §
¹⁰⁴²| MS:inn: they § crossed out and replaced above by § so knocked *1869:*so, knocked

"Your pleasure, great ones?"—"Shelter, rest and food!"
For shelter, there was one bare room above;
1045　For rest therein, three beds of bundled straw:
For food, one wretched starveling fowl, no more—
Meat for one mouth, but mockery for three.
"You have my utmost." How should supper serve?
Peter broke silence: "To the spit with fowl!
1050　And while 'tis cooking, sleep!—since beds there be,
And, so far, satisfaction of a want.
Sleep we an hour, awake at supper-time,
Then each of us narrate the dream he had,
And he whose dream shall prove the happiest, point
1055　The clearliest out the dreamer as ordained
Beyond his fellows to receive the fowl,
Him let our shares be cheerful tribute to,
His the entire meal, may it do him good!"
Who could dispute so plain a consequence?
1060　So said, so done: each hurried to his straw,
Slept his hour's-sleep and dreamed his dream, and woke.
"I," commenced John, "dreamed that I gained the prize
We all aspire to: the proud place was mine,
Throughout the earth and to the end of time
1065　I was the Loved Disciple: mine the meal!"
"But I," proceeded Peter, "dreamed, a word
Gave me the headship of our company,
Made me the Vicar and Vice-gerent, gave
The keys of heaven and hell into my hand,
1070　And o'er the earth, dominion: mine the meal!"
"While I," submitted in soft under-tone
The Iscariot—sense of his unworthiness

1043| MS:ones?"—"Shelter, food and rest!" *CP1869:*ones?"—"Shelter, rest and food!"
1044| MS:above, *P1869:*above; 　1045| MS:straw, *P1869:*straw: 　1049| MS:silence.
"To *1872:*silence: "To 　1050| MS:sleep!— § punctuation added in revision §
1051| MS:satisfaction for § crossed out and replaced above by § of 　1055| MS:clearliest
to § crossed out and replaced above by § out 　1058| MS:meal—may *P1869:*meal, may
1062| MS:"I" commenced John "dreamed *P1869:*"I," commenced John, "dreamed
1066| MS:"But I" proceeded Peter "dreamed a *P1869:*"But I," proceeded Peter, "dreamed, a
1068| MS:I was § last two words crossed out and replaced above by two words § Made me
<> Viceregent, held § crossed out § *P1869:*and Vice-regent *1889a:*and Vice-gerent
1069| MS:of Heaven and Hell *1872:*of heaven and hell 　1073| MS:Turning his

Turning each eye up to the inmost white—
With long-drawn sigh, yet letting both lips smack,
1075 "I have had just the pitifullest dream
That ever proved man meanest of his mates,
And born foot-washer and foot-wiper, nay
Foot-kisser to each comrade of you all!
I dreamed I dreamed; and in that mimic dream
1080 (Impalpable to dream as dream to fact)
Methought I meanly chose to sleep no wink
But wait until I heard my brethren snore;
Then stole from couch, slipped noiseless o'er the planks,
Slid downstairs, furtively approached the hearth,
1085 Found the fowl duly brown, both back and breast,
Hissing in harmony with the cricket's chirp,
Grilled to a point; said no grace but fell to,
Nor finished till the skeleton lay bare.
In penitence for which ignoble dream,
1090 Lo, I renounce my portion cheerfully!
Fie on the flesh—be mine the ethereal gust,
And yours the sublunary sustenance!
See that whate'er be left ye give the poor!"
Down the two scuttled, one on other's heel,
1095 Stung by a fell surmise; and found, alack,
A goodly savour, both the drumstick bones,
And that which henceforth took the appropriate name
O' the Merry-thought, in memory of the fact

---

§ crossed out and replaced above by § each eyes § altered to § eye   1074| MS:Yet—
§ word and dash crossed out and replaced above by two words § With long-drawn sigh—yet
< > smack— *CP1869:*sigh, yet < > smack,   1076| MS:mates *P1869:*mates,
1077| MS:The § altered to § And < > foot-washer § *foot* written over illegible word §
1082| MS:brethren breathe; § last word written over word, perhaps *snore* § *1889a:*brethren
snore;   1083| MS:noiseless to the door, *1889a:*noiseless o'er the planks,
1087| MS:point,—said *P1869:*point; said   1088| MS:the bones § crossed out and
replaced above by § skeleton lay picked and § last two words crossed out §
1091| MS:gust, § last word written over illegible word §   1093| MS:See, that < > left, ye
*1872:*See that < > left ye   1094| MS:scuttled, on on *P1869:*scuttled, one on
1095| MS:found, too late § last two words crossed out §   1096| MS:drumstick-bones,
*1872:*drumstick bones,   1098| MS:merry-thought < > fact. *P1869:* < > fact *1872:*the

48

That to keep wide awake is man's best dream.

1100 So,—as was said once of Thucydides
And his sole joke, "The lion, lo, hath laughed!"—
Just so, the Governor and all that's great
I' the city, never meant that Innocence
Should quite starve while Authority sat at meat;
1105 They meant to fling a bone at banquet's end:
Wished well to our Pompilia—in their dreams,
Nor bore the secular sword in vain—asleep.
Just so the Archbishop and all good like him
Went to bed meaning to pour oil and wine
1110 I' the wounds of her, next day,—but long ere day,
They had burned the one and drunk the other, while
Just so, again, contrariwise, the priest
Sustained poor Nature in extremity
By stuffing barley-bread into her mouth,
1115 Saving Pompilia (grant the parallel)
By the plain homely and straightford way
Taught him by common sense. Let others shriek
"Oh what refined expedients did we dream
Proved us the only fit to help the fair!"

Merry-thought   1099-1102| MS:§ marginal note that new ¶ begins after line 1099
§ is the § crossed out and replaced above by § our best < > / Just   P1869:So,—as was
said once of Thucydides/ And his sole joke, "The lion, lo, hath laughed!"—/ Just
1889a:is man's best 1889a:dream DC,Bru:dream. 1889:dream.   1103| MS:the
City < > that she should starve— § last three words and dash crossed out and replaced above
by § Innocence P1869:the city   1104-5| MS:§ lines crowded between 1103-6 in
continuous line with break indicated between meat and They § Amid § crossed out § Should
starve thus § written over they so § while < > meat § illegible blot § / < > end:
P1869:meat./ < > end, 1872:Should quite starve while < > meat;/ < > end:
1107| MS:asleep: 1872:asleep.   1110| MS:her, next day,— § last two words, comma and
dash inserted above line § < > ere dawned the day § last three words crossed out and replaced
above by word and comma § day,   1111| MS:other: while 1872:other, while
1112| MS:again, not otherwise § last two words crossed out and replaced above by word and
comma § contrariwise,   1113| MS:poor nature 1869:poor Nature   1114| MS:§
crowded between lines 1113-15 § mouth. P1869:mouth,   1115| MS:Saving
§ written in margin § (Pompilia) § both parentheses crossed out § —if you § last
two words crossed out § P1869:Saving Pompilia (grant   1117| MS:common-sense
1872:common sense   1118| MS:"Oh, what CP1869:"Oh what

1120   He cried "A carriage waits, jump in with me!"

And now, this application pardoned, lords,—
This recreative pause and breathing-while,—
Back to beseemingness and gravity!
For Law steps in: Guido appeals to Law,
1125   Demands she arbitrate,—does well for once.
O Law, of thee how neatly was it said
By that old Sophocles, thou hast thy seat
I' the very breast of Jove, no meanlier throned!
Here is a piece of work now, hitherto
1130   Begun and carried on, concluded near,
Without an eye-glance cast thy sceptre's way;
And, lo the stumbling and discomfiture!
Well may you call them "lawless" means, men take
To extricate themselves through mother-wit
1135   When tangled haply in the toils of life!
Guido would try conclusions with his foe,
Whoe'er the foe was and whate'er the offence;
He would recover certain dowry-dues:
Instead of asking Law to lend a hand,
1140   What pother of sword drawn and pistol cocked,
What peddling with forged letters and paid spies,
Politic circumvention!—all to end
As it began—by loss of the fool's head,
First in a figure, presently in a fact.

1120| MS:§ crowded between lines 1119-21 § cried—"A   P1869:cried "A
1120-21| MS:§ marginal note that new ¶ begins §   1121| MS:pardoned, lords
§ written over *sirs* § ,—   1122| MS:breathing while,—   CP1869:breathing-while,—
1124| MS:in,—Guido <> law,   P1869:in: Guido   CP1869:to Law,   1126| MS:Oh,
Law—of   P1869:O Law, of   1128| MS:no meaner § altered to § meanlier
1131| MS:way   P1869:way;   1133| MS:"lawless," means men   1872:"lawless" means,
men   1134| MS:To help § crossed out and replaced above by § extricate <>
through simple § crossed out §   1136| MS:his wife § crossed out and
replaced above by § foe—   P1869:foe,   1137-39| MS:§ crowded between 1136-40
in continuous line with breaks indicated between *offence;* and *He* and *dowry-dues:* and
Instead §   1137| MS:Whoever   P1869:Whoe'er   1139| MS:asking law
CP1869:asking Law   1140| MS:cocked—   P1869:cocked,   1141| MS:what piddling
with   P1869:what peddling with   1142| MS:circumvention,—to what § last two words
crossed out and replaced above by two words § all to end,   P1869:circumvention!—all to
end   1143| MS:head   P1869:head,   1144| MS:First, § word and comma inserted in
margin § In § altered to § in a figure, first and § last two words crossed out and replaced
above by § in a fact. presently § transposed to § presently in a fact.   P1869:First in a figure

¹¹⁴⁵ It is a lesson to mankind at large.
How other were the end, would men be sage
And bear confidingly each quarrel straight,
O Law, to thy recipient mother-knees!
How would the children light come and prompt go,
¹¹⁵⁰ This with a red-cheeked apple for reward,
The other, peradventure red-cheeked too
I' the rear, by taste of birch for punishment.
No foolish brawling murder any more!
Peace for the household, practise for the Fisc,
¹¹⁵⁵ And plenty for the exchequer of my lords!
Too much to hope, in this world: in the next,
Who knows? Since, why should sit the Twelve enthroned
To judge the tribes, unless the tribes be judged?
And 'tis impossible but offences come:
¹¹⁶⁰ So, all's one lawsuit, all one long leet-day!

Forgive me this digression—that I stand
Entranced awhile at Law's first beam, outbreak
O' the business, when the Count's good angel bade
"Put up thy sword, born enemy to the ear,
¹¹⁶⁵ And let Law listen to thy difference!"
And Law does listen and compose the strife,

^{1145|}   MS:§ crowded between 1144-46 §   ^{1146|}   MS:sage § written over illegible word §
^{1148|}   MS:recipient mother-lap § *lap* crossed out and replaced above by § knees,—
*P1869:*mother-knees!   ^{1149|}   MS:How happy § crossed out § <> the human § crossed
out § children light § inserted above line § <> and prompt § inserted above line §
^{1150|}   *CP1869:*This, with   *1889a:*This with   ^{1151-53|}   MS:The other red-cheeked too by
taste of birch/ For punishment. No foolish murders more! § altered to § The other
peradventure § inserted above § red-cheeked too/ By gentle § inserted above § taste of birch for
punishment./ No foolish brawling § inserted above § murders any § inserted above § more!
P1869:/ I' the rear, by taste <> / <> murders   *CP1869:*other, peradventure <> ///
1872:// <> murder   ^{1154|}   MS:What § crossed out § peace § altered to § Peace
^{1156|}   MS:hope, for § crossed out and replaced above by § in this life § crossed out and
replaced above by § world   ^{1157|}   MS:Perhaps § crossed out and replaced above by two
words § Who knows? Since, wherefore § crossed out and replaced above by two words § why
should <> enthroned § *en* blotted; perhaps written over illegible word §   ^{1158|}   MS:the
world § crossed out and replaced above by § tribes   ^{1159|}   MS:come? § question
mark crossed out and replaced by § :   ^{1160-61|}   MS:§ marginal note that new
¶ begins §   ^{1161|}   MS:stood   *P1869:*stand   ^{1162|}   MS:at § over *as* § Laws
first § transposed to § at first Laws § original order restored § <> outbroke
*P1869:*at Law's   *CP1869:*outbreak   ^{1163|}   MS:business, and § crossed out and replaced
above by § when   ^{1166|}   MS:And Law did listen   *CP1869:*And Law does listen

Settle the suit, how wisely and how well!
On our Pompilia, faultless to a fault,
Law bends a brow maternally severe,
1170 Implies the worth of perfect chastity,
By fancying the flaw she cannot find.
Superfluous sifting snow, nor helps nor harms:
'Tis safe to censure levity in youth,
Tax womanhood with indiscretion, sure!
1175 Since toys, permissible to-day, become
Follies to-morrow: prattle shocks in church:
And that curt skirt which lets a maiden skip,
The matron changes for a trailing robe.
Mothers may aim a blow with half-shut eyes
1180 Nodding above their spindles by the fire,
And chance to hit some hidden fault, else safe.
Just so, Law hazarded a punishment—
If applicable to the circumstance,
Why, well! if not so apposite, well too.
1185 "Quit the gay range o' the world," I hear her cry,
"Enter, in lieu, the penitential pound:
Exchange the gauds of pomp for ashes, dust!
Leave each mollitious haunt of luxury!
The golden-garnished silken-couched alcove,

1167| MS:Settled the suit—how *P1869:*suit, how *CP1869:*Settle the   1169| MS:She
§ crossed out and replaced in margin by § Law   1170| MS:Implies the
§ written over *Her* § the value of a perfect white pure § last six words crossed out
and replaced above by four words and comma § worth of perfect chastity,   1171| MS:By
fancying § *ing* added in revision § of § crossed out § the speck § crossed out and
replaced above by § flaw < > find, § comma crossed out and replaced by § .
1172| MS:—Superfluous *P1869:*Superfluous   1173| MS:Tis *P1869:*'Tis
1174| MS:sure— *P1869:*sure!   1177| MS:maiden leap, *P1869:*maiden skip,
1178| MS:robe. *P1869:*robe.   1179| MS:Will § crossed out § mothers § altered to §
Mothers risk § crossed out and replaced above by two words § should risk thus much with
*P1869:*Mothers may risk thus much with *1872:*Mothers may aim a blow with
1181| MS:§ crowded between lines 1180-82 § On the chance < > else missed § crossed out §
safe. *1872:*And chance   1182| *P1869:*so, law *CP1869:*so, Law   1184| MS:well—if
*P1869:*opposite *CP1869:*apposite *1872:*well! if   1185| MS:gay range o' the § last
three words inserted above § world," methinks § crossed out § I hear the voice § last two
words crossed out and replaced below line by same two words and dash § the voice—
*CP1869:*hear her cry,   1186| MS:Enter, in lieu, § last two words and commas inserted
above line §   1187| MS:dust:— *1872:*dust!   1188| MS:Then old § last two words
crossed out and replaced above by three words § Leave the § crossed out § each < > luxury,

1190

The many-columned terrace that so tempts
Feminine soul put foot forth, extend ear
To fluttering joy of lover's serenade,—
Leave these for cellular seclusion! mask
And dance no more, but fast and pray! avaunt—
1195 Be burned, thy wicked townsman's sonnet-book!
Welcome, mild hymnal by . . . some better scribe!
For the warm arms were wont enfold thy flesh,
Let wire-shirt plough and whipcord discipline!"
If such an exhortation proved, perchance,
1200 Inapplicable, words bestowed in waste,
What harm, since Law has store, can spend nor miss?

And so, our paragon submits herself,
Goes at command into the holy house,
And, also at command, comes out again:
1205 For, could the effect of such obedience prove
Too certain, too immediate? Being healed,
Go blaze abroad the matter, blessed one!
Art thou sound forthwith? Speedily vacate
The step by pool-side, leave Bethesda free
1210 To patients plentifully posted round,
Since the whole need not the physician! Brief,

---

*1872:*luxury!   ¹¹⁹¹| MS:Thy § crossed out § Feminine § written over illegible word §
soul put § last two words inserted above line § foot to step § last two words crossed out §
forth, give them § last two words crossed out and replaced above by two words § nor stop ear
*1872:*forth, extend ear   ¹¹⁹²| MS:§ word crossed out illegibly and replaced above by two
words § To fluttering <> lover's § several words, perhaps four, crossed out illegibly §
serenade, *1872:*serenade,—   ¹¹⁹³| MS:seclusion; mask *1872:*seclusion! mask
¹¹⁹⁴| MS:pray; avaunt— *1872:*pray! avaunt—   ¹¹⁹⁵| MS:Be burned, § last two words
and comma added in margin § Thy § altered to § thy <> townsman's Sonnet-book!
*P1869:*townsman's sonnet-book!   ¹¹⁹⁶| MS:Welcome, § word crossed out illegibly and
replaced above by § mild <> by . . . a § altered to § some better scribe § over *man* § !
¹¹⁹⁷| MS:arms, were <> thy waist, , *CP1869:*thy flesh, *1889a:*arms were
¹¹⁹⁸| MS:whip- cord discipline! *P1869:*discipline!" *1869:*discipline " *1872:*discipline!"
*1889a:*whipcord   ¹²⁰¹| MS:What matter § crossed out and replaced above by two words §
harm, since <> miss! *P1869:*law <> miss? *1889a:*since Law   ¹²⁰¹⁻²| MS:§ marginal
note that new ¶ begins §   ¹²⁰²| MS:so our *P1869:*so, our   ¹²⁰³| MS:house
*1872:*house,   ¹²⁰⁵| MS:For, § word and comma added in margin §   ¹²⁰⁸| MS:thou
whole § crossed out and replaced above by § sound   ¹²⁰⁹| MS:by the § crossed out §
¹²¹⁰| MS:patients therein § inserted above line; crossed out § plentifully § partially crossed

She may betake her to her parents' place.
Welcome her, father, with wide arms once more,
Motion her, mother, to thy breast again!
1215 For why? Since Law relinquishes the charge,
Grants to your dwelling-place a prison's style,
Rejoice you with Pompilia! golden days,
Redeunt Saturnia regna. Six weeks slip,
And she is domiciled in house and home
1220 As though she thence had never budged at all.
And thither let the husband,—joyous, ay,
But contrite also—quick betake himself,
Proud that his dove which lay among the pots
Hath mued those dingy feathers,—moulted now,
1225 Shows silver bosom clothed with yellow gold!
So shall he tempt her to the perch she fled,
Bid to domestic bliss the truant back.

But let him not delay! Time fleets how fast,
And opportunity, the irrevocable,
1230 Once flown will flout him! Is the furrow traced?
If field with corn ye fail preoccupy,
Darnel for wheat and thistle-beards for grain,
Infelix lolium, carduus horridus,
Will grow apace in combination prompt,
1235 Defraud the husbandman of his desire.
Already—hist—what murmurs 'monish now
The laggard?—doubtful, nay, fantastic bruit

---

out and altered to § plenty § original word restored §   1212| MS:The Law § last two
words crossed out and replaced above by two words § She may   1214| MS:Receive §
crossed out and replaced above by § Motion   1215| MS:why? The Law relinquishes its
charge,   *1872:*why? Since Law relinquishes the charge,   1217| MS:But gives you
back Pompilia; golden   *1872:*Rejoice you with Pompilia! golden   1218| MS:*regna!*
Six   *1872:regna.* Six   1221| MS:husband, joyous—ay,   *1872:*husband,—joyous,
ay,   1222| MS:also quick < > himself—   *P1869:*also—quick < >
himself,   1225| MS:gold: *P1869:*gold.   *1872:*gold!   1226| MS:Quick § over
illegible word § , let him § last two words crossed out and replaced above by two words § he
shall tempt her back § crossed out § to the § added above line § < > fled—   *P1869:*fled,
*1872:*So shall he tempt   1227| MS:back!   *1872:*back.   1227-28| MS:§ marginal note
that new ¶ begins §   1228| MS:O let   *1872:*But let   1230| MS:flout you! Is
*P1869:*flout him! Is   1231| MS:If ye § crossed out and replaced above by five words §
field with corn ye fail   1232| MS:and thistle-seed § *seed* crossed out and replaced above

Of such an apparition, such return
Interdum, to anticipate the spouse,
1240 Of Caponsacchi's very self! 'Tis said,
When nights are lone and company is rare,
His visitations brighten winter up.
If so they did—which nowise I believe—
(How can I?—proof abounding that the priest,
1245 Once fairly at his relegation-place,
Never once left it) still, admit he stole
A midnight march, would fain see friend again,
Find matter for instruction in the past,
Renew the old adventure in such chat
1250 As cheers a fireside! He was lonely too,
He, too, must need his recreative hour.
Shall it amaze the philosophic mind
If he, long wont the empurpled cup to quaff,
Have feminine society at will,
1255 Being debarred abruptly from all drink
Save at the spring which Adam used for wine,
Dreads harm to just the health he hoped to guard,
And, trying abstinence, gains malady?
Ask Tozzi, now physician to the Pope!
1260 "Little by little break"—(I hear he bids
Master Arcangeli my antagonist,
Who loves good cheer, and may indulge too much:

---

by § beards   1239| MS:spouse,—   *P1869:*spouse,   1240| MS:said *1872:*said,
1243| MS:If it § crossed out and replaced above by § so they did § last two words over *were
so* § —which scarcely § crossed out and replaced above by § nowise   1244| MS:With
evidence § last two words crossed out and replaced above by four words § How can I?—proof
1872:(How   1245| MS:relegation-place *1889a:*relegation-place,   1246| MS:it—
still *1872:*it) still   1250| MS:fireside? He <> too— *P1869:*too, *1869:*fireside! He
1252| MS:Should it *1872:*Shall it   1253-55| MS:If one, was wont <> / Being
*P1869:*quaff,/ (His feminine society at home)/ Being *CP1869:*quaff,/ Have feminine society
at will,/ Being *1889a:*If he, long wont <> //   1256| MS:wine— *P1869:*wine,
1257| MS:Dread consequence § crossed out and replaced above by § harm to just the § last
two words added above line § <> hopes § over illegible word § *P1869:*hoped
*1872:*Dreads   1258| MS:And meaning abstinence gain *P1869:*And, meaning
abstinence, gain *1872:*gains *1889a:*And, trying abstinence   1259| MS:Ask Tozzi
now *CP1869:*Ask Tozzi, now   1260| MS:by little" break—(I hear him bid *P1869:*by
little break"—(I hear he bids   1262| MS:cheer—and <> much— *1872:*cheer,

So I explain the logic of the plea
Wherewith he opened our proceedings late)—
1265 "Little by little break a habit, Don,
Become necessity to feeble flesh!"
And thus, nocturnal taste of intercourse
(Which never happened,—but, suppose it did)
May have been used to dishabituate
1270 By sip and sip this drainer to the dregs
O' the draught of conversation,—heady stuff,
Brewage which, broached, it took two days and nights
To properly discuss i' the journey, Sirs!
Such power has second-nature, men call use,
1275 That undelightful objects get to charm
Instead of chafe: the daily colocynth
Tickles the palate by repeated dose,
Old sores scratch kindly, the ass makes a push,
Although the mill-yoke-wound be smarting yet,
1280 For mill-door bolted on a holiday:
Nor must we marvel here if impulse urge
To talk the old story over now and then,
The hopes and fears, the stoppage and the haste,—
Subjects of colloquy to surfeit once.
1285 "Here did you bid me twine a rosy wreath!"
"And there you paid my lips a compliment!"
"Here you admired the tower could be so tall!"

---

and <>much: 1263| MS:of that § crossed out and replaced above by §
the   1264| MS:opened the § crossed out and replaced above by § our
1265| MS:habit, friend! CP1869:habit, Don! 1872:habit, Don,   1267| MS:thus
nocturnal P1869:thus, nocturnal   1268| MS:§ crowded between lines 1267-69 §
Which <> did, P1869:(Which <> did)   1269| MS:Might § crossed out and replaced
above by § May   1271| MS:Of § altered to § O'   1272| MS:That § crossed out §
brewage § altered to § Brewage which, § word and punctuation added above line §
P1869:which broached 1872:which, broached   1273| MS:discuss o' the
P1869:journey, sirs! CP1869:journey, Sirs 1872:discuss i' the   1274| MS:Such is the
second-nature men call use CP1869:second-nature, men call use, 1872:Such power has
second-nature   1278| 1872:push DC,BrU:push, 1889:push,   1279| MS:§ crowded
between lines 1278-80 § mill-yoke wound is smarting P1869:mill-yoke-wound be smarting
1280| MS:For the § crossed out § bolted mill-door § transposed to § mill-door bolted <>
holiday— 1872:holiday: 1281| MS:And must we marvel if the impulse pricks
P1869:impulse prick CP1869:impulse urge 1872:Nor must we marvel here if impulse
1284| MS:once? 1872:once.   1286| MS:lips the § crossed out and
replaced above by § a   1287| MS:There you 1872:Here you

"And there you likened that of Lebanon
To the nose of the beloved!" Trifles! still,
1290 *"Forsan et hæc olim,"*—such trifles serve
To make the minutes pass in winter-time.

Husband, return then, I re-counsel thee!
For, finally, of all glad circumstance
Should make a prompt return imperative,
1295 What in the world awaits thee, dost suppose?
O' the sudden, as good gifts are wont befall,
What is the hap of our unconscious Count?
That which lights bonfire and sets cask a-tilt,
Dissolves the stubborn'st heart in jollity.
1300 O admirable, there is born a babe,
A son, an heir, a Franceschini last
And best o' the stock! Pompilia, thine the palm!
Repaying incredulity with faith,
Ungenerous thrift of each marital debt
1305 With bounty in profuse expenditure,
Pompilia scorns to have the old year end
Without a present shall ring in the new—
Bestows on her too-parsimonious lord
An infant for the apple of his eye,
1310 Core of his heart, and crown completing life,
True *summum bonum* of the earthly lot!
"We," saith ingeniously the sage, "are born
Solely that others may be born of us."

1289| MS:To the § added above line § nose of § altered to § o' the
beloved!"—Trifles—yet § crossed out § still, *1872:*of the beloved!" Trifles!
still, 1290| MS:*olim,*"—of some § last two words crossed out § such may § crossed out
and replaced above by § trifles 1291-92| MS:§ marginal note that new ¶ begins §
1292| MS:recounsel *P1869:*re-counsel 1295| MS:what in § altered to § i' *1872:*in
1297| MS:of the inconscious *P1869:*unconscious *1872:*of our unconscious
1299| MS:jollity— *P1869:*jollity. 1304| MS:marital due *CP1869:*marital debt
1305| MS:With § over illegible word § bounteous § altered to § bounty and § crossed out §
1306| MS:Pompilia will not have *1872:*Pompilia scorns to have 1308| MS:Bestows
upon her parcimonious *P1869:*parsimonious *1872:*Bestows on her too-parsimonious
1310| MS:heart, the crown *CP1869:*heart, and crown 1311| MS:The
summum <> earthly § written over illegible word § *1872:*True *summum*
1312| MS:"We § over illegible word § 1313| MS:us—" *P1869:*us."

So, father, take thy child, for thine that child,
1315 Oh nothing doubt! In wedlock born, law holds
Baseness impossible: since *"filius est*
Quem nuptiæ demonstrant," twits the text
Whoever dares to doubt.

                    Yet doubt he dares!
O faith, where art thou flown from out the world?
1320 Already on what an age of doubt we fall!
Instead of each disputing for the prize,
The babe is bandied here from that to this.
Whose the babe? *"Cujum pecus?"* Guido's lamb?
"An Meliboei?" Nay, but of the priest!
1325 *"Non sed Ægonis!"* Someone must be sire:
And who shall say, in such a puzzling strait,
If there were not vouchsafed some miracle
To the wife who had been harassed and abused
More than enough by Guido's family
1330 For non-production of the promised fruit
Of marriage? What if Nature, I demand,
Touched to the quick by taunts upon her sloth,
Had roused herself, put forth recondite power,
Bestowed this birth to vindicate her sway,
1335 Like the strange favour, Maro memorized
As granted Aristæus when his hive
Lay empty of the swarm? not one more bee—
Not one more babe to Franceschini's house!

1314| MS:that child— P1869:that child, 1316| MS:impossible, since
1872:impossible: since 1317| MS:*demonstrant,*—twits P1869:*demonstrant,"*
twits 1318| MS:§ marginal note that new ¶ begins between *doubt.* and *Yet*
§ 1319| MS:faith where 1889a:faith, where 1320| MS:Already § written
in margin over illegible word § < > doubt is this § last two words crossed out
§ 1321| MS:§ crowded between lines 1320-22 § 1322| MS:this
P1869:this. 1323| MS:the lamb § crossed out and replaced above by § babe? G § crossed
out § 1325| MS:*"Non, sed* P1869:*"Non sed* 1331| MS:marriage. What if nature
CP1869:if Nature 1869:marriage? What 1333| MS:forth unusual § crossed out and
replaced above by § recondite 1334| MS:her § followed by illegible erasure § sway
P1869:sway, CP1869:sway? 1872:sway, 1335| MS:Ay put § last two words crossed
out and replaced above by three words § Repeat § crossed out § Like to the favour < >
memorized, 1872:Like the strange favor < > memorized 1336| MS:Was granted
1872:As granted 1337| MS:swarm, not 1872:swarm? not 1338| MS:house—

And lo, a new birth filled the air with joy,
1340 Sprung from the bowels of the generous steer,
A novel son and heir rejoiced the Count!
Spontaneous generation, need I prove
Were facile feat to Nature at a pinch?
Let whoso doubts, steep horsehair certain weeks
1345 In water, there will be produced a snake;
Spontaneous product of the horse, which horse
Happens to be the representative—
Now that I think on't—of Arezzo's self,
The very city our conception blessed:
1350 Is not a prancing horse the City-arms?
What sane eye fails to see coincidence?
Cur ego, boast thou, my Pompilia, then,
Desperem fieri sine conjuge
Mater—how well the Ovidian distich suits!—
1355 *Et parere intacto dummodo*
Casta viro? Such miracle was wrought!
Note, further, as to mark the prodigy,
The babe in question neither took the name
Of Guido, from the sire presumptive, nor
1360 Giuseppe, from the sire potential, but
Gaetano—last saint of our hierarchy,
And newest namer for a thing so new!

---

*1872:*house!   1340| MS:steed, *CP1869:*steed! *1872:*steer,   1341| MS:Just as a son
*P1869:*Just so a   *1872:*A novel son   1343| MS:It § crossed out and replaced above by §
Were <> nature   *CP1869:*to Nature   1344| MS:certain days § crossed out § weeks,
*1889a:*weeks   1345| MS:snake: *P1869:*snake;   1346| MS:A second product <>
horse—which horse *P1869:*the horse, which horse   *1872:*Spontaneous product
1348| MS:self *1872:*self,   1349| MS:city where § crossed out § <> blessed! *1872:*blessed:
1351| MS:eye sees not such coincidence? *1872:*eye fails to see coincidence?   1354| MS:the
Ovidian language § crossed out and replaced above by § distich   1356| MS:*viro?*
but language baffles here. *1872:viro?* a miracle was wrought! *1889a:viro?* Such
miracle   1357| MS:And § crossed out and replaced in margin by word and comma §
Note,   1359| MS:Of Guido from *CP1869:*Of Guido, from   1360| MS:Giuseppe
from *CP1869:*Giuseppe, from   1361| MS:of the hierarchy, *1872:*of our
hierarchy,   1362| MS:§ crowded between 1361-63 § new: *1872:*new!

What other motive could have prompted choice?

Therefore be peace again: exult, ye hills!
¹³⁶⁵ Ye vales rejoicingly break forth in song!
Incipe, parve puer, begin, small boy,
Risu cognoscere patrem, with a laugh
To recognize thy parent! Nor do thou
Boggle, oh parent, to return the grace!
¹³⁷⁰ *Nec anceps hære, pater, puero*
Cognoscendo—one may well eke out the prayer!
In vain! The perverse Guido doubts his eyes,
Distrusts assurance, lets the devil drive.
Because his house is swept and garnished now,
¹³⁷⁵ He, having summoned seven like himself,
Must hurry thither, knock and enter in,
And make the last worse than the first, indeed!
Is he content? We are. No further blame
O' the man and murder! They were stigmatized
¹³⁸⁰ Befittingly: the Court heard long ago
My mind o' the matter, which, outpouring full,
Has long since swept like surge, i' the simile
Of Homer, overborne both dyke and dam,
And whelmed alike client and advocate:
¹³⁸⁵ His fate is sealed, his life as good as gone,
On him I am not tempted to waste word.
Yet though my purpose holds,—which was and is

1363-64| MS:§ marginal note that new ¶ begins §   1366| MS:*puer,*—begin,
poor § crossed out and replaced above by § small *P1869:puer,* begin   1367| MS:a
smile *1872:*a laugh   1369| MS:Boggle, o Parent <> grace— *P1869:*Boggle,
oh parent *1872:*grace!   1371| MS:one might well <> the phrase § crossed
out and replaced above by § prayer! *1872:*one may well   1373| MS:drive;
*1872:*drive.   1374| MS:Whether § crossed out and replaced above by § Because
<> now *P1869:*now,   1375| MS:And § crossed out and replaced in margin by word
and comma § He,   1376| MS:They § crossed out and replaced in margin by § Must
hurry there § altered to § thither, and § crossed out §   1377| MS:last and far § last two
words crossed out §   1378| MS:are: § crossed out § no § altered to § No further word
§ crossed out §   1379| MS:On § altered to § O' <> stigmatised *P1869:*stigmatized
1380| MS:the Court has § altered to § heard   1381| MS:My full § crossed out § <> on
the matter, that § altered to § which *P1869:*o'   1382| MS:Had § altered to §
Has long since swept, § word and comma added above line § like the § crossed out §
surge i' *1872:*swept like surge, i'   1384| MS:Had § altered to § And

60

And solely shall be to the very end,
To draw the true *effigies* of a saint,
1390 Do justice to perfection in the sex,—
Yet let not some gross pamperer of the flesh
And niggard in the spirit's nourishment,
Whose feeding hath offuscated his wit
Rather than law,—he never had, to lose—
1395 Let not such advocate object to me
I leave my proper function of attack!
"What's this to Bacchus?"—(in the classic phrase,
Well used, for once) he hiccups probably.
O Advocate o' the Poor, thou born to make
1400 Their blessing void—*beati pauperes!*
By painting saintship I depicture sin:
Beside my pearl, I prove how black thy jet,
And, through Pompilia's virtue, Guido's crime.

Back to her, then,—with but one beauty more,
1405 End we our argument,—one crowning grace
Pre-eminent 'mid agony and death.
For to the last Pompilia played her part,
Used the right means to the permissible end,
And, wily as an eel that stirs the mud
1410 Thick overhead, so baffling spearman's thrust,
She, while he stabbed her, simulated death,
Delayed, for his sake, the catastrophe,
Obtained herself a respite, four days' grace,
Whereby she told her story to the world,

1389| MS:true *effigies* § altered to § *effigiem*   *1872:effigies*   1391| MS:Still let < > of flesh
*P1869:*Yet, let < > o' the flesh   *1872:*Yet let < > of   1392| MS:the spirit's § added
above line §   1396| MS:proper business § crossed out and replaced above by § function
1399| MS:to prove § crossed out §   1400| MS:blessing null § crossed out and
replaced above by § void < > *pauperes!—*   *P1869:pauperes!*   1401| MS:sin,   *1872:*sin:
1402| MS:Beside the pearl I < > black the jet,   *CP1869:*pearl, I   *1872:*Beside my pearl < >
black thy jet,   1403| MS:And through   *1872:*And, through   1403-4| MS:§ marginal
note that new ¶ begins §   1405| MS:argument,—a crowning   *P1869:*argument,—one
crowning   1410| MS:spear-man's stroke § crossed out and replaced above by § thrust,
*P1869:*spearman's   1413| MS:Obtained thereby § crossed out and replaced above by §
herself < > four good § crossed out §   1414| MS:Wherein § altered to § Whereby

¹⁴¹⁵ Enabled me to make the present speech,
And, by a full confession, saved her soul.

Yet hold, even here would malice leer its last,
Gurgle its choked remonstrance: snake, hiss free!
Oh, that's the objection? And to whom?—not her
¹⁴²⁰ But me, forsooth—as, in the very act
Of both confession and (what followed close)
Subsequent talk, chatter and gossipry,
Babble to sympathizing he and she
Whoever chose besiege her dying bed,—
¹⁴²⁵ As this were found at variance with my tale,
Falsified all I have adduced for truth,
Admitted not one peccadillo here,
Pretended to perfection, first and last,
O' the whole procedure—perfect in the end,
¹⁴³⁰ Perfect i' the means, perfect in everything,
Leaving a lawyer nothing to excuse,
Reason away and show his skill about!
—A flight, impossible to Adamic flesh,
Just to be fancied, scarcely to be wished,
¹⁴³⁵ And, anyhow, unpleadable in court!
"How reconcile," gasps Malice, "that with this?"

Your "this," friend, is extraneous to the law,
Comes of men's outside meddling, the unskilled

---

¹⁴¹⁵| MS:make this § altered to § the ¹⁴¹⁶⁻¹⁷| MS:§ marginal note that new ¶ begins §
¹⁴¹⁷| MS:here spent § crossed out and replaced above by § would <> leers § altered to § leer
¹⁴¹⁸| MS:Gurgles § altered to § Gurgle ¹⁴²⁰| MS:forsooth,—that § crossed out and
replaced above by word and comma § as, ¹⁴²¹| MS:Of not § crossed out and replaced
above by § both confession but § crossed out and replaced above by § and what <> close,
*P1869:*and, what *1872:*and (what <> close) ¹⁴²⁵| MS:That talk § last two words
crossed out and replaced above by two words § As this was § altered to § were <> tale—
*P1869:*tale, ¹⁴²⁶| MS:all I had § altered to § have adduced for § written over illegible
word, perhaps *as* § ¹⁴²⁷| MS:one part § crossed out § ¹⁴²⁸| MS:to a § crossed
out § ¹⁴³¹| MS:Leaving a § written above word illegibly crossed out, possibly *the* §
¹⁴³⁵| MS:And, certainly not § last two words crossed out and replaced above by word and
comma § anyhow, unpleaded § altered to § unpleadable in a § crossed out §
¹⁴³⁶| MS:reconcile" gasps Malice "this with that?" § transposed to § that with this?"
*1889a:*reconcile," gasps Malice, "that ¹⁴³⁶⁻³⁷| MS:§ marginal
note that new ¶ begins § ¹⁴³⁸| MS:of mere § altered to § men's

Interposition of such fools as press
1440 Out of their province. Must I speak my mind?
Far better had Pompilia died o' the spot
Than found a tongue to wag and shame the law,
Shame most of all herself,—could friendship fail
And advocacy lie less on the alert:
1445 But no, they shall protect her to the end!
Do I credit the alleged narration? No!
Lied our Pompilia then, to laud herself?
Still, no! Clear up what seems discrepancy?
The means abound: art's long, though time is short;
1450 So, keeping me in compass, all I urge
Is—since, confession at the point of death,
Nam in articulo mortis, with the Church
Passes for statement honest and sincere,
Nemo presumitur reus esse,—then,
1455 If sure that all affirmed would be believed,
'Twas charity, in her so circumstanced,
To spend the last breath in one effort more
For universal good of friend and foe:
And,—by pretending utter innocence,
1460 Nay, freedom from each foible we forgive,—
Re-integrate—not solely her own fame,

But do the like kind office for the priest
Whom telling the crude truth about might vex,
Haply expose to peril, abbreviate
¹⁴⁶⁵ Indeed the long career of usefulness
Presumably before him: while her lord,
Whose fleeting life is forfeit to the law,—
What mercy to the culprit if, by just
The gift of such a full certificate
¹⁴⁷⁰ Of his immitigable guiltiness,
She stifled in him the absurd conceit
Of murder as it were a mere revenge
—Stopped confirmation of that jealousy
Which, did she but acknowledge the first flaw,
¹⁴⁷⁵ The faintest foible, had emboldened him
To battle with the charge, baulk penitence,
Bar preparation for impending fate!
Whereas, persuade him that he slew a saint
Who sinned not even where she may have sinned,
¹⁴⁸⁰ You urge him all the brisklier to repent
Of most and least and aught and everything!
Still, if this view of mine content you not,

---

above by § solely   ¹⁴⁶²| MS:like § over illegible word §   ¹⁴⁶³| MS:Whom the
crude truth might treat less courteously: *P1869:*courteously,   *1872:*Whom telling the crude
truth about might vex,   ¹⁴⁶⁴| MS:Indeed, expose to danger or cut short § last four
words crossed out and replaced above by two words § peril, abbreviate   *1872:*Haply expose
¹⁴⁶⁵| MS:The life and long   *1872:*Indeed the long   ¹⁴⁶⁶| MS:him,—while
*P1869:*him: while   ¹⁴⁶⁷| MS:Whose fleeting § added above line § life will soon be § last
three words crossed out and replaced above by § is   ¹⁴⁶⁸| MS:What kindness
§ crossed out and replaced above by § mercy <> if thereby § altered to § by   *CP1869:*if, by
¹⁴⁶⁸⁻⁷⁰| MS:§ lines crowded in margin; marks indicate placement §   ¹⁴⁷¹| MS:him that
§ crossed out and replaced above by § the   ¹⁴⁷²| MS:a just § crossed out and replaced
above by § mere revenge—   *P1869:*revenge!   *1872:*revenge   ¹⁴⁷³| MS:That § crossed
out and replaced above by § Stopped confirmation § over illegible word, perhaps
satisfaction § of the § altered to § that violence § crossed out   *P1869:*—Stopped
¹⁴⁷⁴| MS:Which, if § crossed out and replaced above by § had she   *1872:*Which, did she
¹⁴⁷⁵| MS:foible, might embolden   *1872:*foible had emboldened   ¹⁴⁷⁶| MS:with his
judge, § written above illegibly crossed out word § baulk   *1872:*with the charge, baulk
¹⁴⁷⁷| MS:And fail § last two words crossed out and replaced above by § Bar prepare § altered
to § preparation himself § crossed out § for what § crossed out § <> fate.   *1872:*fate!
¹⁴⁷⁸| MS:Whereas—persuade him he has slain a   *P1869:*Whereas, persuade   *1872:*him that
he slew a   ¹⁴⁷⁹| MS:not in the little she did sin,   *1872:*not even where she may have
sinned,   ¹⁴⁸⁰| MS:the louder § crossed out and replaced above by § brisklier
¹⁴⁸²| MS:Next,—if this view of mine, § last two words and comma added above line §

Lords, nor excuse the genial falsehood here,
We come to our *Triarii*, last resource:
1485 We fall back on the inexpugnable,
Submitting,—she confessed before she talked!
The sacrament obliterates the sin:
What is not,—was not, therefore, in a sense.
Let Molinists distinguish, "Souls washed white
1490 But red once, still show pinkish to the eye!"
We say, abolishment is nothingness,
And nothingness has neither head nor tail,
End nor beginning! Better estimate
Exorbitantly, than disparage aught
1495 Of the efficacity of the act, I hope!

Solvuntur tabulæ? May we laugh and go?
Well,—not before (in filial gratitude
To Law, who, mighty mother, waves adieu)
We take on us to vindicate Law's self!
1500 For,—yea, Sirs,—curb the start, curtail the stare!—

content ye not, *1872:*Still, if <> mine content you not, ¹⁴⁸³| MS:§ crowded between lines 1482-84 § ¹⁴⁸⁴| MS:§ word illegibly crossed out; replaced in margin by § 'Tis come<>resource, *1872:*We come<>resource: ¹⁴⁸⁵| MS:We § added in margin § Fall § altered to § fall back on § added above word illegibly crossed out § ¹⁴⁸⁶| MS:Admit § altered to § Submit that § crossed out and replaced below by word, comma and dash § you,—she *1872:*Submitting,—she ¹⁴⁸⁷| MS:This § altered to § The Sacrament § altered to § sacrament obliterates all § crossed out and replaced above by § the ¹⁴⁸⁸| MS:Who then, § last two words and comma crossed out § what § altered to § What is not, clearly never was § last three words crossed out and replaced above by six words, dash, comma and period § —was not, in a certain sense. *1872:*was not, therefore, in a sense. ¹⁴⁸⁹| MS:distinguish, "Which is § last two words crossed out and replaced above by two words § Souls grown white *1869:*distinguish, "Souls washed white ¹⁴⁹⁰| MS:Were red *1872:*But red ¹⁴⁹¹| MS:nothingness *CP1869:*nothingness, *1869:*nothingness *1872:*nothingness, ¹⁴⁹²| MS:tail *1872:*tail, ¹⁴⁹³| MS:beginning;—else a doubt be cast § last five words crossed out and replaced above by three words § better doubt § crossed out § estimate *1872:*beginning! Better ¹⁴⁹⁴| MS:§ crowded between lines 1493-95 § ¹⁴⁹⁵| MS:On § altered to § Of <> act, § next three words illegibly crossed out and replaced above by two words and exclamation point § I hope! ¹⁴⁹⁵⁻⁹⁶| MS:§ marginal note that new ¶ begins § *1889a:*§ no ¶ § *1889:*§ no ¶ ; emended to restore ¶ ; see Editorial Notes § ¹⁴⁹⁷| MS:before; in *P1869:*before,—in *1869:*before (in ¹⁴⁹⁸| MS:adieu,— *1869:*adieu) ¹⁴⁹⁹| MS:self— *1872:*self! ¹⁵⁰⁰| MS:For,—oh, § crossed out and replaced above by word and comma § yea, <> start, restrain § crossed out and replaced above by § curtail *P1869:*sirs *CP1869:*yea, Sirs

Remains that we apologize for haste
I' the Law, our lady who here bristles up
"Blame my procedure? Could the Court mistake?
(Which were indeed a misery to think)
1505 Did not my sentence in the former stage
O' the business bear a title plain enough?
Decretum"—I translate it word for word—
" 'Decreed: the priest, for his complicity
I' the flight and deviation of the dame,
1510 As well as for unlawful intercourse,
Is banished three years:' crime and penalty,
Declared alike. If he be taxed with guilt,
How can you call Pompilia innocent?
If both be innocent, have I been just?"

1515 Gently, O mother, judge men—whose mistake
Is in the mere misapprehensiveness!
The Titulus a-top of your decree
Was but to ticket there the kind of charge
You in good time would arbitrate upon.
1520 Title is one thing,—arbitration's self,
Probatio, quite another possibly.
Subsistit, there holds good the old response,
Responsio tradita, we must not stick,
Quod non sit attendenus Titulus,
1525 To the Title, sed Probatio, but the Proof,

1501| MS:apologise *P1869:*apologize   1502| MS:the Law, our § last two words added above line § lady of us all, § last three words and comma crossed out § who here § added above line §   1503| MS:"And my procedure? Did I then § last two words crossed out and replaced above by two words § the Court   *1872:*"Blame my procedure? Could the
1507| MS:Decretum"—I recite § crossed out and replaced above by § translate
1511| MS:years:' p § crossed out § crime   *1889a:*years: crime § emended to § years:' § see Editorial Notes §   1512| MS:guilt   *1872:*guilt,   1514| MS:If he be   *P1869:*If they be   *1872:*If both be   1514-15| MS:§ no ¶ §   *CP1869:*§ marginal note that new ¶ begins §
1515| MS:men! Their § crossed out and replaced above by dash and word § —whose   *1872:*men—whose   1516| MS:the poor misapprehensiveness.   *1872:*the mere misapprehensiveness!   1517| MS:atop   *CP1869:*a-top   1522| MS:Subsistit—there < > response   *P1869:Subsistit,* there   *CP1869:*response,   1523| MS:not name § crossed out and replaced above by § stick,   1525| MS:but the § crossed out and replaced above

Resultans ex processu, the result
O' the Trial, and the style of punishment,
Et pœna per sententiam imposita.
All is tentative, till the sentence come:
1530   An indication of what men expect,
But nowise an assurance they shall find.
Lords, what if we permissibly relax
The tense bow, as the law-god Phœbus bids,
Relieve our gravity at labour's close?
1535   I traverse Rome, feel thirsty, need a draught,
Look for a wine-shop, find it by the bough
Projecting as to say "Here wine is sold!"
So much I know,—"sold:" but what sort of wine?
Strong, weak, sweet, sour, home-made or foreign drink?
1540   That much must I discover by myself.
"Wine is sold," quoth the bough, "but good or bad,
Find, and inform us when you smack your lips!"
Exactly so, Law hangs her title forth,
To show she entertains you with such case

---

by § to Proof, *1872:*but the Proof,   1526–30| MS:§ the following five lines were revised
on the blank page facing the MS text. The original is referred to as MSA and the revision as
MSB § MSA:*Resultans ex processu,* through the Cause. § last three words and period crossed
out and replaced above by two words § and result/ § lines 1527-28 crowded between lines
1526-29 in continuous line with break indicated between *punishment,* and *Et* § O' the Trial
§ last three words added in margin § : and the style of punishment,/ *Et pœna per
sententiam imposita./* Yet to be tried § last four words crossed out § simply § altered to §
Simply tentative, till the sentence come,—/ Mere indication of what men expect,—/
MSB:*Resultans ex processu,* and result/ O' the Trial, and the style of punishment,/ Et poena
per sententiam imposita;/ —Simply tentative till the sentence come,/ Mere indication §
shorthand marks perhaps for *et cetera* ; line breaks off § *P1869://* Et pœna per sententiam
imposita;/ All is tentative, till < > / *1872:processu,* the result // < > imposita./ < >
come:/ An indication 1531| MS:And nowise an § added above line § *1872:*But nowise
1532| MS:Just so—that § last three words crossed out and replaced above by three words §
Lords, what § over illegible word, perhaps *just* § if   1533| MS:bow as < > bids
*P1869:*bow, as < > bids,   1534| MS:at the § crossed out § close § written over illegible
word § of this § crossed out and replaced above by § speech?— *1872:*at labour's close?
1537| MS:to tell § crossed out and replaced above by § say   1538| MS:know, then:§ word
crossed out and replaced above by dash, word and quotation marks § —"sold:"
1539| MS:— § added in margin § Strong *P1869:*Strong   1541| MS:sold" quoth the
bough "but *P1869:*sold," quoth the bough, "but   1542| MS:Find, out § crossed out §
and tell § crossed out and replaced above by § inform < > lips"! *P1869:*lips!"
1543| MS:so, I § crossed out and replaced above by § Law hang § altered to § hangs my
§ crossed out and replaced above by § her Title forth," *P1869:*title forth,
1544| MS:show I § altered to § she entertain § altered to § entertains you with an § altered

67

¹⁵⁴⁵ About such crime. Come in! she pours, you quaff.
You find the Priest good liquor in the main,
But heady and provocative of brawls:
Remand the residue to flask once more,
Lay it low where it may deposit lees,
¹⁵⁵⁰ I' the cellar: thence produce it presently,
Three years the brighter and the better!

                                    Thus,
Law's son, have I bestowed my filial help,
And thus I end, *tenax proposito;*
Point to point as I purposed have I drawn
¹⁵⁵⁵ Pompilia, and implied as terribly
Guido: so, gazing, let the world crown Law—
Able once more, despite my impotence,
And helped by the acumen of the Court,
To eliminate, display, make triumph truth!
¹⁵⁶⁰ What other prize than truth were worth the pains?

There's my oration—much exceeds in length
That famed panegyric of Isocrates,

---

to § such ease § altered to § case   ^{1545|} MS:crime: come in, I § crossed out and replaced
above by § she pour § altered to § pours it § crossed out § , you taste § crossed out § quaff.
*1869:*in! she   *1872:*crime. Come   ^{1546|} MS:You § written over illegible word §
^{1547|} MS:brawls:— *P1869:*brawls. *1872:*brawls: ^{1549|} MS:it down § altered to §
low   ^{1550|} MS:cellar,—thence <> presently *P1869:*cellar: thence <>
presently,   ^{1551|} MS:better. § ¶ § Thus *P1869:*better! § ¶ § Thus,
^{1553|} MS:*proposito—* *P1869:proposito;*   · ^{1554|} MS:purposed I have drawn
§ transposed to § have I drawn   ^{1556|} MS:Guido; so <> world praise § crossed out and
replaced above by § crown Law *P1869:*Guido: so <> Law—   ^{1557|} MS:Assisting,
even through § last three words crossed out and replaced above by five words § Able § next
word illegibly crossed out § once more, despite   ^{1558|} MS:§ crowded between lines
1557-59 § the court, *P1869:*the Court,   ^{1559|} MS:eliminate and clarify the § last three
words crossed out and replaced below by three words and commas § , display, make triumph
truth— *P1869:*truth!   ^{1560|} MS:prize than truth § last two words added below
line § were <> pains? I have said. § last three words and period crossed out §
^{1560-61|} MS:§ line drawn with notation(*small line*) §   ^{1561|} MS:oration—scarce exceeds
*P1869:*oration—much exceeds   ^{1562|} MS:famed Panegyric *1872:*panegyric

68

They say it took him fifteen years to pen.
But all those ancients could say anything!
¹⁵⁶⁵ He put in just what rushed into his head:
While I shall have to prune and pare and print.
This comes of being born in modern times
With priests for auditory. Still, it pays.

^{1563|} MS:They vaunt § crossed out and replaced above by § say   ^{1564|} MS:But he—
those Pagans § crossed out and replaced above by § ancients <> anything;
*P1869:*anything! *CP1869:*But all those   ^{1565|} MS:in all that § last two words crossed
out and replaced above by two words § just what <> head, *1872:*head:
^{1566|} MS:pare—well, well— § last two words and dashes crossed out and replaced above by
two words and period § and print.   ^{1567|} MS:This § crossed out and restored §

X

THE POPE

Like to Ahasuerus, that shrewd prince,
I will begin,—as is, these seven years now,
My daily wont,—and read a History
(Written by one whose deft right hand was dust
5   To the last digit, ages ere my birth)
Of all my predecessors, Popes of Rome:
For though mine ancient early dropped the pen,
Yet others picked it up and wrote it dry,
Since of the making books there is no end.
10   And so I have the Papacy complete
From Peter first to Alexander last;
Can question each and take instruction so.
Have I to dare?—I ask, how dared this Pope?
To suffer?—Suchanone, how suffered he?
15   Being about to judge, as now, I seek
How judged once, well or ill, some other Pope;
Study some signal judgment that subsists
To blaze on, or else blot, the page which seals
The sum up of what gain or loss to God
20   Came of His one more Vicar in the world.
So, do I find example, rule of life;
So, square and set in order the next page,
Shall be stretched smooth o'er my own funeral cyst.

Eight hundred years exact before the year
25   I was made Pope, men made Formosus Pope,

---

³| MS:a history   *P1869:*a History   ⁴⁻⁵| MS:§ inserted between 3-6 § / <> digit ages
P1869:/ <> digit, ages   ⁶| MS:of Rome;   *P1869:*of Rome: ⁷⁻¹⁰| MS:§ inserted
in margin § drops the pen / <> pick <> write <> / <> end: *P1869:*dropped the
pen, / <> picked <> wrote <> / <> end.   ¹²| MS:I question   *P1869:*Can
question   ¹³| MS:dare,—I ask, How   *P1869:*ask, how   *1889a:*dare?—I
¹⁴| MS:suffer? How § crossed out and replaced above by word and comma § Suchanone,
¹⁵| MS:judge as   *P1869:*judge, as   ¹⁶| MS:other Pope,   *P1869:*other Pope;
¹⁸| MS:on or <> blot the   *P1869:*on, or <> blot, the   ²⁰| MS:of his <> world:
*P1869:*of His <> world.   ²¹| MS:So do <> life   *P1869:*So, do <> life;
²²| MS:So square <> order my own § last two words crossed out and replaced above by two
words § the next page.   *P1869:*So, square <> page,   ²³| MS:Soon to § last two words
crossed out and replaced above by § Shall <> my own § inserted above line §
²⁴| MS:§ marginal note that new ¶ begins §   ²⁵| MS:made pope   *P1869:*made Pope

Say Sigebert and other chroniclers.
Ere I confirm or quash the Trial here
Of Guido Franceschini and his friends,
Read,—How there was a ghastly Trial once
30 Of a dead man by a live man, and both, Popes:
Thus—in the antique penman's very phrase.

"Then Stephen, Pope and seventh of the name,
Cried out, in synod as he sat in state,
While choler quivered on his brow and beard,
35 'Come into court, Formosus, thou lost wretch,
That claimedst to be late Pope as even I!'

"And at the word the great door of the church
Flew wide, and in they brought Formosus' self,
The body of him, dead, even as embalmed
40 And buried duly in the Vatican
Eight months before, exhumed thus for the nonce.
They set it, that dead body of a Pope,
Clothed in pontific vesture now again,
Upright on Peter's chair as if alive.

45 "And Stephen, springing up, cried furiously
'Bishop of Porto, wherefore didst presume
To leave that see and take this Roman see,

---

²⁶| MS:Saith Sigebert, with § crossed out and replaced above by § say   *P1869:*Say Sigebert
and other   ²⁷| MS:the sentence § crossed out and replaced above by § trial   *P1869:*the
Trial   ²⁸| MS:his gang § crossed out §   ²⁹| MS:Which § crossed out § Read,—
how < > trial   *P1869:*ghastly Trial   *1872:*Read,—How   ³⁰| MS:Of a § crossed out
§ < > by a § crossed out § < > man and both men, § last word and comma inserted above §
Popes: *P1869:*Of a dead < > by a live man, and both, Popes: ³²| MS:Then Stephen
Pope < > name   *P1869:*"Then Stephen, Pope < > name,   ³³| MS:out in < > state
*P1869:*out, in < > state,   ³⁴| MS:(While < > beard)   *P1869:*While < > beard,
³⁶| MS:late the Pope I am!'   *P1869:*the Pope as I!'   *1889a:*late Pope as even I!'
³⁷| MS:§ marginal note that new paragraph begins §   *P1869:*word, the   *1889a:*word the
⁴²| MS:a pope § over *man* §   *P1869:*a Pope,   ⁴⁴⁻⁴⁵| MS:§ no ¶ §   *1872:*§ ¶ §
⁴⁴| MS:on Peter's Chair   *P1869:*on Peter's chair   ⁴⁵| MS:And Stephen § written over
perhaps *Pope* § < > up cried   *P1869:*up, cried   ⁴⁷| MS:this see of Rome,

Exchange the lesser for the greater see,
—A thing against the canons of the Church?'

50 "Then one—(a Deacon who, observing forms,
Was placed by Stephen to repel the charge,
Be advocate and mouthpiece of the corpse)—
Spoke as he dared, set stammeringly forth
With white lips and dry tongue,—as but a youth,
55 For frightful was the corpse-face to behold,—
How nowise lacked there precedent for this.

"But when, for his last precedent of all,
Emboldened by the Spirit, out he blurts
'And, Holy Father, didst not thou thyself
60 Vacate the lesser for the greater see,
Half a year since change Arago for Rome?'
'—Ye have the sin's defence now, Synod mine!'
Shrieks Stephen in a beastly froth of rage:
'Judge now betwixt him dead and me alive!
65 Hath he intruded, or do I pretend?
Judge, judge!'—breaks wavelike one whole foam of wrath.

"Whereupon they, being friends and followers,
Said 'Ay, thou art Christ's Vicar, and not he!
Away with what is frightful to behold!
70 This act was uncanonic and a fault.'

"Then, swallowed up in rage, Stephen exclaimed
'So, guilty! So, remains I punish guilt!

*P1869:*this Roman see,   48| MS:§ inserted between 47-49 §   49| MS:the Church?
*P1869:*the Church?'   50| MS:Then he, the Deacon *P1869:*Then one, (a Deacon
*1872:*one—(a   51| MS:repel this charge *P1869:*repel the charge,   52| MS:corpse,
*1869:*corpse) *1872:*corpse)—   56-57| MS:§ no ¶ § *1872:*§ ¶ §   57| MS:when
for *P1869:*when, for   60| MS:see *P1869:*see,   62| MS:Ye < > now synod
or *P1869:*—Ye *1889a:*now, Synod   63| MS:rage *P1869:*rage: 65| MS:he obtruded
or *P1869:*he intruded or *1889a:*intruded, or   67| MS:they, his friends < > followers
all, *P1869:*they, being friends < > followers,   68| MS:art Christ's Vicar and not he:
*P1869:*art Christ's Vicar, and not he!   70| MS:uncanonic, null and void § last three
words crossed out and replaced above by three words, period and quotation marks § and a
fault." *P1869:*uncanonic and   71| MS:Then swallowed < > rage Stephen
*P1869:*Then, swallowed < > rage, Stephen   72| MS:guilt. *P1869:*guilt!

He is unpoped, and all he did I damn:
The Bishop, that ordained him, I degrade:
75 Depose to laics those he raised to priests:
What they have wrought is mischief nor shall stand,
It is confusion, let it vex no more!
Since I revoke, annul and abrogate
All his decrees in all kinds: they are void!
80 In token whereof and warning to the world,
Strip me yon miscreant of those robes usurped,
And clothe him with vile serge befitting such!
Then hale the carrion to the market-place:
Let the town-hangman chop from his right hand
85 Those same three fingers which he blessed withal;
Next cut the head off once was crowned forsooth:
And last go fling them, fingers, head and trunk,
To Tiber that my Christian fish may sup!'
—Either because of ΙΧΘΥΣ which means Fish
90 And very aptly symbolizes Christ,
Or else because the Pope is Fisherman,
And seals with Fisher's-signet.

                    "Anyway,
So said, so done: himself, to see it done,
Followed the corpse they trailed from street to street
95 Till into Tiber wave they threw the thing.
The people, crowded on the banks to see,

73| MS:unpoped and P1869:unpoped, and   74| MS:The Bishop that < > him I
1869:The Bishop, that < > him, I   77| MS:more P1869:more!   79| MS:kinds,
they are void. P1869:kinds: they are void!   81| MS:usurped P1869:usurped,
82| MS:such, P1869:such!   83| MS:market-place, P1869:market-place;
1889a:market-place: 85| MS:withal, P1869:withal;   86| MS:off, once < >
forsooth, P1869:forsooth: 1889a:off once   87| MS:And then go fling all,
fingers head and trunk P1869:And last go < > fingers, head and trunk, 1872:fling
them, fingers   88–93| MS:In Tiber that the Christian < > sup § over
perhaps live § ! / § ¶ § So < > himself to < > done P1869:that my Christian < >
sup!' / —Either because of ΙΧΘΥΣ which means Fish / And very aptly symbolizes Christ, /
Or else because the Pope is Fisherman / And seals with Fisher's-signet. Anyway, / So < >
himself, to < > done, 1872:To Tiber < > / / / < > is Fisherman, / < > with Fisher's-signet.
§ ¶ § Anyway,   94| MS:Following P1869:corpse, they 1872:Followed < > corpse
they   96| MS:people crowding < > see P1869:people, crowded < > see,

Were loud or mute, wept or laughed, cursed or jeered,
According as the deed addressed their sense;
A scandal verily: and out spake a Jew
100   'Wot ye your Christ had vexed our Herod thus?'

"Now when, Formosus being dead a year,
His judge Pope Stephen tasted death in turn,
Made captive by the mob and strangled straight,
Romanus, his successor for a month,
105   Did make protest Formosus was with God,
Holy, just, true in thought and word and deed.
Next Theodore, who reigned but twenty days,
Therein convoked a synod, whose decree
Did reinstate, repope the late unpoped,
110   And do away with Stephen as accursed.
So that when presently certain fisher-folk
(As if the queasy river could not hold
Its swallowed Jonas, but discharged the meal)
Produced the timely product of their nets,
115   The mutilated man, Formosus,—saved
From putrefaction by the embalmer's spice,
Or, as some said, by sanctity of flesh,—
'Why, lay the body again,' bade Theodore,
'Among his predecessors, in the church
120   And burial-place of Peter!' which was done.
'And,' addeth Luitprand, 'many of repute,
Pious and still alive, avouch to me
That, as they bore the body up the aisle,

97| MS:§ first four words inserted above §   98| MS:sense, *P1869:*sense;
99| MS:verily, and *P1869:*verily: and   100| MS:ye that Christ had vexed King Herod
*P1869:*ye your Christ had vexed our Herod   103| MS:Thrown into § last two words
crossed out § <> captive and straight strangled by the mob, § transposed to § captive by the
mob and strangled straight,   104| MS:Theodore § crossed out and replaced above by §
Romanus   113| MS:swallowed Jonas but *P1869:*swallowed Jonas, but
114| MS:nets *P1869:*nets,   115| MS:man, Formosus, saved *P1869:*man, Formosus,—
saved   116| MS:spice *P1869:*spice,   117| MS:But much more by a sanctity
*P1869:*Or, as some said, by sanctity   118| MS:again' bade Theodore *1889a:*again,'
bade Theodore,   120| MS:done: *P1869:*done.   121| MS:addeth Luitprand 'many
of repute *P1869:*repute, *1889a:*addeth Luitprand, 'many   122| MS:alive avouch
*P1869:*alive, avouch   123| MS:That as <> aisle *1872:*That, as <> aisle,

The saints in imaged row bowed each his head
125 For welcome to a brother-saint come back.'
As for Romanus and this Theodore,
These two Popes, through the brief reign granted each,
Could but initiate what John came to close
And give the final stamp to: he it was
130 Ninth of the name, (I follow the best guides)
Who,—in full synod at Ravenna held
With Bishops seventy-four, and present too
Eude King of France with his Archbishopry,—
Did condemn Stephen, anathematize
135 The disinterment, and make all blots blank,
'For,' argueth here Auxilius in a place
De Ordinationibus, 'precedents
Had been, no lack, before Formosus long,
Of Bishops so transferred from see to see,—
140 Marinus, for example:' read the tract.

"But, after John, came Sergius, reaffirmed
The right of Stephen, cursed Formosus, nay
Cast out, some say, his corpse a second time.
And here,—because the matter went to ground,
145 Fretted by new griefs, other cares of the age,—
Here is the last pronouncing of the Church,
Her sentence that subsists unto this day.

124| MS:The imaged saints in row   *P1869:*The saints in imaged row   125| MS:In
welcome   *P1869:*For welcome   127| MS:two Popes through   *P1869:*two Popes,
through   128| MS:what had close by § last three words crossed out §   129| MS:was,
*1872:*was   130| MS:§ inserted between 129-31 § name, I follow—   *P1869:*name, (I
follow the best guides)   131| MS:Who, in < > Ravenna sat   *P1869:*Who,—in < >
Ravenna held   132| MS:seventy four   *P1869:*seventy-four   133| MS:Eudes < >
Archbishopry,   *P1869:*Eude < > Archbishopry,—   135| MS:blank.   *1889a:*blank,
136| MS:argueth here § inserted above §   137| MS:*De ordinationibus Papæ,*—
'precedents   *P1869:De Ordinationibus,* 'precedents   138| MS:long § over illegible
word § ,   139| MS:Of Bishops thus transferred   *P1869:*Of Bishops so transferred
141| MS:But after John came   *P1869:*But, after John, came   144| MS:here, because
< > ground   *P1869:*here,—because ground,   145| MS:Fretted § over illegible word § of
§ crossed out and replaced above by § by < > other cares § over illegible erasure § < > age,
*P1869:*age,—   146| MS:the Church   *P1869:*the Church,   147| MS:And sentence

Yet constantly opinion hath prevailed
I' the Church, Formosus was a holy man."

150   Which of the judgments was infallible?
Which of my predecessors spoke for God?
And what availed Formosus that this cursed,
That blessed, and then this other cursed again?
"Fear ye not those whose power can kill the body
155   And not the soul," saith Christ, "but rather those
Can cast both soul and body into hell!"

John judged thus in Eight Hundred Ninety Eight,
Exact eight hundred years ago to-day
When, sitting in his stead, Vice-gerent here,
160   I must give judgment on my own behoof.
So worked the predecessor: now, my turn!

In God's name! Once more on this earth of God's,
While twilight lasts and time wherein to work,
I take His staff with my uncertain hand,
165   And stay my six and fourscore years, my due
Labour and sorrow, on His judgment-seat,
And forthwith think, speak, act, in place of Him—
The Pope for Christ. Once more appeal is made
From man's assize to mine: I sit and see
170   Another poor weak trembling human wretch
Pushed by his fellows, who pretend the right,
Up to the gulf which, where I gaze, begins

*P1869:*Her sentence   149| MS:In *P1869:*I'   150–54| MS:of my predecessors spoke
the truth § last two words crossed out and replaced above by two words § for God? / "Fear
*P1869:*of the judgments was infallible? / Which of my predecessors spoke for God? / And
what availed Formosus that this cursed, / That blessed, and then this other cursed again? /
"Fear   155| MS:soul,"—saith Christ—§ last two words and dashes inserted above §
"but *P1869:*soul," saith Christ, "but   158| MS:Exact § in margin § Eight < > to-day.
*P1869:*eight < > to-day   159| MS:stead, and both for Christ § replaced above by § God
§ last five words crossed out and replaced above by § Vice-gerent here,   162| MS:of His
§ altered to § God's,   164| MS:take his < > hand *1869:*take His < > hand,
165| MS:my five and *P1869:*my six and   166| MS:on his *P1869:*on His
167| MS:of him *P1869:*of Him—   172| MS:where I shall be led § last four words

From this world to the next,—gives way and way,
Just on the edge over the awful dark:
175   With nothing to arrest him but my feet.
He catches at me with convulsive face,
Cries "Leave to live the natural minute more!"
While hollowly the avengers echo "Leave?
None! So has he exceeded man's due share
180   In man's fit license, wrung by Adam's fall,
To sin and yet not surely die,—that we,
All of us sinful, all with need of grace,
All chary of our life,—the minute more
Or minute less of grace which saves a soul,—
185   Bound to make common cause with who craves time,
—We yet protest against the exorbitance
Of sin in this one sinner, and demand
That his poor sole remaining piece of time
Be plucked from out his clutch: put him to death!
190   Punish him now! As for the weal or woe
Hereafter, God grant mercy! Man be just,
Nor let the felon boast he went scot-free!"
And I am bound, the solitary judge,
To weigh the worth, decide upon the plea,
195   And either hold a hand out, or withdraw
A foot and let the wretch drift to the fall.
Ay, and while thus I dally, dare perchance
Put fancies for a comfort 'twixt this calm

---

crossed out §   174| MS:dark *P1869:*dark: 175| MS:feet— *P1869:*feet.
176| MS:Catches <> with his convulsive *P1869:*He catches <> with convulsive
180| MS:licence wrung <> fall *P1869:*licence, wrung <> fall,   182| MS:us
guilty § crossed out and replaced above by § sinful and with *P1869:*sinful,
all with   183–85| MS:of that grace the <> more, / Bound therefore § crossed
out § *P1869:*of our life,—the <> more / Or minute less of grace which saves a
soul,—/ Bound   187| MS:Of this <> demand his sole *P1869:*Of sin in this
<> demand   188| MS:Remaining <> time to purchase heaven *P1869:*That his
poor sole remaining <> time   189| MS:clutch: punish him now! *P1869:*clutch: put
him to death!   190| MS:Put him to death! As *P1869:*Punish him now! As
191| MS:mercy! Man was just, *P1869:*mercy! Man be just,   192| MS:scot-free.
*P1869:*scot-free!"   193| MS:the sole tribunal here, *P1869:*the solitary judge,
194| MS:weigh its worth <> upon such plea, *P1869:*weigh the worth <> upon the plea,
195| MS:out or *P1869:*out, or   197| MS:while even § crossed out §
198| MS:fancies like a <> twixt my face *P1869:*fancies for a <> 'twixt this calm

And yonder passion that I have to bear,—
200 As if reprieve were possible for both
Prisoner and Pope,—how easy were reprieve!
A touch o' the hand-bell here, a hasty word
To those who wait, and wonder they wait long,
I' the passage there, and I should gain the life!—
205 Yea, though I flatter me with fancy thus,
I know it is but nature's craven-trick.
The case is over, judgment at an end,
And all things done now and irrevocable:
A mere dead man is Francheschini here,
210 Even as Formosus centuries ago.
I have worn through this sombre wintry day,
With winter in my soul beyond the world's,
Over these dismalest of documents
Which drew night down on me ere eve befell,—
215 Pleadings and counter-pleadings, figure of fact
Beside fact's self, these summaries to-wit,—
How certain three were slain by certain five:
I read here why it was, and how it went,
And how the chief o' the five preferred excuse,
220 And how law rather chose defence should lie,—
What argument he urged by wary word
When free to play off wile, start subterfuge,
And what the unguarded groan told, torture's feat
When law grew brutal, outbroke, overbore

199| MS:And yon pale § crossed out and replaced above by § black passion that it hates to
bear, P1869:And yonder passion that I have to bear,— 200-202| MS:How still reprieve
is possible for both,—/ A <> of P1869:As if reprieve were possible for both/ Prisoner and
Pope,—how easy were reprieve! / A <> o' 204| MS:In <> I have gained § over
illegible word, possibly *found* § the life! P1869:I shall gain CP1869:I' <> I should gain
the life!— 205| MS:thus P1869:thus, 206| MS:craven-trick—
P1869:craven-trick. 207| MS:judgment absolute, § word crossed out and replaced above
by three words § at an end, 208| MS:things ended § crossed out and replaced above by
two words § done now and irrevocable, P1869:irrevocable: 209| MS:here P1869:here,
212| MS:A winter P1869:With winter 214| MS:draw <> eve be come,—
P1869:drew <> eve befell,— 215| MS:counterpleadings P1869:counter-pleadings
217| MS:five, P1869:five: 218| MS:was and <> went P1869:was, and <> went,
219| MS:of P1869:o' 221| MS:Such argument P1869:What argument
223| MS:And here the <> groan was torture's P1869:And what the <> groan told,

225 And glutted hunger on the truth, at last,—
No matter for the flesh and blood between.
All's a clear rede and no more riddle now.
Truth, nowhere, lies yet everywhere in these—
Not absolutely in a portion, yet
230 Evolvible from the whole: evolved at last
Painfully, held tenaciously by me.
Therefore there is not any doubt to clear
When I shall write the brief word presently
And chink the hand-bell, which I pause to do.
235 Irresolute? Not I, more than the mound
With the pine-trees on it yonder! Some surmise,
Perchance, that since man's wit is fallible,
Mine may fail here? Suppose it so,—what then?
Say,—Guido, I count guilty, there's no babe
240 So guiltless, for I misconceive the man!
What's in the chance should move me from my mind?
If, as I walk in a rough country-side,
Peasants of mine cry "Thou art he can help,
Lord of the land and counted wise to boot:
245 Look at our brother, strangling in his foam,
He fell so where we find him,—prove thy worth!"
I may presume, pronounce, "A frenzy-fit,
A falling-sickness or a fever-stroke!
Breathe a vein, copiously let blood at once!"

---

torture's   225-27| MS:truth, blood and all,— / There's a <> now—   P1869:truth, at
last,— / No matter for the flesh and blood between. / All's a <> now.
228| MS:nowhere, and § crossed out and replaced above by § lies <> these   P1869:nowhere
<> these—   229| MS:a part, no less   P1869:a portion, yet   230-32| MS:Evolvable
<> whole: so held by me. / Therefore   P1869:Evolvible <> whole:evolved at last/
Painfully, held tenaciously by me. / Therefore   234| MS:handbell   P1869:hand-bell
235| MS:Irresolute? Not I more the   P1869:Irresolute? Not I, more than the
236| MS:yonder. Some   P1869:yonder! Some   237| MS:Since the best wit
of man is fallible, mine   P1869:Perchance, that since man's wit is fallible,
238| MS:Also may <> here? Why, suppose it so,—   P1869:Mine may <> here?
Suppose it so,—what then?   239| MS:Guido I doom as guilty   P1869:Say,—Guido,
I count guilty   240| MS:Guiltless, so much I <> man: P1869:So guiltless,
for I <> man!   241| MS:Well, what is there should   P1869:What's in the chance
should   242| MS:If as <> country-side   P1869:If, as <> country-side,
243| P1869:cry, "Thou   CP1869:cry "Thou   244| MS:to-boot,   P1869:to boot:
247| MS:I might presume and say "A   P1869:I may presume, pronounce, "A
248| MS:fever-stroke—   P1869:fever-stroke!   249| MS:once!   P1869:once!"

80

250 So perishes the patient, and anon
I hear my peasants—"All was error, lord!
Our story, thy prescription: for there crawled
In due time from our hapless brother's breast
The serpent which had stung him: bleeding slew
255 Whom a prompt cordial had restored to health."
What other should I say than "God so willed:
Mankind is ignorant, a man am I:
Call ignorance my sorrow, not my sin!"
So and not otherwise, in after-time,
260 If some acuter wit, fresh probing, sound
This multifarious mass of words and deeds
Deeper, and reach through guilt to innocence,
I shall face Guido's ghost nor blench a jot.
"God who set me to judge thee, meted out
265 So much of judging faculty, no more:
Ask Him if I was slack in use thereof!"
I hold a heavier fault imputable
Inasmuch as I changed a chaplain once,
For no cause,—no, if I must bare my heart,—
270 Save that he snuffled somewhat saying mass.
For I am ware it is the seed of act,
God holds appraising in His hollow palm,
Not act grown great thence on the world below,
Leafage and branchage, vulgar eyes admire.
275 Therefore I stand on my integrity,
Nor fear at all: and if I hesitate,

251| MS:Reproach my   *P1869:*I hear my   252| MS:prescription, for
*P1869:*prescription: for   253| MS:brother's heart   *P1869:*brother's breast
254| MS:him,—bleeding   *P1869:*him: bleeding   255| MS:When a <> restored
the sick."   *P1869:*Whom a <> restored to health."   256| MS:willed—
*P1869:*willed: 257| MS:Man is an ignorant, none other I,   *P1869:*Mankind
is ignorant, a man am I: 258| MS:sorrow and not sin!"   *P1869:*sorrow
not my sin!"   *1889a:*sorrow, not   259| MS:otherwise in after time
*P1869:*otherwise, in after-time,   260| MS:fresh probe shall sound   *P1869:*fresh
probing, sound   262| MS:Deeper and   *P1869:*Deeper, and   263| MS:I would tell
Guido's ghost, nor <> jot,   *P1869:*I shall face Guido's ghost nor <> jot.
266| MS:Ask him   *P1869:*Ask Him   267| MS:I think a heaver   *P1869:*I hold a
heavier   269| MS:my breast,—   *P1869:*my heart,—   271| MS:seeds of act
*P1869:*seed of act,   272| MS:in his   *P1869:*in His   273| MS:below   *P1869:*below,
274| MS:branchage vulgar   *P1869:*branchage, vulgar   276| MS:Fear not at <>

It is because I need to breathe awhile,
Rest, as the human right allows, review
Intent the little seeds of act, my tree,—
280   The thought, which, clothed in deed, I give the world
At chink of bell and push of arrased door.

O pale departure, dim disgrace of day!
Winter's in wane, his vengeful worst art thou,
To dash the boldness of advancing March!
285   Thy chill persistent rain has purged our streets
Of gossipry; pert tongue and idle ear
By this, consort 'neath archway, portico.
But wheresoe'er Rome gathers in the grey,
Two names now snap and flash from mouth to mouth—
290   (Sparks, flint and steel strike) Guido and the Pope.
By this same hour to-morrow eve—aha,
How do they call him?—the sagacious Swede
Who finds by figures how the chances prove,
Why one comes rather than another thing,
295   As, say, such dots turn up by throw of dice,
Or, if we dip in Virgil here and there
And prick for such a verse, when such shall point.
Take this Swede, tell him, hiding name and rank,
Two men are in our city this dull eve;
300   One doomed to death,—but hundreds in such plight
Slip aside, clean escape by leave of law

hesitate   *P1869:*Nor fear at < > hesitate,   279| MS:The little seed of fact § altered to §
act the spreading tree,   *P1869:*Intent the little seeds of act, the tree,—   *1872:*act, my tree,—
280| MS:thought I clothe in § illegible erasure § deed to give   *P1869:*thought, to clothe in
deed, and give   *1872:*thought, which, clothed in deed, I give   282| MS:departure, of the
ignoble § last three words crossed out and replaced above by three words § dim disgrace of
day,   *P1869:*day!   283| MS:his sullen § crossed out and replaced above by § vengeful
285| MS:Thy dull § crossed out and replaced above by § chill < > purged the place § last
two words crossed out and replaced above by § our streets   286| MS:gossipry, pert
*P1869:*gossipry; pert   287| MS:House and § last two words inserted in margin §
Consort 'neath palace § crossed out § < > portico,—   *P1869:*By this, consort < > portico.
288| MS:But § over *And* § wheresoe'er § *soe'er* inserted above § < > grey, two words § last
two words crossed out §   290| MS:Sparks flint < > strike,—Guido   *P1869:*(Sparks, flint
< > strike) Guido   292| MS:do we call him, the   *P1869:*do they call him?—the
293| MS:chances should § inserted above § go,   *P1869:*chances prove,   294| MS:And §
altered to § Why   295| MS:up in throw of dice   *P1869:*up by throw of dice,
296| MS:if you dip   *CP1869:*if we dip   299| MS:eve   *P1869:*eve;   300| MS:death,

Which leans to mercy in this latter time;
Moreover in the plenitude of life
Is he, with strength of limb and brain adroit,
305 Presumably of service here: beside,
The man is noble, backed by nobler friends:
Nay, they so wish him well, the city's self
Makes common cause with who—house-magistrate,
Patron of hearth and home, domestic lord—
310 But ruled his own, let aliens cavil. Die?
He'll bribe a gaoler or break prison first!
Nay, a sedition may be helpful, give
Hint to the mob to batter wall, burn gate,
And bid the favourite malefactor march.
315 Calculate now these chances of escape!
"It is not probable, but well may be."
Again, there is another man, weighed now
By twice eight years beyond the seven-times-ten,
Appointed overweight to break our branch.
320 And this man's loaded branch lifts, more than snow,
All the world's cark and care, though a bird's nest
Were a superfluous burthen: notably
Hath he been pressed, as if his age were youth,
From to-day's dawn till now that day departs,

---

but *P1869:*death,—but   304| MS:adroit *P1869:*adroit,   305| MS:Presumably
§ over illegible word, possibly *Seem* § beside *P1869:*beside,   306| MS:noble,
backed by < > friends, *CP1869:*friends: *1872:*noble, backed, by *1889a:*noble,
backed by   307| MS:And, for who wish *P1869:*Nay, for *1872:*Nay, so they wish
*1889a:*Nay, they so wish   308| MS:with the house-magistrate, *1872:*with who—
house-magistrate,   309| MS:Rules § crossed out and replaced above by § Laws of the
§ inserted above § hearth < > domestic right, *P1869:*The lord of hearth < > domestic judge
*1872:*Patron of < > domestic lord—   310| MS:Who ruled < > let men cavil *1872:*But
ruled < > let aliens cavil   311| MS:Why, bribe *P1869:*He'll bribe
312| MS:sedition once was helpful, gave *P1869:*sedition may be helpful, give
313| MS:mob that battered down the § last two words crossed out and replaced above by two
words § wall, burned gate *P1869:*mob to batter wall, burn gate,   314| MS:And bade a
favorite *P1869:*And bids the favourite *CP1869:*bid   315| MS:escape,—
*P1869:*escape!   316| MS:It is not certain, probable, but may be. *P1869:*It is not
probable, but well may *CP1869:*"It is < > be."   319| MS:branch,— *P1869:*breaks
our branch. *CP1869:*break   320| MS:And this same loaded branch lifts § over *bears* §
*P1869:*And this man's loaded   321| MS:care, when a *P1869:*care, though a
322| MS:burthen,—notably *P1869:*burthen: notably   323| MS:pressed as < > youth
*P1869:*pressed, as < > youth,   324| MS:From this day's dawn < > that it departs

83

³²⁵ Trying one question with true sweat of soul
"Shall the said doomed man fitlier die or live?"
When a straw swallowed in his posset, stool
Stumbled on where his path lies, any puff
That's incident to such a smoking flax,
³³⁰ Hurries the natural end and quenches him!
Now calculate, thou sage, the chances here,
Say, which shall die the sooner, this or that?
"That, possibly, this in all likelihood."
I thought so: yet thou tripp'st, my foreign friend!
³³⁵ No, it will be quite otherwise,—to-day
Is Guido's last: my term is yet to run.

But say the Swede were right, and I forthwith
Acknowledge a prompt summons and lie dead:
Why, then I stand already in God's face
³⁴⁰ And hear "Since by its fruit a tree is judged,
Show me thy fruit, the latest act of thine!
For in the last is summed the first and all,—
What thy life last put heart and soul into,
There shall I taste thy product." I must plead
³⁴⁵ This condemnation of a man to-day.

Not so! Expect nor question nor reply
At what we figure as God's judgment-bar!
None of this vile way by the barren words
Which, more than any deed, characterize
³⁵⁰ Man as made subject to a curse: no speech—

---

*P1869:*From to-day's dawn <> that day departs, ³²⁵| MS:with such sweat
*P1869:*with true sweat ³²⁸| MS:Tripped upon § last two words crossed out and
replaced above by two words § Stumbled on ³²⁹| MS:incidental § altered to § incident
to the § crossed out and replaced above by two words § such a ³³⁰| MS:him.
*P1869:*him! ³³¹| MS:calculate in turn these § altered to § the chances here § over
perhaps *too* § , *P1869:*calculate, thou sage, the ³³³| MS:possibly, but § crossed out §
this in all § inserted above § ³³⁴| MS:trippest, egregious friend § over illegible
erasure § ! *P1869:*tripp'st, my foreign friend! ³³⁷| MS:right and *P1869:*right, and
³³⁸| MS:lie § over *died* § dead, *P1869:*dead: ³³⁹| MS:Why then <> face.
*P1869:*Why, then <> face ³⁴¹| MS:thine, *P1869:*thine! ³⁴²| MS:all,
*P1869:*all,— ³⁴⁴| MS:So shall *P1869:*There shall ³⁴⁵| MS:"This <> to-day."
*P1869:*This <> to-day. ³⁴⁶| MS:so! Nor <> reply expect *P1869:*so! Expect nor <>
reply ³⁴⁷| MS:At that we *P1869:*At what we ³⁴⁸| MS:of the vile *P1869:*of this
vile ³⁴⁹| MS:That, more *P1869:*Which, more ³⁵⁰| MS:speech *P1869:*speech—

That still bursts o'er some lie which lurks inside,
As the split skin across the coppery snake,
And most denotes man! since, in all beside,
In hate or lust or guile or unbelief,
355 Out of some core of truth the excrescence comes,
And, in the last resort, the man may urge
"So was I made, a weak thing that gave way
To truth, to impulse only strong since true,
And hated, lusted, used guile, forwent faith."
360 But when man walks the garden of this world
For his own solace, and, unchecked by law,
Speaks or keeps silence as himself sees fit,
Without the least incumbency to lie,
—Why, can he tell you what a rose is like,
365 Or how the birds fly, and not slip to false
Though truth serve better? Man must tell his mate
Of you, me and himself, knowing he lies,
Knowing his fellow knows the same,—will think
"He lies, it is the method of a man!"
370 And yet will speak for answer "It is truth"
To him who shall rejoin "Again a lie!"
Therefore these filthy rags of speech, this coil
Of statement, comment, query and response,
Tatters all too contaminate for use,
375 Have no renewing: He, the Truth, is, too,

351| MS:o'er the lie that lurks inside   *P1869:*o'er some lie that lurks inside,   *CP1869:*lie
which lurks   352| MS:As his split   *P1869:*As the split   353| MS:man since
*P1869:*man! since   354| MS:His hate <> or disbelief,   *P1869:*In hate <> or unbelief,
355| MS:excrescence shows § crossed out § winds,   *P1869:*excrescence comes,
356| MS:resort, excuse may § illegible word crossed out § be   *P1869:*resort, the man may
urge   357| MS:made, the weak   *P1869:*made, a weak   358| MS:truth, an impulse
*P1869:*truth, to impulse   359| MS:forewent   *P1869:*forwent   *1889a:*forewent
DC,BrU:forwent   *1889:*forwent   361| MS:and unchecked by law   *P1869:*and,
unchecked by law,   362| MS:or is silent as he sees most fit   *P1869:*or keeps silence as
himself sees fit,   364| MS:Why   *P1869:*—Why   366| MS:better. Man
*P1869:*better? Man   367| MS:lies   *P1869:*lies,   368| MS:And that his <> will say
*P1869:*Knowing his <> will think   369| MS:He <> man,   *P1869:*"He <> man!"
370| MS:And I shall fitly answer   *P1869:*And yet will speak for answer   371| MS:To
one who <> lie!"   *P1869:*To him who   *1889a:*lie!' § emended to § lie!" § see Editorial
Notes §   372| MS:Therefore this filthy rags   *P1869:*this speak for rags   *CP1869:*this
filthy rags   *1872:*these   375| MS:And past § last two words crossed out and

85

The Word. We men, in our degree, may know
There, simply, instantaneously, as here
After long time and amid many lies,
Whatever we dare think we know indeed
380 —That I am I, as He is He,—what else?

But be man's method for man's life at least!
Wherefore, Antonio Pignatelli, thou
My ancient self, who wast no Pope so long
But studiedst God and man, the many years
385 I' the school, i' the cloister, in the diocese
Domestic, legate-rule in foreign lands,—
Thou other force in those old busy days
Than this grey ultimate decrepitude,—
Yet sensible of fires that more and more
390 Visit a soul, in passage to the sky,
Left nakeder than when flesh-robe was new—
Thou, not Pope but the mere old man o' the world,
Supposed inquisitive and dispassionate,
Wilt thou, the one whose speech I somewhat trust,
395 Question the after-me, this self now Pope,
Hear his procedure, criticize his work?
Wise in its generation is the world.

This is why Guido is found reprobate.
I see him furnished forth for his career,

---

replaced above by two words § Have no   376| MS:The Word. And man, in due degree
P1869:The Word. We men, in our degree   377–79| MS:here/ Whatever   P1869:here/
After long time and amid many lies, / Whatever   380–81| MS:§ ¶ §   1869:§ no ¶ §
1889:§ no ¶ ; emended to restore ¶ ; see Editorial Notes §   381| MS:But the man's
P1869:But be man's   383| MS:self who   P1869:self, who   384| MS:studied
DC,BrU:studiedst   1889:studiedst   385| MS:In <> in the cloister, diocese   P1869:I'
<> i' the cloister, in the diocese   386| MS:legate-life in <> lands   P1869:legate-rule
in <> lands,—   390| MS:soul in   P1869:soul, in   391| MS:Nakeder <>
when fleshly robes were whole—   P1869:Left nakeder <> when flesh-robe was new—
392| MS:not the Pope but the old man of   P1869:not Pope but the mere old man o'
393| MS:Supposed sagacious and   P1869:Supposed inquisitive and   394| MS:speech I
can somewhat   P1869:speech I somewhat   395| MS:Speak to the after-me, the self
that's Pope,   P1869:Question the after-me, this self now Pope,   398| MS:why Guido I
call reprobate,   P1869:why Guido is found reprobate.   399| MS:I find him <> career

On starting for the life-chance in our world,
With nearly all we count sufficient help:
Body and mind in balance, a sound frame,
A solid intellect: the wit to seek,
Wisdom to choose, and courage wherewithal
To deal in whatsoever circumstance
Should minister to man, make life succeed.
Oh, and much drawback! what were earth without?
Is this our ultimate stage, or starting-place
To try man's foot, if it will creep or climb,
'Mid obstacles in seeming, points that prove
Advantage for who vaults from low to high
And makes the stumbling-block a stepping-stone?
So, Guido, born with appetite, lacks food:
Is poor, who yet could deftly play-off wealth:
Straitened, whose limbs are restless till at large.
He, as he eyes each outlet of the cirque
And narrow penfold for probation, pines
After the good things just outside its grate,
With less monition, fainter conscience-twitch,
Rarer instinctive qualm at the first feel

*P1869:*I see him <> career,　　　400| 　MS:world　*P1869:*world,　　　401| 　MS:all God
counts <> help;　*P1869:*all we count <> help:　　　402| 　MS:balance, the sound frame
*P1869:*balance, a sound frame,　　　403| 　MS:The solid § inserted above § intellect: its
match § last two words crossed out § a wit to § illegible erasure § seek § over illegible erasure
§ ,　*P1869:*A solid intellect: the wit　　　404| 　MS:Judgment to choose, courage to force an
§ last two words crossed out and replaced above by § deal for good　*P1869:*Wisdom to
choose, and courage wherewithal　　　405| 　MS:Of both with what of earthly circumstance
*P1869:*To deal with whatsoever circumstance　*1872:*deal in whatsoever　　　406| 　MS:life
success.　*P1869:*life succeed.　　　407| 　MS:Oh, and § over *with* § much <> were
life exempt § crossed out and replaced above by § without?　*P1869:*were earth
without?　　　408| 　MS:this the ultimate　*P1869:*this our ultimate　　　409| 　MS:That
tries the foot if <> climb　*P1869:*To try man's foot, if <> climb,
410| 　MS:Mid　*P1869:*'Mid　411| 　MS:Advantage to who　*P1869:*Advantage for who
412| 　MS:Turning § crossed out and replaced above by two words § And makes <>
stepping-stone.　*P1869:*stepping-stone?　　　413| 　MS:So Guido with much appetite lacks
food,　*P1869:*So, Guido, born with appetite, lacks　*1872:*food:　　　414| 　MS:poor who
<> play off wealth,　*P1869:*poor, who　*CP1869:*play-off　*1872:*wealth:
415| 　MS:Straitened whose <> large—　*P1869:*Straitened, whose <> large:
*1889a:*large.　　　416| 　MS:And, as <> cirque　*P1869:*cirque,　*1872:*He, as <> cirque
417| 　MS:His narrow　*P1869:*The narrow　*1872:*And narrow　　　418| 　MS:outside the
grate,　*P1869:*outside its grate,　　　420| 　MS:first § over illegible word § sense　*P1869:*first

Of greed unseemly, prompting grasp undue,
Than nature furnishes her main mankind,—
Making it harder to do wrong than right
The first time, careful lest the common ear
425   Break measure, miss the outstep of life's march.
Wherein I see a trial fair and fit
For one else too unfairly fenced about,
Set above sin, beyond his fellows here:
Guarded from the arch-tempter all must fight,
430   By a great birth, traditionary name,
Diligent culture, choice companionship,
Above all, conversancy with the faith
Which puts forth for its base of doctrine just
"Man is born nowise to content himself,
435   But please God." He accepted such a rule,
Recognized man's obedience; and the Church,
Which simply is such rule's embodiment,
He clave to, he held on by,—nay, indeed,
Near pushed inside of, deep as layman durst,
440   Professed so much of priesthood as might sue
For priest's-exemption where the layman sinned,—
Got his arm frocked which, bare, the law would bruise.
Hence, at this moment, what's his last resource,
His extreme stay and utmost stretch of hope
445   But that,—convicted of such crime as law

---

feel   421| MS:Of the unseemly over § crossed out § greed and undue grasp § transposed
to § grasp undue,—   *P1869:*undue,   *1872:*Of greed unseemly, prompting grasp
422| MS:furnishes the main mankind   *P1869:*mankind,—   *1872:*furnishes her main
424-26| MS:time, miss the outstep of life's march. / Herein   *P1869:*time, careful lest the
common ear/ Break measure, miss <> / Wherein   427| MS:Of one   *P1869:*For one
428| MS:sin beyond <> here,   *P1869:*sin, beyond   *1872:*here: 429| MS:arch-foe man
needs must fight   *P1869:*arch-tempter, all must fight,   *1889a:*arch-tempter all
433| MS:doctrine this   *P1869:*doctrine just   434| MS:himself   *1889a:*himself,
435| MS:please God"—he   *P1869:*please God." He   436| MS:Recognized man obeys
here,—took § crossed out and replaced above by § and the Church   *P1869:*Recognized man's
obedience; and the Church,   437| MS:is that rule's   *P1869:*is such rules'
*CP1869:*rule's   439| MS:He pushed   *P1869:*Near pushed   440| MS:might plead
§ crossed out §   441| MS:priests' exemption from § crossed out and replaced above by §
where   *P1869:*priest's-exemption   442| MS:Thrust his <> bruise: *P1869:*Got his <>
bruise.   443| MS:Hence at this juncture § last two words crossed out and replaced above
by two words § the moment what's   *P1869:*Hence, at this moment, what's
444| MS:and solitary § crossed out and replaced above by three words § utmost stretch of
445| MS:that, convicted of § over illegible erasure §   *P1869:*that,—convicted

Wipes not away save with a worldling's blood,—
Guido, the three-parts consecrate, may 'scape?
Nay, the portentous brothers of the man
Are veritably priests, protected each
450 May do his murder in the Church's pale,
Abate Paul, Canon Girolamo!
This is the man proves irreligiousest
Of all mankind, religion's parasite!
This may forsooth plead dinned ear, jaded sense,
455 The vice o' the watcher who bides near the bell,
Sleeps sound because the clock is vigilant,
And cares not whether it be shade or shine,
Doling out day and night to all men else!
Why was the choice o' the man to niche himself
460 Perversely 'neath the tower where Time's own tongue
Thus undertakes to sermonize the world?
Why, but because the solemn is safe too,
The belfry proves a fortress of a sort,
Has other uses than to teach the hour:
465 Turns sunscreen, paravent and ombrifuge
To whoso seeks a shelter in its pale,
—Ay, and attractive to unwary folk
Who gaze at storied portal, statued spire,
And go home with full head but empty purse,

446| MS:with the § crossed out and replaced above by § a <> blood, *P1869:*blood,—
447| MS:scape: *P1869:*'scape? 449| MS:protectedly § altered to § protected both
§ crossed out § 450| MS:do his § over illegible word § <> the churches *P1869:*the
Church's 451-54| MS:Abate Paul, Canon Girolamo!/ This § illegible word crossed out
and replaced above by § one forsooth would § crossed out § pleads dulled brain § last two
words crossed out and replaced above by three words § dinned sense § last two
words crossed out and replaced by § ear, jaded sense § over perhaps *ear* § , *P1869:*This is the man proves
irreligiousest / Of all mankind, religion's parasite! / This may forsooth plead
455| MS:of <> bell *P1869:*o' <> bell, 456-58| MS:clock wakes, beats his brain, /
Doling *P1869:*clock is vigilant, / And cares not whether it be shade or shine, / Doling
459| MS:of *P1869:*o' 460| MS:neath § over *near* § *P1869:*'neath
461| MS:Teaches the world, § last three words and comma crossed out and replaced
above by three words § Thus undertakes to 462-64| MS:Because the solemn
Belfrey is <> / Has <> hour, *P1869:*Why, but because the solemn is <> / The belfry
proves a fortress of a sort, / Has *1872:*/ / hour: 465-67| MS:Is sunscreen <> /
Ay <> to a crowd of § last three words crossed out and replaced above by § unwary
*P1869:*Turns sunscreen <> / To whoso seeks a shelter in its pale, / —Ay
468| MS:Who gape § altered to § gaze at the § crossed out § <> portal, splendid § crossed out
and replaced above by § statued 469| MS:To go <> with a § crossed out § <> head

470   Nor dare suspect the sacristan the thief!
     Shall Judas,—hard upon the donor's heel,
     To filch the fragments of the basket,—plead
     He was too near the preacher's mouth, nor sat
     Attent with fifties in a company?
475   No,—closer to promulgated decree,
     Clearer the censure of default. Proceed!

     I find him bound, then, to begin life well;
     Fortified by propitious circumstance,
     Great birth, good breeding, with the Church for guide,
480   How lives he? Cased thus in a coat of proof,
     Mailed like a man-at-arms, though all the while
     A puny starveling,—does the breast pant big,
     The limb swell to the limit, emptiness
     Strive to become solidity indeed?
485   Rather, he shrinks up like the ambiguous fish,
     Detaches flesh from shell and outside show,
     And steals by moonlight (I have seen the thing)
     In and out, now to prey and now to skulk.
     Armour he boasts when a wave breaks on beach,
490   Or bird stoops for the prize: with peril nigh,—
     The man of rank, the much-befriended-man,
     The man almost affiliate to the Church,

---

and empty poke § crossed out § purse   *P1869:*And go <> head but empty   *1889a:*purse,
470| MS:thief.   *P1869:*thief!   471| MS:Shall Judas, hard <> heel   *P1869:*Shall
Judas,—hard <> heel,   472| MS:filch § over illegible erasure § <> basket, plead
*P1869:*fill the <> basket,—plead   *CP1869:*filch the   473| MS:nor heard § crossed out
and replaced above by § sat   474| MS:Seated § crossed out and replaced above by §
Attent   475| MS:closest   *P1869:*closer   476-77| MS:§ no ¶ §   *P1869:*§ ¶ §
477| MS:bound then to <> well   *P1869:*bound, then, to <> well;   479| MS:breeding,
and the <> guide.   *1889a:*breeding, with the <> guide,   481| MS:man-at-arms and
all   *P1869:*man-at-arms, though all   482| MS:starveling, does   *P1869:*starveling,—
does   483| MS:Each § over illegible word, perhaps *The* § limb swell up § crossed out §
*P1869:*The limb   484| MS:to be that solidity which seems?   *P1869:*to become solidity
which seems?   *CP1869:*solidity indeed?   485| MS:Rather he <> fish   *P1869:*Rather,
he <> fish,   486| MS:and show outside   *P1869:*outside,   *CP1869:*and outside show,
488| MS:and now to hide,   *P1869:*and now to skulk.   484| MS:beach   *P1869:*beach,
490| MS:A hawk § crossed out and replaced above by § bird <> for a prize: the § erased §
*P1869:*Or bird <> for the prize   491| MS:much befriended man   *P1869:*much-
befriended   *1889a:*much-befriended-man   492| MS:affiliate by the   *P1869:*affiliate to the

Such is to deal with, let the world beware!
Does the world recognize, pass prudently?
495   Do tides abate and sea-fowl hunt i' the deep?
Already is the slug from out its mew,
Ignobly faring with all loose and free,
Sand-fly and slush-worm at their garbage-feast,
A naked blotch no better than they all:
500   Guido has dropped nobility, slipped the Church,
Plays trickster if not cut-purse, body and soul
Prostrate among the filthy feeders—faugh!
And when Law takes him by surprise at last,
Catches the foul thing on its carrion-prey,
505   Behold, he points to shell left high and dry,
Pleads "But the case out yonder is myself!"
Nay, it is thou, Law prongs amid thy peers,
Congenial vermin; that was none of thee,
Thine outside,—give it to the soldier-crab!

510   For I find this black mark impinge the man,
That he believes in just the vile of life.
Low instinct, base pretension, are these truth?
Then, that aforesaid armour, probity
He figures in, is falsehood scale on scale;
515   Honour and faith,—a lie and a disguise,
Probably for all livers in this world,
Certainly for himself! All say good words
To who will hear, all do thereby bad deeds
To who must undergo; so thrive mankind!

493| MS:with let   *P1869:*with, let   495| MS:hunt elsewhere?   *P1869:*hunt i' the deep?
496| MS:the thing from   *P1869:*the slug from   497| MS:fares <> all the loose and free
*P1869:*faring <> all loose and free,   502| MS:Prostrate § over illegible word §
503| MS:when law § followed by illegible erasure §   *P1869:*when Law   507| MS:thou
we prong   *P1869:*thou, Law prongs   510| MS:this § illegible word or words erased and
replaced above by four words § black mark runs through denotes § crossed out § the
*P1869:*mark impinge the   511| MS:life—   *P1869:*life.   512| MS:propension, these
are truth? § transposed to § propension, are these truth?   *P1869:*pretension
513| MS:Then that   *P1869:*Then, that   514| MS:scale.   *P1869:*scale;
515| MS:faith, a   *P1869:*faith,—a   517| MS:Past question for himself: one says good
*P1869:*Certainly for himself! All say good   518| MS:hear, one does thereby ill § crossed
out and replaced above by § bad   *P1869:*hear, all do thereby   519| MS:who will §

520 See this habitual creed exemplified
Most in the last deliberate act; as last,
So, very sum and substance of the soul
Of him that planned and leaves one perfect piece,
The sin brought under jurisdiction now,
525 Even the marriage of the man: this act
I sever from his life as sample, show
For Guido's self, intend to test him by,
As, from a cup filled fairly at the fount,
By the components we decide enough
530 Or to let flow as late, or staunch the source.

He purposes this marriage, I remark,
On no one motive that should prompt thereto—
Farthest, by consequence, from ends alleged
Appropriate to the action; so they were:
535 The best, he knew and feigned, the worst he took.
Not one permissible impulse moves the man,
From the mere liking of the eye and ear,
To the true longing of the heart that loves,
No trace of these: but all to instigate,

---

crossed out and replaced above by § must <> thrive § over *live* § mankind.
*P1869:*mankind!   520| MS:habitual trait exemplified *P1869:*habitual creed
exemplified   521| MS:deliberate § inserted above line § act, of the man § last three
words crossed out § as *P1869:*act; as   523| MS:That planned § followed by illegible
erasure § and leaves this § crossed out and replaced above by § one <> piece, the same
*P1869:*Of him that <> piece,   524| MS:Which brings § illegible erasure § sin under
*P1869:*The sin brought under   527| MS:For Guido and intend *P1869:*For Guido's
self, intend   528| MS:As from <> fairly from the fount *P1869:*As, from <> fairly at
the fount,   529| MS:components I decide *P1869:*components we decide
530| MS:Shall I let flow as late § last two words inserted above § or <> the living § crossed
out § source? *P1869:*Or to let <> late, or <> source.   531| MS:purposes to marry
§ last two words crossed out and replaced above by two words § a marriage, I perceive
§ crossed out and replaced above by § remark, *P1869:*purposes this marriage
532| MS:On the worst § last two words crossed out and replaced above by two words § no
one motives § altered to § motive   533| MS:—Furthest, by consequence § followed by
illegible erasure § , from those § crossed out and replaced above by § ends *P1869:*Farthest
534| MS:were,— *P1869:*were: 535| MS:He knew and feigned § last two words
inserted above § the best and § crossed out and replaced above by § he took. the worst; of all.
§ semi-colon, two words and period crossed out; line transposed to § The best he knew and
feigned the worst he took. *P1869:*best, he <> feigned, the   536| MS:No one <>
impulse § illegible erasure § *P1869:*Not one   537| MS:ear *P1869:*ear,
538| MS:heart that's love, *P1869:*heart that loves,   539| MS:Not a trace: all that

92

540 Is what sinks man past level of the brute
Whose appetite if brutish is a truth.
All is the lust for money: to get gold,—
Why, lie, rob, if it must be, murder! Make
Body and soul wring gold out, lured within
545 The clutch of hate by love, the trap's pretence!
What good else get from bodies and from souls?
This got, there were some life to lead thereby,
—What, where or how, appreciate those who tell
How the toad lives: it lives,—enough for me!
550 To get this good,—with but a groan or so,
Then, silence of the victims,—were the feat.
He foresaw, made a picture in his mind,—
Of father and mother stunned and echoless
To the blow, as they lie staring at fate's jaws
555 Their folly danced into, till the woe fell;
Edged in a month by strenuous cruelty
From even the poor nook whence they watched the wolf
Feast on their heart, the lamb-like child his prey;
Plundered to the last remnant of their wealth,
560 (What daily pittance pleased the plunderer dole)

---

instigates,—and so *P1869:*No trace of these: but all to instigate,   540| MS:Sinks the
man past the level *P1869:*Is what sinks man past level <> brute, *1889a:*brute
541| MS:truth,— *P1869:*truth.   543| MS:Lie, rob, and, if <> murder—make
*P1869:*Why, lie, rob, if <> murder! Make   545| MS:The grasp § crossed out and
replaced above by § clutch   548| MS:What <> appreciate you who *P1869:*—What
<> appreciate those who   549| MS:lives:he lives <> me: *P1869:*lives: it lives <> me!
550| MS:And to get this with just a <> so *P1869:*To get this good,—with but a <> so,
551| MS:Then silence <> victims were success § crossed out and replaced above by two
words § the feat: *P1869:*Then, silence <> victims,—were the feat.   552| MS:made the
picture <> mind, *P1869:*made a picture <> mind,—   553| MS:Father *P1869:*Of
father   554| MS:blow as stones lie, staring at the § crossed out § *P1869:*blow, as they
lie   555| MS:into,—till the trap fell: *P1869:*into, till the woe
fell;   556| MS:Chased § crossed out and replaced above by § Edged <> strenuous
villany § crossed out §   557| MS:even the strand wherefrom § last two words crossed out
and replaced above by three words § poor nook whence   558| MS:heart, his sport § last
two words crossed out and replaced above by two words § the lamb-like <> prey,—
*P1869:*prey;   559| MS:Robbed so § last two words crossed out and replaced above by §
Plundered   560| MS:And § written over by § That sorry § last two words crossed out
and replaced above by three words § What poor § crossed out § daily <> the thief to dole
apace § last four words crossed out and replaced above by § plunderer dole § last word

Hunted forth to go hide head, starve and die,
And leave the pale awe-stricken wife, past hope
Of help i' the world now, mute and motionless,
His slave, his chattel, to first use, then destroy.
565 All this, he bent mind how to bring about,
Put plain in act and life, as painted plain,
So have success, reach crown of earthly good,
In this particular enterprise of man,
By marriage—undertaken in God's face
570 With all these lies so opposite God's truth,
For end so other than man's end.

                              Thus schemes
Guido, and thus would carry out his scheme:
But when an obstacle first blocks the path,
When he finds none may boast monopoly
575 Of lies and trick i' the tricking lying world,—
That sorry timid natures, even this sort
O' the Comparini, want nor trick nor lie
Proper to the kind,—that as the gor-crow treats
The bramble-finch so treats the finch the moth,
580 And the great Guido is minutely matched
By this same couple,—whether true or false
The revelation of Pompilia's birth,

---

restored §, *P1869:*(What < > dole)   561| MS:Hunted to Rome, there § crossed out §
to hide head < > die,— *P1869:*Hunted forth to go hide < > die,   562| MS:So leave
*1872:*And leave   563| MS:in *P1869:*i'   564| MS:slave,—his < > to use then
destroy— *P1869:*slave, his < > to use and then destroy: *1872:*to first use, then destroy
*1889a:*destroy.   566| MS:This put in < > life as *P1869:*Put this in < > life, as
*1872:*Put plain in   567| MS:Such § written over perhaps *This* § were success, the crown
< > good *P1869:*And have success < > good, *1872:*So have success, reach crown
569| MS:A marriage *1872:*By marriage   570| MS:those < > opposite the truth
*P1869:*truth, *CP1869:*opposite God's truth, *1872:*these   571| MS:For ends quite
other than this end. So schemes *P1869:*For ends so other than such end. § ¶ § Thus schemes
*CP1869:*than man's end. *1872:*For end   572| MS:and so would *P1869:*and thus
would   574| MS:he discovers none monopolise *P1869:*he finds there is no monopoly
*1872:*finds none may boast monopoly   575| MS:Lies < > in *P1869:*Of lies < > i'
577| MS:Of *P1869:*O'   579| MS:The bramble § inserted above § finch < > the finch
the butter § crossed out § *P1869:*bramble-finch   580| MS:matched,— *P1869:*matched
581-83| MS:§ inserted in continuous line between 580 and 584 §   581| MS:same story
whether *P1869:*same couple,—whether   582| MS:This revelation < >

Which in a moment brings his scheme to nought,—
Then, he is piqued, advances yet a stage,
585 Leaves the low region to the finch and fly,
Soars to the zenith whence the fiercer fowl
May dare the inimitable swoop. I see.
He draws now on the curious crime, the fine
Felicity and flower of wickedness;
590 Determines, by the utmost exercise
Of violence, made safe and sure by craft,
To satiate malice, pluck one last arch-pang
From the parents, else would triumph out of reach,
By punishing their child, within reach yet,
595 Who, by thought, word or deed, could nowise wrong
I' the matter that now moves him. So plans he,
Always subordinating (note the point!)
Revenge, the manlier sin, to interest
The meaner,—would pluck pang forth, but unclench
600 No gripe in the act, let fall no money-piece.
Hence a plan for so plaguing, body and soul,
His wife, so putting, day by day, hour by hour,
The untried torture to the untouched place,
As must precipitate an end foreseen,
605 Goad her into some plain revolt, most like
Plunge upon patent suicidal shame,
Death to herself, damnation by rebound

---

birth *P1869:*The revelation <> birth, ⁵⁸⁴| MS:—Why, he <> advances
*P1869:*Then, he <> advances ⁵⁸⁶| MS:the nobler fowl *P1869:*the fiercer
fowl ⁵⁸⁷| MS:swoop, I see: *P1869:*swoop. I see. ⁵⁸⁹| MS:wickedness,
*P1869:*wickedness; ⁵⁹⁰| MS:Determines by *CP1869:*Determines, by
⁵⁹¹| MS:violence made <> craft *P1869:*violence, made <> craft, ⁵⁹²| MS:pluck
§ over illegible word § ⁵⁹³| MS:parents in their triumph *P1869:*parents, else would
triumph ⁵⁹⁴| MS:child within *P1869:*child, within ⁵⁹⁵| MS:Who nowise
wronged him, thought nor word nor deed, *P1869:*nowise could have wronged, thought,
word or deed, *1872:*Who, by thought, word or deed, could nowise wrong ⁵⁹⁶| MS:In
<> him,—so *P1869:*I' <> him. So ⁵⁹⁷| MS:subordinating,—note the point,
*P1869:*subordinating (note the point!) ⁵⁹⁹| MS:meaner,—pluck the pang
*P1869:*meaner,—would pluck pang ⁶⁰⁰| MS:money-piece! *P1869:*money-piece.
⁶⁰¹| MS:plaguing body and soul *P1869:*plaguing, body and soul, ⁶⁰²| MS:putting
§ crossed out and replaced above by *lay*, and then restored § day by day and hour by hour
*P1869:*putting, day by day and hour by hour, *1889a:*by day, hour by ⁶⁰³| MS:The
happy § crossed out and replaced above by § novel torture to § over *on* § *P1869:*The untried
torture ⁶⁰⁴| MS:precipitate an unnatural § crossed out § ⁶⁰⁶| MS:Some

To those whose hearts he, holding hers, holds still:
Such plan as, in its bad completeness, shall
610 Ruin the three together and alike,
Yet leave himself in luck and liberty,
No claim renounced, no right a forfeiture,
His person unendangered, his good fame
Without a flaw, his pristine worth intact,—
615 While they, with all their claims and rights that cling,
Shall forthwith crumble off him every side,
Scorched into dust, a plaything for the winds.
As when, in our Campagna, there is fired
The nest-like work that overruns a hut;
620 And, as the thatch burns here, there, everywhere,
Even to the ivy and wild vine, that bound
And blessed the home where men were happy once,
There rises gradual, black amid the blaze,
Some grim and unscathed nucleus of the nest,—
625 Some old malicious tower, some obscene tomb
They thought a temple in their ignorance,
And clung about and thought to lean upon—
There laughs it o'er their ravage,—where are they?
So did his cruelty burn life about,
630 And lay the ruin bare in dreadfulness,
Try the persistency of torment so

---

§ crossed out and replaced above by two words § Plunge upon   609| MS:Such a plan as
in its completeness shall § over *could* §   *P1869:*as, in its completeness, shall   *1872:*Such
plan as, in its bad completeness   612| MS:right in forfeiture,   *P1869:*right a forfeiture,
614| MS:pristine self intact   *P1869:*pristine worth intact,—   615| MS:they and all <>
claims, and § inserted above § <> cling   *P1869:*they, with all <> claims and <> cling,
616| MS:Shall § over illegible word § <> side   *P1869:*side,   617| MS:winds,—
*P1869:*winds.   618| MS:when in our Campagna there   *P1869:*when, in our Compagna,
there   619| MS:that lets some peasant house   *P1869:*that lets a peasant house;
*1889a:*that overruns a hut;   620| MS:And as the poor § crossed out § thatch blazes §
crossed out and replaced above by § burns   *P1869:*And, as   622| MS:the hut where
*1889a:*the home where   624| MS:The grim <> nest   *P1869:*Some grim <> nest,—
625| MS:The old <> tower, the obscene   *P1869:*Some old <> tower, some obscene
626| MS:§ inserted between lines 625-27 §   627| MS:They § crossed out and replaced
in margin by § So clung   *CP1869:*And clung   628| MS:ravage and where
*P1869:*ravage,—where   629-31| MS:So cold calm cruelty turned § altered to § turns
winch and wheel, / Tried § altered to § Tries the § crossed out and replaced above by §
its persistency   *P1869:*So did his cruelty burn life about, / And lay the ruin bare in

Upon the wife, that, at extremity,
Some crisis brought about by fire and flame,
The patient frenzy-stung must needs break loose,
635 Fly anyhow, find refuge anywhere,
Even in the arms of who should front her first,
No monster but a man—while nature shrieked
"Or thus escape, or die!" The spasm arrived,
Not the escape by way of sin,—O God,
640 Who shall pluck sheep Thou holdest, from Thy hand?
Therefore she lay resigned to die,—so far
The simple cruelty was foiled. Why then,
Craft to the rescue, let craft supplement
Cruelty and show hell a masterpiece!
645 Hence this consummate lie, this love-intrigue,
Unmanly simulation of a sin,
With place and time and circumstance to suit—
These letters false beyond all forgery—
Not just handwriting and mere authorship,
650 But false to body and soul they figure forth—
As though the man had cut out shape and shape
From fancies of that other Aretine,
To paste below—incorporate the filth

dreadfulness, / Try the persistency   632-33| MS:On the wife, harmless in thought, word
and deed, / With § crossed out § To this and that, at some extremity, / Some < > by scrape
of screw,   P1869:O' the wife, that, at some fierce extremity, / Some < > by fire and flame,
1872:Upon the < > at extremity, /   634| MS:patient stung to frenzy should § over
shall § break   P1869:frenzy should break   1872:patient frenzy-stung must needs break
636| MS:who might § crossed out and replaced above by § may front her first   P1869:who
might front her first,   1872:who should front   637| MS:shrieked § ed blotted and
almost illegible §   638| MS:spasm arrive § over illegible word § —   P1869:arrived,
639| MS:sin,—O God   P1869:sin,—O God,   640| MS:Who plucks that sheep thou
holdest from thy   P1869:Who shall pluck sheep Thou holdest, from Thy   641| MS:she
was § crossed out and replaced above by § is resigned   P1869:she lay resigned
642| MS:cruelty was § crossed out and replaced above by illegible word § foiled: why
P1869:cruelty was foiled. Why   643| MS:rescue, craft shall supplement   P1869:craft
should supplement   1872:rescue, let craft supplement   645| MS:love-intrigue
1869:love-intrigue,   646| MS:The unmanly < > a man,   P1869:Unmanly < > a sin,
647| MS:A place, a time, a circumstance   P1869:With place and time and circumstance
650| MS:soul they § over that § < > forth   P1869:forth—   651| MS:and shape.
P1869:and shape   653| MS:And § crossed out and replaced above by § To pasted
§ altered to § paste them as indivisible and § last four words crossed out and replaced above

With cherub faces on a missal-page!

655 Whereby the man so far attains his end
That strange temptation is permitted,—see!
Pompilia wife, and Caponsacchi priest,
Are brought together as nor priest nor wife
Should stand, and there is passion in the place,
660 Power in the air for evil as for good,
Promptings from heaven and hell, as if the stars
Fought in their courses for a fate to be.
Thus stand the wife and priest, a spectacle,
I doubt not, to unseen assemblage there.
665 No lamp will mark that window for a shrine,
No tablet signalize the terrace, teach
New generations which succeed the old
The pavement of the street is holy ground;
No bard describe in verse how Christ prevailed
670 And Satan fell like lightning! Why repine?
What does the world, told truth, but lie the more?

A second time the plot is foiled; nor, now,
By corresponding sin for countercheck,
No wile and trick that baffle trick and wile,—
675 The play o' the parents! Here the blot is blanched

by word and dash § below—   654| MS:From two pure § last three words crossed out
and replaced above by two words § With cherub <> missal-page: P1869:missal-page!
654-55| MS:§ no ¶ §   P1869:§ ¶ §   655| MS:far affects § crossed out and replaced above
by § attains his end § written over illegible erasure §   656| MS:A strange   P1869:That
strange   657| MS:Pompilia, wife, and Caponsacchi, priest,   1889a:Pompilia wife, and
Caponsacchi priest,   659| MS:Should § followed by one word written over another,
both illegible § , and   P1869:Should stand, and   662| MS:for what § crossed out and
replaced above by § the § crossed out and replaced by § a fate should fall. § last two
words crossed out and replaced above by two words § to be.   663| MS:There stand the
priest and wife § last three words transposed to § wife and priest   P1869:Thus stand
666| MS:Nor tablet § erasure of word perhaps *will* §   667| MS:generations that succeed
<> old,   P1869:generations which succeed   DC,BrU:old   1889:old   668| MS:ground:
P1869:ground;   669| MS:bard shall ever sing § last two words crossed out and replaced
above by three words § put in verse   P1869:bard describe in   670| MS:lightning. Why
P1869:lightning! Why   671| MS:told § over illegible erasure §   671-72| MS:§ no
¶ §   P1869:§ ¶ §   672| MS:foiled, nor now   P1869:foiled; nor, now,
674| MS:and wile,   P1869:and wile,—   675| MS:of the parents,—how the blot was

By God's gift of a purity of soul
That will not take pollution, ermine-like
Armed from dishonour by its own soft snow.
Such was this gift of God who showed for once
680 How He would have the world go white: it seems
As a new attribute were born of each
Champion of truth, the priest and wife I praise,—
As a new safeguard sprang up in defence
Of their new noble nature: so a thorn
685 Comes to the aid of and completes the rose—
Courage to-wit, no woman's gift nor priest's,
I' the crisis; might leaps vindicating right.
See how the strong aggressor, bad and bold,
With every vantage, preconcerts surprise,
690 Leaps of a sudden at his victim's throat
In a byeway,—how fares he when face to face
With Caponsacchi? Who fights, who fears now?
There quails Count Guido armed to the chattering teeth,
Cowers at the steadfast eye and quiet word
695 O' the Canon of the Pieve! There skulks crime
Behind law called in to back cowardice:
While out of the poor trampled worm the wife,
Springs up a serpent!

But anon of these.

---

blanched   *P1869:*parents! Here the blot is blanched   *1872:*o'   677| MS:That would
not   *P1869:*That will not   678| MS:Armed against all § last two words crossed out and
replaced above by § from <> by its own § last two words inserted above § soft § over *a* §
snow: *P1869:*snow.   679| MS:Today § crossed out and replaced above by two words §
Such was this is § crossed out and replaced above by § of God's gift § transposed to § gift of
God's,—who showed sometimes § crossed out §   *P1869:*of God who   680| MS:How he
<> white,—there seems   *P1869:*How He <> white: it seems   682| MS:Champion
§ over perhaps *Man* § of truth, this priest <> praise,   *P1869:*truth, the priest <> praise,—
683| MS:And a   *P1869:*As a   684| MS:Of the new admirable § crossed out and replaced
above by § stainless nature; so   *P1869:*Of their new noble nature: so   685| MS:rose:
*P1869:*rose—   686| MS:to wit   *P1869:*to-wit   687| MS:In the crisis, might <>
right;   *P1869:*In the crisis; might <> right.   *CP1869:*I'   690| MS:Flies of
*1872:*Leaps of   693| MS:quails Count Guido, armed   DC,BrU:quails Count Guido
armed   *1889:*quails Count Guido armed   695| MS:Of the peaceful Canon at the Pieve!
—skulks   *P1869:*O' the Canon at the Pieve! There skulks crime   *1889a:*the Canon of the
696| MS:cowardice!   DC,BrU:cowardice: *1889:*cowardice: 698| MS:serpent . . . but

Him I judge now,—of him proceed to note,
700   Failing the first, a second chance befriends
Guido, gives pause ere punishment arrive.
The law he called, comes, hears, adjudicates,
Nor does amiss i' the main,—secludes the wife
From the husband, respites the oppressed one, grants
705   Probation to the oppressor, could he know
The mercy of a minute's fiery purge!
The furnace-coals alike of public scorn,
Private remorse, heaped glowing on his head,
What if,—the force and guile, the ore's alloy,
710   Eliminate, his baser soul refined—
The lost be saved even yet, so as by fire?
Let him, rebuked, go softly all his days
And, when no graver musings claim their due,
Meditate on a man's immense mistake
715   Who, fashioned to use feet and walk, deigns crawl—
Takes the unmanly means—ay, though to ends
Man scarce should make for, would but reach thro' wrong,—
May sin, but nowise needs shame manhood so:
Since fowlers hawk, shoot, nay and snare the game,
720   And yet eschew vile practice, nor find sport
In torch-light treachery or the luring owl.

But how hunts Guido? Why, the fraudful trap—
Late spurned to ruin by the indignant feet
Of fellows in the chase who loved fair play—
725   Here he picks up its fragments to the least,
Lades him and hies to the old lurking-place
Where haply he may patch again, refit

*P1869:*serpent! § ¶ § But <> these! DC,BrU:these. *1889:*these.   699| MS:now,—
and thus proceed   *P1869:*now,—of him proceed   702| MS:adjudicates—
*P1869:*adjudicates,   703| MS:in *P1869:*i'   705| MS:Escape to *P1869:*Probation
to   708| MS:head *P1869:*head,   709| MS:if, the *P1869:*if,—the
710| MS:soul burnt clean, *P1869:*soul refined—   712| MS:Let the man but go
*P1869:*Let him, rebuked, go   715| MS:Who fashioned *P1869:*Who, fashioned
717| MS:for, shall but <> wrong, *P1869:*for, would but <> wrong,—   718| MS:but
must not needs <> so— *P1869:*so: *1889a:*but nowise needs   719| MS:game—
*P1869:*game,   720| MS:practice nor *P1869:*practice, nor   721-22| MS:§ no ¶ §
P1869:§ ¶ §   722| MS:trap, *P1869:*trap—   725| MS:up the fragments <> least

The mischief, file its blunted teeth anew,
Make sure, next time, first snap shall break the bone.
730 Craft, greed and violence complot revenge:
Craft, for its quota, schemes to bring about
And seize occasion and be safe withal:
Greed craves its act may work both far and near,
Crush the tree, branch and trunk and root, beside,
735 Whichever twig or leaf arrests a streak
Of possible sunshine else would coin itself,
And drop down one more gold piece in the path:
Violence stipulates "Advantage proved
And safety sure, be pain the overplus!
740 Murder with jagged knife! Cut but tear too!
Foiled oft, starved long, glut malice for amends!"
And what, craft's scheme? scheme sorrowful and strange
As though the elements, whom mercy checked,
Had mustered hate for one eruption more,
745 One final deluge to surprise the Ark
Cradled and sleeping on its mountain-top:
Their outbreak-signal—what but the dove's coo,
Back with the olive in her bill for news
Sorrow was over? 'Tis an infant's birth,

---

*P1869:*least, DC,BrU:up its fragments *1889:*up its fragments   728| MS:The old
mischief, file the blunted *P1869:*The mischief, file its blunted   729| MS:time, a snap
*1872:*time, first snap   731| MS:Craft for its quota schemes <> about, *P1869:*Craft, for
its quota, schemes <> about   732| MS:Seize the occasion *P1869:*And seize occasion
733| MS:craves that one act <> and wide § crossed out and replaced above by § near,
*P1869:*craves its act   734| MS:Break the tree branch <> root beside *P1869:*Crush
the tree, branch <> root beside, *1889a:*beside. DC,BrU:root, beside. *1889:*root, beside.
§ emended to § beside, § see Editorial Notes §   737| *P1869:*path. *1872:*path:
738| MS:stipulates,—advantage *P1869:*stipulates, "Advantage proved, *CP1869:*stipulates
"Advantage DC,BrU:proved *1889:*proved   739| MS:pain my overplus— *P1869:*pain
the overplus!   740| MS:knife,—cut *P1869:*knife! Cut   741| MS:malice at this last!
*P1869:*last!" *CP1869:*malice for amends!"   742| MS:And craft did seize the occasion—
sad § last five words crossed out and replaced above by four words § does scheme,—sorrowful
scheme *P1869:*And, last, craft schemes,—sorrowful scheme *CP1869:*scheme sorrowful
*1872:*And what, craft's scheme? scheme   743| MS:elements whom <> checked
*P1869:*elements, whom <> checked,   745| MS:Last and § altered and transposed
to § And last worst deluge should surprise *P1869:*One final deluge to surprise
747| MS:The out-break-signal <> dove's flight *P1869:*For outbreak-signal <> dove's
flight *CP1869:*The outbreak-signal <> dove's coo,— *1869:*coos *1872:*Their
outbreak-signal <> dove's coo,   749| MS:over! 'Tis *P1869:*is over? 'Tis *CP1869:*was

⁷⁵⁰ Guido's first born, his son and heir, that gives
The occasion: other men cut free their souls
From care in such a case, fly up in thanks
To God, reach, recognize His love for once:
Guido cries "Soul, at last the mire is thine!
⁷⁵⁵ Lie there in likeness of a money-bag
My babe's birth so pins down past moving now,
That I dare cut adrift the lives I late
Scrupled to touch lest thou escape with them!
These parents and their child my wife,—touch one,
⁷⁶⁰ Lose all! Their rights determined on a head
I could but hate, not harm, since from each hair
Dangled a hope for me: now—chance and change!
No right was in their child but passes plain
To that child's child and through such child to me.
⁷⁶⁵ I am a father now,—come what, come will,
I represent my child; he comes between—
Cuts sudden off the sunshine of this life
From those three: why, the gold is in his curls!
Not with old Pietro's, Violante's head,
⁷⁷⁰ Not his grey horror, her more hideous black—
Go these, devoted to the knife!"

                           'Tis done:
Wherefore should mind misgive, heart hesitate?
He calls to counsel, fashions certain four
Colourless natures counted clean till now,
⁷⁷⁵ —Rustic simplicity, uncorrupted youth,
Ignorant virtue! Here's the gold o' the prime

---

^{751|}   MS:The glad § crossed out §   ^{753|}   MS:recognise his   *P1869:*recognize His
^{754|}   MS:cries, Soul   *CP1869:*cries "Soul   ^{755|}   *P1869:*money-bag,   *1889a:*money-bag
^{756|}   MS:This babe's birth so § inserted above § pins me § crossed out § down <> now
*P1869:*so pins down <> now,   *1872:*My babe's   ^{757|}   MS:adrift § written over illegible
word §   ^{758|}   MS:them: *P1869:*them!   ^{759|}   MS:These Parents and <> wife,
touch one   *P1869:*These parents and   *CP1869:*wife,—touch   *1889a:*one,
^{760|}   MS:all,—their <> on the head   *P1869:*all! Their <> on her head   *CP1869:*on a head
^{762|}   MS:hope of mine: now   *P1869:*hope for me: now   ^{763|}   MS:What right <> passes
now   *P1869:*No right   *1889a:*passes plain   ^{764|}   MS:me?   *P1869:*me.
^{765|}   MS:am the father   *1872:*am a father   ^{766|}   MS:child, he   *P1869:*child; he
^{768-70|}   MS:why the <> curls, / Not that grey horror, that more   *P1869:*why, the <>
curls! / Not with old Pietro's, Violante's head, / Not his grey horror, her more
^{771|}   MS:Go then, devoted to the dark!" § ¶ § 'Tis   *P1869:*Go these, devoted to the knife!"
§ ¶ § 'Tis   ^{774|}   MS:counted white till   *P1869:*counted clean till   ^{776|}   MS:The

When Saturn ruled, shall shock our leaden day—
The clown abash the courtier! Mark it, bards!
The courtier tries his hand on clownship here,
⁷⁸⁰ Speaks a word, names a crime, appoints a price,—
Just breathes on what, suffused with all himself,
Is red-hot henceforth past distinction now
I' the common glow of hell. And thus they break
And blaze on us at Rome, Christ's birthnight-eve!
⁷⁸⁵ Oh angels that sang erst "On the earth, peace!
To man, good will!"—such peace finds earth to-day!
After the seventeen hundred years, so man
Wills good to man, so Guido makes complete
His murder! what is it I said?—cuts loose
⁷⁹⁰ Three lives that hitherto he suffered cling,
Simply because each served to nail secure,
By a corner of the money-bag, his soul,—
Therefore, lives sacred till the babe's first breath
O'erweights them in the balance,—off they fly!

⁷⁹⁵ So is the murder managed, sin conceived
To the full: and why not crowned with triumph too?
Why must the sin, conceived thus, bring forth death?
I note how, within hair's-breadth of escape,
Impunity and the thing supposed success,
⁸⁰⁰ Guido is found when the check comes, the change,

---

clown's rude § last three words crossed out and replaced above by § Ignorant virtue: here's
the age o' *P1869:*virtue! Here's the gold o' ⁷⁷⁷| MS:ruled shall shock § over perhaps
shame § *P1869:*ruled, shall ⁷⁷⁸| MS:courtier! Trow ye, bards? *P1869:*courtier! Mark
it, bards! ⁷⁸⁰| MS:crime and notes the pay, *P1869:*crime, appoints a price,—
⁷⁸¹| MS:on to suffuse with *P1869:*on what, suffused with ⁷⁸²| MS:Red-heat
henceforward past *P1869:*Is red-hot henceforth past ⁷⁸³| MS:In *CP1869:*I'
⁷⁸⁴| MS:at Rome, Christ's Birthnight eve! *P1869:*at Rome, Christ's Birthnight-eve!
*1872:*birthnight-eve! ⁷⁸⁵| MS:peace— *P1869:*peace! ⁷⁸⁶| MS:to-day,—
*CP1869:*to-day! ⁷⁸⁹| MS:murder,—what is it I say? cuts *P1869:*murder! what is it I
said?—cuts ⁷⁹⁰| MS:cling *P1869:*cling, ⁷⁹²| MS:soul, *P1869:*soul,—
⁷⁹³| MS:Therefore lives *P1869:*Therefore, lives ⁷⁹⁴| MS:fly. *P1869:*fly!
⁷⁹⁴⁻⁹⁵| MS:§ no ¶ § *P1869:*§ ¶ § ⁷⁹⁵| MS:So is § over *was* § <> managed,
wickedness § crossed out § ⁷⁹⁶| MS:full: and § inserted above § why not a § crossed
out and replaced by § perfect § crossed out § crowned with § last two words inserted above §
⁷⁹⁷| MS:Why the plan § last two words crossed out and replaced above by § must
⁷⁹⁸| MS:how within *P1869:*how, within ⁷⁹⁹| MS:thing he calls § last two words
crossed out and replaced above by § supposed success *P1869:*success, ⁸⁰⁰| MS:Stands

The monitory touch o' the tether—felt
By few, not marked by many, named by none
At the moment, only recognized aright
I' the fulness of the days, for God's, lest sin
805 Exceed the service, leap the line: such check—
A secret which this life finds hard to keep,
And, often guessed, is never quite revealed—
Needs must trip Guido on a stumbling-block
Too vulgar, too absurdly plain i' the path!
810 Study this single oversight of care,
This hebetude that marred sagacity,
Forgetfulness of all the man best knew,—
How any stranger having need to fly,
Needs but to ask and have the means of flight.
815 Why, the first urchin tells you, to leave Rome,
Get horses, you must show the warrant, just
The banal scrap, clerk's scribble, a fair word buys,
Or foul one, if a ducat sweeten word,—
And straight authority will back demand,
820 Give you the pick o' the post-house!—how should he,
Then, resident at Rome for thirty years,
Guido, instruct a stranger! And himself

---

§ crossed out and replaced above by § Gets Guido when <> comes and the   *P1869:*Guido is
found when <> comes, the   801| MS:That monitory <> of   *P1869:*The monitory
<> o'   804| MS:In <> days for God's check § over illegible word § sign § crossed
out § lest   *P1869:*I' <> days, for God's, lest   805| MS:leap the limit § crossed out and
replaced above by two words § line traced here: *P1869:*leap the line: such check—
806| MS:The secret of § crossed out and replaced above by § which <> life finds § over *is* §
*P1869:*A secret   807| MS:Yet, somehow guessed, shall § crossed out and replaced above
by § is never be § crossed out and replaced above by § quite revealed.   *P1869:*And, often
guessed   *1872:*revealed—   808| MS:Guido must needs trip on   *1872:*Needs must trip
Guido on   809| MS:vulgar, all § crossed out § too absurdly § inserted above § <> in
*P1869:*i'   810-15| MS:This <> of sagacity, / Forgetfulness of what the <> knew / One
has to ask <> / Why, the first stranger § crossed out and replaced above by § urchin
*P1869:*Study this <> of care, / This hebetude that mars sagacity, / <> knew! / Here is a
stranger who, with need to fly, / Needs but to ask <> / Why   *1872:*/ <> marred<> / <>
of all the <> knew,— / How any stranger having need <> / / Why   817| MS:scrap, of
§ crossed out and replaced above by § clerk's scribble a   *P1869:*scribble, a   818| MS:Or
a foul <> ducat follow § crossed out and replaced above by § sweeten such,—   *P1869:*Or
foul <> sweeten wood,—   *CP1869:*word,—   819| MS:And there's authority will
§ over *with* §   *P1869:*And straight authority   820-22| MS:of the post-house: how I hear
§ last three words crossed out and replaced above by three words § in such wise / Guido
instructs some § crossed out and replaced above by § a   *P1869:*o' the post-house!—in such

104

Forgets just this poor paper scrap, wherewith
Armed, every door he knocks at opens wide
825 To save him: horsed and manned, with such advance
O' the hunt behind, why, 'twere the easy task
Of hours told on the fingers of one hand,
To reach the Tuscan frontier, laugh at-home,
Light-hearted with his fellows of the place,—
830 Prepared by that strange shameful judgment, that
Satire upon a sentence just pronounced
By the Rota and confirmed by the Granduke,—
Ready in a circle to receive their peer,
Appreciate his good story how, when Rome,
835 The Pope-King and the populace of priests
Made common cause with their confederate
The other priestling who seduced his wife,
He, all unaided, wiped out the affront
With decent bloodshed and could face his friends,
840 Frolic it in the world's eye. Ay, such tale
Missed such applause, and by such oversight!
So, tired and footsore, those blood-flustered five
Went reeling on the road through dark and cold,
The few permissible miles, to sink at length,
845 Wallow and sleep in the first wayside straw,
As the other herd quenched, i' the wash o' the wave,
—Each swine, the devil inside him: so slept they,

---

wise / The resident at Rome for thirty years,/ Guido, instructs a   *1872:*post-house!—how
should he, / Then, resident <> / Guido, instruct a   823| MS:scrap wherewith
*P1869:*scrap, wherewith   825| MS:him, horsed and manned with   *P1869:*him: horsed
and manned, with   826| MS:Of <> why tis the   *P1869:*O' <> why 'twere the
*1872:*why, 'twere   827| MS:hand   *P1869:*hand,   828| MS:the Tuscan Frontier <>
at home   *P1869:*home,   *1872:*the Tuscan frontier   DC,BrU:at-home,   *1889:*at-home,
829| MS:with the best of the land, I see,—   *P1869:*with his fellows of the place,—
833| MS:to salute § crossed out and replaced above by § receive <> peer   *P1869:*peer,
834| MS:Appreciate that good   *P1869:*Appreciate his good   835| MS:The Pope King
*P1869:*The Pope-King   839| MS:With the decent   *P1869:*With decent
841| MS:applause by one such oversight;   *P1869:*applause, all by such oversight!
*1872:*applause, and by   842| MS:So § over *The* § <> footsore, and § crossed out and
replaced above by § those   843| MS:cold   *P1869:*cold,   844| MS:miles to <>
length   *P1869:*miles, to <> length,   845| MS:straw   *P1869:*straw,   846| MS:As
the ancient swine cooled § last three words crossed out and replaced above by three words §
other herd quenched in <> wave   *P1869:*quenched, i' <> wave,   847| MS:Each swine

105

And so were caught and caged—all through one trip,
One touch of fool in Guido the astute!
850 He curses the omission, I surmise,
More than the murder. Why, thou fool and blind,
It is the mercy-stroke that stops thy fate,
Hamstrings and holds thee to thy hurt,—but how?
On the edge o' the precipice! One minute more,
855 Thou hadst gone farther and fared worse, my son,
Fathoms down on the flint and fire beneath!
Thy comrades each and all were of one mind,
Thy murder done, to straightway murder thee
In turn, because of promised pay withheld.
860 So, to the last, greed found itself at odds
With craft in thee, and, proving conqueror,
Had sent thee, the same night that crowned thy hope,
Thither where, this same day, I see thee not,
Nor, through God's mercy, need, to-morrow, see.

865 Such I find Guido, midmost blotch of black
Discernible in this group of clustered crimes
Huddling together in the cave they call
Their palace outraged day thus penetrates.
Around him ranged, now close and now remote,

---

§ over illegible word § the *P1869:*—Each swine, the   848| MS:one fault § crossed out
and replaced above by § trip,   849| MS:Touch of forgetfulness in Guido! Fault
*P1869:*of the fool in Guido:the astute! *CP1869:*in Guido the *1872:*One touch of fool
850| MS:curses at this minute, I   *P1869:*curses the omission, I   851| MS:murder: why
*P1869:*murder. Why   852| MS:This is § over perhaps *was* § *P1869:*It is
853| MS:but where? *P1869:*but how?   854| MS:of the precipice: one <>
more *P1869:*o' the precipice! One <> more,   855| MS:§ inserted between
854-56 § MS:son *P1869:*son,   856| MS:flint beneath § over illegible erasure § :
for why? *P1869:*flint and fire beneath!   857| MS:mind *1872:*mind,
858| MS:Straitway, thy <> to murder *1872:*Thy <> to straightway
murder   859| MS:withheld, *P1869:*withheld.   860| MS:So to the last
greed finds itself *P1869:*So, to the last, greed found itself   861| MS:and proves craft's
conqueror, *P1869:*and, proving conquerer,   862| MS:And sends thee, the § over
perhaps *that* § <> night of thy success § last three words crossed out and replaced above by
four words and comma § that crowns thy hope, *P1869:*Had sent thee <> crowned
864-65| MS:§ no ¶ § *P1869:*§ ¶ §   865| MS:find Guido, central § crossed out and
replaced above by § midmost   866| MS:group, these § crossed out and replaced above
by § of *P1869:*group of   867| MS:in that § altered to § the   868| MS:Arezzo
§ crossed out and replaced above by two words § Their palace, outraged *1889a:*palace
outraged   869| MS:Round him are ranged *CP1869:*Around him ranged

Prominent or obscure to meet the needs
O' the mage and master, I detect each shape
Subsidiary i' the scene nor loathed the less,
All alike coloured, all descried akin
By one and the same pitchy furnace stirred
875 At the centre: see, they lick the master's hand,—
This fox-faced horrible priest, this brother-brute
The Abate,—why, mere wolfishness looks well,
Guido stands honest in the red o' the flame,
Beside this yellow that would pass for white,
880 Twice Guido, all craft but no violence,
This copier of the mien and gait and garb
Of Peter and Paul, that he may go disguised,
Rob halt and lame, sick folk i' the temple-porch!
Armed with religion, fortified by law,
885 A man of peace, who trims the midnight lamp
And turns the classic page—and all for craft,
All to work harm with, yet incur no scratch!
While Guido brings the struggle to a close,
Paul steps back the due distance, clear o' the trap
890 He builds and baits. Guido I catch and judge;
Paul is past reach in this world and my time:
That is a case reserved. Pass to the next,

871| MS:Of the Mage in the middle § last three words crossed out and replaced above by two words § and master, I detect those § crossed out and replaced above by § each shapes § altered to § shape *P1869:*O' the mage   872| MS:in the scene § followed by illegible erasure replaced above by § nor *P1869:*i'   874| MS:pitchy flame, he § last two words crossed out and replaced above by § furnace stirs § altered to §stirred   875| MS:master's foot,— *P1869:*master's hand,—   877| MS:The Abate, why this § crossed out and replaced above by § mere <> well *P1869:*The Abate,—why, mere <> well,   878| MS:And § crossed out § Guido stands § inserted above § <> of the flame *P1869:*flame, *CP1869:*o'
880| MS:This Guido all craft and no violence *P1869:*This Guido, all craft but no violence, *1872:*Twice Guido,   881| MS:the gait and mien § transposed to § mien and gait
882| MS:Of Peter § followed by illegible erasure § <> disguised *P1869:*disguised,
883| MS:lame, and blind § last two words crossed out and replaced above by two words § sick folk in the temple-porch. *P1869:*i' the temple-porch!   886| MS:the § followed by illegible erasure § student's § crossed out and replaced above by § antique page *CP1869:*the classic page   887| MS:with yet <> scratch *P1869:*with, yet <> scratch!
888| MS:While Guido § followed by illegible erasure § <> close *P1869:*close,
889| MS:distance, tempts no trap *P1869:*distance, clear o' the trap   890| MS:baits. Guido has found his fate, § last four words and comma crossed out and replaced above by four words and period § I catch and judge. *P1869:*judge;   891| MS:But § inserted in margin § Paul, is § crossed out § <> time, *P1869:*Paul is <> time: 892| MS:That is

The boy of the brood, the young Girolamo
Priest, Canon, and what more? nor wolf nor fox,
895 But hybrid, neither craft nor violence
Wholly, part violence part craft: such cross
Tempts speculation—will both blend one day,
And prove hell's better product? Or subside
And let the simple quality emerge,
900 Go on with Satan's service the old way?
Meanwhile, what promise,—what performance too!
For there's a new distinctive touch, I see,
Lust—lacking in the two—hell's own blue tint
That gives a character and marks the man
905 More than a match for yellow and red. Once more,
A case reserved: why should I doubt? Then comes
The gaunt grey nightmare in the furthest smoke,
The hag that gave these three abortions birth,
Unmotherly mother and unwomanly
910 Woman, that near turns motherhood to shame,
Womanliness to loathing: no one word,
No gesture to curb cruelty a whit
More than the she-pard thwarts her playsome whelps
Trying their milk-teeth on the soft o' the throat
915 O' the first fawn, flung, with those beseeching eyes,
Flat in the covert! How should she but couch,
Lick the dry lips, unsheath the blunted claw,

---

§ inserted in margin § A < > next   *P1869:*is a < > next,   894| MS:more? Nor
*P1869:*nor   896| MS:craft, a cross   *P1869:*craft: such cross   898| MS:prove the
better   *CP1869:*prove hell's better   899| MS:emerge   *P1869:*emerge,
901| MS:too,   *P1869:*too!   903| MS:the other § crossed out and replaced above by §
two—hell's own § inserted above §   904| MS:gives § over illegible erasure §
906| MS:should I care? Then   *P1869:*should I doubt? Then   909| MS:mother, the
unwomanly   *CP1869:*mother and unwomanly   910| MS:Woman, that § over perhaps
who § turns   *P1869:*that near turns   911| MS:The womanliness to loathing: what,
§ word and comma crossed out § no one § inserted above §   *P1869:*Womanliness
913| MS:the wild beast § last two words crossed out and replaced above by § she-pard
thwarts each § crossed out and replaced above by § her   914| MS:Trying their § over
perhaps *its* § < > of   *P1869:*o'   915| MS:Of < > fawn, flung, § word and comma
inserted above §   *P1869:*O'   916| MS:Captured § crossed out and replaced above by §
Flat < > covert: what does § last two words crossed out and replaced above by two words §
how should   *P1869:*covert! How   917| MS:lips, half § inserted above § unsheathe the
§ followed by illegible erasure replaced above by § blunted   *P1869:*lips, unsheath

Catch 'twixt her placid eyewinks at what chance
Old bloody half-forgotten dream may flit,
920 Born when herself was novice to the taste,
The while she lets youth take its pleasure. Last,
These God-abandoned wretched lumps of life,
These four companions,—country-folk this time,
Not tainted by the unwholesome civic breath,
925 Much less the curse o' the Court! Mere striplings too,
Fit to do human nature justice still!
Surely when impudence in Guido's shape
Shall propose crime and proffer money's-worth
To these stout tall rough bright-eyed black-haired boys,
930 The blood shall bound in answer to each cheek
Before the indignant outcry break from lip!
Are these i' the mood to murder, hardly loosed
From healthy autumn-finish of ploughed glebe,
Grapes in the barrel, work at happy end,
935 And winter near with rest and Christmas play?
How greet they Guido with his final task—
(As if he but proposed "One vineyard more
To dig, ere frost come, then relax indeed!")

918| MS:twixt her placid winking eyelids § last three words crossed out and replaced above
by two words § placid eyewinks at what § over perhaps *an* § old § crossed out §
P1869:'twixt   919-21| MS:Old § inserted in margin § Bloody § altered to § bloody and
§ erased § half-forgotten <> / And let youth <> Last of all   *P1869:*bloody half-forgotten
<> / Born when herself was novice to the taste, / The which she lets youth <> Last,
CP1869:// The while she   922| MS:life   *P1869:*life,   924| MS:Untainted § altered
to § Nor tainted   *P1869:*Not tainted   925| MS:Much less § last two words inserted in
margin § The § altered to § the <> of the court. Just striplings   *P1869:*o' the court! Mere
striplings   *1889a:*the Court   926| MS:still—   *P1869:*still!   927| MS:And here
goes impudence   *P1869:*Surely when impudence   928| MS:Shall § over *Will* § propose
murder for his § last three words crossed out and replaced above by three words § crime and
proffer   929| MS:tall bright-eyed and black-haired   *1889a:*tall rough bright-eyed
black-haired   930| MS:With the § crossed out § blood   *P1869:*The blood
931| MS:indignant speech can break   *P1869:*indignant outcry break   932| MS:Why,
they are just in the mood, loose hardly yet   *P1869:*Are these i' the mood to murder, hardly
loosed   933| MS:From the healthy Autumn labour, the ploughed   *CP1869:*From
healthy autumn-finish, the   *1889a:*autumn-finish of ploughed   934| MS:end
*P1869:*end,   935| MS:winter come with <> play!   *P1869:*play?   *1889a:*winter near
with   937| MS:he said, one <> more to dig   *P1869:*he but proposed "One <> more
938| MS:Ere <> relax with all my heart)—   *P1869:*To dig, ere <> relax indeed!")

"Anywhere, anyhow and anywhy,
940 Murder me some three people, old and young,
Ye never heard the names of,—and be paid
So much!" And the whole four accede at once.
Demur? Do cattle bidden march or halt?
Is it some lingering habit, old fond faith
945 I' the lord o' the land, instructs them,—birthright-badge
Of feudal tenure claims its slaves again?
Not so at all, thou noble human heart!
All is done purely for the pay,—which, earned,
And not forthcoming at the instant, makes
950 Religion heresy, and the lord o' the land
Fit subject for a murder in his turn.
The patron with cut throat and rifled purse,
Deposited i' the roadside-ditch, his due,
Nought hinders each good fellow trudging home,
955 The heavier by a piece or two in poke,
And so with new zest to the common life,
Mattock and spade, plough-tail and waggon-shaft,
Till some such other piece of luck betide,
Who knows? Since this is a mere start in life,
960 And none of them exceeds the twentieth year.

Nay, more i' the background yet? Unnoticed forms

939| MS:§ inserted between 938-40 § "Anywhere anyhow and anywhy *P1869:*"Anywhere,
anyhow and anywhy,   940| MS:people old and young *P1869:*people, old and young,
941| MS:You <> of and *P1869:*Ye <> of,—and   942| MS:once, *P1869:*once.
943| MS:Demur? As cattle do bid march or halt: *P1869:*cattle would, bid <> halt!
*1889a:*Demur? Do cattle bidden march or halt?   945| MS:In <> of the land, compels
§ crossed out and replaced above by § instructs them, birthright badge *P1869:*I' <>
them,—birthright-badge *1872:*o' <> birthright badge § emended to § birthright-badge § see
Editorial Notes §   946| MS:Of the feudal *P1869:*Of feudal   948| MS:All was
done *P1869:*All is done   949| MS:instant, made *P1869:*instant, makes
950| MS:of *P1869:*o'   952| MS:purse *P1869:*purse,   953| MS:in the roadside
ditch his *CP1869:*i' the roadside-ditch, his   954| MS:What hinders *CP1869:*Nought
hinders   955| MS:by the piece *CP1869:*by a piece   956| MS:And going § crossed
out § back with a new zest § last four words inserted above § <> life again § crossed out §
*P1869:*And so with new <> life,   957| MS:plough-tail or waggon-shaft, *P1869:*plough-
tail and waggon-shaft,   958| MS:luck befall § crossed out §   959| MS:knows?
Since is *P1869:*knows? Since this is   960| MS:exceeds § over illegible word §
960-61| MS:§ no ¶ § *P1869:*§ ¶ § *1872:*§ no ¶ § *1889:*§ no ¶ ; emended to restore ¶ ;
see Editorial Notes §   961| MS:Nay, still § crossed out § more in the background, still

110

Claim to be classed, subordinately vile?
Complacent lookers-on that laugh,—perchance
Shake head as their friend's horse-play grows too rough
965 With the mere child he manages amiss—
But would not interfere and make bad worse
For twice the fractious tears and prayers: thou know'st
Civility better, Marzi-Medici,
Governor for thy kinsman the Granduke!
970 Fit representative of law, man's lamp
I' the magistrate's grasp full-flare, no rushlight-end
Sputtering 'twixt thumb and finger of the priest!
Whose answer to the couple's cry for help
Is a threat,—whose remedy of Pompilia's wrong,
975 A shrug o' the shoulder, and facetious word
Or wink, traditional with Tuscan wits,
To Guido in the doorway. Laud to law!
The wife is pushed back to the husband, he
Who knows how these home-squabblings persecute

---

new § last two words crossed out and replaced above by two words § yet, unnoticed
*P1869:*Nay, more i' <> yet? Unnoticed forms   963| MS:Complacent friends that stand
and § last four words crossed out and replaced above by two words § lookers-on that
see,—perchance   *P1869:*that laugh,—perchance   964| MS:Sigh over § last two words
crossed out and replaced above by three words § Shake heads as their comrade's § crossed out
and replaced by § friend's horse-play, grows too § last two words inserted above § rough
and rash, § last two words and comma crossed out § *P1869:*horse-play grows   *CP1869:*head
965| MS:§ inserted between 964-66 § child, he   *P1869:*child he   966| MS:and spoil the
game § last three words crossed out and replaced above by three words § make bad worse
968| MS:Their duty § last two words crossed out and replaced above by § Civility better,
Marzi-Medici   *P1869:*Marzi-Medici,   969| MS:thy cousin the Grand-Duke   *P1869:*thy
kinsman the Granduke!   970| MS:This representative of human § crossed out § law,
man's light § crossed out § *P1869:*Fit representative   971| MS:In the § inserted in
margin § magistrate's grasp § over *hand* § <> no twist of wax § last three words crossed out
and replaced above by § rushlight-end   *P1869:*I' the magistrate's   972| MS:sputtering
§ over illegible word § twixt <> priest,—   *P1869:*'twixt <> priest!   973| MS:to these
Comparini's cry   *1889a:*to the couple's Comparini's cry for help   DC,BrU:couple's cry
*1889:*couple's cry   974| MS:a menace,—whose cure of   *P1869:*a threat,—whose remedy
of   975| MS:of <> word § blotted, perhaps over illegible word § , *CP1869:*o'
976| MS:The § over illegible erasure § wink   *P1869:*Or wink   977| MS:doorway; and
you've law,   *P1869:*doorway. Laud to law!   978| MS:There's the wife pushed
*P1869:*The wife is pushed   979| MS:That knows <> these domestic § crossed out and
replaced above by § home squabblings plague § crossed out § *P1869:*Who knows <>

People who have the public good to mind,
And work best with a silence in the court!

Ah, but I save my word at least for thee,
Archbishop, who art under me, i' the Church,
As I am under God,—thou, chosen by both
985 To do the shepherd's office, feed the sheep—
How of this lamb that panted at thy foot
While the wolf pressed on her within crook's reach?
Wast thou the hireling that did turn and flee?
With thee at least anon the little word!

990 Such denizens o' the cave now cluster round
And heat the furnace sevenfold: time indeed
A bolt from heaven should cleave roof and clear place,
Transfix and show the world, suspiring flame,
The main offender, scar and brand the rest
995 Hurrying, each miscreant to his hole: then flood
And purify the scene with outside day—
Which yet, in the absolutest drench of dark,
Ne'er wants a witness, some stray beauty-beam
To the despair of hell.

First of the first,
1000 Such I pronounce Pompilia, then as now

---

home-squabblings   980| MS:mind,— P1869:mind,   981| MS:And what a lovely
silence P1869:And work best with a silence   981-82| MS:§ no ¶ § P1869:§ ¶ §
982| MS:but I have my <> thee P1869:but I save my <> thee,   983| MS:Archbishop,
who art § last two words inserted above § under me as I § last two words crossed out and
replaced above by three words and comma § in the church, P1869:the Church,
1889a:under, i' § emended to § under me, i' § see Editorial Notes §   984| MS:thou
placed § crossed out and replaced above by § chosen P1869:thou, chosen
989-90| MS:§ no ¶ § P1869:§ ¶ §   990| MS:Such occupants § crossed out and
replaced above by § denizens of the cave now § inserted above § cluster around § crossed
out § CP1869:o'   991| MS:The cauldron and § last three words crossed out § Who
feeds the furnace § last three words crossed out and replaced above by four words § heats the
furnace sevenfold P1869:And heat   996| MS:with outside § inserted above §
998| MS:stray beauty- § word and dash inserted above § beam of God's § last two words
crossed out§   999| MS:Wrestling with § last two words crossed out and replaced above
by four words § To the despair of hell. § marginal note that new paragraph begins §

Perfect in whiteness: stoop thou down, my child,
Give one good moment to the poor old Pope
Heart-sick at having all his world to blame—
Let me look at thee in the flesh as erst,
1005 Let me enjoy the old clean linen garb,
Not the new splendid vesture! Armed and crowned,
Would Michael, yonder, be, nor crowned nor armed,
The less pre-eminent angel? Everywhere
I see in the world the intellect of man,
1010 That sword, the energy his subtle spear,
The knowledge which defends him like a shield—
Everywhere; but they make not up, I think,
The marvel of a soul like thine, earth's flower
She holds up to the softened gaze of God!
1015 It was not given Pompilia to know much,
Speak much, to write a book, to move mankind,
Be memorized by who records my time.
Yet if in purity and patience, if
In faith held fast despite the plucking fiend,
1020 Safe like the signet stone with the new name
That saints are known by,—if in right returned
For wrong, most pardon for worst injury,
If there be any virtue, any praise,—
Then will this woman-child have proved—who knows?—

1001| MS:Splendid of § last two words crossed out and replaced above by two words § Perfect
in whiteness—stand § crossed out and replaced above by § look thou up § crossed
out and replaced above by § down   *P1869:*whiteness—stoop thou   *1872:*whiteness:
stoop   1002| MS:the aged § crossed out and replaced above by two words § poor old
1003-5| MS:all this § crossed out and replaced above by § his <> / Let me enjoy   *P1869:* /
Let me look at thee in the flesh as erst, / Let   1006| MS:vesture! Sword and shield— §
last three words and dash crossed out and replaced above by three words and comma
§ Armed and crowned,   1007| MS:Would not prince § last two words crossed
out § Michael, stand, apart from these § last four words crossed out and replaced
above by five words § yonder, nor crowned nor armed,   *P1869:*yonder, be,
nor   1008| MS:preeminent   *P1869:*pre-eminent   1011| MS:which § over *that*
§ <> shield   *P1869:*shield—   1012| MS:Everywhere, but   *P1869:*Everywhere;
but   1014| MS:of God.   *P1869:*of God!   1015| MS:given to this § last two
words crossed out §   1016| MS:book, to rule a land § last three words crossed out and
replaced above by two words § move mankind,   1019| MS:faith kept § crossed out and
replaced above by § still firm despite <> fiend   *P1869:*faith held fast despite <> fiend,
1020| MS:Held § inserted in margin § Like the white § crossed out § signet-stone
*P1869:*Safe like the   *1872:*signet stone   1022| MS:wrong, forgive wife § last two words
crossed out §   1024| MS:have proved § over *become* § well nigh § last two words crossed

113

¹⁰²⁵ Just the one prize vouchsafed unworthy me,
Seven years a gardener of the untoward ground,
I till,—this earth, my sweat and blood manure
All the long day that barrenly grows dusk:
At least one blossom makes me proud at eve
¹⁰³⁰ Born 'mid the briers of my enclosure! Still
(Oh, here as elsewhere, nothingness of man!)
Those be the plants, imbedded yonder South
To mellow in the morning, those made fat
By the master's eye, that yield such timid leaf,
¹⁰³⁵ Uncertain bud, as product of his pains!
While—see how this mere chance-sown cleft-nursed seed
That sprang up by the wayside 'neath the foot
Of the enemy, this breaks all into blaze,
Spreads itself, one wide glory of desire
¹⁰⁴⁰ To incorporate the whole great sun it loves
From the inch-height whence it looks and longs! My flower,
My rose, I gather for the breast of God,
This I praise most in thee, where all I praise,
That having been obedient to the end

out and replaced above by two words, question mark and dashes § —who knows?—
¹⁰²⁵| MS:Just § inserted in margin § The one reward § crossed out and replaced above by §
prize < > me *P1869:*Just the < > me, ¹⁰²⁶| MS:Ten years the § crossed out and
replaced above by § a < > ground *P1869:*ground, *1872:*Seven years
¹⁰²⁷⁻²⁹| MS:This earth I till, which § crossed out and replaced above by § my < > manure. /
At least this blossom § crossed out and replaced above by § beauty meets my hand at eve—
§ last five words and dash crossed out and replaced above by five words § makes me proud at
eve *P1869:*I till,—this earth, my < > manure / All the long day that barrenly grows dusk:/
At least one blossom makes ¹⁰³⁰| MS:mid the briars *P1869:*'mid the briers
¹⁰³²| MS:Those are the plants, set § crossed out and replaced above by § imbedded yonder in
the § last two words crossed out § *P1869:*Those be ¹⁰³⁴| MS:yield the timid leaf
*P1869:*yield such timid leaf, ¹⁰³⁵| MS:The uncertain bud, product of all the pains—
*P1869:*Uncertain bud, as product of his pains! ¹⁰³⁶| MS:this mere § inserted above §
chance-sown, cleft-nursed seed *P1869:*seed, DC,BrU:chance-sown cleft-nursed seed
*1889:*chance-sown cleft-nursed seed ¹⁰³⁷| MS:This that § inserted above § < > neath
*P1869:*That < > 'neath ¹⁰³⁸| MS:breaks out into one § crossed out and replaced above
by § a blaze, *P1869:*breaks all into blaze, ¹⁰³⁹| MS:itself, in a § last two words crossed
out and replaced above by two words § one wide ¹⁰⁴⁰| MS:whole wide § crossed out
and replaced above by § great < > loves § over illegible word § ¹⁰⁴¹| MS:longs. My
*P1869:*longs! My ¹⁰⁴²| MS:Perfect and true rose gathered for God's breast, *P1869:*My
rose, I gather for the breast of God, ¹⁰⁴³| MS:all is praise, *P1869:*all I praise,

¹⁰⁴⁵ According to the light allotted, law
Prescribed thy life, still tried, still standing test,—
Dutiful to the foolish parents first,
Submissive next to the bad husband,—nay,
Tolerant of those meaner miserable
¹⁰⁵⁰ That did his hests, eked out the dole of pain,—
Thou, patient thus, couldst rise from law to law,
The old to the new, promoted at one cry
O' the trump of God to the new service, not
To longer bear, but henceforth fight, be found
¹⁰⁵⁵ Sublime in new impatience with the foe!
Endure man and obey God: plant firm foot
On neck of man, tread man into the hell
Meet for him, and obey God all the more!
Oh child that didst despise thy life so much
¹⁰⁶⁰ When it seemed only thine to keep or lose,
How the fine ear felt fall the first low word
"Value life, and preserve life for My sake!"
Thou didst . . . how shall I say? . . . receive so long
The standing ordinance of God on earth,
¹⁰⁶⁵ What wonder if the novel claim had clashed
With old requirement, seemed to supersede

---

^{1045|} MS:allotted her § written over by § law, ^{1046|} MS:And law of § last three words
crossed out and replaced above by two words § Prescribed thy <> tried and standing test,
*P1869:*tried, still standing test,— ^{1051|} MS:to law *P1869:*to law, ^{1053|} MS:Of
*P1869:*O' ^{1054|} MS:Bear any more § last two words crossed out and replaced above by
§ longer, but fight now, be sublime § crossed out and replaced above by § found henceforth
*P1869:*To longer bear, but henceforth fight, be found ^{1055|} MS:Sublime § inserted in
margin § In all impatience <> foe. *P1869:*Sublime in new impatience <> foe!
^{1056|} MS:Bear with § last two words crossed out and replaced above by § Endure <>
God: plant § crossed out and then restored § a § crossed out and replaced above by § firm foot
§ crossed out and then restored § ^{1057|} MS:On the face § crossed out and replaced
above by § neck of man, and § crossed out § tread him § crossed out and replaced above by §
man *CP1869:*On neck ^{1058|} MS:That § followed by illegible word, both crossed out
and replaced above by two words § Meet for ^{1060|} MS:lose *P1869:*lose,
^{1061|} MS:Who gave the § last three words crossed out and replaced above by two words §
How felt <> ear for § crossed out and replaced below by § felt § crossed out and replaced
by § prick the small § crossed out and replaced above by three words § distinguished
§ crossed out and replaced by § first low *P1869:*How the <> ear felt fall the
^{1062|} MS:for my sake?" *P1869:*for My sake!" ^{1063|} MS:Thou hadst . . how <> say?
. . receive *P1869:*Thou didst . . how <> receive *1889a:*didst . . . how <> say? . . .
receive ^{1065|} MS:claim should clash *P1869:*claim had clashed ^{1066|} MS:seem

115

Too much the customary law? But, brave,
Thou at first prompting of what I call God,
And fools call Nature, didst hear, comprehend,
1070 Accept the obligation laid on thee,
Mother elect, to save the unborn child,
As brute and bird do, reptile and the fly,
Ay and, I nothing doubt, even tree, shrub, plant
And flower o' the field, all in a common pact
1075 To worthily defend the trust of trusts,
Life from the Ever Living:—didst resist—
Anticipate the office that is mine—
And with his own sword stay the upraised arm,
The endeavour of the wicked, and defend
1080 Him who,—again in my default,—was there
For visible providence: one less true than thou
To touch, i' the past, less practised in the right,
Approved less far in all docility
To all instruction,—how had such an one
1085 Made scruple "Is this motion a decree?"
It was authentic to the experienced ear
O' the good and faithful servant. Go past me
And get thy praise,—and be not far to seek
Presently when I follow if I may!

1090 And surely not so very much apart
Need I place thee, my warrior-priest,—in whom

---

*P1869:*seemed   1067| MS:law? But, brave! § over *no.* §   *P1869:*brave,   1068| MS:call
God   *P1869:*call God,   1069| MS:call nature   *P1869:*call Nature   1072| MS:As the
§ crossed out §   1073| MS:doubt, the § crossed out and replaced above by § even
tree, shrub § over illegible word §   1074| MS:of the field, all § crossed out
and replaced above by § found § crossed out and original restored §   *P1869:*o'
1075| MS:To save § last two words crossed out and replaced above by § recognize
§ crossed out § the glory of that gift, § last five words and comma crossed out
and replaced above by seven words § To worthily defend that trust of trusts   *P1869:*trusts,
*1872:*defend the trust   1078| MS:sword break § crossed out and replaced above by
§ stay   1081| MS:providence: how had § last two words crossed out and replaced
above by § fright § crossed out § <> thou, § erased §   1082| MS:touch in
*CP1869:*touch, i'   1083| MS:Approved in all docility so far   *P1869:*Approved so far in
all docility   *1872:*Approved less far   1084| MS:such one straight   *P1869:*such an one
1085| MS:scruple, "Is   *CP1869:*scruple "Is   1087| MS:Of   *P1869:*O'

What if I gain the other rose, the gold,
We grave to imitate God's miracle,
Greet monarchs with, good rose in its degree?
¹⁰⁹⁵ Irregular noble 'scapegrace—son the same!
Faulty—and peradventure ours the fault
Who still misteach, mislead, throw hook and line,
Thinking to land leviathan forsooth,
Tame the scaled neck, play with him as a bird,
¹¹⁰⁰ And bind him for our maidens! Better bear
The King of Pride go wantoning awhile,
Unplagued by cord in nose and thorn in jaw,
Through deep to deep, followed by all that shine,
Churning the blackness hoary: He who made
¹¹⁰⁵ The comely terror, He shall make the sword
To match that piece of netherstone his heart,
Ay, nor miss praise thereby; who else shut fire
I' the stone, to leap from mouth at sword's first stroke,
In lamps of love and faith, the chivalry
¹¹¹⁰ That dares the right and disregards alike
The yea and nay o' the world? Self-sacrifice,—
What if an idol took it? Ask the Church
Why she was wont to turn each Venus here,—
Poor Rome perversely lingered round, despite
¹¹¹⁵ Instruction, for the sake of purblind love,—
Into Madonna's shape, and waste no whit
Of aught so rare on earth as gratitude!
All this sweet savour was not ours but thine,

---

¹⁰⁹³| MS:miracle *P1869:*'grave <> miracle, *CP1869:*grave ¹⁰⁹⁴| MS:And
§ crossed out § greet § altered to § Greet some § crossed out § monarchs, § crossed
out § with, § word and comma inserted above § good rose § inserted
above § ¹⁰⁹⁵| MS:scapegrace DC,BrU:'scapegrace *1889:*'scapegrace
¹⁰⁹⁷| MS:line *1889a:*line, ¹⁰⁹⁸| MS:to bring § crossed out § ¹¹⁰⁰| MS:maidens!
Better leave *P1869:*maidens! Better bear ¹¹⁰⁶| MS:heart *P1869:*heart,
¹¹⁰⁸| MS:Fast § crossed out § In <> leap out, at § last two words crossed out and replaced
above by four words § from mouth at sword's *P1869:*I' ¹¹⁰⁹| MS:In burning § crossed
out § ¹¹¹¹| MS:The smile § crossed out and replaced above by § yea and frown
§ crossed out and replaced above by § nay of the world,—self-sacrifice,— *P1869:*o' the
world? Self-sacrifice,— ¹¹¹³| MS:each idol § crossed out and replaced above by § Venus
here *CP1869:*here,— ¹¹¹⁵| MS:love, *CP1869:*love,— ¹¹¹⁶| MS:Into a God and
so § last four words crossed out and replaced above by three words § Madonna's shape, and

117

Nard of the rock, a natural wealth we name
1120 Incense, and treasure up as food for saints,
When flung to us—whose function was to give
Not find the costly perfume. Do I smile?
Nay, Caponsacchi, much I find amiss,
Blameworthy, punishable in this freak
1125 Of thine, this youth prolonged, though age was ripe,
This masquerade in sober day, with change
Of motley too,—now hypocrite's disguise,
Now fool's-costume: which lie was least like truth,
Which the ungainlier, more discordant garb
1130 With that symmetric soul inside my son,
The churchman's or the worldling's,—let him judge,
Our adversary who enjoys the task!
I rather chronicle the healthy rage,—
When the first moan broke from the martyr-maid
1135 At that uncaging of the beasts,—made bare
My athlete on the instant, gave such good
Great undisguised leap over post and pale
Right into the mid-cirque, free fighting-place.
There may have been rash stripping—every rag
1140 Went to the winds,—infringement manifold
Of laws prescribed pudicity, I fear,
In this impulsive and prompt self-display!
Ever such tax comes of the foolish youth;
Men mulct the wiser manhood, and suspect

1120| MS:Incense and *P1869:*Incense, and   1125| MS:prolonged though
*1872:*prolonged, though   1127| *P1869:*hypocrite's-disguise, *1872:*hypocrite's disguise,
1128| MS:fool's costume *P1869:*fool's-costume   1131| The Churchman's <> the
Worlding's <> judge *P1869:*The churchman's <> worldling's <> judge,
1132| MS:Thine adversary <> task: *P1869:*Our Adversary <> task! *1872:*Our adversary
1138| MS:the cirque's midst and § last three words altered to § mid-cirque, free
1139| MS:rash work when every § altered to § rash stripping—every
1140| MS:infringements § altered to § infringement much I fear, § last three words and
comma crossed out and replaced above by § manifold   1141| MS:laws our time § last
two words crossed out §   1142| MS:self-display— *P1869:*self-display!
1143-45| MS:§ crowded between 1142-46 and in margin §   1143| MS:Ever § inserted in
margin § Such is the fruit § last three words crossed out and replaced above by two words §
tax comes of the first § crossed out § foolish life wasting § last two words crossed out § youth,
nay love § last two words crossed out § *P1869:*such <> youth;   1144| MS:the wiser

1145   No veritable star swims out of cloud.
      Bear thou such imputation, undergo
      The penalty I nowise dare relax,—
      Conventional chastisement and rebuke.
      But for the outcome, the brave starry birth
1150   Conciliating earth with all that cloud,
      Thank heaven as I do! Ay, such championship
      Of God at first blush, such prompt cheery thud
      Of glove on ground that answers ringingly
      The challenge of the false knight,—watch we long
1155   And wait we vainly for its gallant like
      From those appointed to the service, sworn
      His body-guard with pay and privilege—
      White-cinct, because in white walks sanctity,
      Red-socked, how else proclaim fine scorn of flesh,
1160   Unchariness of blood when blood faith begs!
      Where are the men-at-arms with cross on coat?
      Aloof, bewraying their attire: whilst thou
      In mask and motley, pledged to dance not fight,
      Sprang'st forth the hero! In thought, word and deed,
1165   How throughout all thy warfare thou wast pure,
      I find it easy to believe: and if
      At any fateful moment of the strange
      Adventure, the strong passion of that strait,
      Fear and surprise, may have revealed too much,—
1170   As when a thundrous midnight, with black air
      That burns, rain-drops that blister, breaks a spell,
      Draws out the excessive virtue of some sheathed

---

§ inserted above and then crossed out § manhood   *P1869:*the wiser manhood
1145| MS:cloud: *1889a:*cloud.   1146| MS:thou the § crossed out and replaced below
by § such   1147| MS:nowise must § crossed out and replaced above by § dare
1148| MS:Loving the son, I § last four words crossed out and replaced above by §
Conventional chastise § altered to § chastisement   1149| MS:outcome, the § inserted
above § brave bold § crossed out §   1150| MS:cloud *P1869:*cloud,
1154| MS:knight,—look § crossed out and replaced above by § watch we long,
DC,BrU: long *1889:*long   1155| MS:Exp § crossed out and replaced above by § And
1160| MS:begs? *1872:*begs!   1161| MS:the soldiery § crossed out and replaced above
by § men-at-arms   1163| MS:In the poor frippery § last three words crossed out and
replaced above by three words § mask and motley   1164| MS:Sprangest
*P1869:*Sprang'st   1165| MS:pure *P1869:*pure,   1167| MS:of that § crossed out and
replaced above by § the   1169| MS:surprise may *P1869:*surprise, may
1170| MS:when some § crossed out and replaced above by § a   1172| MS:some flower §

Shut unsuspected flower that hoards and hides
Immensity of sweetness,—so, perchance,
1175 Might the surprise and fear release too much
The perfect beauty of the body and soul
Thou savedst in thy passion for God's sake,
He who is Pity. Was the trial sore?
Temptation sharp? Thank God a second time!
1180 Why comes temptation but for man to meet
And master and make crouch beneath his foot,
And so be pedestaled in triumph? Pray
"Lead us into no such temptations, Lord!"
Yea, but, O Thou whose servants are the bold,
1185 Lead such temptations by the head and hair,
Reluctant dragons, up to who dares fight,
That so he may do battle and have praise!
Do I not see the praise?—that while thy mates
Bound to deserve i' the matter, prove at need
1190 Unprofitable through the very pains
We gave to train them well and start them fair,—
Are found too stiff, with standing ranked and ranged,
For onset in good earnest, too obtuse
Of ear, through iteration of command,
1195 For catching quick the sense of the real cry,—
Thou, whose sword-hand was used to strike the lute,
Whose sentry-station graced some wanton's gate,
Thou didst push forward and show mettle, shame
The laggards, and retrieve the day. Well done!
1200 Be glad thou hast let light into the world

---

crossed out and replaced above by § sheathed   1175| MS:fear draw § crossed out §
1177| MS:Thou barest § crossed out and replaced above by § savedst on thy bosom for
*P1869:*savedst in thy passion for   1178| MS:is Pity: was   *1889a:*is Pity. Was
1185–87| MS:temptations by the head and hair § last five words inserted above § reluctant
dragons, § last two words and comma inserted below § up to who dares fight / That
*P1869:*hair,/ Reluctant < > fight,/ That   1189| MS:in < > proved § altered to § prove
*P1869:*i'   1191| MS:them up to § last two words crossed out and replaced above by two
words § well and   1192| MS:stiff with standing in the § last two words crossed
out §   *P1869:*stiff, with   1195| MS:For § over *To* § catch § altered to § catching at
the first breath § last four words crossed out and replaced above by four words § quick
aright § crossed out § the sense of the battle- § crossed out and replaced above by §
real   1197| MS:Whose watch and § last two words crossed out and replaced above by
two words § sentry station   *P1869:*sentry-station   1200| MS:glad § over illegible

120

Through that irregular breach o' the boundary,—see
The same upon thy path and march assured,
Learning anew the use of soldiership,
Self-abnegation, freedom from all fear,
1205   Loyalty to the life's end! Ruminate,
Deserve the initiatory spasm,—once more
Work, be unhappy but bear life, my son!

And troop you, somewhere 'twixt the best and worst,
Where crowd the indifferent product, all too poor
1210   Makeshift, starved samples of humanity!
Father and mother, huddle there and hide!
A gracious eye may find you! Foul and fair,
Sadly mixed natures: self-indulgent,—yet
Self-sacrificing too: how the love soars,
1215   How the craft, avarice, vanity and spite
Sink again! So they keep the middle course,
Slide into silly crime at unaware,
Slip back upon the stupid virtue, stay
Nowhere enough for being classed, I hope
1220   And fear. Accept the swift and rueful death,
Taught, somewhat sternlier than is wont, what waits
The ambiguous creature,—how the one black tuft
Steadies the aim of the arrow just as well
As the wide faultless white on the bird's breast!
1225   Nay, you were punished in the very part
That looked most pure of speck,—'twas honest love

erasure § *P1869:*world, DC,BrU:world *1889:*world   1201| MS:of *P1869:*o'
1205| MS:end: ruminate, *P1869:*end! Ruminate,   1208| MS:twixt *P1869:*'twixt
1211| MS:hide,— *P1869:*hide!   1212| MS:—A *P1869:*A   1217| MS:into silly
§ inserted above § easy and half- § last three words crossed out and replaced above by two
syllables § at un   1218| MS:back as readily into § last three words crossed out and
replaced above by three words § upon the stupid   1220| MS:the sharp § crossed out
and replaced above by § swift and pitious § crossed out and replaced above by § rueful
death § crossed out and replaced above by § fate § crossed out and original restored § ,
1221| MS:Taught § next word illegibly crossed out and replaced above by two words
§ somewhat sternlier than the rest § last two words crossed out and replaced above
by two words § is wont what chasm § crossed out § betides § crossed out § awaits
*P1869:*Taught, somewhat <> wont, what waits   1224| MS:As the broad § crossed out
and replaced above by three words § wide speckless § crossed out § faultless <> breast.
*1872:*breast!   1226| MS:speck,—the honest *1872:*speck,—'twas honest

Betrayed you,—did love seem most worthy pains,
Challenge such purging, since ordained survive
When all the rest of you was done with? Go!
1230   Never again elude the choice of tints!
White shall not neutralize the black, nor good
Compensate bad in man, absolve him so:
Life's business being just the terrible choice.

So do I see, pronounce on all and some
1235   Grouped for my judgment now,—profess no doubt
While I pronounce: dark, difficult enough
The human sphere, yet eyes grow sharp by use,
I find the truth, dispart the shine from shade,
As a mere man may, with no special touch
1240   O' the lynx-gift in each ordinary orb:
Nay, if the popular notion class me right,
One of well-nigh decayed intelligence,—
What of that? Through hard labour and good will,
And habitude that gives a blind man sight
1245   At the practised finger-ends of him, I do
Discern, and dare decree in consequence,
Whatever prove the peril of mistake.

1227| MS:did it § crossed out and replaced above by § love   1228| MS:purging, as what
should survive   *CP1869:*as ordained survive   *1872:*purging, since ordained survive
1229| MS:with? Dare § crossed out §   1230| MS:again alternate black with white
§ crossed out and replaced above by six words and colon § play § crossed out § elude the
choice of tints: *P1869:*tints!   1231| MS:Good § crossed out and replaced above by §
White <> the black § over *bad* § , nor yet bad § last two words crossed out and replaced
above by § good   1232| MS:The bad § last two words crossed out § compensated
§ altered to § Compensate by good § last two words crossed out and above by
three words and comma § bad in man, absolve the soul § last two words crossed out and
replaced above by two words and colon § him so: 1234| MS:do I class, declare of
§ last three words crossed out and replaced above by three words § see, pronounce on
1236| MS:While I declare: dark   *P1869:*While I pronounce: dark   1238| MS:I in the
main § last three words crossed out and replaced above by three words and comma § find the
truth,   1239| MS:I, a mere man, with   *P1869:*As a mere man may, with
1240| MS:Of <> orb,   *P1869:*O' <> orb: 1241| MS:notion shall decide, § last two
words and comma crossed out and replaced above by § weigh at all § last three words crossed
out § <> right   *P1869:*right,   1242| MS:Absolute, § word and comma crossed out and
replaced above by three words § One well nigh of decayed   *P1869:*One of well nigh decayed
*1889a:*well-nigh   1243| MS:will   *P1869:*will,   1246| MS:Discern and dare § over
illegible word, possibly *now* § shall act § last two words crossed out and replaced above by §
decree in consequence   *P1869:*Discern, and <> consequence,   1247| MS:mistake:

Whence, then, this quite new quick cold thrill,—cloud-like,
This keen dread creeping from a quarter scarce
1250 Suspected in the skies I nightly scan?
What slacks the tense nerve, saps the wound-up spring
Of the act that should and shall be, sends the mount
And mass o' the whole man's-strength,—conglobed so late—
Shudderingly into dust, a moment's work?
1255 While I stand firm, go fearless, in this world,
For this life recognize and arbitrate,
Touch and let stay, or else remove a thing,
Judge "This is right, this object out of place,"
Candle in hand that helps me and to spare,—
1260 What if a voice deride me, "Perk and pry!
Brighten each nook with thine intelligence!
Play the good householder, ply man and maid
With tasks prolonged into the midnight, test
Their work and nowise stint of the due wage
1265 Each worthy worker: but with gyves and whip
Pay thou misprision of a single point
Plain to thy happy self who lift'st the light,
Lament'st the darkling,—bold to all beneath!

---

*P1869:*mistake.   1248| MS:Whence then this other § crossed out and replaced above by
two words § quite new <> thrill, cloud-like   *P1869:*Whence, then, this <> thrill,—
cloud-like,   1249| MS:This keen § last two words inserted in margin § Dread § altered
to § dread <> from what § crossed out and replaced above by § a quarter § followed by
illegible erasure §   1251| MS:wound up   *P1869:*wound-up   1252| MS:mount—
*P1869:*mount   1253| MS:Of § erased § The pride § last two words crossed out and
replaced above by two words § And mass of the whole strength § over perhaps *man* §
confirmed so § over illegible word § late   *P1869:*mass of the whole strength,—conglobed
so late—   *CP1869:*o' the whole man's-strength   1254| MS:Shudderingly moment to
the dust § last six words crossed out and replaced above by five words and question mark §
into dust, one moment's work?   *P1869:*dust, a moment's   1255| MS:stand firmly
§ altered to § firm, go § over *nay* §   1256| MS:arbitrate—   *P1869:*arbitrate,
1258| MS:Say "This <> place"   *P1869:*place,"   *CP1869:*Judge "This
1260| MS:pry—   *P1869:*pry!   1263| MS:the mid § inserted above §   1264| MS:of
the § over *his* §   1265| MS:The well deserving § last three words crossed out and
replaced above by three words § Each worthy worker, but spare § crossed out and replaced
above by § with   *P1869:*worker: but   1266| MS:With whoso stumbled at a § last five
words crossed out and replaced above by seven words § Pay § in margin § Spare § crossed
out § thou misprision of a single   1267| MS:lift   *P1869:*lift'st   1268| MS:Look on
§ last two words crossed out and replaced above by § Lament <> beneath!"

123

What if thyself adventure, now the place
1270 Is purged so well? Leave pavement and mount roof,
Look round thee for the light of the upper sky,
The fire which lit thy fire which finds default
In Guido Franceschini to his cost!
What if, above in the domain of light,
1275 Thou miss the accustomed signs, remark eclipse?
Shalt thou still gaze on ground nor lift a lid,—
Steady in thy superb prerogative,
Thy inch of inkling,—nor once face the doubt
I' the sphere above thee, darkness to be felt?"

1280 Yet my poor spark had for its source, the sun;
Thither I sent the great looks which compel
Light from its fount: all that I do and am
Comes from the truth, or seen or else surmised,
Remembered or divined, as mere man may:
1285 I know just so, nor otherwise. As I know,
I speak,—what should I know, then, and how speak
Were there a wild mistake of eye or brain
As to recorded governance above?
If my own breath, only, blew coal alight
1290 I styled celestial and the morning-star?
I, who in this world act resolvedly,
Dispose of men, their bodies and their souls,
As they acknowledge or gainsay the light

*P1869:*Lament'st < > beneath!   1272| MS:lit the fire which § over illegible erasure §
*CP1869:*lit thy fire   1273| MS:In the work of such an one as Guido here § last nine
words crossed out and replaced above by five words § Guido Franceschini to his cost?
*CP1869:*cost!   1274| MS:if above < > light *P1869:*if, above < > light,
1275| MS:signs, perceive § crossed out and replaced above by § remark   1276| MS:thou
look steadily down § last three words crossed out and replaced above by four words § still
gaze on ground   1277| MS:Rejoice § crossed out and replaced above by § Steady
1278| MS:The inch *P1869:*Thy inch   1279| MS:In < > felt? *P1869:*I' < > felt?"
1279-80| MS:§ no ¶ § *P1869:*§ ¶ §   1280| MS:Yet § inserted in margin § This < > had
first kindled at § last three words crossed out and replaced above by three words and comma §
for its source *P1869:*Yet my poor   1281| MS:Thither § in margin §   1284| MS:may,
*P1869:*may: 1286| MS:know then and *P1869:*know, then, and   1288| MS:In the
recorded governance of § erased § above.— *P1869:*above? *1872:*As to recorded
1289| MS:My < > blew the coal *P1869:*If my < > blew coal   1290| MS:I called
celestial *1872:*I styled celestial   1291| MS:Shall § crossed out § I   1292| MS:men,
the body and the soul, *1872:*men, their bodies and their souls,   1293| MS:gainsay

I show them,—shall I too lack courage?—leave
1295 I, too, the post of me, like those I blame?
Refuse, with kindred inconsistency,
To grapple danger whereby souls grow strong?
I am near the end; but still not at the end;
All to the very end is trial in life:
1300 At this stage is the trial of my soul
Danger to face, or danger to refuse?
Shall I dare try the doubt now, or not dare?

O Thou,—as represented here to me
In such conception as my soul allows,—
1305 Under Thy measureless, my atom width!—
Man's mind, what is it but a convex glass
Wherein are gathered all the scattered points
Picked out of the immensity of sky,
To re-unite there, be our heaven for earth,
1310 Our known unknown, our God revealed to man?
Existent somewhere, somehow, as a whole;

---

this light *P1869:*gainsay the light   1294| MS:too lack § over illegible word §
heart,—desert *P1869:*lack courage,—leave   *CP1869:*courage?—leave   1295| MS:I too
the < > blame, *P1869:*I, too, the   *CP1869:*blame?   1296| MS:Refuse with < >
inconsistency   *CP1869:*Refuse, with < > inconsistency,   1297| MS:To grapple with the
danger < > grow? *CP1869:*Grapple with danger < > grow strong? *1872:*To grapple
danger   1299| MS:All till the *1872:*All to the   1300| MS:the peril to my
*P1869:*the trial to   *CP1869:*trial of my   1301| MS:Danger I face, or danger I refuse?
*P1869:*Danger to face, or danger to refuse?   1303| MS:here § over illegible word § to me
§ last two words crossed out, restored and replaced above by two crossed out words § and
§ followed by illegible word, possibly *was* §   *P1869:*here to me   1304| MS:In this
§ crossed out and replaced above by § such conception, wide § crossed out § as my § inserted
above § life allows § crossed out and replaced above by § lets lie § last two words crossed out
and original restored § ,—   *P1869:*my soul allows,—   *CP1869:*conception as
1305| MS:§ inserted in margin § Under the measureless an atom width, under § crossed out §
*P1869:*Under Thy measureless my atom width!—   *1872:*measureless, my
1306| MS:(Oh § over *The* § mind of man that § over *what* § that little § last four words
crossed out and replaced above by dash and five words § —what is it but § followed by word
illegibly crossed out, possibly *thy* § convex   *P1869:*Man's mind < > but a convex
*1872:*mind, what   1307| MS:the scattered § inserted above §   1308| MS:§ word
illegibly crossed out, possibly *Devised,* and replaced above by two words § Picked out of §
over *in* § of the < > of sky § over illegible erasure §   *P1869:*sky,   1309| MS:reunite
there § over illegible word § , make man's § last two words crossed out and replaced above by
two words § be our heaven on earth   *P1869:*earth, *1872:*re-unite < > heaven for earth,
1310| MS:Our § over *His* § < > Unknown, his § crossed out and replaced above by § our < >
Man,—) *P1869:*unknown < > man?— *CP1869:*man?   1311| MS:whole,

Here, as a whole proportioned to our sense,—
There, (which is nowhere, speech must babble thus!)
In the absolute immensity, the whole
¹³¹⁵ Appreciable solely by Thyself,—
Here, by the little mind of man, reduced
To littleness that suits his faculty,
In the degree appreciable too;
Between Thee and ourselves—nay even, again,
¹³²⁰ Below us, to the extreme of the minute,
Appreciable by how many and what diverse
Modes of the life Thou madest be! (why live
Except for love,—how love unless they know?)
Each of them, only filling to the edge,
¹³²⁵ Insect or angel, his just length and breadth,
Due facet of reflection,—full, no less,
Angel or insect, as Thou framedst things.
I it is who have been appointed here
To represent Thee, in my turn, on earth,
¹³³⁰ Just as, if new philosophy know aught,
This one earth, out of all the multitude
Of peopled worlds, as stars are now supposed,—
Was chosen, and no sun-star of the swarm,

---

*P1869:*whole;   ¹³¹²| MS:As here, a <> sense,   *P1869:*Here, as <> sense,—
¹³¹³| MS:There,—which is nowhere, we § crossed out and replaced above by § speech <>
thus,—   *P1869:*There, (which <> thus!)   ¹³¹⁴| MS:§ inserted between 1313-15 §
¹³¹⁵| MS:Appreciable solely § inserted below §   ¹³¹⁸| MS:Appreciable too in the
degree,—   *P1869:*degree;   *1872:*In the degree appreciable too;   ¹³¹⁹| MS:even again
*P1869:*even, again,   ¹³²¹| MS:Appreciable, by how many and § last three words
inserted above §   *P1869:*Appreciable by   ¹³²²| MS:life thou makest be,—why life
*P1869:*life Thou <> be! (why live   *1872:*life Thou madest be   ¹³²³| MS:know?
*P1869:*know?)   ¹³²⁴| MS:the brim § crossed out § edge   *P1869:*edge,
¹³²⁵| MS:his allotted § crossed out and replaced above by two words § just length and § over
space § breadth   *P1869:*breadth,   ¹³²⁶| MS:Due § over illegible word § <> less
*P1869:*less,   ¹³²⁷| MS:insect as thou <> things,—   *P1869:*insect, as Thou
*1872:*things.   ¹³²⁸| MS:It is I who   *P1869:*I it is who   ¹³²⁹| MS:represent Thee in
my turn on   *P1869:*represent Thee, in my turn, on   ¹³³⁰| MS:as, 'tis held by some
§ last four words crossed out and replaced above by two words § if new philosophy, knows
*P1869:*philosophy know   ¹³³¹| MS:earth, not § crossed out and replaced above by three
words § out of all   ¹³³²| MS:Of peopled § inserted above § worlds which stars
*P1869:*worlds, as stars   ¹³³³| MS:sun star § inserted above § of all § crossed out §

126

For stage and scene of Thy transcendent act
¹³³⁵ Beside which even the creation fades
Into a puny exercise of power.
Choice of the world, choice of the thing I am,
Both emanate alike from Thy dread play
Of operation outside this our sphere
¹³⁴⁰ Where things are classed and counted small or great,—
Incomprehensibly the choice is Thine!
I therefore bow my head and take Thy place.
There is, beside the works, a tale of Thee
In the world's mouth, which I find credible:
¹³⁴⁵ I love it with my heart: unsatisfied,
I try it with my reason, nor discept
From any point I probe and pronounce sound.
Mind is not matter nor from matter, but
Above,—leave matter then, proceed with mind!
¹³⁵⁰ Man's be the mind recognized at the height,—
Leave the inferior minds and look at man!
Is he the strong, intelligent and good
Up to his own conceivable height? Nowise.
Enough o' the low,—soar the conceivable height,
¹³⁵⁵ Find cause to match the effect in evidence,
The work i' the world, not man's but God's; leave man!
Conjecture of the worker by the work:

---

*P1869:*sun-star   ¹³³⁶| MS:power: *P1869:*power.   ¹³³⁷| MS:thing § over *man* §
¹³³⁸| MS:Both § over *Each* § <> from the dread   *1872:*from Thy dread   ¹³⁴¹| MS:is
thine— *P1869:*is Thine!   ¹³⁴²| MS:take thy *P1869:*take Thy   ¹³⁴³| MS:There
is § over *was* § <> of thee *P1869:*of Thee   ¹³⁴⁴⁻⁴⁶| MS:mouth which I find § over
found § / I try *P1869:*of Thee *P1869:*mouth, which <> / I love it with my heart:
unsatisfied,/ I try   ¹³⁴⁷| MS:sound: *P1869:*sound.   ¹³⁴⁹| MS:matter then § over
and § <> mind: *1872:*mind!   ¹³⁵⁰| MS:Man is the <> recognised <> height,
*P1869:*Man's be the <> recognized <> height,—   ¹³⁵¹| MS:Leave all § crossed out §
the other § crossed out and replaced above by § inferior <> Man, *P1869:*man. *1872:*man!
¹³⁵³| MS:height? Nowise: *P1869:*height? Nowise.   ¹³⁵⁴| MS:Leave man § last two
words crossed out and replaced above by four words § Enough of the low,—go on with the
<> height. *P1869:*o' the low,—soar the <> height,   ¹³⁵⁵| MS:Find cause § last two
words written in margin § To <> effect § over illegible erasure § in evidence; not Man's:
§ last two words, and semi-colon crossed out § *P1869:*cause to <> evidence,
¹³⁵⁶| MS:Works in § last two words inserted in margin § the world § last two words inserted
above § Not man's § altered to § man, then God's: leave man. *P1869:*world, not man's <>
God's; leave man: *1872:*The work i' <> man's but God's <> man!   ¹³⁵⁷| MS:the

Is there strength there?—enough: intelligence?
Ample: but goodness in a like degree?
1360 Not to the human eye in the present state,
An isoscele deficient in the base.
What lacks, then, of perfection fit for God
But just the instance which this tale supplies
Of love without a limit? So is strength,
1365 So is intelligence; let love be so,
Unlimited in its self-sacrifice,
Then is the tale true and God shows complete.
Beyond the tale, I reach into the dark,
Feel what I cannot see, and still faith stands:
1370 I can believe this dread machinery
Of sin and sorrow, would confound me else,
Devised,—all pain, at most expenditure
Of pain by Who devised pain,—to evolve,
By new machinery in counterpart,
1375 The moral qualities of man—how else?—
To make him love in turn and be beloved,
Creative and self-sacrificing too,
And thus eventually God-like, (ay,
"I have said ye are Gods,"—shall it be said for nought?)
1380 Enable man to wring, from out all pain,
All pleasure for a common heritage
To all eternity: this may be surmised,

---

workman by the work, _P1869:_the worker by the work: ¹³⁶⁰| MS:present world.
_P1869:_present state,   ¹³⁶¹| MS:inserted between 1360-62 § This isoscele < > base—
_P1869:_base.   _1872:_An isoscele   ¹³⁶²| MS:lacks of the perfection then of God
_P1869:_lacks, then, of perfection fit for God   ¹³⁶⁴| MS:limit, like the strength
_P1869:_limit? So is strength,   ¹³⁶⁵| MS:Like the intelligence, then love is so,   _P1869:_So
is intelligence; then < > so,   _1872:_intelligence; let love be so,   ¹³⁶⁶| MS:§ inserted in
margin § self sacrifice: _P1869:_self-sacrifice: _1872:_self-sacrifice,   ¹³⁶⁷| MS:the § over
that § angel's § inserted above § < > true and § over illegible word § God is § crossed out §
complete.   _P1869:_the tale < > and God shows complete.   ¹³⁷¹| MS:sorrow, that
confounds me   _P1869:_sorrow, would confound me   ¹³⁷²| MS:pain at   _P1869:_pain,
at   ¹³⁷³| MS:by § over illegible word § who devised § last two words inserted above §
pain's § _'s_ crossed out § deviser § crossed out § , —to evolve   _P1869:_by Who < > evolve,
¹³⁷⁴| MS:counterpart,—   _P1869:_counterpart,   ¹³⁷⁵| MS:man, to wit,   _P1869:_man—
how else?—   ¹³⁷⁶| MS:Which make < > beloved,—   _P1869:_To make < >
beloved,   ¹³⁷⁸| MS:eventually God-like,—ay,   _CP1869:_eventually God-like, (ay,
¹³⁷⁹⁻⁸¹| MS:are Gods,"—evolve thereby / All pleasures as a   _P1869:_are Gods,"—shall
it be said for nought?)/ Enable man to wring, from out all pain, / All pleasure for a

The other is revealed,—whether a fact,
Absolute, abstract, independent truth,
1385 Historic, not reduced to suit man's mind,—
Or only truth reverberate, changed, made pass
A spectrum into mind, the narrow eye,—
The same and not the same, else unconceived—
Though quite conceivable to the next grade
1390 Above it in intelligence,—as truth
Easy to man were blindness to the beast
By parity of procedure,—the same truth
In a new form, but changed in either case:
What matter so intelligence be filled?
1395 To a child, the sea is angry, for it roars:
Frost bites, else why the tooth-like fret on face?
Man makes acoustics deal with the sea's wrath,
Explains the choppy cheek by chymic law,—
To man and child remains the same effect
1400 On drum of ear and root of nose, change cause
Never so thoroughly: so my heart be struck,
What care I,—by God's gloved hand or the bare?
Nor do I much perplex me with aught hard,
Dubious in the transmitting of the tale,—
1405 No, nor with certain riddles set to solve.
This life is training and a passage; pass,—
Still, we march over some flat obstacle

1384| MS:Absolutely § altered to § Absolute, abstractedly § altered to § abstract
1385| MS:Historic, and uncoloured by § last three words crossed out and replaced
above by five words, the first of which is crossed out § uncramped not reduced to
suit   1386| MS:reverberate, truth § crossed out and replaced above by §
changed   1390–92| MS:Above, below it, in intelligence / By P1869:Above it in
intelligence,—as truth/ Easy to man were blindness to the beast / By   1393| MS:form,
still changed <> case. P1869:form, but changed <> case: 1394| MS:so
the intelligence 1872:so intelligence   1395| MS:To the child <> angry—for
it roars, P1869:angry, for it roars: 1872:To a child   1396| MS:the fret of
tooth on P1869:the tooth-like fret on   1399| MS:To both, one and the same effect
remains P1869:both, remains one <> effect 1872:To man and child remains the same
1401| MS:so the § crossed out and replaced above by § our heart § over illegible word,
perhaps soul § be § over is § 1872:so my heart   1403| MS:perplex § over illegible
word §   1404| MS:transmitting § over transmission §   1405| MS:solve,—
P1869:solve.   1406| MS:and probation § crossed out and replaced above by two words §
a passage   1407| MS:Why, you march <> flat § over illegible word § P1869:Still, we

We made give way before us; solid truth
In front of it, what motion for the world?
¹⁴¹⁰ The moral sense grows but by exercise.
'Tis even as man grew probatively
Initiated in Godship, set to make
A fairer moral world than this he finds,
Guess now what shall be known hereafter. Deal
¹⁴¹⁵ Thus with the present problem: as we see,
A faultless creature is destroyed, and sin
Has had its way i' the world where God should rule.
Ay, but for this irrelevant circumstance
Of inquisition after blood, we see
¹⁴²⁰ Pompilia lost and Guido saved: how long?
For his whole life: how much is that whole life?
We are not babes, but know the minute's worth,
And feel that life is large and the world small,
So, wait till life have passed from out the world.

¹⁴²⁵ Neither does this astonish at the end,
That whereas I can so receive and trust,
Other men, made with hearts and souls the same,
Reject and disbelieve,—subordinate
The future to the present,—sin, nor fear.
¹⁴³⁰ This I refer still to the foremost fact,

---

march   ¹⁴⁰⁸| MS:You made <> before you; solid   *P1869:*We made <> before us;
solid   ¹⁴⁰⁹| MS:front, how then were motion possible § crossed out §   *P1869:*front of
it, were   *1872:*it, what motion   ¹⁴¹¹| MS:Tis <> grew by probation here   *P1869:*'Tis
<> grew probatively   ¹⁴¹²| MS:in godship   *P1869:*in Godship   ¹⁴¹³| MS:than
what he   *P1869:*than this he   ¹⁴¹⁴| MS:hereafter. Thus,   *1872:*hereafter. Deal
¹⁴¹⁵| MS:Of the <> problem,—as we men may speak,   *P1869:*O' <> problem: as we see
and speak,   *1872:*Thus with the <> see,   ¹⁴¹⁷| MS:way in the world in § crossed out
and replaced above by one word § where God's § altered to § God despite § crossed out and
replaced above by § should   *P1869:*way i'   ¹⁴¹⁹| MS:blood, we'll see   *P1869:*blood, we
see   ¹⁴²⁰| MS:saved and set   *P1869:*saved: how long?   ¹⁴²¹| MS:Glorious for
many a day § last three words crossed out and replaced above by § his whole life <> that?
*P1869:*For <> that whole life?   ^{1422–25}| MS:babes: we know <> / Nor fear § over
illegible word § this world sufficient for our course. § line crossed out and replaced above by
new line § And feel life large and the world small, so wait. / Neither   *P1869:*babes, but
know <> / And feel that life is large <> small, / So wait till life have passed from out the
world. / Neither   *CP1869:*/ / So, wait   ^{1424–25}| MS:§ no ¶ §   *P1869:*§ ¶ §   *1889a:*§ no
¶ §   *1889:*§ no ¶ ; emended to restore ¶ ; see Editorial Notes §   ¹⁴²⁶| *P1869:*That,
whereas   *1872:*That whereas   ¹⁴²⁷| MS:Men made <> same as mine   *P1869:*Men,
made <> mine,   *1872:*Other men <> same,   ¹⁴³⁰| MS:the leading § crossed out and

Life is probation and the earth no goal
But starting-point of man: compel him strive,
Which means, in man, as good as reach the goal,—
Why institute that race, his life, at all?
1435 But this does overwhelm me with surprise,
Touch me to terror,—not that faith, the pearl,
Should be let lie by fishers wanting food,—
Nor, seen and handled by a certain few
Critical and contemptuous, straight consigned
1440 To shore and shingle for the pebble it proves,—
But that, when haply found and known and named
By the residue made rich for evermore,
These,—that these favoured ones, should in a trice
Turn, and with double zest go dredge for whelks,
1445 Mud-worms that make the savoury soup! Enough
O' the disbelievers, see the faithful few!
How do the Christians here deport them, keep
Their robes of white unspotted by the world?
What is this Aretine Archbishop, this
1450 Man under me as I am under God,
This champion of the faith, I armed and decked,
Pushed forward, put upon a pinnacle,
To show the enemy his victor,—see!
What's the best fighting when the couple close?

---

replaced above by § foremost   1431| MS:probation and this § last two words inserted
above § earth is not the § last three words crossed out and replaced above by § no
1432–34| MS:starting-place § altered to § starting-point < > strive § over illegible word § , /
Why < > race his life, at all? § last five words transposed to § race at all, his life?   *P1869:* /
Which means, in man, as good as reach the goal,— / Why < > race, his life, at all?
1435| MS:surprise   *P1869:*surprise,   1436| MS:terror, that the pearl of faith § last six
words altered to § terror,—not that faith the pearl   *P1869:*faith, the pearl,   1437| MS:by
the fishers wanting food § over *work* § ,—   *P1869:*by fishers   1440| MS:To the shore
< > the stone it   *P1869:*To shore < > the pebble it   1441| MS:that when   *P1869:*that,
when   1443| MS:These,—ay these   *CP1869:*ay, these   *1872:*These,—that
these   1444| MS:wilks   *P1869:*whelks,   1445| MS:And § crossed out §
mud § altered to § Mudworms < > the savoury § last two words inserted
above § soup: of § crossed out § Enough   *P1869:*Mud-worms < > soup. Enough
*1872:*soup! Enough   1446| MS:Of the Disbelievers   *CP1869:*O' the disbelievers
1451| MS:faith I arm and deck   *P1869:*faith, I armed and decked,   1453| MS:To show
§ crossed out and replaced above by § scare the enemy with § inserted above § his victor,—see
*P1869:*To show the enemy his victor,—see!   1454| MS:What § altered to § What's the
§ over *his* § best fight § altered to § fighting amounts to § last two words crossed out and

131

¹⁴⁵⁵ Pompilia cries, "Protect me from the wolf!"
He—"No, thy Guido is rough, heady, strong,
Dangerous to disquiet: let him bide!
He needs some bone to mumble, help amuse
The darkness of his den with: so, the fawn
¹⁴⁶⁰ Which limps up bleeding to my foot and lies,
—Come to me, daughter!—thus I throw him back!"
Have we misjudged here, over-armed our knight,
Given gold and silk where plain hard steel serves best,
Enfeebled whom we sought to fortify,
¹⁴⁶⁵ Made an archbishop and undone a saint?
Well, then, descend these heights, this pride of life,
Sit in the ashes with a barefoot monk
Who long ago stamped out the worldly sparks,
By fasting, watching, stone cell and wire scourge,
¹⁴⁷⁰ —No such indulgence as unknits the strength—
These breed the tight nerve and tough cuticle,
And the world's praise or blame runs rillet-wise
Off the broad back and brawny breast, we know!
He meets the first cold sprinkle of the world,
¹⁴⁷⁵ And shudders to the marrow. "Save this child?

---

replaced above by three words § is § crossed out § when the   ¹⁴⁵⁵| MS:This poor girl
cries, protect <> the fiend!   *P1869:*Pompilia cries, "Protect <> fiend!"   *1872:*the wolf!"
¹⁴⁵⁶| MS:"Ay, but this Guido is a heady   *P1869:*"No, for thy Guido is one heady
*1872:*He—"No, thy <> is rough, heady   ¹⁴⁵⁷| MS:Dangerous brute § over perhaps
man § to deal with § last two words crossed out and replaced above by § disquiet <> bide:
*P1869:*Dangerous to <> bide!   ¹⁴⁵⁸| MS:some prey § crossed out and replaced above by
§ bone to mumble, help § over *and* §   ¹⁴⁵⁹| MS:with,—so this fawn   *P1869:*with: so,
the fawn   ¹⁴⁶¹| MS:—Look at § last two words written over illegible word or words §
me, daughter,—thus I throw thee back!"   *P1869:*—Come to me <> throw him back!"
*1872:*daughter!—thus   ¹⁴⁶²| MS:overarmed the knight,   *P1869:*over-armed
*1872:*over-armed our knight,   ¹⁴⁶³| MS:silk to boot where plain steel serves   *P1869:*silk
where the plain <> serves best,   *1872:*plain hard steel   ¹⁴⁶⁵| MS:Made a § altered to §
an saint § crossed out and replaced above by § arch   ¹⁴⁶⁶| MS:Well then   *1872:*Well,
then   ¹⁴⁶⁸| MS:Who has § crossed out and replaced above by two words § long ago put
§ crossed out and replaced above by § stamped out the greedy § crossed out and replaced
above by § worldly sparks; we boast,— § last two words, comma and dash crossed out §
*P1869:*sparks.   *1872:*sparks,   ¹⁴⁶⁹| MS:Fasting and prayer § crossed out and replaced
above by § watching, the stone cell and the § crossed out and replaced above by § wire
*P1869:*watching, stone   *1872:*By fasting, watching   ¹⁴⁷⁰| MS:strength § over illegible
word § —   ¹⁴⁷¹| MS:cuticle   *P1869:*cuticle,   ¹⁴⁷²| MS:Let § crossed out § the <>
run rillet wise   *P1869:*Let <> rillet-wise   *1872:*And the <> runs   ¹⁴⁷⁴| MS:He faces
§ crossed out and replaced above by § meets world   *1872:*world,   ¹⁴⁷⁵| MS:marrow,

Oh, my superiors, oh, the Archbishop's self!
Who was it dared lay hand upon the ark
His betters saw fall nor put finger forth?
Great ones could help yet help not: why should small?
1480 I break my promise: let her break her heart!"
These are the Christians not the worldlings, not
The sceptics, who thus battle for the faith!
If foolish virgins disobey and sleep,
What wonder? But, this time, the wise that watch,
1485 Sell lamps and buy lutes, exchange oil for wine,
The mystic Spouse betrays the Bridegroom here.
To our last resource, then! Since all flesh is weak,
Bind weaknesses together, we get strength:
The individual weighed, found wanting, try
1490 Some institution, honest artifice
Whereby the units grow compact and firm!
Each props the other, and so stand is made
By our embodied cowards that grow brave.
The Monastery called of Convertites,
1495 Meant to help women because these helped Christ,—
A thing existent only while it acts,
Does as designed, else a nonentity,—
For what is an idea unrealized?—
Pompilia is consigned to these for help.

"Save   *1872:*marrow. "Save   1476| MS:superiors, oh the Archbishop here,—
*P1869:*superiors, oh, the < > here!   *1872:*the Archbishop's self!   1477| MS:it dared
§ over *laid* § lay § over *his* §   1478| MS:betters let § crossed out and replaced above by §
saw   1479| MS:They all § last two words crossed out and replaced above by two words §
Since Law < > help and will § last two words crossed out and replaced above by two words §
yet help < > should I?   *P1869:*Great ones could < > should small?   1480| MS:heart."
*P1869:*heart!"   1481-83| MS:the infidel! / The foolish   *P1869:*the worldlings, not < > /
The sceptics, who thus battle for the faith!/ If foolish   1484| MS:wonder? But the < >
watch, this time   *1872:*wonder? But, this time, the < > watch,   1487| MS:On to < >
resource,—all < > weak   *P1869:*To < > resource, then! Since all < > weak,
1488| MS:together you get   *P1869:*together, we get   1491| MS:firm: *1872:*firm!
1492| MS:and both § crossed out and replaced above by § so < > made: *P1869:*made
1493| MS:Embodied < > brave: to-wit,   *P1869:*By our embodied < > brave.
1494| MS:of Convertites—   *P1869:*of Convertites,   1495| MS:§ inserted between
1494-96 § helped Christ   *P1869:*helped Christ,—   1497| MS:as § over illegible word §
non-entity.   *P1869:*nonentity,   *1872:*nonentity,—   1498| MS:unrealised?
*P1869:*unrealized?—   1499| MS:This poor child is < > these § over illegible word § for

133

They do help: they are prompt to testify
To her pure life and saintly dying days.
She dies, and lo, who seemed so poor, proves rich.
What does the body that lives through helpfulness
To women for Christ's sake? The kiss turns bite,
The dove's note changes to the crow's cry: judge!
"Seeing that this our Convent claims of right
What goods belong to those we succour, be
The same proved women of dishonest life,—
And seeing that this Trial made appear
Pompilia was in such predicament,—
The Convent hereupon pretends to said
Succession of Pompilia, issues writ,
And takes possession by the Fisc's advice."
Such is their attestation to the cause
Of Christ, who had one saint at least, they hoped:
But, is a title-deed to filch, a corpse
To slander, and an infant-heir to cheat?
Christ must give up his gains then! They unsay
All the fine speeches,—who was saint is whore.
Why, scripture yields no parallel for this!
The soldiers only threw dice for Christ's coat;
We want another legend of the Twelve
Disputing if it was Christ's coat at all,

---

help: *P1869:*Pompilia is < > help.   1500| MS:help,—they § over illegible word § it is
who § last three words crossed out and replaced above by three words § are prompt to
*P1869:*help they   *1872:*help: they   1501| MS:days: *P1869:*days.   1502|
*P1869:*rich   *1872:*rich!   *1889a:*rich   DC,BrU:rich.   *1889:*rich.   1503| MS:lives in
helpfulness *P1869:*lives through helpfulness   1504| MS:sake? The § followed by word
illegibly crossed out and replaced above by § kiss turns brute § over illegible word, crossed
out and replaced above by § bite *P1869:*bite,   1505| MS:There is the dove's note
changed to < > cry— *P1869:*The dove's note changes to < > cry: judge!
1506| MS:"For seeing that the Convent *P1869:*"Seeing that this our Convent
1507| MS:those they succour, grant § crossed out § *P1869:*those we succour
1508| MS:same but women *P1869:*same proved women   1509| MS:makes
*P1869:*made   1510| MS:Pompilia stood in < > predicament *P1869:*Pompilia was in
< > predicament,—   1512| MS:of Pompilia,—issues writ *P1869:*of Pompilia, issues
writ,   1513| MS:advice. *P1869:*advice."   1514| MS:We have their *P1869:*Such is
their   1515| MS:Of Christ,—he had < > they knew: *P1869:*Of Christ, who had < >
they hoped: 1516| MS:There is a title- § over illegible erasure § < > filch § over
illegible erasure § *P1869:*But, is   1517| MS:cheat,— *P1869:*cheat?
1518| MS:then,—they *P1869:*then! They   1519| MS:speeches,—call the saint a whore.
*P1869:*speeches,—who was saint is whore.   1523| MS:Disputing that it

Claiming as prize the woof of price—for why?
1525 The Master was a thief, purloined the same,
Or paid for it out of the common bag!
Can it be this is end and outcome, all
I take with me to show as stewardship's fruit,
The best yield of the latest time, this year
1530 The seventeen-hundredth since God died for man?
Is such effect proportionate to cause?
And still the terror keeps on the increase
When I perceive . . . how can I blink the fact?
That the fault, the obduracy to good,
1535 Lies not with the impracticable stuff
Whence man is made, his very nature's fault,
As if it were of ice the moon may gild
Not melt, or stone 'twas meant the sun should warm
Not make bear flowers,—nor ice nor stone to blame:
1540 But it can melt, that ice, can bloom, that stone,
Impassible to rule of day and night!
This terrifies me, thus compelled perceive,
Whatever love and faith we looked should spring
At advent of the authoritative star,
1545 Which yet lie sluggish, curdled at the source,—
These have leapt forth profusely in old time,
These still respond with promptitude to-day,
At challenge of—what unacknowledged powers
O' the air, what uncommissioned meteors, warmth

---

*P1869:*Disputing if it   1524| MS:Claiming it as a prize: the <> price—for why?
*P1869:*Claiming as prize <> price—for why?   1526| MS:bag. *P1869:*bag!
1530| MS:seventeenth hundredth *P1869:*seventeen-hundredth   1531| MS:to such cause?
*P1869:*to cause?   1533| MS:perceive . . how *1889a:*perceive . . . how
1534| MS:fault, this obduracy to good *P1869:*fault, the obduracy to good,
1535| MS:not with § over *in* §   1536| Whence man § last two words over illegible
erasure §   1537| MS:ice, the *1889a:*ice the   1538| MS:or rock the sun was
meant to warm *P1869:*or stone, 'twas meant the sun should warm *1889a:*stone
'twas   1539| MS:make bear § crossed out and then restored § grass § crossed
out and replaced above by § flowers,—nor sun's nor moon's the blame: *P1869:*nor
ice nor stone to blame: 1540| MS:melt this ice, and bloom, this rock,
*P1869:*melt, that ice, and bloom, that stone, *1872:*ice, can bloom   1542| MS:That
terrifies *P1869:*This terrifies   1544| MS:star *P1869:*star,   1545| MS:And shall
§ crossed out and replaced above by § yet <> source, *P1869:*Which <> source,—
1547| MS:to-day *P1869:*to-day,   1548| MS:of what <> powers of the air § last three
words crossed out § , *P1869:*of—what <> powers   1549| MS:What <> meteors, law

135

1550 By law, and light by rule should supersede?
For see this priest, this Caponsacchi, stung
At the first summons,—"Help for honour's sake,
Play the man, pity the oppressed!"—no pause,
How does he lay about him in the midst,
1555 Strike any foe, right wrong at any risk,
All blindness, bravery and obedience!—blind?
Ay, as a man would be inside the sun,
Delirious with the plenitude of light
Should interfuse him to the finger-ends—
1560 Let him rush straight, and how shall he go wrong?
Where are the Christians in their panoply?
The loins we girt about with truth, the breasts
Righteousness plated round, the shield of faith,
The helmet of salvation, and that sword
1565 O' the Spirit, even the word of God,—where these?
Slunk into corners! Oh, I hear at once
Hubbub of protestation! "What, we monks
We friars, of such an order, such a rule,
Have not we fought, bled, left our martyr-mark
1570 At every point along the boundary-line
'Twixt true and false, religion and the world,
Where this or the other dogma of our Church
Called for defence?" And I, despite myself,
How can I but speak loud what truth speaks low,
1575 "Or better than the best, or nothing serves!
What boots deed, I can cap and cover straight
With such another doughtiness to match,

*P1869:*O' the air, what <> meteors, warmth   1550| MS:And <> rule were sent to
supersede? *P1869:*By law, and light by rule should supersede?   1551| MS:this
Caponsacchi, quick § crossed out § stung   1553| MS:oppressed,—" no
*P1869:*oppressed!"—no   1554| MS:There does *P1869:*How does   1555| MS:foe
to right at *P1869:*foe, right wrong at   1556| MS:obedience!—blind?
*CP1869:*obedience!—blind?   1559| MS:Has interfused *P1869:*Should interfuse
1560| MS:him go straight *P1869:*him rush straight   1562-65| MS:§ inserted between
1561-63 and in margin §   1563| MS:faith *P1869:*faith,   1565| MS:Of *P1869:*O'
1566| MS:corners: oh *P1869:*corners! Oh   1567| MS:protestation,—what
*P1869:*protestation! "What   1570| MS:boundary line *CP1869:*boundary-line
1573| MS:defence? And *P1869:*defence?" And   1574| MS:truth breathes low,
*P1869:*truth speaks low,   1575| MS:serves: *P1869:*serves!   1576| MS:boots
a deed I *P1869:*boots deed, I   1577| MS:match *P1869:*match,

Done at an instinct of the natural man?"
Immolate body, sacrifice soul too,—
1580 Do not these publicans the same? Outstrip!
Or else stop race you boast runs neck and neck,
You with the wings, they with the feet,—for shame!
Oh, I remark your diligence and zeal!
Five years long, now, rounds faith into my ears,
1585 "Help thou, or Christendom is done to death!"
Five years since, in the Province of To-kien,
Which is in China as some people know,
Maigrot, my Vicar Apostolic there,
Having a great qualm, issues a decree.
1590 Alack, the converts use as God's name, not
Tien-chu but plain *Tien* or else mere *Shang-ti*,
As Jesuits please to fancy politic,
While, say Dominicans, it calls down fire,—
For *Tien* means heaven, and *Shang-ti*, supreme prince,
1595 While *Tien-chu* means the lord of heaven: all cry,
"There is no business urgent for despatch
As that thou send a legate, specially
Cardinal Tournon, straight to Pekin, there

1578| MS:Done for a vanity by the <> man? *P1869:*Done at an instinct of the
<> man?" 1579| MS:sacrifice the soul,— *P1869:*sacrifice soul too,—
1580| MS:Outstrip *P1869:*Outstrip! 1581| MS:Or stop § over *stay* § that
race you *P1869:*Or else stop race, you *1889a:*race you 1582| MS:wings,—
they *P1869:*wings, they 1584| MS:long in my ears rings faith her peal,
*P1869:*long, now, rounds faith into my ears, 1585| MS:Help now, or <> death!
P1869:"Help thou, or <> death!" 1586| MS:For whereas § crossed out and replaced
above by three words § Five years since in *P1869:*since, in 1587| MS:as the whole
world knows *P1869:*as some people know, 1588| MS:And § crossed out § Maigrot my
§ inserted above § *P1869:*Maigrot, my 1589| MS:Hath a <> qualm and issues a
decree— *P1869:*Having a <> qualm, issues a decree. 1590| MS:It is observed § last
three words crossed out and replaced above by four words § For why? The converts
*P1869:*Alack, the converts 1591–92| MS:§ written in one continuous line § *Tien* nor
Shang-ti, as Jesuits recommend, as politic, § altered to § Tien-chu, but plain Tien or else
mere Shang-ti, / As Jesuits please to fancy politic, *P1869:*§ names italicized §
1593| MS:But Tien-chu § last two words crossed out § , which § altered to § While should
§ crossed out and replaced above by three words § Dominicans say it <> fire from heaven,—
*P1869:*While, say Dominicans, it <> fire,— 1594–95| MS:§ inserted between 1593-96
and in margin § 1594| MS:§ names not underlined § prince *P1869:*§ names in italics §
prince, 1595| MS:While Tien-chu <> of Heaven: you say *P1869:*While Tien-chu
<> of heaven: all cry, 1596| MS:There *P1869:*"There 1597| MS:that I send a
legate,—specially *P1869:*that thou send a legate, specially 1598| MS:Cardinal

To settle and compose the difference!"
1600　So have I seen a potentate all fume
For some infringement of his realm's just right,
Some menace to a mud-built straw-thatched farm
O' the frontier; while inside the mainland lie,
Quite undisputed-for in solitude,
1605　Whole cities plague may waste or famine sap:
What if the sun crumble, the sands encroach,
While he looks on sublimely at his ease?
How does their ruin touch the empire's bound?

And is this little all that was to be?
1610　Where is the gloriously-decisive change,
Metamorphosis the immeasurable
Of human clay to divine gold, we looked
Should, in some poor sort, justify its price?
Had an adept of the mere Rosy Cross
1615　Spent his life to consummate the Great Work,
Would not we start to see the stuff it touched
Yield not a grain more than the vulgar got
By the old smelting-process years ago?
If this were sad to see in just the sage
1620　Who should profess so much, perform no more,
What is it when suspected in that Power
Who undertook to make and made the world,

Tournon straight　*P1869:*Cardinal Tournon, straight　1599|　MS:difference.
*P1869:*difference!"　1602|　MS:to some mud-built strawthatched　*P1869:*to a mud-built
straw-thatched　1603-5|　MS:On <> lie / <> sap,—　*P1869:*O' <> lie, / Quite
undisputed—for in solitude, / <> sap—　*CP1869:* / <> undisputed-for <> / <> sap:
1606|　MS:§ inserted between 1605-7 § Let the sun crumble and the　*P1869:*What if the sun
crumble, the　1607|　MS:ease:　*P1869:*ease?　1608-9|　MS:§ no ¶ §　*P1869:*§ ¶ §
1610|　*P1869:*gloriously decisive　*CP1869:*gloriously-decisive　1611|　MS:The
immeasurable metamorphosis　*1872:*Metamorphosis the immeasurable
1613|　MS:Should in <> sort § illegible word crossed out and replaced above by § justify the
§ illegible word crossed out § the price?　*P1869:*justify its price?　*CP1869:*Should, in <>
sort, justify　1614|　MS:Had a mere adept of the Rosy　*1872:*Had an adept of the mere
Rosy　1615|　MS:the Great Work　*P1869:*the Great Work,　1616|　MS:not one start
*P1869:*not we start　1617|　MS:not one grain　*P1869:*not a grain　1619|　MS:in just
§ inserted above § the mere § crossed out §　1620|　MS:more　*P1869:*more,
1622|　MS:That that undertook <> world,—　*P1869:*Who undertook <> world,

138

Devised and did effect man, body and soul,
Ordained salvation for them both, and yet . . .
1625   Well, is the thing we see, salvation?

                                                        I
Put no such dreadful question to myself,
Within whose circle of experience burns
The central truth, Power, Wisdom, Goodness,—God:
I must outlive a thing ere know it dead:
1630   When I outlive the faith there is a sun,
When I lie, ashes to the very soul,—
Someone, not I, must wail above the heap,
"He died in dark whence never morn arose."
While I see day succeed the deepest night—
1635   How can I speak but as I know?—my speech
Must be, throughout the darkness, "It will end:
The light that did burn, will burn!" Clouds obscure—
But for which obscuration all were bright?
Too hastily concluded! Sun-suffused,
1640   A cloud may soothe the eye made blind by blaze,—
Better the very clarity of heaven:
The soft streaks are the beautiful and dear.
What but the weakness in a faith supplies
The incentive to humanity, no strength
1645   Absolute, irresistible, comports?
How can man love but what he yearns to help?
And that which men think weakness within strength,

---

¹⁶²³| MS:soul,— *P1869:*soul,   ^{1624–26}| MS:both, and . . . § ¶ § I / Put   *P1869:*both,
and yet . . / Well, is the thing we see, salvation? § ¶ § I / Put   *1889a:*yet . . .
¹⁶²⁸| MS:truth, Power, wisdom   *P1869:*truth, Power, Wisdom   ^{1629–31}| MS:One must
outlive the thing one knows for dead: / When I lie <> soul,   *P1869:*I must outlive a thing
ere know it dead: / When I outlive the faith there is a sun, / <> soul,—
¹⁶³²| MS:Something, not me, must   *P1869:*Someone, not I, must   ¹⁶³³| MS:He <>
arose;   *P1869:*"He <> arose."   ¹⁶³⁴| MS:Now, I   *P1869:*While I
^{1635–40}| MS:know,—my <> / Is, that § crossed out § the light did § inserted above §
burns § altered to § burn, therefore § crossed out and replaced above by two
words § will burn: clouds obscure? / I know not vain that, § last five words crossed out
and replaced above by three words and colon § Too hastily concluded: all § crossed out §
sun-suffused / <> may help § crossed out and replaced above by § soothe <> blaze,
*P1869:*know?—my <> / Must be, throughout the darkness, "It will end:" / The light
that did burn, will burn!" Clouds obscure— / But for which obscuration all were bright? /
<> concluded! Sun-suffused, / <> blaze,—   *1889a:* / end: ¹⁶⁴¹| MS:heaven,—
*P1869:*heaven: ^{1646–49}| MS:§ inserted in left margin § but when he <> help? / What is

139

But angels know for strength and stronger yet—
What were it else but the first things made new,
1650 But repetition of the miracle,
The divine instance of self-sacrifice
That never ends and aye begins for man?
So, never I miss footing in the maze,
No,—I have light nor fear the dark at all.

1655 But are mankind not real, who pace outside
My petty circle, world that's measured me?
And when they stumble even as I stand,
Have I a right to stop ear when they cry,
As they were phantoms who took clouds for crags,
1660 Tripped and fell, where man's march might safely move?
Beside, the cry is other than a ghost's,
When out of the old time there pleads some bard,
Philosopher, or both, and—whispers not,
But words it boldly. "The inward work and worth
1665 Of any mind, what other mind may judge
Save God who only knows the thing He made,
The veritable service He exacts?
It is the outward product men appraise.

---

it <> new,   *P1869:*but what he <> help? / And that which men think weakness within
strength, / But angels know for strength and stronger yet— / What were it   1650| MS:A
repetition   *P1869:*But repetition   1652–54| MS:man? / No   *P1869:*man? / So, never I
miss footing in the maze, / No   1654–55| MS:§ no ¶ §   *P1869:*§ ¶ §   1655| MS:real,
those men outside   *P1869:*real, who pace outside   1656–62| MS:circle, all the world to
me, / <> ears <> cry? / When <> there stoops some man   *P1869:*circle, the world
measured me/ And when they stumble even as I stand, / <> cry,/ As they were phantoms,
took the clouds for crags, / Tripped and fell, where the march of man might move? / Beside,
the cry is other than a ghost's, / When <> there pleads some bard,   *1872:* / /
<> ear <> / / <> men <> / / When   *1889a:*circle, world that's measured me/ / / <>
phantoms who took clouds <> / <> fell, where man's march might safely move? / / When
1663| MS:Philosopher or bard and   *P1869:*Philosopher, or both and   *1872:*both, and
1664| MS:But thus pleads boldly   *P1869:*But words it boldly   1665| MS:any mind what
*P1869:*any mind, what   1666| MS:Save God's who only knows what § replaced above
by § the thing he made   *P1869:*Save God <> thing He made,   1667| MS:And how
much § last three words crossed out and replaced above by two words § The veritable service
he exacts: therefrom § crossed out §   *P1869:*service He exacts?   1668| MS:It is § last two
words inserted in margin § The <> product all may estimate blame § last four words
crossed out and replaced above by two words and colon § we appraise: *P1869:*is the <>

Behold, an engine hoists a tower aloft:
1670 'I looked that it should move the mountain too!'
Or else 'Had just a turret toppled down,
Success enough!'—may say the Machinist
Who knows what less or more result might be:
But we, who see that done we cannot do,
1675 'A feat beyond man's force,' we men must say.
Regard me and that shake I gave the world!
I was born, not so long before Christ's birth
As Christ's birth haply did precede thy day,—
But many a watch before the star of dawn:
1680 Therefore I lived,—it is thy creed affirms,
Pope Innocent, who art to answer me!—
Under conditions, nowise to escape,
Whereby salvation was impossible.
Each impulse to achieve the good and fair,
1685 Each aspiration to the pure and true,
Being without a warrant or an aim,
Was just as sterile a felicity
As if the insect, born to spend his life
Soaring his circles, stopped them to describe
1690 (Painfully motionless in the mid-air)
Some word of weighty counsel for man's sake,
Some 'Know thyself' or 'Take the golden mean!'
—Forwent his happy dance and the glad ray,
Died half an hour the sooner and was dust.

---

product men appraise.   1669| MS:aloft—   *P1869:*aloft: 1670| MS:too'
*P1869:*too!'   1672–75| MS:the Machinist: / Man says § last two words crossed out § 'A
*P1869:*the Mac / Who knows what less or more result might be: / But we, who see that
done we cannot do, / 'A   *CP1869:*the Machinist   1676| MS:the earth § crossed out and
replaced above by § world!   1677| MS:birth,   *1889a:*birth   1679| MS:As poet
or philosopher or both § line crossed out and replaced above by § But many a watch
before the star of dawn.   *P1869:*watch, before <> dawn: *1889a:*watch before
1680–82| MS:affirms,— / Under   *P1869:*affirms, / Pope Innocent, who art to answer me!— /
Under   1684| MS:Each § over perhaps *Such* § aspiration § crossed out and replaced
above by two words § impulse to   1686| MS:aim   *P1869:*aim,   1688| MS:insect
born <> life § over illegible word §   *P1869:*insect, born   1689–91| MS:describe / Some
<> sake   *P1869:*describe / (Painfully motionless in the mid-air) / Some <> sake,
1692–94| MS:mean," / Died   *P1869:*mean!' / —Forwent his happy dance and the glad ray,/

1695 I, born to perish like the brutes, or worse,
Why not live brutishly, obey brutes' law?
But I, of body as of soul complete,
A gymnast at the games, philosopher
I' the schools, who painted, and made music,—all
1700 Glories that met upon the tragic stage
When the Third Poet's tread surprised the Two,—
Whose lot fell in a land where life was great
And sense went free and beauty lay profuse,
I, untouched by one adverse circumstance,
1705 Adopted virtue as my rule of life,
Waived all reward, loved but for loving's sake,
And, what my heart taught me, I taught the world,
And have been teaching now two thousand years.
Witness my work,—plays that should please, forsooth!
1710 'They might please, they may displease, they shall teach,
For truth's sake,' so I said, and did, and do.
Five hundred years ere Paul spoke, Felix heard,—
How much of temperance and righteousness,
Judgment to come, did I find reason for,
1715 Corroborate with my strong style that spared
No sin, nor swerved the more from branding brow
Because the sinner was called Zeus and God?
How nearly did I guess at that Paul knew?

Died   1695| MS:brutes or P1869:brutes, or   1696| MS:obey my law? 1889a:obey
brutes' law?   1699| MS:In the schools, a painter, a musician, all P1869:I' the schools,
who painted, and made music,—all   1700| MS:that gathered § crossed out and replaced
above by § met on § altered to § upon   1701| MS:the Third Poet § altered to § Poet's
stood there by § last two words crossed out and replaced above by two words § tread
surprised   1703| MS:sense was free and beauty was profuse, 1869:sense went free and
beauty lay profuse,   1706| MS:reward, and loved for 1889a:reward, loved but for
1707| MS:§ line heavily revised § And what I saw, loved, first strove the world should see
§ line altered to § And what my heart taught me I taught the world to love § last two words
crossed out § P1869:And, what <> me, I <> world,   1708| MS:teaching these
§ crossed out and replaced above by § now   1709| MS:my plays,—things meant to § last
four words crossed out and replaced above by four words § work,—plays that should
1711| MS:All § crossed out § for § altered to § For the § crossed out § truth's <> said and did
and P1869:said, and did, and   1712| MS:§ inserted between 1711-13 §
1714| MS:come do I find § over perhaps tell § P1869:come, did I
1715| MS:Corroborate in that strong P1869:Corroborate with my strong
1716| MS:swerved the more § last two words inserted above §   1717| MS:sinner was
§ crossed out and replaced above by § is called P1869:sinner was called   1718| MS:that

142

How closely come, in what I represent
1720 As duty, to his doctrine yet a blank?
And as that limner not untruly limns
Who draws an object round or square, which square
Or round seems to the unassisted eye,
Though Galileo's tube display the same
1725 Oval or oblong,—so, who controverts
I rendered rightly what proves wrongly wrought
Beside Paul's picture? Mine was true for me.
I saw that there are, first and above all,
The hidden forces, blind necessities,
1730 Named Nature, but the thing's self unconceived:
Then follow,—how dependent upon these,
We know not, how imposed above ourselves,
We well know,—what I name the gods, a power
Various or one: for great and strong and good
1735 Is there, and little, weak and bad there too,
Wisdom and folly: say, these make no God,—
What is it else that rules outside man's self?
A fact then,—always, to the naked eye,—
And so, the one revealment possible
1740 Of what were unimagined else by man.
Therefore, what gods do, man may criticize,
Applaud, condemn,—how should he fear the truth?—
But likewise have in awe because of power,
Venerate for the main munificence,

---

he knew   *P1869:*that Paul knew?   1719| MS:As it is so § uncertain § untrue § last five
words crossed out and replaced above by § How closely come, in what   1720| MS:As
§ over *Man's* § duty, to the doctrine yet in blank?   *P1869:*As duty, to his doctrine yet a blank?
1722| MS:Who draws § last two words over illegible erasure §   1724| MS:§ written
between 1723-25 §   1730| MS:Named § over illegible erasure § nature   *CP1869:*Named
Nature   1732| MS:ourselves   *P1869:*ourselves,   1733| MS:the Gods,   *P1869:*the
gods,   1734| MS:one, for   *P1869:*one; for   *1872:*one: for   1735| MS:weak, and
*P1869:*weak and   1736| MS:no God,   *P1869:*no God,—   1737| MS:it then that
*P1869:*it else that   1738| MS:always to   *P1869:*always, to   1739| MS:Therefore
§ crossed out and replaced above by § And, as § altered to § so   *1872:*And so
1740| MS:man,   *P1869:*man.   1741| MS:—Therefore what <> criticise,
*P1869:*Therefore, what <> criticize,   1742| MS:how should § over *can* § he but speak
truth?   *P1869:*how should he fear the truth?   *1889a:*truth?—   1743| MS:awe and
venerate § last two words crossed out and replaced above by three words and comma §
because of power,   1744| MS:Venerate § inserted in margin; followed by word

1745   And give the doubtful deed its due excuse
From the acknowledged creature of a day
To the Eternal and Divine. Thus, bold
Yet self-mistrusting, should man bear himself,
Most assured on what now concerns him most—
1750   The law of his own life, the path he prints,—
Which law is virtue and not vice, I say,—
And least inquisitive where search least skills,
I' the nature we best give the clouds to keep.
What could I paint beyond a scheme like this
1755   Out of the fragmentary truths where light
Lay fitful in a tenebrific time?
You have the sunrise now, joins truth to truth,
Shoots life and substance into death and void;
Themselves compose the whole we made before:
1760   The forces and necessity grow God,—
The beings so contrarious that seemed gods,
Prove just His operation manifold
And multiform, translated, as must be,
Into intelligible shape so far
1765   As suits our sense and sets us free to feel.
What if I let a child think, childhood-long,
That lightning, I would have him spare his eye,
Is a real arrow shot at naked orb?
The man knows more, but shuts his lids the same:
1770   Lightning's cause comprehends nor man nor child.

---

inserted above line and illegibly crossed out § <> main mercy and § last two words
crossed out §   1745| MS:deed the due   *P1869:*deed its due   1746| creatures
*P1869:*creature   1747| MS:and Divine: so, bold   *P1869:*and Divine. Thus, bold
1748| MS:self-mistrusting should   *P1869:*self-mistrusting, should   1750| MS:life,—
the   *P1869:*life, the   1751| MS:§ inserted between 1750-52 §   1752| MS:where
least search skills,   *1889a:*where search least skills,   1753| MS:The nature   *P1869:*I'
the nature   1754| MS:What but a scheme like this behoved me paint   *P1869:*What
could I paint beyond a scheme like this   *1872:*schene   *1889a:*scheme
1757| MS:sunrise,—which joins   *P1869:*sunrise now, joins   1758| MS:void,
*P1869:*void;   1759| MS:themselves make now the <> before.   *P1869:*Themselves
compose the <> before: 1760| MS:The force and all necessity grows God,—
*P1869:*The forces and necessity grow God,—   1762| MS:just his operation multiform
§ crossed out §   *P1869:*just His   1765| MS:us right to feel: *P1869:*us free to
*1889a:*feel.   1766| MS:let the child <> childhood long,   *P1869:*let a child <>
childhood-long,   1767| MS:The lightning I   *P1869:*That lightning, I
1768| MS:at idle orb?   *P1869:*at naked orb?   1770| MS:The first cause

Why then, my scheme, your better knowledge broke,
Presently re-adjusts itself, the small
Proportioned largelier, parts and whole named new:
So much, no more two thousand years have done!
1775 Pope, dost thou dare pretend to punish me,
For not descrying sunshine at midnight,
Me who crept all-fours, found my way so far—
While thou rewardest teachers of the truth,
Who miss the plain way in the blaze of noon,—
1780 Though just a word from that strong style of mine,
Grasped honestly in hand as guiding-staff,
Had pricked them a sure path across the bog,
That mire of cowardice and slush of lies
Wherein I find them wallow in wide day!"

1785 How should I answer this Euripides?
Paul,—'tis a legend,—answered Seneca,
But that was in the day-spring; noon is now:
We have got too familiar with the light.
Shall I wish back once more that thrill of dawn?
1790 When the whole truth-touched man burned up, one fire?
—Assured the trial, fiery, fierce, but fleet,
Would, from his little heap of ashes, lend
Wings to that conflagration of the world
Which Christ awaits ere He makes all things new:

---

*P1869:*Lightning's cause   1771| MS:then my   *1869:*then, my   1772| MS:readjusts
*1872:*re-adjusts   1774| MS:done. *P1869:*done!   1775| MS:And do you dare
*P1869:*Pope, dost thou dare   1776| MS:§ inserted between 1775-78 §   1777| MS:§
inserted in right margin § Who crept on all fours < > far, *P1869:*Me who crept
all-fours < > far—   1778| MS:Reward your bishops, priests, and friars here
*P1869:*While thou rewardest teachers of the truth,   1779| MS:plain path
in *P1869:*plain way in   1780| MS:While just *P1869:*Though just a word
from *CP1869:*a help from § original reading restored §   1781| MS:guiding
staff *CP1869:*guiding-staff,   1782| MS:across that bog *P1869:*across the bog,
1783| MS:and maze of *P1869:*and slush of   1784| MS:day?" *1889a:*day!"
1784-85| MS:§ no ¶ § *P1869:*§ ¶ § *1889a:*§ no ¶ § *1889:*§ no ¶ ; emended to restore ¶ ; see
Editorial Notes §   1786| MS:legend, answered Seneca *P1869:*legend,—answered
Seneca,   1787| MS:day spring,—noon < > now *P1869:*day-spring; noon *1889a:*now:
1790| MS:up one fire *P1869:*up, one fire?   1791| MS:Assured < > fiery fierce, and
fleet, *P1869:*—Assured < > fiery, fierce, but fleet,   1792| MS:Would from < > ashes
lend *P1869:*Would, from < > ashes, lend   1793| MS:to the conflagration
*1872:*to that conflagration   1794| MS:ere he < > new— *P1869:*ere He

145

¹⁷⁹⁵ So should the frail become the perfect, rapt
From glory of pain to glory of joy; and so,
Even in the end,—the act renouncing earth,
Lands, houses, husbands, wives and children here,—
Begin that other act which finds all, lost,
¹⁸⁰⁰ Regained, in this time even, a hundredfold,
And, in the next time, feels the finite love
Blent and embalmed with the eternal life.
So does the sun ghastlily seem to sink
In those north parts, lean all but out of life,
¹⁸⁰⁵ Desist a dread mere breathing-stop, then slow
Re-assert day, begin the endless rise.
Was this too easy for our after-stage?
Was such a lighting-up of faith, in life,
Only allowed initiate, set man's step
¹⁸¹⁰ In the true way by help of the great glow?
A way wherein it is ordained he walk,
Bearing to see the light from heaven still more
And more encroached on by the light of earth,
Tentatives earth puts forth to rival heaven,
¹⁸¹⁵ Earthly incitements that mankind serve God
For man's sole sake, not God's and therefore man's.
Till at last, who distinguishes the sun
From a mere Druid fire on a far mount?
More praise to him who with his subtle prism

---

*1889a:*new: ¹⁷⁹⁶| MS:so *P1869:*so,   ¹⁷⁹⁸| MS:husbands wives < > here,
*P1869:*husbands, wives < > here,—   ¹⁷⁹⁹| MS:all lost *P1869:*all, lost,
¹⁸⁰⁰⁻¹⁸⁰²| MS:An hundred fold in this time and the next / Blends *P1869:*Regained, in
this time even, a hundredfold, / And, in the next time, feels the finite love / Blent
¹⁸⁰³| MS:sun sink, say who § followed by illegible word, last four words crossed out and
replaced above by four words § steadily seem to die *P1869:*sun ghastlily seem to sink
¹⁸⁰⁴| MS:parts, dip all *P1869:*parts, lean all   ¹⁸⁰⁵| MS:breathing-while, then
*P1869:*breathing-stop, then   ¹⁸⁰⁷⁻⁹| MS:Was not § crossed out § < > for the
after-stage?— / Only *P1869*| MS:for our after-stage?/ Was such a lighting-up of faith, in
life, / Only   ¹⁸¹⁰| MS:glow, *P1869:*glow?   ¹⁸¹¹| MS:The way he walks in,—'tis
the trial's gist,— *P1869:*A way wherein it is ordained he walk,   ¹⁸¹³| MS:light § over
illegible erasure §   ¹⁸¹⁴⁻¹⁷| MS:§ 1814, 1815 inserted between 1813-17 § Earth's tentatives
put < > / Earth's motives for doing God's § 's crossed out § service, / Till at last who < >
sun § over illegible word § *P1869:*Tentatives earth puts < > / Earthly incitements that
mankind serve God / For man's sole sake, not God's and therefore man's, / < > last, who
1872: / / < > man's.   ¹⁸¹⁸| MS:From the mere < > on the far hill? *P1869:*From a
mere < > on a far mount?   ¹⁸¹⁹| MS:his new-found prism *P1869:*his subtle prism

146

¹⁸²⁰ Shall decompose both beams and name the true.
In such sense, who is last proves first indeed;
For how could saints and martyrs fail see truth
Streak the night's blackness? Who is faithful now?
Who untwists heaven's white from the yellow flare
¹⁸²⁵ O' the world's gross torch, without night's foil that helped
Produce the Christian act so possible
When in the way stood Nero's cross and stake,—
So hard now when the world smiles "Right and wise!
Faith points the politic, the thrifty way,
¹⁸³⁰ Will make who plods it in the end returns
Beyond mere fool's-sport and improvidence.
We fools dance thro' the cornfield of this life,
Pluck ears to left and right and swallow raw,
—Nay, tread, at pleasure, a sheaf underfoot,
¹⁸³⁵ To get the better at some poppy-flower,—
Well aware we shall have so much less wheat
In the eventual harvest: you meantime
Waste not a spike,—the richlier will you reap!
What then? There will be always garnered meal
¹⁸⁴⁰ Sufficient for our comfortable loaf,
While you enjoy the undiminished sack!"
Is it not this ignoble confidence,
Cowardly hardihood, that dulls and damps,

---

^{1821|} MS:indeed, *P1869:*indeed; *1889a:*indeed: ^{1822|} MS:For saints and martyrs
cannot but see *P1869:*For how could saints and martyrs fail see
^{1823|} MS:blackness,—who <> now *P1869:*blackness? Who <> now, *1889a:*now?
^{1824|} MS:Untwists the pure white *P1869:*Untwists heaven's pure white *1889a:*Who
untwists heaven's white   ^{1825|} MS:Of <> without a foil to help. *P1869:*O' <> help
*1889a:*without night's foil that helped   ^{1826|} MS:O splendid Christian act so
*P1869:*Produce the Christian act, so *1889a:*act so   ^{1828|} MS:hard when all the <>
smiles, "Rightly done, *P1869:*hard now that the <> smiles "Rightly done! *1889a:*now
when the <> smiles "Right and wise!   ^{1829|} MS:It is the *1889a:*Faith points the
^{1830|} MS:Will clearly make you in *1889a:*Will make who plods it in
^{1831|} MS:Beyond our fool's play and improvidence,— *P1869:*our fool's-sport and
improvidence: *1889a:*Beyond mere fool's-sport and improvidence.   ^{1832|} MS:fools go
thro' <> life *P1869:*fools dance thro' <> life,   ^{1834|} MS:Nay, tread at *P1869:*—Nay,
tread, at   ^{1836|} MS:much wheat less *1889a:*much less wheat   ^{1837|} MS:harvest,—
you meanwhile *P1869:*harvest: you meantime   ^{1838|} MS:spike,—and rich reward will
reap: *P1869:*spike,—the richlier will you reap!   ^{1840|} MS:Enough to make our
*P1869:*Sufficient for our   ^{1841|} MS:you go feast on the undiminished prize—
*P1869:*you enjoy the <> prize!" *1889a:*undiminished sack!"   ^{1843|} MS:hardihood

147

Makes the old heroism impossible?

1845 Unless . . . what whispers me of times to come?
What if it be the mission of that age
My death will usher into life, to shake
This torpor of assurance from our creed,
Re-introduce the doubt discarded, bring
1850 That formidable danger back, we drove
Long ago to the distance and the dark?
No wild beast now prowls round the infant camp:
We have built wall and sleep in city safe:
But if some earthquake try the towers that laugh
1855 To think they once saw lions rule outside,
And man stand out again, pale, resolute,
Prepared to die,—which means, alive at last?
As we broke up that old faith of the world,
Have we, next age, to break up this the new—
1860 Faith, in the thing, grown faith in the report—
Whence need to bravely disbelieve report
Through increased faith i' the thing reports belie?
Must we deny,—do they, these Molinists,
At peril of their body and their soul,—
1865 Recognized truths, obedient to some truth
Unrecognized yet, but perceptible?—
Correct the portrait by the living face,
Man's God, by God's God in the mind of man?
Then, for the few that rise to the new height,
1870 The many that must sink to the old depth,

---

that < > damps   *P1869:*hardihood, that < > damps,   1844| MS:impossible . . unless
*P1869:*impossible?   1844–45| MS:§ no ¶ §   *P1869:*§ ¶ §   1845| MS: . . What is it
whispers   *P1869:*Unless . . what whispers   *1889a:*Unless . . . what   1846| MS:of
next age   *P1869:*of that age,   *1889a:*age   1847| MS:Waiting my death to begin life
*P1869:*My death will usher into life   1848| MS:creed   *P1869:*creed,   1850| MS:The
formidable   *1872:*That formidable   1851| MS:dark.   *P1869:*dark?
1852| MS:camp,   *P1869:*camp;   *1872:*camp: 1854| MS:if the earthquake < > towers,
that   *1872:*if some earthquake   *1889a:*towers that   1856| MS:Till man   *1872:*And man
1857| MS:die,—that is, alive   *1889a:*die,—which means, alive   1858| MS:world
*P1869:*world,   1860| MS:Faith in the thing grown   *P1869:*Faith, in the thing, grown
1862| MS:faith in thing   *1872:*faith i' the thing   1864| MS:§ inserted between 1863-65 §
soul,   *P1869:*soul,—   1865| MS:Received truths, in obedience to   *P1869:*Recognized
truths, obedient to   1866| MS:perceptible,   *P1869:*perceptible?—
1867| MS:§ inserted between 1866-68 §   1870| MS:that sink < > depth again,

148

The multitude found fall away! A few,
E'en ere new law speak clear, may keep the old,
Preserve the Christian level, call good good
And evil evil, (even though razed and blank
1875 The old titles,) helped by custom, habitude,
And all else they mistake for finer sense
O' the fact than reason warrants,—as before,
They hope perhaps, fear not impossibly.
At least some one Pompilia left the world
1880 Will say "I know the right place by foot's feel,
I took it and tread firm there; wherefore change?"
But what a multitude will surely fall
Quite through the crumbling truth, late subjacent,
Sink to the next discoverable base,
1885 Rest upon human nature, settle there
On what is firm, the lust and pride of life!
A mass of men, whose very souls even now
Seem to need re-creating,—so they slink
Worm-like into the mud, light now lays bare,—
1890 Whose future we dispose of with shut eyes
And whisper—"They are grafted, barren twigs,
Into the living stock of Christ: may bear

---

*P1869:*that must sink <> depth,　　　　1871| MS:multitude that falls away!
*P1869:*multitude found fall away!　　　　1872| MS:ere the new <> speaks clear, keep
*P1869:*speak　*1872:*ere new law speak clear, may keep　　　　1874| MS:And evil evil, even
*P1869:*And evil evil, (even　　　1875| MS:titles stand,—thro' custom　*P1869:*stand,) thro'
*1872:*titles,) helped by custom　　　　1876| MS:all they take　*P1869:*they
may mistake　*1872:*all else they mistake　　　　1877| MS:Of the fact than reason　*CP1869:*O'
*1889a:*fact that reason § emended to § than § see Editorial Notes §　　　　1878| MS:Would
hope　*P1869:*They hope　　　　1879| MS:Surely some one Pompilia in the　*1872:*At
least some one Pompilia left the　　　　1880| MS:Would say　*P1869:*Will say
1881| MS:and I tread firm; wherefore　*P1869:*and tread firm there; wherefore
1882| MS:multitude would fall forthwith,　*P1869:*multitude will fall, perchance,
*1872:*multitude will surely fall　　　　1883| MS:truth subjacent late　*P1869:*late,
*1872:*truth, late subjacent,　　　　1885| MS:nature, take their stand　*1872:*nature, settle
there　　　　1886| MS:is fact, the lusts and prides of　*P1869:*lust and pride　*1872:*is
firm, the　　　　1887| MS:The mass　*1872:*A mass　　　　1888| MS:recreating
*P1869:*re-creating　　　　1889| MS:the depths light　*P1869:*the mud light　*1872:*mud, light
1891| MS:"They are baptised,—grafted, the barren twigs　*1872:*And whisper—"They
are grafted, barren twigs,　　　　1892| MS:of Christ: will bear　*P1869:*of Christ: may bear

One day, till when they lie death-like, not dead,"—
Those who with all the aid of Christ succumb,
1895   How, without Christ, shall they, unaided, sink?
Whither but to this gulf before my eyes?
Do not we end, the century and I?
The impatient antimasque treads close on kibe
O' the very masque's self it will mock,—on me,
1900   Last lingering personage, the impatient mime
Pushes already,—will I block the way?
Will my slow trail of garments ne'er leave space
For pantaloon, sock, plume and castanet?
Here comes the first experimentalist
1905   In the new order of things,—he plays a priest;
Does he take inspiration from the Church,
Directly make her rule his law of life?
Not he: his own mere impulse guides the man—
Happily sometimes, since ourselves allow
1910   He has danced, in gaiety of heart, i' the main
The right step through the maze we bade him foot.
But if his heart had prompted him break loose
And mar the measure? Why, we must submit,

1893| MS:death-like not *P1869:*death-like, not   1894| MS:§ inserted
between 1893-95 § of Christ lie thus, *1872:*of Christ succumb,   1895| MS:What
will they do, whither, unaided *P1869:*How, without Christ, whither   *1872:*without
Christ, shall they, unaided   1896-98| MS:What but this here rehearsed before
my eyes— / The impatient § inserted above § <> treads even § crossed out and replaced
above by § close on the heel § last two words crossed out and replaced above by § kibe
*P1869:*but to this rehearsed <> eyes? / Do not we end, the century and I? / The
*1872:*Whither but to this gulf before <> / / The   1899| MS:§ inserted between
1898-1900 § Of the very § inserted above § <> will personage § crossed out § <> me
*P1869:*O' <> me,   1900-1902| MS:Of the § last two words crossed out § last § altered to §
Last lingering masquer whom it mocks § last four words crossed out § personage, they press
then § last three words crossed out and replaced above by § the first pushing § inserted
above § mime— / Will that § crossed out and replaced above by § my slow-trail <> ne'er
give place § last two words crossed out § *P1869:*personage, the impatient mime / Pushes
already,—will I block the way? / Will *CP1896:*/ / <> slow trail   1903| MS:For the
new mime and mirthful interlude § last six words crossed out and replaced above by six
words and question mark § pantaloon, sock, that § crossed out § plume and castanet?
1906| MS:Does he take § last three words over illegible erasure §   1908| MS:guides his
course— *P1869:*guides the man—   1909| MS:ourselves admit *1872:*ourselves allow
1911| MS:step in the maze we had bade *P1869:*we bade *1872:*step through the
1912| MS:What if <> prompted to break *1872:*But if *1889a:*prompted him break
1913| MS:the figure? Why <> submit *P1869:*the measure? Why *1872:*submit,

And thank the chance that brought him safe so far.
1915 Will he repeat the prodigy? Perhaps.
Can he teach others how to quit themselves,
Show why this step was right while that were wrong?
How should he? "Ask your hearts as I asked mine,
And get discreetly through the morrice too;
1920 If your hearts misdirect you,—quit the stage,
And make amends,—be there amends to make!"
Such is, for the Augustin that was once,
This Canon Caponsacchi we see now.
"But my heart answers to another tune,"
1925 Puts in the Abate, second in the suite,
"I have my taste too, and tread no such step!
You choose the glorious life, and may, for me!
I like the lowest of life's appetites,—
So you judge,—but the very truth of joy
1930 To my own apprehension which decides.
Call me knave and you get yourself called fool!
I live for greed, ambition, lust, revenge;
Attain these ends by force, guile: hypocrite,
To-day, perchance to-morrow recognized
1935 The rational man, the type of common sense."
There's Loyola adapted to our time!
Under such guidance Guido plays his part,

1914| MS:him safely through. *1872:*him safe so far. 1917| MS:Prove why <> right,
while *1872:*Show why <> right while 1918-22| MS:he? Ask <> mine / This is, for
that Saint Bernard that was once *P1869:*he? "Ask <> mine, / And get discreetly through
the morrice so;/ If your hearts misdirect you,—quit the stage, / And make amends,—be there
amends to make." / Such is, for the saint <> once, *CP1869:* / / / / <> the Augustine
1872:/ morrice too; / / make!" / *1889a:* / / / / <> Augustin 1923| MS:The Canon
*P1869:*This Canon 1924| MS:"And my <> tune" *CP1869:*tune," *1872:*"But my
1926| MS:too, for the opposite § last three words crossed out and replaced above by four
words § and choose no such step: *P1869:*and tread no such step! 1927| MS:You live
the <> may for me *P1869:*You choose the <> may, for me, *1872:*me!
1928| MS:Who like *1872:*I like 1929| MS:What you call,—and the *P1869:*you
judge,—but the *1872:*So you 1930| MS:which must judge,— *P1869:*judge.
*1872:*which decides. 1931| MS:fool. *P1869:*fool! 1932| MS:revenge,
*P1869:*revenge; 1933| MS:these ends § inserted above § <> guile,—hypocrite
*P1869:*guile: hypocrite, 1934| MS:To-day,—perchance *P1869:*To-day, perchance
1935| MS:sense" *P1869:*sense." 1937| MS:Under his guidance *P1869:*Under such

He also influencing in the due turn
These last clods where I track intelligence
¹⁹⁴⁰ By any glimmer, these four at his beck
Ready to murder any, and, at their own,
As ready to murder him,—such make the world!
And, first effect of the new cause of things,
There they lie also duly,—the old pair
¹⁹⁴⁵ Of the weak head and not so wicked heart,
With the one Christian mother, wife and girl,
—Which three gifts seem to make an angel up,—
The world's first foot o' the dance is on their heads!

Still, I stand here, not off the stage though close
¹⁹⁵⁰ On the exit: and my last act, as my first,
I owe the scene, and Him who armed me thus
With Paul's sword as with Peter's key. I smite
With my whole strength once more, ere end my part,
Ending, so far as man may, this offence.
¹⁹⁵⁵ And when I raise my arm, who plucks my sleeve?
Who stops me in the righteous function,—foe
Or friend? Oh, still as ever, friends are they
Who, in the interest of outraged truth
Deprecate such rough handling of a lie!
¹⁹⁶⁰ The facts being proved and incontestable,
What is the last word I must listen to?
Perchance—"Spare yet a term this barren stock
We pray thee dig about and dung and dress

---

guidance   ¹⁹⁴²| MS:him,—these are the world: *P1869:*world!   *1872:*him,—such make the world!   ¹⁹⁴³| MS:And, the first effect § over illegible erasure § < > new state § crossed out and replaced above by § cause   *P1869:*And, first   ¹⁹⁴⁴| MS:duly: the *CP1869:*duly,—the   ¹⁹⁴⁶| MS:And the   *1872:*With the   ¹⁹⁴⁷| MS:Which < > gifts make < > up,   *P1869:*—Which < > gifts seem to make < > up,—   ¹⁹⁴⁸⁻⁴⁹| MS:§ ¶ § *1872:*§ no ¶ §   *1889:*§ no ¶ ; emended to restore ¶ ; see Editorial Notes §   ¹⁹⁴⁸| MS:The first < > of < > heads.   *P1869:*heads!   *1872:*The world's first < > o'   ¹⁹⁵⁰| MS:act as my first   *P1869:*act, as my first,   ¹⁹⁵²| MS:keys,—I   *P1869:*key,—I   *CP1869:*key. I   ¹⁹⁵³| MS:more then end   *P1869:*more, then end   *1872:*more, ere end   ¹⁹⁵⁵| MS:arm, what plucks   *1872:*arm, who plucks   ¹⁹⁵⁶| MS:What stops < > foes   *P1869:*Who stops < > foe   ¹⁹⁵⁷| MS:friends? O   *1889a:*friend? Oh   ¹⁹⁵⁸| MS:of the outraged *P1869:*of outraged   ¹⁹⁶⁰| MS:proved here incontestably   *P1869:*incontestable *CP1869:*proved and incontestable,   ¹⁹⁶²| MS:Is it "Spare < > barren tree   *P1869:*barren stock,   *1872:*Perchance—"Spare   *1889a:*stock   ¹⁹⁶³| MS:We mean to dig   *P1869:*We

Till he repent and bring forth fruit even yet!"
1965 Perchance—"So poor and swift a punishment
Shall throw him out of life with all that sin:
Let mercy rather pile up pain on pain
Till the flesh expiate what the soul pays else!"
Nowise! Remonstrants on each side commence
1970 Instructing, there's a new tribunal now
Higher than God's—the educated man's!
Nice sense of honour in the human breast
Supersedes here the old coarse oracle—
Confirming none the less a point or so
1975 Wherein blind predecessors worked aright
By rule of thumb: as when Christ said,—when, where?
Enough, I find it pleaded in a place,—
"All other wrongs done, patiently I take:
But touch my honour and the case is changed!
1980 I feel the due resentment,—*nemini*
Honorem trado is my quick retort."
Right of Him, just as if pronounced to-day!
Still, should the old authority be mute
Or doubtful or in speaking clash with new,
1985 The younger takes permission to decide.
At last we have the instinct of the world
Ruling its household without tutelage:
And while the two laws, human and divine,
Have busied finger with this tangled case,

---

pray thee dig   1964| MS:yet? *P1869:*yet?" *1872:*yet!"   1965| MS:Or also § last
two words crossed out and replaced above by two words § Is it "So <> punishment?
*P1869:*punishment   *1872:*Perchance—"So   1966| MS:You throw <> sin?
*P1869:*Shall throw   *1872:*sin: 1968| MS:else?" *1872:*else!"   1969| MS:Nowise:
remonstrance on all sides begins   *P1869:*Nowise! Remonstrance   *1872:*Nowise!
Remonstrants on each side commence   1970| MS:Instruct me there's   *P1869:*me, there's
*1872:*Instructing, there's   1971| MS:man's,—   *P1869:*man's!
1974| MS:Confirming handsomely a   *1872:*Confirming none the less a
1975| MS:Wherein the predecessor   *1872:*Wherein blind predecessors
1977| MS:Enough we find it in a pleading here,—   *P1869:*Enough I find   *CP1869:*Enough,
I   *1872:*it pleaded in a place,—   1979| MS:changed. *P1869:*changed!
1981| MS:*trado,* is   *1889a:trado* is   1982| MS:Right, just as right as   *P1869:*Right of
Him, just as   1983| MS:mute, *1889a:*mute   1984| MS:doubtful, or
*1889a:*doubtful or   1985| MS:takes it on him to   *P1869:*takes permission to
1987| MS:tutelage, *1872:*tutelage: 1989| MS:busied noddle with this knotty §

1990 In pushes the brisk junior, cuts the knot,
Pronounces for acquittal. How it trips
Silverly o'er the tongue! "Remit the death!
Forgive, . . . well, in the old way, if thou please,
Decency and the relics of routine
1995 Respected,—let the Count go free as air!
Since he may plead a priest's immunity,—
The minor orders help enough for that,
With Farinacci's licence,—who decides
That the mere implication of such man,
2000 So privileged, in any cause, before
Whatever Court except the Spiritual,
Straight quashes law-procedure,—quash it, then!
Remains a pretty loophole of escape
Moreover, that, beside the patent fact
2005 O' the law's allowance, there's involved the weal
O' the Popedom: a son's privilege at stake,
Thou wilt pretend the Church's interest,
Ignore all finer reasons to forgive!
But herein lies the crowning,cogency—
2010 (Let thy friends teach thee while thou tellest beads)
That in this case the spirit of culture speaks,
Civilization is imperative.

---

crossed out and replaced above by § tangled   *P1869:*busied finger with   1990| MS:In
§ inserted in margin § The brisk youth § crossed out and replaced above by §
Junior pushes, in and § last two words crossed out § cuts the § crossed out and
then restored §   *P1869:*In the brisk   *1872:*In pushes the brisk junior, cuts
1992| MS:O'er the silverly § transposed to § Silverly o'er the tongue "You
will § last two words crossed out § Remit the death;   *P1869:*tongue! "Remit the death!
1993| MS:Forgive, . . well <> if you please—   *P1869:*if thou please,   *1889a:*Forgive, . . .
well   1994| MS:Decency's sake, the   *P1869:*Decency and the   1995| MS:Respected,
let <> air   *P1869:*Respected,—let <> air!   1996| MS:immunity,   *P1869:*immunity,—
1997| MS:that   *P1869:*that,   1998| MS:With Farinaccio's licence,—he decides
*P1869:*With Farinacci's licence,— who decides   1999| MS:man   *P1869:*man,
2002| MS:quashes the procedure,— quash it then;   *P1869:*quash it, then!   *1872:*quashes
law-procedure,— quash   2003| MS:It proves a   *1872:*Remains a   2005| MS:Of
*P1869:*O'   2006| MS:Of the Popedom,— a <> privilege § over illegible word §
*P1869:*O' the Popedom: a   2007| MS:You may pretend the Churche's dignity § crossed
out and replaced above by § interest,   *P1869:*Thou may'st pretend the Church's
*CP1869:*Thou wilt pretend   2008| MS:forgive: *P1869:*forgive!   2009| MS:the
proper cogency   *P1869:*cogency—   *1872:*the crowning cogency—
2010| MS:(Let us but teach you while you tell your beads)   *P1869:*(Let
thy friends teach thee while thou tellest your beads)   *CP1869:*tellest beads

To her shall we remand all delicate points
Henceforth, nor take irregular advice
2015 O' the sly, as heretofore: she used to hint
Remonstrances, when law was out of sorts
Because a saucy tongue was put to rest,
An eye that roved was cured of arrogance:
But why be forced to mumble under breath
2020 What soon shall be acknowledged as plain fact,
Outspoken, say, in thy successor's time?
Methinks we see the golden age return!
Civilization and the Emperor
Succeed to Christianity and Pope.
2025 One Emperor then, as one Pope now: meanwhile,
Anticipate a little! We tell thee 'Take
Guido's life, sapped society shall crash,
Whereof the main prop was, is, and shall be
—Supremacy of husband over wife!'
2030 Does the man rule i' the house, and may his mate
Because of any plea dispute the same?
Oh, pleas of all sorts shall abound, be sure,
One but allowed validity,—for, harsh
And savage, for, inept and silly-sooth,
2035 For, this and that, will the ingenious sex
Demonstrate the best master e'er graced slave:

2015| MS:On <> heretofore,—she   *P1869:*O' <> heretofore: she
2016| MS:Apologies when law was difficult   *P1869:*was out of sorts
*1872:*Remonstrances, when   2018| MS:that § over illegible erasure § <>
of impudence,   *CP1869:*of arrogance: 2020| MS:What all § crossed out and replaced
above by three words § soon shall be acknowledged to be § last two words crossed out §
the plain truth   *CP1869:*plain fact,   *1889a:*acknowledged as plain   2021| MS:in
your successor's   *P1869:*in thy successor's   2022| MS:Methinks I see <> return,—
*P1869:*Methinks we see <> return!   2024| MS:Succeed the Christianity
*P1869:*Succeed thy Christianity   *1872:*Succeed to Christianity   2025| MS:now.
Meanwhile,   *P1869:*now: meanwhile,   2026| MS:She anticipates a little and tells you,
Take § over perhaps *Here* §   *CP1869:*little to tell thee 'Take   *1872:*Anticipate a little! We
tell   2027| MS:Count Guido's life you sap society,   *P1869:*life, and sap   *1872:*Guido's
life, sapped society shall crash,   2028| MS:shall prove   *1872:*shall be
2029| MS:wife.   *P1869:*wife!'   2030| MS:Shall the <> in the house, or may   *P1869:*i'
*1872:*Does the <> house, and may   2031| MS:same—   *P1869:*same?
2032| MS:For pleas   *CP1869:*Oh, pleas   2033| MS:If once allowed <> for harsh
*P1869:*for, harsh   *1872:*One but allowed   2034| MS:for inept   *P1869:*for, inept
2035| MS:For this and that will   *P1869:*For, this and that, will   2036| MS:ere <>

And there's but one short way to end the coil,—
Acknowledge right and reason steadily
I' the man and master: then the wife submits
2040 To plain truth broadly stated. Does the time
Advise we shift—a pillar? nay, a stake
Out of its place i' the social tenement?
One touch may send a shudder through the heap
And bring it toppling on our children's heads!
2045 Moreover, if ours breed a qualm in thee,
Give thine own better feeling play for once!
Thou, whose own life winks o'er the socket-edge,
Wouldst thou it went out in such ugly snuff
As dooming sons dead, e'en though justice prompt?
2050 Why, on a certain feast, Barabbas' self
Was set free, not to cloud the general cheer:
Neither shalt thou pollute thy Sabbath close!
Mercy is safe and graceful. How one hears
The howl begin, scarce the three little taps
2055 O' the silver mallet silent on thy brow,—
'His last act was to sacrifice a Count
And thereby screen a scandal of the Church!
Guido condemned, the Canon justified
Of course,—delinquents of his cloth go free!'
2060 And so the Luthers chuckle, Calvins scowl,

---

slave, *P1869:*e'er <> slave: ²⁰³⁸| MS:By giving right *1872:*Acknowledge right
²⁰³⁹| MS:To the <> submits: *P1869:*submits. *1872:*I' the <> submits
²⁰⁴⁰| MS:There it is broadly stated,—nor the *1872:*To plain truth broadly stated. Does the
²⁰⁴¹| MS:Admits we <> pillar? Nay *P1869:*pillar? nay *1872:*Advise we
²⁰⁴²| MS:in the tenement, one touch *1869:*i' *1872:*i' the social tenement?
²⁰⁴³| MS:Whereto might send *P1869:*Whereto may send *1872:*One touch may
²⁰⁴⁴| MS:our heads perchance. *1872:*on our children's heads! ²⁰⁴⁵| MS:Moreover if
this breed <> in you, *P1869:*Moreover if <> thee, *CP1869:*Moreover, if *1872:*if ours
breed ²⁰⁴⁶| MS:Give your own feelings <> once,—deal death? *P1869:*Give thine
own *1872:*own better feeling <> once! ²⁰⁴⁷| MS:You, whose <> socket-edge
*P1869:*Thou, whose <> socket-edge, ²⁰⁴⁸| MS:Would you it *P1869:*Would'st thou it
²⁰⁴⁹| MS:sons to death though justice were? *P1869:*death, though justice bade? *1872:*sons
dead, e'en though justice prompt? ²⁰⁵⁰| MS:feast Barabbas' *P1869:*feast, Barabbas'
²⁰⁵¹| MS:free not <> cheer; *P1869:*cheer. *1872:*free, not <> cheer: ²⁰⁵²| MS:Nor
§ inserted in margin § Trouble not pollute § inserted above § your own § crossed out §
sabbath *P1869:*Neither shalt thou pollute thy Sabbath ²⁰⁵⁵| MS:Of <> mallet ended
on your brow,— *P1869:*O' <> on thy brow,— *1872:*mallet silent on ²⁰⁵⁶| MS:a
man *P1869:*a Count ²⁰⁵⁷| MS:the church: *P1869:*the Church!
²⁰⁵⁸| MS:justified. *P1869:*justified ²⁰⁵⁹| MS:free, *P1869:*free!' ²⁰⁶⁰| MS:so

So thy hand helps Molinos to the chair
Whence he may hold forth till doom's day on just
These *petit-maître* priestlings,—in the choir
Sanctus et Benedictus, with a brush
2065 Of soft guitar-strings that obey the thumb,
Touched by the bedside, for accompaniment!
Does this give umbrage to a husband? Death
To the fool, and to the priest impunity!
But no impunity to any friend
2070 So simply over-loyal as these four
Who made religion of their patron's cause,
Believed in him and did his bidding straight,
Asked not one question but laid down the lives
This Pope took,—all four lives together made
2075 Just his own length of days,—so, dead they lie,
As these were times when loyalty's a drug,
And zeal in a subordinate too cheap
And common to be saved when we spend life!
Come, 'tis too much good breath we waste in words:
2080 The pardon, Holy Father! Spare grimace,
Shrugs and reluctance! Are not we the world,
Art not thou Priam? Let soft culture plead
Hecuba-like, *'non tali'* (Virgil serves)
'Auxilio' and the rest! Enough, it works!
2085 The Pope relaxes, and the Prince is loth,
The father's bowels yearn, the man's will bends,

---

your Luthers and your Calvins come, *P1869:*so the Luthers and the Calvins *1872:*the
Luthers chuckle, Calvins scowl, 2061| MS:So your hand *P1869:*So thy hand
2063| MS:*petit-maitre*—priestlings <> the Choir *P1869:petit-maître* priestlings <>
the choir, *1889a:*choir 2064| MS:*et Benedictus,*—with *P1869:et Benedictus,* with
2066| MS:accompaniment. *P1869:*accompaniment! 2069| MS:This husband too § last
three words crossed out and replaced above by four words § But no impunity to
2070| MS:As simply *P1869:*So simply 2071| MS:their Patron's *P1869:*their patron's
2072| MS:straight *P1869:*straight, 2074| MS:made *1872:*make § emended to § made
§ see Editorial Notes § 2075| MS:so dead they are, *P1869:*so, dead they lie,
2076| MS:These being the times *P1869:*As these were times 2078| MS:life.
*CP1869:*life! 2080| MS:pardon, Holy Father! spare *P1869:*pardon, Holy Father! Spare
2081| MS:reluctance. Are *P1869:*reluctance! Are 2082| MS:Bid you, our Priam, let
*P1869:*bid thee, our *1872:*Art not thou Priam? let *1889a:*thou Priam? Let
2083| MS:'non tali' *P1869:'non tali'* 2084| MS:Auxilio <> rest: enough, it works:
P1869:'Auxilio' <> rest! Enough, it works! 2086| MS:The man's will bends, The
Father's heart flows over § last three words crossed out and replaced above by two words §

157

Reply is apt. Our tears on tremble, hearts
Big with a benediction, wait the word
Shall circulate thro' the city in a trice,
Set every window flaring, give each man
O' the mob his torch to wave for gratitude.
Pronounce then, for our breath and patience fail!"

I will, Sirs: but a voice other than yours
Quickens my spirit. "*Quis pro Domino?*
Who is upon the Lord's side?" asked the Count.
I, who write—
                    "On receipt of this command,
Acquaint Count Guido and his fellows four
They die to-morrow: could it be to-night,
The better, but the work to do, takes time.
Set with all diligence a scaffold up,
Not in the customary place, by Bridge
Saint Angelo, where die the common sort;
But since the man is noble, and his peers
By predilection haunt the People's Square,
There let him be beheaded in the midst,
And his companions hanged on either side:
So shall the quality see, fear and learn.
All which work takes time: till to-morrow, then,

2090

2095

2100

2105

bowels yearn, § transposed to § The Father's <> yearn, the man's <> bends,   *P1869:*father's
2087| MS:Speak the § last two words crossed out and replaced above by two words § Reply is
apt: § inserted § word § crossed out § ; our tears now § crossed out and replaced above by §
on   *P1869:*apt. Our   2088| MS:benediction wait   *P1869:*benediction, wait
2090| MS:every house-face flaring, give   *P1869:*every window flaring, give
2091| MS:Of   *P1869:*O'   2092| MS:Pronounce it, for <> fail!   *P1869:*fail!"
*1872:*Pronounce then, for   2093| MS:will, Sirs: for a   *1872:*will, Sirs: but a
2094-97| MS:spirit. "Quis pro Domino? / I, § inserted § am, § word and comma crossed out §
who write— § ¶ § On <> command   *P1869:*spirit. "*Quis pro Domino?* / Who is upon the
Lord's side?" asked the Count. / I, who write— § ¶ § "On <> command,
2099| MS:but I want work done takes   *P1869:*but the work to do, takes
2100| MS:up   *P1869:*up,   2101| MS:place, the Bridge   *P1869:*place, by Bridge
2102| MS:Saint Angelo where <> sort,   *P1869:*Saint Angelo, where <> sort;
2104| MS:haunt Del Popolo,   *P1869:*haunt the People's Square,   2105| MS:midst
*P1869:*midst,   2106| MS:side,—   *P1869:*side: 2108| MS:to-morrow then

Let there be prayer incessant for the five!"

2110 For the main criminal I have no hope
Except in such a suddenness of fate.
I stood at Naples once, a night so dark
I could have scarce conjectured there was earth
Anywhere, sky or sea or world at all:
2115 But the night's black was burst through by a blaze—
Thunder struck blow on blow, earth groaned and bore,
Through her whole length of mountain visible:
There lay the city thick and plain with spires,
And, like a ghost disshrouded, white the sea.
2120 So may the truth be flashed out by one blow,
And Guido see, one instant, and be saved.
Else I avert my face, nor follow him
Into that sad obscure sequestered state
Where God unmakes but to remake the soul
2125 He else made first in vain; which must not be.
Enough, for I may die this very night
And how should I dare die, this man let live?

Carry this forthwith to the Governor!

---

*P1869:*tomorrow, then,   2109| MS:five."   *P1869:*five!"   2110| MS:§ marginal note
that new paragraph begins §   2113| MS:have conjectured   *P1869:*have scarce
conjectured   2116| MS:blow earth   *P1869:*blow, earth   2117| MS:visible,
*P1869:*visible: 2118| MS:plain § over illegible erasure §

XI

GUIDO

You are the Cardinal Acciaiuoli, and you,
Abate Panciatichi—two good Tuscan names:
Acciaiuoli—ah, your ancestor it was
Built the huge battlemented convent-block
5   Over the little forky flashing Greve
That takes the quick turn at the foot o' the hill
Just as one first sees Florence: oh those days!
'Tis Ema, though, the other rivulet,
The one-arched brown brick bridge yawns over,—yes,
10   Gallop and go five minutes, and you gain
The Roman Gate from where the Ema's bridged:
Kingfishers fly there: how I see the bend
O'erturreted by Certosa which he built,
That Senescal (we styled him) of your House!
15   I do adjure you, help me, Sirs! My blood
Comes from as far a source: ought it to end
This way, by leakage through their scaffold-planks
Into Rome's sink where her red refuse runs?
Sirs, I beseech you by blood-sympathy,
20   If there be any vile experiment
In the air,—if this your visit simply prove,
When all's done, just a well-intentioned trick
That tries for truth truer than truth itself,
By startling up a man, ere break of day,
25   To tell him he must die at sunset,—pshaw!
That man's a Franceschini; feel his pulse,
Laugh at your folly, and let's all go sleep!

Title: MS:Guido Franceschini Again § last two words crossed out §   ¹| MS:and you
*P1869:*and you,   ³| MS:was, *1889a:*was   ⁸| MS:'Tis Ema though <> rivulet
P1869:'Tis Ema, though <> rivulet,   ⁹| MS:one-arched, brown <> yes *P1869:*yes,
*1872:*one-arched brown   ¹⁰| MS:minutes and *P1869:*minutes, and   ¹³| MS:built
*P1869:*built,   ¹⁴| MS:your House. *P1869:*your House!   ¹⁶| MS:source,—ought
*P1869:*source: ought   ¹⁷| MS:way by *P1869:*way, by   ²¹| MS:air, if
*CP1869:*air,—if   ²²| MS:trick *P1869:*trick, DC,BrU:trick *1889:*trick
²³| MS:itself *P1869:*itself,   ²⁴| MS:man ere <> day *P1869:*man, ere <> day,

You have my last word,—innocent am I
As Innocent my Pope and murderer,
30 Innocent as a babe, as Mary's own,
As Mary's self,—I said, say and repeat,—
And why, then, should I die twelve hours hence? I—
Whom, not twelve hours ago, the gaoler bade
Turn to my straw-truss, settle and sleep sound
35 That I might wake the sooner, promptlier pay
His due of meat-and-drink-indulgence, cross
His palm with fee of the good-hand, beside,
As gallants use who go at large again!
For why? All honest Rome approved my part;
40 Whoever owned wife, sister, daughter,—nay,
Mistress,—had any shadow of any right
That looks like right, and, all the more resolved,
Held it with tooth and nail,—these manly men
Approved! I being for Rome, Rome was for me.
45 Then, there's the point reserved, the subterfuge
My lawyers held by, kept for last resource,
Firm should all else,—the impossible fancy!—fail,
And sneaking burgess-spirit win the day.
The knaves! One plea at least would hold,—they laughed,—
50 One grappling-iron scratch the bottom-rock
Even should the middle mud let anchor go!
I hooked my cause on to the Clergy's,—plea
Which, even if law tipped off my hat and plume,
Revealed my priestly tonsure, saved me so.

31| MS:self, I <> repeat, P1869:self,—I <> repeat,— 32| MS:why then should
P1869:why, then, should 36| MS:dues 1872:due 38| MS:again: P1869:again!
39| MS:part, P1869:part; 41| MS:had the mere § last two words crossed out and
replaced above by § any 42| MS:and all <> resolved P1869:and, all <> resolved,
44| MS:Approved,—I P1869:Approved! I 46| MS:resource P1869:resource,
47| MS:fancy!—drop— P1869:fancy!—fail,— 1872:fail, 48| MS:day: 1889a:day.
49| MS:The knaves! § last two words and exclamation point inserted in margin § One <>
hold, they said, P1869:they laughed, 1872:hold,—they laughed,—
50| MS:grappling iron <> bottom rock P1869:bottom-rock CP1869:grappling-iron
51| MS:anchor slide— P1869:anchor go— 1872:anchor go! 52| MS:And hook my
1872:I hooked my 53| MS:even should law tip off P1869:even if law tipped off
54| MS:Showed the Pope my priestly-tonsure, <> so,— P1869:Would show my priestly

55 The Pope moreover, this old Innocent,
Being so meek and mild and merciful,
So fond o' the poor and so fatigued of earth,
So . . . fifty thousand devils in deepest hell!
Why must he cure us of our strange conceit

60 Of the angel in man's likeness, that we loved
And looked should help us at a pinch? He help?
He pardon? Here's his mind and message—death!
Thank the good Pope! Now, is he good in this,
Never mind, Christian,—no such stuff's extant,—

65 But will my death do credit to his reign,
Show he both lived and let live, so was good?
Cannot I live if he but like? "The law!"
Why, just the law gives him the very chance,
The precise leave to let my life alone,

70 Which the archangelic soul of him (he says)
Yearns after! Here they drop it in his palm,
My lawyers, capital o' the cursed kind,—
Drop life to take and hold and keep: but no!
He sighs, shakes head, refuses to shut hand,

75 Motions away the gift they bid him grasp,
And of the coyness comes—that off I run
And down I go, he best knows whither! mind,
He knows, who sets me rolling all the same!
Disinterested Vicar of our Lord,

80 This way he abrogates and disallows,
Nullifies and ignores,—reverts in fine
To the good and right, in detriment of me!

---

tonsure, *1872:*Revealed my <> so.   57| MS:of *P1869:*o'   58| MS:So . . fifty
*1889a:*So . . . fifty   60| MS:likeness that *P1869:*likeness, that   61| MS:pinch.
He *P1869:*pinch? He   62| MS:death, *1872:*death!   66| MS:live so *P1869:*live,
so   68| MS:Why just *P1869:*Why, just   69| MS:alone *P1869:*alone,
70| MS:angelic <> him, he says, *P1869:*him (he says) *1872:*archangelic
71| MS:after,—here *P1869:*after! Here   72| MS:of <> kind, *P1869:*kind,—
*CP1869:*o'   73| MS:A life <> and keep § over *save* §   *1872:*Drop life
76| MS:comes that <> I roll § crossed out §   *1872:*comes—that   77| MS:he
well § crossed out and replaced above by § best <> whither,—blame §
crossed out § mind *P1869:*mind, *1872:*whither! mind,   78| MS:Who
§ crossed out and replaced above by § He knows and § over illegible word §
sets <> the while § crossed out §   *P1869:*He knows, and *1872:*knows, who sets
80| MS:disallows *P1869:*disallows,   82| MS:right in *P1869:*right, in

Talk away! Will you have the naked truth?
He's sick of his life's supper,—swallowed lies:
85 So, hobbling bedward, needs must ease his maw
Just where I sit o' the door-sill. Sir Abate,
Can you do nothing? Friends, we used to frisk:
What of this sudden slash in a friend's face,
This cut across our good companionship
90 That showed its front so gay when both were young?
Were not we put into a beaten path,
Bid pace the world, we nobles born and bred,
We body of friends with each his scutcheon full
Of old achievement and impunity,—
95 Taking the laugh of morn and Sol's salute
As forth we fared, pricked on to breathe our steeds
And take equestrian sport over the green
Under the blue, across the crop,—what care?
If we went prancing up hill and down dale,
100 In and out of the level and the straight,
By the bit of pleasant byeway, where was harm?
Still Sol salutes me and the morning laughs:
I see my grandsire's hoof-prints,—point the spot
Where he drew rein, slipped saddle, and stabbed knave
105 For daring throw gibe—much less, stone—from pale:
Then back, and on, and up with the cavalcade.
Just so wend we, now canter, now converse,
Till, 'mid the jauncing pride and jaunty port,
Something of a sudden jerks at somebody—

83| MS:away will *P1869:*away! Will   86| MS:on *P1869:*o'   87| MS:nothing?
Friends we *P1869:*nothing? Friends, we   90| MS:Showing its gay front when we both
*P1869:*That showed its front so gay when both   91| MS:we not put *P1869:*we put
93–95| MS:The body <> / Taking *P1869:*/ Of old achievent and impunity,—/ Taking
CP1869:/ <> achievement <> / Taking *1872:*We body <> / / Taking
98| MS:crop § over illegible word §   99| MS:So we go prancing <> dale *P1869:*we
went prancing <> dale, *1872:*If we   100| MS:straight *P1869:*straight,
101–3| MS:bye way, where's the harm?/ I *P1869:*byeway, where was harm?/ Still Sol salutes
me and the morning laughs:/ I   105| MS:Who dared throw stone § crossed out and
replaced above by § gibe from pale, then vaulted § crossed out § back and on *P1869:*For
daring throw gibe—much less, stone—from pale, *1872:*pale: 106–8| MS:And up with
the cavalcade; just so wend we/ Till, mid mid § crossed out § the sportive mouth § last two
words crossed out and replaced above by two words § jauncing pride and jaunty grace

110 A dagger is out, a flashing cut and thrust,
Because I play some prank my grandsire played,
And here I sprawl: where is the company? Gone!
A trot and a trample! only I lie trapped,
Writhe in a certain novel springe just set
115 By the good old Pope: I'm first prize. Warn me? Why?
Apprise me that the law o' the game is changed?
Enough that I'm a warning, as I writhe,
To all and each my fellows of the file,
And make law plain henceforward past mistake,
120 "For such a prank, death is the penalty!"
Pope the Five Hundredth (what do I know or care?)
Deputes your Eminency and Abateship
To announce that, twelve hours from this time, he needs
I just essay upon my body and soul
125 The virtue of his brand-new engine, prove
Represser of the pranksome! I'm the first!
Thanks. Do you know what teeth you mean to try
The sharpness of, on this soft neck and throat?
I know it,—I have seen and hate it,—ay,
130 As you shall, while I tell you! Let me talk,
Or leave me, at your pleasure! talk I must:
What is your visit but my lure to talk?
Nay, you have something to disclose?—a smile,

---

*P1869:*Then back, and on, and up with the cavalcade;/ Just so wend we, now canter, now converse,/ Till 'mid <> jaunty port, *1872:*cavalcade./ / Till ¹¹⁰| MS:thrust *P1869:*thrust, ¹¹²| MS:company? Gone, *P1869:*company? Gone!
¹¹³| MS:A-trot <> trample,—only <> trapped *P1869:*A trot <> trample! only <> trapped, ¹¹⁵⁻¹⁷| MS:me? Why?/ Enough <> as I lie *P1869:*me? Why?/ Apprize me that the law o' the game is changed?/ Enough <> as I writhe, *1889a:*/ Apprise <> / Enough ¹¹⁸| MS:file *P1869:*file, ¹¹⁹| MS:And the law's plain *P1869:*And make law plain ¹²⁰| MS:prank death <> penalty." *P1869:*prank, death <> penalty!" ¹²¹| MS:the Five Hundredth . . what <> care? *1872:*the Five Hundredth (what <> care?) ¹²²| MS:your Eminence *1872:*your Eminency ¹²³| MS:that twelve <> time he *P1869:*that, twelve <> time, he ¹²⁴| MS:I shall essay *P1869:*I just essay ¹²⁵| MS:bran-new engine, brave *P1869:*brand-new engine, prove ¹²⁶| MS:pranksome! I make proof *P1869:*pranksome! I'm the first! ¹²⁷| MS:First . . do you guess § crossed out and replaced above by § know <> you bid me try *P1869:*Thanks. Do <> you mean to try ¹²⁸| MS:of on *P1869:*of, on ¹²⁹| MS:hate the same, *P1869:*hate it,—ay, ¹³⁰| MS:you: let me talk! *P1869:*talk, *1872:*you! Let ¹³¹| MS:pleasure: talk I must, *P1869:*pleasure! talk I must: ¹³³| MS:You have a something to disclose,—a smile *P1869:*disclose?—a smile, *1872:*Nay,

At end of the forced sternness, means to mock
135 The heart-beats here? I call your two hearts stone!
Is your charge to stay with me till I die?
Be tacit as your bench, then! Use your ears,
I use my tongue: how glibly yours will run
At pleasant supper-time . . . God's curse! . . . to-night
140 When all the guests jump up, begin so brisk
"Welcome, his Eminence who shrived the wretch!
Now we shall have the Abate's story!"

Life!
How I could spill this overplus of mine
Among those hoar-haired, shrunk-shanked odds and ends
145 Of body and soul old age is chewing dry!
Those windlestraws that stare while purblind death
Mows here, mows there, makes hay of juicy me,
And misses just the bunch of withered weed
Would brighten hell and streak its smoke with flame!
150 How the life I could shed yet never shrink,
Would drench their stalks with sap like grass in May!
Is it not terrible, I entreat you, Sirs?—
With manifold and plenitudinous life,
Prompt at death's menace to give blow for threat,
155 Answer his "Be thou not!" by "Thus I am!"—
Terrible so to be alive yet die?

How I live, how I see! so,—how I speak!

---

you have something   134| MS:sternness means   CP1869:sternness, means
135| MS:here: I <> stone: P1869:here? I <> stone!   139| MS:supper-time . .
God's curse! . . to-night   1889a:supper-time . . . God's curse! . . . to-night
142| MS:story!—" Life! P1869:story!" § ¶ § Life!   144| MS:shrunk-shanked,
odds   1889a:shrunk-shanked odds   145| MS:soul, old <> dry,
P1869:dry!   1889a:soul old   146| MS:windlestraws P1869:windle-straws
1889a:windlestraws   147-49| MS:there, and misses all the same § last three words crossed
out and replaced above by three words § just the bunch,/ Would <> flame.   P1869:there,
makes hay of juicy me,/ And misses, just the bunch of withered weed,/ Would <> flame!
1872:/ <> misses just   1889a:/ <> weed   150| MS:never miss P1869:never
shrink,   1872:life, I   1889a:life I   152| MS:you, Sirs? 1889a:you, Sirs?—
153| MS:Such manifold <> life   P1869:life,   1889a:With manifold   155-57| MS:his
"Be not!" by "Thus feel I am!"/ § no ¶ § How <> see! Therefore I speak—   P1869:his "Be
thou not!" by "Thus I am!"—/ Terrible so to be alive yet die?/ § ¶ § How <> see! so,—how

166

Lucidity of soul unlocks the lips:
I never had the words at will before.
160 How I see all my folly at a glance!
"A man requires a woman and a wife:"
There was my folly; I believed the saw.
I knew that just myself concerned myself,
Yet needs must look for what I seemed to lack,
165 In a woman,—why, the woman's in the man!
Fools we are, how we learn things when too late!
Overmuch life turns round my woman-side:
The male and female in me, mixed before,
Settle of a sudden: I'm my wife outright
170 In this unmanly appetite for truth,
This careless courage as to consequence,
This instantaneous sight through things and through,
This voluble rhetoric, if you please,—'tis she!
Here you have that Pompilia whom I slew,
175 Also the folly for which I slew her!
                                        Fool!
And, fool-like, what is it I wander from?
What did I say of your sharp iron tooth?
Ah,—that I know the hateful thing! this way.
I chanced to stroll forth, many a good year gone,
180 One warm Spring eve in Rome, and unaware
Looking, mayhap, to count what stars were out,
Came on your fine axe in a frame, that falls
And so cuts off a man's head underneath,
Mannaia,—thus we made acquaintance first:
185 Out of the way, in a by-part o' the town,
At the Mouth-of-Truth o' the river-side, you know:

I speak!   159–61| MS:before./ A <> wife.   P1869:before./ How I see all my folly at a
glance!/ "A <> wife:"   162| MS:my bane, I was born man and strong: P1869:my
folly; I believed the saw: 1889a:saw.   167| MS:Much life <> round the woman side of
me,   P1869:Overmuch life <> round my woman-side;   1889a:woman-side:
169| MS:Settles <> sudden, I'm   P1869:Settle <> sudden: I'm   171| MS:consequence
P1869:consequence,   173| MS:rhetoric if <> she,   P1869:rhetoric, if <> she!
175| MS:her,—I   P1869:her! § ¶ § Fool!   176–78| MS:Am a fool, what <> / Ah <>
thing: this   P1869:And, fool-like, what <> / What, of the sharpness of your iron tooth?/
Ah   1872:What did I say of your sharp iron <> / Ah <> thing! this   181| MS:out
P1869:out,   182| MS:your huge axe   1872:your fine axe   184| MS:first,
1872:first: 185| MS:bye-part of   P1869:o'   1889a:by-part   186| MS:the Mouth of

167

One goes by the Capitol: and wherefore coy,
Retiring out of crowded noisy Rome?
Because a very little time ago
190 It had done service, chopped off head from trunk
Belonging to a fellow whose poor house
The thing must make a point to stand before—
Felice Whatsoever-was-the-name
Who stabled buffaloes and so gained bread,
195 (Our clowns unyoke them in the ground hard by)
And, after use of much improper speech,
Had struck at Duke Some-title-or-other's face,
Because he kidnapped, carried away and kept
Felice's sister who would sit and sing
200 I' the filthy doorway while she plaited fringe
To deck the brutes with,—on their gear it goes,—
The good girl with the velvet in her voice.
So did the Duke, so did Felice, so
Did Justice, intervening with her axe.
205 There the man-mutilating engine stood
At ease, both gay and grim, like a Swiss guard
Off duty,—purified itself as well,
Getting dry, sweet and proper for next week,—
And doing incidental good, 'twas hoped,
210 To the rough lesson-lacking populace
Who now and then, forsooth, must right their wrongs!
There stood the twelve-foot-square of scaffold, railed
Considerately round to elbow-height,

Truth on   *P1869:*the Mouth-of-Truth o'   188| MS:of § followed by word illegibly
crossed out and replaced above by § crowded   190| MS:trunk,   *1889a:*trunk
192| MS:thing had made a <> before.   *1872:*thing must make a   *1889a:*before—
195| MS:(People unyoke   *P1869:*(Our clowns unyoke   197| MS:Had spat in Duke
Some- § over illegible word § <> face   *P1869:*Had struck at Duke <> face,
199| MS:sister that would   *1872:*sister who would   200| MS:In   *P1869:*I'
202| MS:voice   *P1869:*voice.   203| MS:So did Felice § crossed out and replaced above
by § the   205| MS:man-mutilating business § crossed out and replaced above by §
engine   206| MS:grim like   *CP1869:*grim, like   207| MS:duty,—being purified as
*P1869:*duty,—purified itself as   209| MS:good, belike,   *P1869:*good, 'twas hoped
DC,BrU:hoped,   *1889:*hoped,   210| MS:To the gross § crossed out and replaced above
by § rough lesson-lacking multitude § crossed out §   211| MS:and then;   *P1869:*and
then,   213| MS:elbow-height   *P1869:*elbow-height: *1872:*elbow-height,

For fear an officer should tumble thence
215 And sprain his ankle and be lame a month
Through starting when the axe fell and head too!
Railed likewise where the steps whereby 'twas reached.
All of it painted red: red, in the midst,
Ran up two narrow tall beams barred across,
220 Since from the summit, some twelve feet to reach,
The iron plate with the sharp shearing edge
Had slammed, jerked, shot, slid,—I shall soon find which!—
And so lay quiet, fast in its fit place,
The wooden half-moon collar, now eclipsed
225 By the blade which blocked its curvature: apart,
The other half,—the under half-moon board
Which, helped by this, completes a neck's embrace,—
Joined to a sort of desk that wheels aside
Out of the way when done with,—down you kneel,
230 In you're pushed, over you the other drops,
Tight you're clipped, whiz, there's the blade cleaves its best,
Out trundles body, down flops head on floor,
And where's your soul gone? That, too, I shall find!
This kneeling-place was red, red, never fear!
235 But only slimy-like with paint, not blood,
For why? a decent pitcher stood at hand,
A broad dish to hold sawdust, and a broom
By some unnamed utensil,—scraper-rake,—
Each with a conscious air of duty done.
240 Underneath, loungers,—boys and some few men,—
Discoursed this platter, named the other tool,

---

²¹⁴| MS:—Suppose an *P1869:*(Suppose an *1872:*For fear an ²¹⁵| MS:a week
*P1869:*a month, DC,BrU:month *1889a:*month ²¹⁶| MS:falls <> too? *P1869:*fell
<> too?) *1872:*too! ²¹⁸| MS:painted red: red in the midst *P1869:*painted red: red,
in the midst, ²²²| MS:Had . . slammed <> shot or slid <> which. *P1869:*which!
*1872:*Had slammed <> shot, slid *1889a:*which!— ²²³| MS:There it lay *1872:*And
so lay ²²⁴| MS:eclipses *P1869:*eclipsed ²²⁵| MS:apart *P1869:*apart,
²²⁷| MS:That, helped *P1869:*Which, helped ²³⁰| MS:you're wheeled, over
*1872:*you're pushed, over ²³¹| MS:tight you are clipped <> blade on you, *1872:*tight
you're clipped <> blade cleaves its best, ²³³| MS:find. *P1869:*find!
²³⁴| *1889a:*kneeling place DC,BrU:kneeling-place *1889:*kneeling-place
²³⁸| MS:With § crossed out and replaced above by § By <> utensil, scraper-rake,
*P1869:*utensil,—scraper-rake,— ²⁴⁰| MS:Underneath loungers, boys <> men,
*P1869:*Underneath, loungers,—boys <> men,— ²⁴¹| MS:platter and the

Just as, when grooms tie up and dress a steed,
Boys lounge and look on, and elucubrate
What the round brush is used for, what the square,—
245 So was explained—to me the skill-less then—
The manner of the grooming for next world
Undergone by Felice What's-his-name.
There's no such lovely month in Rome as May—
May's crescent is no half-moon of red plank,
250 And came now tilting o'er the wave i' the west,
One greenish-golden sea, right 'twixt those bars
Of the engine—I began acquaintance with,
Understood, hated, hurried from before,
To have it out of sight and cleanse my soul!
255 Here it is all again, conserved for use:
Twelve hours hence, I may know more, not hate worse.

That young May-moon-month! Devils of the deep!
Was not a Pope then Pope as much as now?
Used not he chirrup o'er the Merry Tales,
260 Chuckle,—his nephew so exact the wag
To play a jealous cullion such a trick
As wins the wife i' the pleasant story! Well?
Why do things change? Wherefore is Rome un-Romed?
I tell you, ere Felice's corpse was cold,
265 The Duke, that night, threw wide his palace-doors,
Received the compliments o' the quality
For justice done him,—bowed and smirked his best,

*1872:*platter, named   242| MS:as when <> steed   *P1869:*as, when <> steed,
243| MS:Boys and men § last two words crossed out and replaced above by two words §
lounge and <> on, lucubrate aloud   *P1869:*on, and elucubrate   245| MS:explained to
<> skilless man   *P1869:*explained—to <> skill-less man—   *1872:*skill-less then—
249| MS:plank   *P1869:*plank,   250| MS:wave, the west   *P1869:*wave i' the west,
251| MS:twixt   *P1869:*'twixt   252| MS:engine I   *P1869:*engine—I
253| MS:before   *P1869:*before,   254| MS:soul: *P1869:*soul!   255| MS:use,
*P1869:*use: 256| MS:hence I   *1872:*hence, I   256–57| MS:§ no ¶ §   *P1869:*§ ¶ §
257| MS:The young   *P1869:*That young   258| MS:not the Pope   *P1869:*not a Pope
259| MS:the Merry Tales   *P1869:*the Merry Tales,   261| MS:Would play the jealous
*P1869:*To play a jealous   262| MS:wins his wife in <> story: well?   *P1869:*wins the
wife i' <> story! Well?   264| MS:cold   *P1869:*cold,   265| MS:palace doors,
*P1869:*palace-doors,   266| MS:of   *P1869:*o'   267| MS:On the justice   *P1869:*For

And in return passed round a pretty thing,
A portrait of Felice's sister's self,
270 Florid old rogue Albano's masterpiece,
As—better than virginity in rags—
Bouncing Europa on the back o' the bull:
They laughed and took their road the safelier home.
Ah, but times change, there's quite another Pope,
275 I do the Duke's deed, take Felice's place,
And, being no Felice, lout and clout,
Stomach but ill the phrase "I lose my head!"
How euphemistic! Lose what? Lose your ring,
Your snuff-box, tablets, kerchief!—but, your head?
280 I learnt the process at an early age;
'Twas useful knowledge, in those same old days,
To know the way a head is set on neck.
My fencing-master urged "Would you excel?
Rest not content with mere bold give-and-guard,
285 Nor pink the antagonist somehow-anyhow!
See me dissect a little, and know your game!
Only anatomy makes a thrust the thing."
Oh Cardinal, those lithe live necks of ours!
Here go the vertebræ, here's *Atlas*, here
290 *Axis*, and here the symphyses stop short,
So wisely and well,—as, o'er a corpse, we cant,—
And here's the silver cord which . . . what's our word?

---

justice   268| MS:a masterpiece § crossed out and replaced above by two words § pretty
thing,   269| MS:Minature § crossed out and replaced above by two words § A portrait
270-72| MS:masterpiece,/ Bouncing <> bull,—   *P1869:*masterpiece,/ As—better than
virginity in rags—/ Bouncing <> bull: 276| MS:Who, being no Felice lout
*P1869:*And, being no Felice, lout   277| MS:phrase, "I <> head."   *P1869:*phrase "I
<> head!"   *1889a:*lost   DC,BrU: lose   *1889:*lose   279| MS:kerchief,—but your
head!   *CP1869:*kerchief!—but, your head?   280| MS:age,   *P1869:*age;
281-83| MS:knowledge in <> / My fencing master   *P1869:*knowledge, in <> / To know
the way a head is set on neck./ My   *1889a:*/ / My fencing-master   284| MS:bold
cut § crossed out and replaced above by § give and thrust § crossed out and replaced
above by § guard   *P1869:*give-and-guard,   285| MS:somehow anyhow,—
*P1869:*somehow-anyhow,—   *1872:*somehow-anyhow!   286| MS:game,   *P1869:*game!
287| MS:thing.   *P1869:*thing."   289| MS:here's atlas   *P1869:*here's *Atlas*
291| MS:well, as o'er a corpse we   *P1869:*well,—as, o'er a corpse, we
292| MS:which . . what's the word?   *P1869:*which . . . what's our word?

171

Depends from the gold bowl, which loosed (not "lost")
Lets us from heaven to hell,—one chop, we're loose!
²⁹⁵ "And not much pain i' the process," quoth a sage:
Who told him? Not Felice's ghost, I think!
Such "losing" is scarce Mother Nature's mode.
She fain would have cord ease itself away,
Worn to a thread by threescore years and ten,
³⁰⁰ Snap while we slumber: that seems bearable.
I'm told one clot of blood extravasate
Ends one as certainly as Roland's sword,—
One drop of lymph suffused proves Oliver's mace,—
Intruding, either of the pleasant pair,
³⁰⁵ On the arachnoid tunic of my brain.
That's Nature's way of loosing cord!—but Art,
How of Art's process with the engine here,
When bowl and cord alike are crushed across,
Bored between, bruised through? Why, if Fagon's self,
³¹⁰ The French Court's pride, that famed practitioner,
Would pass his cold pale lightning of a knife,
Pistoja-ware, adroit 'twixt joint and joint,
With just a "See how facile, gentlefolk!"—
The thing were not so bad to bear! Brute force
³¹⁵ Cuts as he comes, breaks in, breaks on, breaks out
O' the hard and soft of you: is that the same?
A lithe snake thrids the hedge, makes throb no leaf:
A heavy ox sets chest to brier and branch,

---

²⁹⁴| MS:Lets you from <> chop, you're loose!   *P1869:*Lets us from <> chop, we're loose!
²⁹⁵| MS:in <> quoth the sage: *P1869:*i'   *1889a:*quoth a sage: ²⁹⁷| MS:losing is
scarce Mother Nature's way § crossed out §   *P1869:*"losing"   ²⁹⁸| MS:away
*P1869:*away,   ³⁰⁰| MS:while you slumber <> bearable: *P1869:*while we slumber
*1889a:*bearable.   ³⁰²| MS:Ends you as <> sword,   *P1869:*Ends one as <> sword,—
³⁰³| MS:One ounce of <> mace   *P1869:*One drop of <> mace,—   ³⁰⁵| MS:of the
brain.   *P1869:*of my brain.   ³⁰⁶| MS:cord,—but   *P1869:*cord!—but
³⁰⁷| MS:here?   *1872:*here,   ³⁰⁸| MS:across   *P1869:*across,   ³⁰⁹| MS:self
*P1869:*self,   ³¹⁰| MS:That famed practioner the French Court pays,   *P1869:*The
French Court's pride, that famed practioner,   ³¹²| MS:and joint   *CP1869:*and joint,
³¹³| MS:gentlefolks!"   *P1869:*gentlefolks!"—   *1889a:*gentlefolk!"—   ³¹⁴| MS:Not so
bad were the thing to bear: brute   *P1869:*The thing were not so bad to bear! Brute
³¹⁶| MS:Of hard   *P1869:*O' the hard   ³¹⁷| MS:hedge, nor throb one leaf—
*P1869:*hedge, makes throb no leaf—   *CP1869:*leaf: ³¹⁸| MS:to briar and bough,

Bursts somehow through, and leaves one hideous hole
320 Behind him!

          And why, why must this needs be?
Oh, if men were but good! They are not good,
Nowise like Peter: people called him rough,
But if, as I left Rome, I spoke the Saint,
—"Petrus, quo vadis?"—doubtless, I should hear,
325 "To free the prisoner and forgive his fault!
I plucked the absolute dead from God's own bar,
And raised up Dorcas,—why not rescue thee?"
What would cost one such nullifying word?
If Innocent succeeds to Peter's place,
330 Let him think Peter's thought, speak Peter's speech!
I say, he is bound to it: friends, how say you?
Concede I be all one bloodguiltiness
And mystery of murder in the flesh,
Why should that fact keep the Pope's mouth shut fast?
335 He execrates my crime,—good!—sees hell yawn
One inch from the red plank's end which I press,—
Nothing is better! What's the consequence?
How should a Pope proceed that knows his cue?
Why, leave me linger out my minute here,
340 Since close on death comes judgment and comes doom,
Not crib at dawn its pittance from a sheep
Destined ere dewfall to be butcher's-meat!
Think, Sirs, if I have done you any harm,

---

*P1869:*and branch,   *1869:*brier   ³¹⁹| MS:Burst somehow *P1869:*Bursts somehow
³²⁰| MS:him: and   *P1869:*him! § ¶ § And   ³²²| MS:call *P1869:*called
³²³| MS:left Rome, I met the *P1869:*left Rome, I spoke the   ³²⁴| MS:—"Petrus, quo
vadis?" "Guido," I *P1869:*—"Petrus, quo vadis?"—doubtless, I   ³²⁵| MS:fault!"
*P1869:*fault!   ³²⁷| MS:Raised up Jairus daughter,—why not thee? *1869:*And raised up
Dorcas,—why not rescue thee?"   ³²⁹| MS:place *P1869:*place,   ³³⁰| MS:speech.
*P1869:*speech!   ³³⁹| MS:my moment § crossed out and replaced above by § minute
³⁴⁰| MS:comes <> and such § over illegible word § doom,   *P1869:*come <> and the doom,
*1872:*comes <> and comes doom,   ³⁴¹| MS:Nor cribs *1872:*Nor crib *1889a:*Not crib
³⁴²| MS:Because § crossed out and replaced above by § Destined ere dewfall destined
§ crossed out and replaced above by two words § to be butcher's meat.
*P1869:*butcher's-meat!   ³⁴³| MS:if I had done <> harm *P1869:*harm, *1872:*if I have

And you require the natural revenge,
345 Suppose, and so intend to poison me,
—Just as you take and slip into my draught
The paperful of powder that clears scores,
You notice on my brow a certain blue:
How you both overset the wine at once!
350 How you both smile! "Our enemy has the plague!
Twelve hours hence he'll be scraping his bones bare
Of that intolerable flesh, and die,
Frenzied with pain: no need for poison here!
Step aside and enjoy the spectacle!"
355 Tender for souls are you, Pope Innocent!
Christ's maxim is—one soul outweighs the world:
Respite me, save a soul, then, curse the world!
"No," venerable sire, I hear you smirk,
"No: for Christ's gospel changes names, not things,
360 Renews the obsolete, does nothing more!
Our fire-new gospel is re-tinkered law,
Our mercy, justice,—Jove's rechristened God,—
Nay, whereas, in the popular conceit,
'Tis pity that old harsh Law somehow limps,
365 Lingers on earth, although Law's day be done,
Else would benignant Gospel interpose,
Not furtively as now, but bold and frank
O'erflutter us with healing in her wings,

___

done   344–46| MS:required <> / —Just <> take it, slip   P1869:require <> /
Suppose, and so intend to poison me,/ —Just <> take and slip   348–51| MS:blue:/
How you both pause, "Our enemy has the plague—/ Twelve   P1869:blue:/ How you both
overset the wine at once!/ How you both smile! "Our enemy has the plague!/ Twelve
352| MS:flesh, so die,   P1869:flesh, and die,   354| MS:Put powder up, § last three
words crossed out § step § altered to § Step <> spectacle!   P1869:spectacle!"
356| MS:Christ lays it down—one   P1869:Christ's maxim is—one   357| MS:soul, let
the world wag!   P1869:soul, then, curse the world!   358| MS:"No," verily I think I
<> smirk   P1869:"No," venerable sire, I <> smirk,   359| MS:"No, for <> names
not   P1869:"No: for <> names, not   360| MS:obsolete, and § written over by § does
nothing more § over else § ,   P1869:more!   361| MS:retinkered   1872:re-tinkered
362| MS:Our mercy's justice   P1869:Our mercy, justice   364| MS:Tis pity the old law
still somehow   P1869:'Tis pity that the old law somehow   CP1869:that old harsh Law
365| MS:although its day be done,   P1869:although law's day be done,—
CP1869:although Law's   1872:Although <> done, lingers <> earth,—   1889a:Lingers
<> earth, although <> done,   366| MS:interpose   P1869:benignant gospel interpose,
CP1869:benignant Gospel   368–70| MS:wings—/ We like to put it, on the contrary,

174

Law being harshness, Gospel only love—
370 We tell the people, on the contrary,
Gospel takes up the rod which Law lets fall;
Mercy is vigilant when justice sleeps!
Does Law permit a taste of Gospel-grace?
The secular arm allow the spiritual power
375 To act for once?—no compliment so fine
As that our Gospel handsomely turn harsh,
Thrust victim back on Law the nice and coy!"
Yes, you do say so, else you would forgive
Me whom Law does not touch but tosses you!
380 Don't think to put on the professional face!
You know what I know: casuists as you are,
Each nerve must creep, each hair start, sting and stand,
At such illogical inconsequence!
Dear my friends, do but see! A murder's tried,
385 There are two parties to the cause: I'm one,
—Defend myself, as somebody must do:
I have the best o' the battle: that's a fact,
Simple fact,—fancies find no place just now.
What though half Rome condemned me? Half approved:
390 And, none disputes, the luck is mine at last,
All Rome, i' the main, acquitting me: whereon,

---

*P1869:*wings,—/ Law is all harshness, Gospel were all love!—/ We <> contrary,—
*1872:*wings,/ Law being harshness, Gospel only love—/ We tell the people, on *1889a:*/ /
<> contrary,   371| MS:which law <> fall,   *P1869:*fall;   *CP1869:*which Law
372-74| MS:sleeps—/ The <> allows   *P1869:*sleeps;/ Does Law let Guido taste the
Gospel-grace?/ The <> allow   *1872:*Does Law permit a taste of Gospel-grace?/ The
375| MS:once,—what compliment so fit   *P1869:*once?—what <> so fine   *1872:*once?—no
compliment   376| MS:As doing the harsh § inserted above § deed whence law shrunk,
*P1869:*As that the Gospel handsomely be harsh,   *1872:*that our Gospel handsomely turn
harsh,   377| MS:Pressing § crossed out and replaced above by § Urging a victim on the
<> coy?"   *P1869:*Thrust back Law's victim on   *1872:*Thrust victim back on Law the <>
coy!"   378| MS:so,—else   *1889a:*so, else   379| MS:whom law dares not
*P1869:*whom Law   *1872:*whom Law does not   380| MS:face—   *P1869:*face!
381| MS:know,—being casuists both;   *P1869:*know,—casuists as you are,   *1889a:*know:
casuists   382| MS:stand   *P1869:*stand,   383-85| MS:inconsequence!/ There <> to
a cause   *P1869:*inconsequence!/ Dear my friends, do but see! A murder's tried,/ There <>
to the cause   386| MS:Defend § over illegible word §   387| MS:of the battle—,
that's   *P1869:*o' the battle: that's   388| MS:Simple § over illegible word § fact fancies
<> place beside;   *P1869:*fact,—fancies <> beside: *1872:*place just now.
389| MS:Suppose half <> me,—half approved,   *P1869:*What though half <> me? Half
approved: 390| MS:And none   *P1869:*And, none   391| MS:All Rome acquits me

What has the Pope to ask but "How finds Law?"
"I find," replies Law, "I have erred this while:
Guilty or guiltless, Guido proves a priest,
395 No layman: he is therefore yours, not mine:
I bound him: loose him, you whose will is Christ's!"
And now what does this Vicar of our Lord,
Shepherd o' the flock,—one of whose charge bleats sore
For crook's help from the quag wherein it drowns?
400 Law suffers him employ the crumpled end:
His pleasure is to turn staff, use the point,
And thrust the shuddering sheep, he calls a wolf,
Back and back, down and down to where hell gapes!
"Guiltless," cries Law—"Guilty" corrects the Pope!
405 "Guilty," for the whim's sake! "Guilty," he somehow thinks,
And anyhow says: 'tis truth; he dares not lie!

Others should do the lying. That's the cause
Brings you both here: I ought in decency
Confess to you that I deserve my fate,
410 Am guilty, as the Pope thinks,—ay, to the end,
Keep up the jest, lie on, lie ever, lie
I' the latest gasp of me! What reason, Sirs?
Because to-morrow will succeed to-day

---

in the main,—and now   *P1869:*All Rome, i' the main, acquits me: whereupon
*1872:*acquitting me: whereon,   393| MS:replies Law "I <> erred through haste, § last
two words and comma crossed out and replaced above by two words and colon § this while:
*P1869:*replies Law, "I   394| MS:priest *P1869:*priest,   395| MS:layman,—
therefore § inserted above § he is yours not mine: I bound— § last two words crossed out §
*P1869:*layman: he is therefore yours,   396| MS:I bound him, § last three words and
comma inserted in margin § loose him, you; your will *P1869:*him: loose him, you whose
will   397| MS:of the Lord, *1872:*of our Lord,   398| MS:of the *P1869:*o'
400| MS:him put forth the <> end,— *1872:*him employ the *1889a:*end:
402| MS:shuddering § followed by word illegibly crossed out § , he § last two words crossed
out and replaced above by two words § sheep he calls a § inserted above § *1872:*sheep, he
403| MS:Back and back, down § last three words inserted above § <> to damnation
§ crossed out § . . there it gapes! *P1869:*to where hell gapes!   404| MS:"Guiltless"
quoth Law <> Pope, *P1869:*"Guiltless," cries Law <> Pope!   405| MS:thinks
*P1869:*thinks,   406-7| MS:§ no ¶ § *1872:*§ ¶ §   406| MS:anyhow speaks: 'tis
*P1869:*anyhow says: 'tis   407| MS:'Tis I should *P1869:*Others should
408| MS:here,—I *P1869:*here: I   411| MS:Carry the *P1869:*Keep up the
412| MS:In <> me,—your reason *P1869:*I' <> me! What reason   413| MS:to-day,

For you, though not for me: and if I stick
415 Still to the truth, declare with my last breath,
I die an innocent and murdered man,—
Why, there's the tongue of Rome will wag apace
This time to-morrow: don't I hear the talk!
"So, to the last he proved impenitent?
420 Pagans have said as much of martyred saints!
Law demurred, washed her hands of the whole case.
Prince Somebody said this, Duke Something, that.
Doubtless the man's dead, dead enough, don't fear!
But, hang it, what if there have been a spice,
425 A touch of . . . eh? You see, the Pope's so old,
Some of us add, obtuse: age never slips
The chance of shoving youth to face death first!"
And so on. Therefore to suppress such talk
You two come here, entreat I tell you lies,
430 And end, the edifying way. I end,
Telling the truth! Your self-styled shepherd thieves!
A thief—and how thieves hate the wolves we know:
Damage to theft, damage to thrift, all's one!
The red hand is sworn foe of the black jaw.
435 That's only natural, that's right enough:
But why the wolf should compliment the thief
With shepherd's title, bark out life in thanks,
And, spiteless, lick the prong that spits him,—eh,

P1869:to-day   414| MS:you if not   P1869:you, though not   415| MS:last cry,
P1869:last breath,   417| MS:the talk of Rome § letter crossed out § will treat the truth
P1869:the tongue of Rome will wag a-pace   1889a:apace   418| MS:to-morrow,—don't
I hear them talk!   P1869:hear the talk!   1889a:to-morrow: don't   420| MS:saints:
P1869:saints!   422| MS:this, Duke Something that,—   P1869:this, Duke Something,
that.   423| MS:fear,   P1869:fear!   425| MS:of . . eh? you   P1869:eh?
You   1889a:of . . . eh   426| MS:obtuse,—age   1889a:obtuse: age   427| MS:first,"
P1869:first!" 429| MS:tell the lies,   P1869:tell you lies,   430| MS:And end the < > end
P1869:And end, the < > end,   431| MS:truth: your < > shepherd is   P1869:truth! Your
CP1869:shepherd thieves!   432| MS:and that thieves hate wolves   P1869:and how
thieves hate the wolves   433–36| MS:theft or thrift, all's one—red hand/ Is sworn foe of
black jaw: that's right enough:/ But that the   P1869:theft, damage to thrift, all's one!/ The
red hand is < > of the black jaw!/ That's only natural, that's right enough:/ But why the
1889a:/ < > jaw.   437| MS:With the shepherd's < > out breath in   P1869:out life in
1872:With shepherd's   438| MS:And dying, § word and comma inserted above § lick
the point that < > him,—why,   P1869:And spiteless, lick the prong that < > him,—eh,

177

Cardinal? My Abate, scarcely thus!
440 There, let my sheepskin-garb, a curse on't, go—
Leave my teeth free if I must show my shag!
Repent? What good shall follow? If I pass
Twelve hours repenting, will that fact hold fast
The thirteenth at the horrid dozen's end?
445 If I fall forthwith at your feet, gnash, tear,
Foam, rave, to give your story the due grace,
Will that assist the engine half-way back
Into its hiding-house?—boards, shaking now,
Bone against bone, like some old skeleton bat
450 That wants, at winter's end, to wake and prey!
Will howling put the spectre back to sleep?
Ah, but I misconceive your object, Sirs!
Since I want new life like the creature,—life,
Being done with here, begins i' the world away:
455 I shall next have "Come, mortals, and be judged!"
There's but a minute betwixt this and then:
So, quick, be sorry since it saves my soul!
Sirs, truth shall save it, since no lies assist!
Hear the truth, you, whatever you style yourselves,
460 Civilization and society!
Come, one good grapple, I with all the world!
Dying in cold blood is the desperate thing;
The angry heart explodes, bears off in blaze

*CP1869:*And, spiteless   439| MS:Cardinal, no! Abate   *P1869:*Cardinal? My Abate
440| MS:sheepskin garb   *P1869:*sheepskin-garb   443| MS:fact hook fast   *1872:*fact
hold fast   448| MS:hiding-house, that's shaking now   *P1869:*hiding-house?—boards,
shaking now,   449| MS:against bone like   *P1869:*against bone, like
450| MS:wants, now winter's done, to < > and live,   *P1869:*winter's dead, to < > and prey!
*1872:*wants, at winter's end, to   451| MS:Will that § crossed out and replaced above
by § howling   453–56| MS:I want life < > life being done/ And the world away: come,
mortals, and be judged!/ There's < > then,   *P1869:*Since I want new life < > life/ Being
done with here, begins i' the world away:/ I shall next have "Come, mortals, and be
judged!"/ There's < > then: DC,BrU:life,   *1889a:*life,   457| MS:I should be < > soul.
*P1869:*So, quick, be < > soul!   458| MS:lies do good § last two words crossed out §
assist.   *P1869:*assist!   459| MS:Come, all of you § last four words crossed out and
replaced above by four words § Hear the truth, you   460| MS:society,—   *P1869:*society!
462| MS:thing,   *P1869:*thing;   463| MS:But angry hearts explode, bear   *P1869:*The

The indignant soul, and I'm combustion-ripe.
465　Why, you intend to do your worst with me!
That's in your eyes! You dare no more than death,
And mean no less. I must make up my mind.
So Pietro,—when I chased him here and there,
Morsel by morsel cut away the life
470　I loathed,—cried for just respite to confess
And save his soul: much respite did I grant!
Why grant me respite who deserve my doom?
Me—who engaged to play a prize, fight you,
Knowing your arms, and foil you, trick for trick,
475　At rapier-fence, your match and, maybe, more.
I knew that if I chose sin certain sins,
Solace my lusts out of the regular way
Prescribed me, I should find you in the path,
Have to try skill with a redoubted foe;
480　You would lunge, I would parry, and make end.
At last, occasion of a murder comes:
We cross blades, I, for all my brag, break guard,
And in goes the cold iron at my breast,
Out at my back, and end is made of me.
485　You stand confessed the adroiter swordsman,—ay,
But on your triumph you increase, it seems,
Want more of me than lying flat on face:
I ought to raise my ruined head, allege
Not simply I pushed worse blade o' the pair,
490　But my antagonist dispensed with steel!
There was no passage of arms, you looked me low,

---

angry heart explodes, bears　　465| 　MS:me, *P1869:*me!　　466| 　MS:eyes,—you < >
death　*P1869:*eyes! You < > death,　　467| 　MS:less,—I mind.　*P1869:*less. I < > mind!
*1889a:*mind.　　468| 　MS:So Pietro when　*P1869:*So Pietro,—when
470| 　MS:loathed, cried　*P1869:*loathed,—cried　　473| 　MS:you　*P1869:*you,
474| 　MS:you trick for trick　*P1869:*you, trick for trick,　　475| 　MS:rapier fence < > may
be　*P1869:*rapier-fence　*1889a:*maybe　　477| 　MS:my lusts § over illegible word,
perhaps *wants* §　　479| 　MS:to cross swords § last two words crossed out and replaced
above by two words § try skill　　480–82| 　MS:Let him § last two words crossed out and
replaced above by two words § You would < > and so § crossed out and replaced above
by § make end./ We < > guard　*P1869:*end./ At last, occasion of a murder comes:/
We < > guard,　　489| 　MS:of　*CP1869:*o'　　490| 　MS:steel:　*P1869:*steel!

With brow and eye abolished cut and thrust
Nor used the vulgar weapon! This chance scratch,
This incidental hurt, this sort of hole
495   I' the heart of me? I stumbled, got it so!
Fell on my own sword as a bungler may!
Yourself proscribe such heathen tools, and trust
To the naked virtue: it was virtue stood
Unarmed and awed me,—on my brow there burned
500   Crime out so plainly intolerably red,
That I was fain to cry—"Down to the dust
With me, and bury there brow, brand and all!"
Law had essayed the adventure,—but what's Law?
Morality exposed the Gorgon shield!
505   Morality and Religion conquer me.
If Law sufficed would you come here, entreat
I supplement law, and confess forsooth?
Did not the Trial show things plain enough?
"Ah, but a word of the man's very self
510   Would somehow put the keystone in its place
And crown the arch!" Then take the word you want!

I say that, long ago, when things began,
All the world made agreement, such and such
Were pleasure-giving profit-bearing acts,
515   But henceforth extra-legal, nor to be:
You must not kill the man whose death would please
And profit you, unless his life stop yours
Plainly, and need so be put aside:
Get the thing by a public course, by law,

492| MS:cut-and-thrust *1889a:*cut and thrust   493| MS:weapon: this *P1869:*weapon!
This   495| MS:In <> so, *P1869:*I' <> so!   496| MS:may, *P1869:*may!
498| MS:So the *P1869:*To the   500| MS:plainly, intolerably *1872:*intolerably, red,
*1889a:*plainly intolerably red,   501| MS:cry—"down *P1869:*cry—"Down
504| MS:Morality must bare the Gorgon-shield, *P1869:*the Gorgon-shield! *1869:*Morality
exposed the *1872:*the Gorgon shield!   506| MS:Unless you say so, why § last five
words crossed out and replaced above by five words § If Law sufficed, would you
*P1869:*sufficed would   507| MS:supplement the Law, confess *P1869:*supplement law,
and confess   509| MS:Ah *P1869:*"Ah   511| MS:arch: then *P1869:*arch!" Then
511-12| MS:§ no ¶ § *P1869:* § ¶ §   514| MS:acts *P1869:*acts,   515| MS:extralegal
*P1869:*extra-legal   517| MS:life stopped yours *P1869:*life stop yours
518| MS:and needed so *P1869:*and need so   519| MS:The same thing *P1869:*Get the

520　Only no private bloodshed as of old!
　　All of us, for the good of every one,
　　Renounced such licence and conformed to law:
　　Who breaks law, breaks pact therefore, helps himself
　　To pleasure and profit over and above the due,
525　And must pay forfeit,—pain beyond his share:
　　For, pleasure being the sole good in the world,
　　Anyone's pleasure turns to someone's pain,
　　So, law must watch for everyone,—say we,
　　Who call things wicked that give too much joy,
530　And nickname mere reprisal, envy makes,
　　Punishment: quite right! thus the world goes round.
　　I, being well aware such pact there was,
　　I, in my time who found advantage come
　　Of law's observance and crime's penalty,—
535　Who, but for wholesome fear law bred in friends,
　　Had doubtless given example long ago,
　　Furnished forth some friend's pleasure with my pain,
　　And, by my death, pieced out his scanty life,—
　　I could not, for that foolish life of me,
540　Help risking law's infringement,—I broke bond,
　　And needs must pay price,—wherefore, here's my head,
　　Flung with a flourish! But, repentance too?
　　But pure and simple sorrow for law's breach
　　Rather than blunderer's-ineptitude?
545　Cardinal, no! Abate, scarcely thus!
　　'Tis the fault, not that I dared try a fall

---

thing 　　520| MS:old: P1869:old! 　　521| MS:us for <> one P1869:us, for <>
one, 　　522| MS:law, P1869:law: 　　523| MS:pact, therefore 1889a:pact therefore
526| MS:For pleasure is the 1872:For, pleasure being the 　　528| MS:So, let law watch
for everyone, say P1869:everyone,—say 1872:So, law must watch 　　529| MS:Calling §
crossed out and replaced above by two words § Who call 　　530| MS:nickname the reprisal
envy P1869:reprisal, envy 1872:nickname mere reprisal 　　531| MS:right,—thus
P1869:right! thus 　　533| MS:Who in my time have found advantage too 1872:I, in my
time who found advantage come 　　534| MS:In law's 1872:Of law's 　　535| MS:fear
this bred P1869:fear law bred 　　537| MS:friends P1869:friend's 　　538| MS:And by
my death pieced <> life, P1869:And, by my death, pieced <> life,— 　　539| MS:I,
could not for <> me P1869:I could not, for <> me, 　　541| MS:wherefore here's
P1869:wherefore, here's 　　543| MS:for law's § over illegible word §
544-46| MS:blunderer's ineptitude?/ The fault is not <> I dared § written above line §
trying § altered to § try a fall with law § last two words crossed out §
P1869:blunderer's-ineptitude?/ Cardinal, no! Abate, scarcely thus!/ 'Tis the fault, not

181

With Law and straightway am found undermost,
But that I failed to see, above man's law,
God's precept you, the Christians, recognize?
⁵⁵⁰ Colly my cow! Don't fidget, Cardinal!
Abate, cross your breast and count your beads
And exorcize the devil, for here he stands
And stiffens in the bristly nape of neck,
Daring you drive him hence! You, Christians both?
⁵⁵⁵ I say, if ever was such faith at all
Born in the world, by your community
Suffered to live its little tick of time,
'Tis dead of age, now, ludicrously dead;
Honour its ashes, if you be discreet,
⁵⁶⁰ In epitaph only! For, concede its death,
Allow extinction, you may boast unchecked
What feats the thing did in a crazy land
At a fabulous epoch,—treat your faith, that way,
Just as you treat your relics: "Here's a shred
⁵⁶⁵ Of saintly flesh, a scrap of blessed bone,
Raised King Cophetua, who was dead, to life
In Mesopotamy twelve centuries since,
Such was its virtue!"—twangs the Sacristan,
Holding the shrine-box up, with hands like feet
⁵⁷⁰ Because of gout in every finger joint:
Does he bethink him to reduce one knob,
Allay one twinge by touching what he vaunts?
I think he half uncrooks fist to catch fee,
But, for the grace, the quality of cure,—

^{547|} MS:and straightway am § last two words written above line §   ^{548|} MS:that I fail
to see above < > law   *P1869:*see, above < > law,   *1872:*that I failed to
^{549|} MS:God's will which § last two words crossed out and replaced above by § precept < >
the Christians recognize?   *1872:*the Christians, recognize?   ^{551|} MS:cross yourself § *self*
crossed out and replaced above by § breast   ^{553|} MS:bristly nape of § last two words
added above line § neck of him § last two words crossed out §   *P1869:*neck,
^{554|} MS:hence. What, Christians   *P1869:*hence! You, Christians   ^{556|} MS:world and
your   *P1869:*world, by your   ^{557|} MS:Suffered § added in margin § To § altered to § to
< > little moment § crossed out and replaced above by § tick   ^{558|} MS:age now
*1872:*age, now   ^{560|} MS:concede us death,   *P1869:*concede its death,
^{563|} MS:epoch: treat your faith, I say,   *P1869:*epoch,—treat your faith, that way,
^{564|} MS:here's   *P1869:*relics: "Here's   ^{565|} MS:bone   *P1869:*bone,
^{566|} MS:Raised King Cophetua up to life again   *P1869:*Raised King Cophetua, who was
dead, to life   ^{568|} MS:virtue,"—quoth the   *P1869:*virtue!"—twangs the
^{570|} MS:finger-joint: *1889a:*finger joint: ^{574|} MS:the grace, the § last two words

575 Cophetua was the man put that to proof!
     Not otherwise, your faith is shrined and shown
     And shamed at once: you banter while you bow!
     Do you dispute this? Come, a monster-laugh,
     A madman's laugh, allowed his Carnival
580 Later ten days than when all Rome, but he,
     Laughed at the candle-contest: mine's alight,
     'Tis just it sputter till the puff o' the Pope
     End it to-morrow and the world turn Ash.
     Come, thus I wave a wand and bring to pass
585 In a moment, in the twinkle of an eye,
     What but that—feigning everywhere grows fact,
     Professors turn possessors, realize
     The faith they play with as a fancy now,
     And bid it operate, have full effect
590 On every circumstance of life, to-day,
     In Rome,—faith's flow set free at fountain-head!
     Now, you'll own, at this present, when I speak,
     Before I work the wonder, there's no man
     Woman or child in Rome, faith's fountain-head,
595 But might, if each were minded, realize
     Conversely unbelief, faith's opposite—
     Set it to work on life unflinchingly,
     Yet give no symptom of an outward change:
     Why should things change because men disbelieve?
600 What's incompatible, in the whited tomb,
     With bones and rottenness one inch below?
     What saintly act is done in Rome to-day

---

added above line § <> cure, *CP1869:*cure,—   576| MS:otherwise your faith, is
*P1869:*otherwise, your faith is   579| MS:mad man's *P1869:*madman's
580| MS:but me, *P1869:*but he,   581| MS:candle-contest: I'm alight, *P1869:*candle-
contest: mine's alight,   582| MS:just I sputter <> of *P1869:*just it sputter <> o'
583| MS:End me to-morrow *P1869:*End it to-morrow   586| MS:that feigning
suddenly § crossed out and replaced above by § everywhere *P1869:*that—
feigning   591| MS:fountain-head: *P1869:*fountain-head!   592| MS:present when
*1889a:*present, when   595| MS:might if <> minded realize *P1869:*might, if <>
minded, realize   597| MS:Let it go work <> unflinchingly *P1869:*Set it to work <>
unflinchingly,   599| MS:should life § crossed out and replaced above by § things <>
because you disbelieve? *P1869:*because men disbelieve? *1889a:*disbelieve § emended to §
disbelieve? § see Editorial Notes §   600| MS:incompatible in <> tomb
*P1869:*incompatible, in <> tomb,   601| MS:With the dead man's § last three words
crossed out § bones and rottenness § last two words added above line §

But might be prompted by the devil,—"is"
I say not,—"has been, and again may be,—"
605 I do say, full i' the face o' the crucifix
You try to stop my mouth with! Off with it!
Look in your own heart, if your soul have eyes!
You shall see reason why, though faith were fled,
Unbelief still might work the wires and move
610 Man, the machine, to play a faithful part.
Preside your college, Cardinal, in your cape,
Or,—having got above his head, grown Pope,—
Abate, gird your loins and wash my feet!
Do you suppose I am at loss at all
615 Why you crook, why you cringe, why fast or feast?
Praise, blame, sit, stand, lie or go!—all of it,
In each of you, purest unbelief may prompt,
And wit explain to who has eyes to see.
But, lo, I wave wand, make the false the true!
620 Here's Rome believes in Christianity!
What an explosion, how the fragments fly
Of what was surface, mask and make-believe!
Begin now,—look at this Pope's-halberdier
In wasp-like black and yellow foolery!
625 He, doing duty at the corridor,

604-7| MS:not,—has <> be,—/ Look into your own heart if you have P1869:not,—"has
<> be,"—/ I do say, full i' the face o' the crucifix/ You try to stop my mouth with! Off with
it!/ Look in your own heart if your soul have CP1869:/ / / <> heart, if 1889a:be,—"
608| MS:why though <> fled P1869:why, though <> fled, 609| MS:still may work
P1869:still might work 610| MS:Man the machine to <> part— P1869:Man, the
machine, to <> part. 611-15| MS:§ first two lines crowded between lines 610-16 in
continuous line with break indicated between cape,— and Abate § your College <>
cape,—/ Abate <> feet,—/ Why <> feast, P1869:college <> cape,/ Or,—having
got above his head, grown Pope,—/ Abate <> feet!/ Do you suppose I am at loss at
all/ Why <> feast? 616| MS:stand, lie § added above line § or go, or § crossed
out § live, or § crossed out § die, all of it P1869:go!—all of it, 617| MS:All
§ crossed out and replaced above by two words § In each of it § crossed out and replaced
above by two words § you purest P1869:you, purest 618| MS:And so § last two words
added in margin § Explain P1869:And wit explain 619| MS:wand, make the
1889a:wand, made § emended to § make § see Editorial Notes § 621| MS:fragments fall
§ crossed out and replaced by § fly 622| MS:and a mere lie § last three words
crossed out and replaced above by § make-believe! 623| MS:Begin now,— § last two
words, comma and dash added above line § Look § altered to § look at this fellow, the § last
two words crossed out § 624| MS:Wasp-like in § altered to § In wasp-like
625| MS:the golden door, § last two words crossed out and replaced by § corridor

Wakes from a muse and stands convinced of sin!
Down he flings halbert, leaps the passage-length,
Pushes into the presence, pantingly
Submits the extreme peril of the case
630 To the Pope's self,—whom in the world beside?—
And the Pope breaks talk with ambassador,
Bids aside bishop, wills the whole world wait
Till he secure that prize, outweighs the world,
A soul, relieve the sentry of his qualm!
635 His Altitude the Referendary,—
Robed right, and ready for the usher's word
To pay devoir,—is, of all times, just then
'Ware of a master-stroke of argument
Will cut the spinal cord . . . ugh, ugh! . . . I mean,
640 Paralyse Molinism for evermore!
Straight he leaves lobby, trundles, two and two,
Down steps to reach home, write, if but a word
Shall end the impudence: he leaves who likes
Go pacify the Pope: there's Christ to serve!
645 How otherwise would men display their zeal?
If the same sentry had the least surmise
A powder-barrel 'neath the pavement lay
In neighbourhood with what might prove a match,
Meant to blow sky-high Pope and presence both—

---

*P1869:*corridor,   626| MS:Wakes § over illegible word § <> muse and § crossed out
and replaced above by § to stands § altered to § stand   *P1869:*muse and stands
627| MS:halberk § altered to § halbert <> passage length,   *P1869:*passage-length,
631| MS:ambassadors,   *P1869:*ambassador,   632| MS:bishops   *P1869:*bishop
633| MS:prize outweighs the world   *P1869:*prize, outweighs the world,   634| MS:A
human § crossed out § <> qualm.   *P1869:*qualm!   635| MS:the Referendary
*P1869:*the Referendary,—   636| MS:usher's world § altered to § word
637| MS:devoir, is   *P1869:*devoir,—is   638| MS:Ware of a subtle piece § last two words
crossed out and replaced above by § masterstroke   *P1869:*'Ware <> master-stroke
639| MS:cord . . ugh, ugh! . . I   *1889a:*cord . . . ugh, ugh! . . . I
640| MS:forevermore: *P1869:*for evermore!   641| MS:trundles two and two
*CP1869:*trundles, two and two,   642| MS:Down staircase, to <> write if   *P1869:*Down
steps, to   *1872:*Down steps to <> write, if   643| MS:impudence,—he
*P1869:*impudence: he   645| MS:otherwise do men   *P1869:*otherwise would men
646| MS:If that same   *P1869:*If the same   647| MS:Some § over illegible word §
powder-barrel neath   *P1869:*That powder-barrel 'neath   *CP1869:*A powder-barrel
648| MS:might be § crossed out and replaced above by § prove a match   *P1869:*match,

650 Would he not break through courtiers, rank and file,
Bundle up, bear off and save body so,
The Pope, no matter for his priceless soul?
There's no fool's-freak here, nought to soundly swinge,
Only a man in earnest, you'll so praise
655 And pay and prate about, that earth shall ring!
Had thought possessed the Referendary
His jewel-case at home was left ajar,
What would be wrong in running, robes awry,
To be beforehand with the pilferer?
660 What talk then of indecent haste? Which means,
That both these, each in his degree, would do
Just that,—for a comparative nothing's sake,
And thereby gain approval and reward,—
Which, done for what Christ says is worth the world,
665 Procures the doer curses, cuffs and kicks.
I call such difference 'twixt act and act,
Sheer lunacy unless your truth on lip
Be recognized a lie in heart of you!
How do you all act, promptly or in doubt,
670 When there's a guest poisoned at supper-time
And he sits chatting on with spot on cheek?
"Pluck him by the skirt, and round him in the ears,
Have at him by the beard, warn anyhow!"
Good, and this other friend that's cheat and thief
675 And dissolute,—go stop the devil's feast,

650| MS:courtiers rank   *P1869:*courtiers, rank   651| MS:up and bear < >
so   *P1869:*up, bear < > so,   652| MS:Of the   *P1869:*O'   *1872:*The
653| MS:fool's freak   *P1869:*fool's-freak there   *CP1869:*fool's-freak here
654| MS:earnest you'll   *P1869:*earnest, you'll   655| MS:about that < >
ring.   *CP1869:*about, that < > ring!   657| MS:A jewel case
*P1869:*His jewel-case   658| MS:Explain § crossed out and replaced above by § Where
would   *P1869:*What would   659| MS:pilferer,   *P1869:*pilferer?   660| MS:Who
talk < > means   *P1869:*What talk < > means,   662| MS:that, for   *P1869:*that,—for
663| MS:reward,   *P1869:*reward,—   664| MS:Which done < > world   *P1869:*Which,
done < > world,   665-67| MS:kicks./ § word illegibly crossed out and replaced above by
two words § Its lunacy   *P1869:*kicks./ I call such difference 'twixt act and act,/ Sheer lunacy
668| MS:lie in § added above line §   671-74| MS:spot on brow?/ § lines 672-73 written
in continuous line § And § in margin § Round him in the ears,/ Have at him by the beard,
warn anyhow!/ Pluck him by the skirt, § transposed to § Pluck < > And Round < > / /
Good   *P1869:/* "Pluck < > and round < > / < > anyhow!"   *CP1869:*spot on cheek?
675| MS:dissolute, go < > feast, § written over illegible erasure §   *P1869:*dissolute,—go

Withdraw him from the imminent hell-fire!
Why, for your life, you dare not tell your friend
"You lie, and I admonish you for Christ!"
Who yet dare seek that same man at the Mass
680 To warn him—on his knees, and tinkle near,—
He left a cask a-tilt, a tap unturned,
The Trebbian running: what a grateful jump
Out of the Church rewards your vigilance!
Perform that self-same service just a thought
685 More maladroitly,—since a bishop sits
At function!—and he budges not, bites lip,—
"You see my case: how can I quit my post?
He has an eye to any such default.
See to it, neighbour, I beseech your love!"
690 He and you know the relative worth of things,
What is permissible or inopportune.
Contort your brows! You know I speak the truth:
Gold is called gold, and dross called dross, i' the Book:
Gold you let lie and dross pick up and prize!
695 —Despite your muster of some fifty monks
And nuns a-maundering here and mumping there,
Who could, and on occasion would, spurn dross,
Clutch gold, and prove their faith a fact so far,—
I grant you! Fifty times the number squeak
700 And gibber in the madhouse—firm of faith,
This fellow, that his nose supports the moon;
The other, that his straw hat crowns him Pope:
Does that prove all the world outside insane?
Do fifty miracle-mongers match the mob
705 That acts on the frank faithless principle,
Born-baptized-and-bred Christian-atheists, each

679| MS:man out at mass *P1869:*man at the Mass   684| MS:selfsame
*P1869:*self-same   685| MS:a Bishop *P1869:*a bishop   686| MS:function,—why he
< > not,—bites *P1869:*function!—and he < > not, bites   692| MS:brows,—you
*P1869:*brows! You   693| MS:dross called dross,—what then? *P1869:*dross called dross,
i' the Book: 694| MS:prize *P1869:*prize!   695| MS:Despite *P1869:*—Despite
696| MS:there *P1869:*there,   697| MS:could and < > would spurn dross
*P1869:*could, and < > would, spurn dross,   698| MS:gold and *P1869:*gold, and
700| MS:madhouse firm *P1869:*madhouse—firm   701| MS:fellow that < > moon,
*P1869:*fellow, that *1889a:*moon;   702| MS:That worthy, his old straw < > Pope,—
*P1869:*The other, that his straw < > him Pope: 706| MS:Born, bred and baptized

With just as much a right to judge as you,—
As many senses in his soul, and nerves
I' neck of him as I,—whom, soul and sense,
710   Neck and nerve, you abolish presently,—
I being the unit in creation now
Who pay the Maker, in this speech of mine,
A creature's duty, spend my last of breath
In bearing witness, even by my worst fault,
715   To the creature's obligation, absolute,
Perpetual: my worst fault protests, "The faith
Claims all of me: I would give all she claims,
But for a spice of doubt: the risk's too rash:
Double or quits, I play, but, all or nought,
720   Exceeds my courage: therefore, I descend
To the next faith with no dubiety—
Faith in the present life, made last as long
And prove as full of pleasure as may hap,
Whatever pain it cause the world." I'm wrong?
725   I've had my life, whate'er I lose: I'm right?
I've got the single good there was to gain.
Entire faith, or else complete unbelief!
Aught between has my loathing and contempt,
Mine and God's also, doubtless: ask yourself,
730   Cardinal, where and how you like a man!

---

§ transposed to § Born, baptized and bred   *P1869:*Born-baptized-and-bred
708| MS:soul, and § crossed out and replaced above by § or nerves   *1872:*soul, and nerves
709| MS:In <> I,—whose § altered to § whom, nerves and § last two words crossed out and replaced above by three words and comma § soul and sense,   *P1869:*I'   710| MS:nerve you <> presently   *P1869:*nerve, you <> presently,—   712| MS:Who at this moment § last three words crossed out § <> Maker there § crossed out and replaced above by § in <> mine   *CP1869:*the Maker, in <> mine,   713| MS:my dying § crossed out and replaced above by two words § last of   714| MS:fault   *1872:*fault,   717| MS:would acquit such § last two words crossed out and replaced above by three words § give all she claims   *P1869:*claims,   719| MS:but all or nought   *P1869:*but, all or nought,
720| MS:therefore, this descent   *P1869:*therefore, I descend   723| MS:may be *P1869:*be,   *CP1869:*may hap,   724| MS:pain I cause the world: I'm   *P1869:*pain it cause the world." I'm   727| MS:unbelief,—   *1872:*unbelief!   729| MS:And § crossed out and replaced above by three words § As mine, so § crossed out and replaced in margin by § Mine § *And* restored § God's too, I feel certain: § last four words crossed out and replaced above by two words and commas § also, doubtless, ask yourself   *P1869:*Mine and God's <> doubtless: ask yourself,   730| MS:Cardinal, where and § last two words added above line § <> like the § crossed out and replaced by § a man,   *P1869:*man!

Why, either with your feet upon his head,
Confessed your caudatory, or, at large,
The stranger in the crowd who caps to you
But keeps his distance,—why should he presume?
735 You want no hanger-on and dropper-off,
Now yours, and now not yours but quite his own,
According as the sky looks black or bright.
Just so I capped to and kept off from faith—
You promised trudge behind through fair and foul,
740 Yet leave i' the lurch at the first spit of rain.
Who holds to faith whenever rain begins?
What does the father when his son lies dead,
The merchant when his money-bags take wing,
The politician whom a rival ousts?
745 No case but has its conduct, faith prescribes:
Where's the obedience that shall edify?
Why, they laugh frankly in the face of faith
And take the natural course,—this rends his hair
Because his child is taken to God's breast,
750 That gnashes teeth and raves at loss of trash
Which rust corrupts and thieves break through and steal,
And this, enabled to inherit earth
Through meekness, curses till your blood runs cold!

731| MS:Why either <> head *P1869:*Why, either <> head,   732| MS:or at large
*1872:*or, at large,   733| MS:The gallant § crossed out and replaced above by § stranger
<> who must § crossed out §   734| MS:distance, what w § last word and fragment
crossed out and replaced above by two words § why should he to you § last two words
crossed out § *P1869:*distance,—why   735| MS:dropper-off *P1869:*dropper-off,
736| MS:yours and <> own *P1869:*yours, and <> own,   738| MS:and declined the
§ last two words crossed out and replaced above by three words § kept off from faith
*P1869:*faith—   739| MS:You and the rest are bound to take up cross/ And § last ten
words crossed out; two lines combined § promised § crowded between lines § trudge behind
through fair and foul,   740| MS:Yet § over illegible word § <> in <> first cloud that
comes. § last three words crossed out and replaced above by three words and colon § spit of
rain: *P1869:*i' <> rain.   741| MS:faith's skirt now that rain *P1869:*faith whenever
rain   742| MS:What says § crossed out and replaced above by § does
745| MS:conduct faith *P1869:*conduct, faith   746| MS:Wants but of § last three words
crossed out and replaced above by three words § Now for obedience <> edify!
*P1869:*Where's the obedience <> edify?   747| MS:they spit frankly in the faith of face
§ transposed to § face of faith *P1869:*they laugh frankly   748| MS:course,—one rends
*P1869:*course,—this rends   750| MS:The other gnashes teeth at loss of gold § crossed
out § *P1869:*That gnashes teeth, and raves at *CP1869:*teeth and   751| MS:That
rust <> steal *P1869:*Which rust <> steal,   753| MS:cold: *P1869:*cold!

Down they all drop to my low level, rest
755 Heart upon dungy earth that's warm and soft,
And let who please attempt the altitudes.
Each playing prodigal son of heavenly sire,
Turning his nose up at the fatted calf,
Fain to fill belly with the husks, we swine
760 Did eat by born depravity of taste!

Enough of the hypocrites. But you, Sirs, you—
Who never budged from litter where I lay,
And buried snout i' the draff-box while I fed,
Cried amen to my creed's one article—
765 "Get pleasure, 'scape pain,—give your preference
To the immediate good, for time is brief,
And death ends good and ill and everything!
What's got is gained, what's gained soon is gained twice,
And,—inasmuch as faith gains most,—feign faith!"
770 So did we brother-like pass word about:
—You, now,—like bloody drunkards but half-drunk,
Who fool men yet perceive men find them fools,—
Vexed that a titter gains the gravest mouth,—
O' the sudden you must needs re-introduce
775 Solemnity, straight sober undue mirth

754| MS:all slip § crossed out and replaced above by § drop <> level, ease   1889a:level,
rest   755| MS:Heart on the dungy <> soft   P1869:Heart upon dungy <>
soft,   756| MS:who will go try the altitudes: P1869:will, attempt the altitudes:
CP1869:altitudes.   1889a:who please attempt   757-59| MS:We have the prodigal son
and heir § last two words crossed out § <> sire/ § illegible fragment § Fain <> husks we
P1869:sire,/ Turning his nose up at the fatted calf,/ Fain   1872:Each is the prodigal <> / /
<> husks, we   1889a:Each playing prodigal   760| MS:eat with § crossed out and
replaced by § by such § crossed out and replaced above by § some depravity   P1869:by
born depravity   760-61| MS:§ no ¶ § P1869:§ ¶ §   761| MS:hypocrites: but you
<> you   P1869:hypocrites. But you <> you—   762-64| MS:lay,/ Said amen
P1869:lay,/ And buried snout i' the draff-box while I fed,/ Cried amen   765| MS:Get
<> giving preference   P1869:"Get <> give your preference   766| MS:good,—for <>
brief   P1869:good, for <> brief,   767| MS:everything,   P1869:everything:
1872:everything!   769| MS:And inasmuch <> feign faith!   P1869:And,—inasmuch
<> feign faith!"   770| MS:about—   P1869:about: 771| MS:Till now, like
P1869:—You, now,—like   772| MS:men and perceive <> fools,   1872:fools,—
perceive <> fools,   1872:fools,—   773| MS:And that <> gravest face § crossed out
and replaced above by § mouth,   P1869:mouth,—   1872:Vexed that   774| MS:You on
the sudden must   P1869:O' the sudden you must   775| MS:Solemnity, and sober

By a blow dealt me your boon companion here
Who, using the old licence, dreamed of harm
No more than snow in harvest: yet it falls!
You check the merriment effectually
780 By pushing your abrupt machine i' the midst,
Making me Rome's example: blood for wine!
The general good needs that you chop and change!
I may dislike the hocus-pocus,—Rome,
The laughter-loving people, won't they stare
785 Chap-fallen!—while serious natures sermonize
"The magistrate, he beareth not the sword
In vain; who sins may taste its edge, we see!"
Why my sin, drunkards? Where have I abused
Liberty, scandalized you all so much?
790 Who called me, who crooked finger till I came,
Fool that I was, to join companionship?
I knew my own mind, meant to live my life,
Elude your envy, or else make a stand,
Take my own part and sell you my life dear.
795 But it was "Fie! No prejudice in the world
To the proper manly instinct! Cast your lot
Into our lap, one genius ruled our births,
We'll compass joy by concert; take with us
The regular irregular way i' the wood;
800 You'll miss no game through riding breast by breast,
In this preserve, the Church's park and pale,
Rather than outside where the world lies waste!"
Come, if you said not that, did you say this?

---

*P1869:*Solemnity, must sober   *1872:*Solemnity, straight sober   776| MS:dealt your
*1889a:*dealt me your   778| MS:falls—   *P1869:*falls!   781-83| MS:wine!/ I <>
hocus pocus   *P1869:*wine!/ The general good needs that you chop and change!/ I <>
hocus-pocus   784| MS:laughter-loving of them, won't   *P1869:*laughter-loving people,
won't   785| MS:Chap-fallen, while   *P1869:*Chap-fallen!—while
787| MS:Vainly, who laughs § crossed out and replaced above by § sins   *P1869:*In vain; who
790| MS:came   *P1869:*came,   791| MS:to make § replaced above by § join
companionship, § comma altered to § ?   792| MS:Cast in my lot and feast at Rome
with you? § line crossed out and replaced above by § I knew my own mind, meant to take my
way   *P1869:*to live my life,   794| MS:dear   *P1869:*dear: *1872:*dear.
799| MS:wood,   *P1869:*wood;   801| MS:the Churches   *P1869:*the Church's
802| MS:world is waste!"   *1872:*world lies waste!"   803| MS:that did <> this—

Give plain and terrible warning, "Live, enjoy?
805 Such life begins in death and ends in hell!–
Dare you bid us assist your sins, us priests
Who hurry sin and sinners from the earth?
No such delight for us, why then for you?
Leave earth, seek heaven or find its opposite!"
810 Had you so warned me, not in lying words
But veritable deeds with tongues of flame,
That had been fair, that might have struck a man,
Silenced the squabble between soul and sense,
Compelled him to make mind up, take one course
815 Or the other, peradventure!—wrong or right,
Foolish or wise, you would have been at least
Sincere, no question,—forced me choose, indulge
Or else renounce my instincts, still play wolf
Or find my way submissive to your fold,
820 Be red-crossed on my fleece, one sheep the more.
But you as good as bade me wear sheep's wool
Over wolf's skin, suck blood and hide the noise
By mimicry of something like a bleat,—
Whence it comes that because, despite my care,
825 Because I smack my tongue too loud for once,
Drop baaing, here's the village up in arms!
Have at the wolf's throat, you who hate the breed!
Oh, were it only open yet to choose—

*P1869:*that, did <> this?   804| MS:Give § added in margin § Plain § altered to § plain
805| MS:hell: *P1869:*hell!   806| MS:assist you to your sins   *1872:*assist your sins, us
priests   808| MS:delights   *P1869:*delight   809| MS:Leave them, seek
*P1869:*Leave earth, seek   811| MS:flame   *P1869:*flame,   814| MS:him make his
mind   *1872:*him to make mind   815| MS:peradventure,—wrong or right
*P1869:*peradventure!—wrong or right,   818| MS:Or else § added in margin § renounce
§ added above line § My   *P1869:*my   819| MS:Or drop § crossed out and replaced
above by three words § find my way <> to the fold,   *1872:*to your fold,   820| MS:red
crossed on the fleece one   *P1869:*red-crossed <> fleece, one   *1872:*on my fleece
822| MS:wolf's shag, suck   *P1869:*wolf's skin, suck   826| MS:arms,   *P1869:*arms!
827| MS:throat, we who   *P1869:*throat, you who   *1889a:*wolf s § emended to § wolf's § see
Editorial Notes §   828| MS:Oh were <> choose   *P1869:*Oh, were <> choose—

One little time more—whether I'd be free
830   Your foe, or subsidized your friend forsooth!
Should not you get a growl through the white fangs
In answer to your beckoning! Cardinal,
Abate, managers o' the multitude,
I'd turn your gloved hands to account, be sure!
835   You should manipulate the coarse rough mob:
'Tis you I'd deal directly with, not them,—
Using your fears: why touch the thing myself
When I could see you hunt, and then cry "Shares!
Quarter the carcase or we quarrel; come,
840   Here's the world ready to see justice done!"
Oh, it had been a desperate game, but game
Wherein the winner's chance were worth the pains!
We'd try conclusions!—at the worst, what worse
Than this Mannaia-machine, each minute's talk
845   Helps push an inch the nearer me? Fool, fool!

You understand me and forgive, sweet Sirs?
I blame you, tear my hair and tell my woe—
All's but a flourish, figure of rhetoric!
One must try each expedient to save life.
850   One makes fools look foolisher fifty-fold
By putting in their place men wise like you,
To take the full force of an argument
Would buffet their stolidity in vain.
If you should feel aggrieved by the mere wind
855   O' the blow that means to miss you and maul them,

829| MS:more whether *P1869:*more—whether   833| MS:of *P1869:*o'
835| MS:mob, *P1869:*mob: 836| MS:them, *CP1869:*them—   838| MS:hunt and
*1872:*hunt, and   842| MS:chance is worth the pains, *CP1869:*chance were worth the
pains *1889a:*pains!   843| MS:So, try conclusions,—at *P1869:*Ride, try <> what's
worse *CP1869:*To try conclusions!—at *1872:*We'd try <> what worse   844| MS:this
the red machine <> talk, *P1869:*this Mannaia machine *CP1869:*this Mannaia-machine
*1872:*talk   845| MS:push a little § last two words crossed out and replaced above by
three words § an inch the nearer,—oh, fool *P1869:*nearer me? Fool   848| MS:rhetoric,
*P1869:*rhetoric!   850| MS:I make <> fifty fold *P1869:*One makes <> fifty-fold
851| MS:place the wise like you *1872:*place men wise like you,   853| MS:That buffets
<> vain— *P1869:*Would buffet <> vain.   855| MS:Of <> that ought to *P1869:*O'

That's my success! Is it not folly, now,
To say with folk, "A plausible defence—
We see through notwithstanding, and reject?"
Reject the plausible they do, these fools,
860   Who never even make pretence to show
One point beyond its plausibility
In favour of the best belief they hold!
"Saint Somebody-or-other raised the dead:"
Did he? How do you come to know as much?
865   "Know it, what need? The story's plausible,
Avouched for by a martyrologist,
And why should good men sup on cheese and leeks
On such a saint's day, if there were no saint?"
I praise the wisdom of these fools, and straight
870   Tell them my story—"plausible, but false!"
False, to be sure! What else can story be
That runs—a young wife tired of an old spouse,
Found a priest whom she fled away with,—both
Took their full pleasure in the two-days' flight,
875   Which a grey-headed greyer-hearted pair,
(Whose best boast was, their life had been a lie)
Helped for the love they bore all liars. Oh,
Here incredulity begins! Indeed?
Allow then, were no one point strictly true,
880   There's that i' the tale might seem like truth at least
To the unlucky husband,—jaundiced patch—
Jealousy maddens people, why not him?
Say, he was maddened, so forgivable!

<> that means to   856| MS:success. Is *P1869:*success! Is   857| MS:folks
*1889a:*folk   858| MS:notwithstanding and reject." *P1869:*notwithstanding, and
reject?"   859| MS:fools *P1869:*fools,   860| MS:even made pretense *P1869:*even
make pretence   863| MS:Saint Somebody or other <> dead: *P1869:*"Saint
Somebody-or-other <> dead:"   865| MS:Know *P1869:*"Know   868–70| MS:day if
there was no saint?/ I tell my *P1869:*day, if there were no saint?"/ I praise the wisdom of
these fools, and straight/ Tell them my   874| MS:Taking their pleasure <> two-days
*P1869:*Took their full pleasure <> two-days' *1872:*two-day's *1889a:*two-days'
875| MS:Helped by § last two words crossed out and replaced above by three words § Which
a grey headed greyer hearted pair *P1869:*grey-headed greyer-hearted pair,
876| MS:Whose <> was their <> lie, *CP1869:*(Whose <> was, their <> lie)
877| MS:liars—Oh, *P1869:*liars. Oh,   880| MS:in *P1869:*i'   881| MS:patch,—
*1889a:*patch—   883| MS:maddened and forgiveable! *P1869:*maddened, so, forgivable!

194

Humanity pleads that though the wife were true,
885 The priest true, and the pair of liars true,
They might seem false to one man in the world!
A thousand gnats make up a serpent's sting,
And many sly soft stimulants to wrath
Compose a formidable wrong at last
890 That gets called easily by some one name
Not applicable to the single parts,
And so draws down a general revenge,
Excessive if you take crime, fault by fault.
Jealousy! I have known a score of plays,
895 Were listened to and laughed at in my time
As like the everyday-life on all sides,
Wherein the husband, mad as a March hare,
Suspected all the world contrived his shame.
What did the wife? The wife kissed both eyes blind,
900 Explained away ambiguous circumstance,
And while she held him captive by the hand,
Crowned his head,—you know what's the mockery,—
By half her body behind the curtain. That's
Nature now! That's the subject of a piece
905 I saw in Vallombrosa Convent, made
Expressly to teach men what marriage was!
But say "Just so did I misapprehend,
Imagine she deceived me to my face,"
And that's pretence too easily seen through!

---

*1872:*so forgivable!   885| MS:And the priest   *P1869:*The priest   888| MS:As many
*P1869:*And many   889| MS:last,   *1889a:*last   891| MS:the thousand parts,
*P1869:*the single parts,   892| MS:draw   *P1869:*draws   893| MS:§ word crossed out
illegibly and replaced above by § Excessive <> take them fault by   *P1869:*take crime, fault
by   894| MS:plays   *P1869:*plays,   896| MS:everyday life   *P1869:*everyday-life
897| MS:a march   *P1869:*a March   898| MS:shame;   *1872:*shame.   899| MS:On
the other hand, § last four words and comma crossed out and replaced above by four words
and question mark § What did the wife? the   *P1869:*wife? The   900| MS:circumstances,
*P1869:*circumstance,   902| MS:Made his head, you <> mockery,   *P1869:*Crowned his
head,—you <> mockery,—   906| MS:was.   *P1869:*was!   907| MS:say—and just
so I misapprehend—   *P1869:*say "And just so did I misapprehend!"   *CP1869:*say "Just
*1872:*misapprehend,   908| MS:Or just so she <> face   *P1869:*Or "Just <> face!"
*1872:*Imagine she   *1889a:*face,"   909| MS:That's a pretense   *P1869:*And that's

910 All those eyes of all husbands in all plays,
At stare like one expanded peacock-tail,
Are laughed at for pretending to be keen
While horn-blind: but the moment I step forth—
Oh, I must needs o' the sudden prove a lynx
915 And look the heart, that stone-wall, through and through!
Such an eye, God's may be,—not yours nor mine.

Yes, presently . . . what hour is fleeting now?
When you cut earth away from under me,
I shall be left alone with, pushed beneath
920 Some such an apparitional dread orb
As the eye of God, since such an eye there glares:
I fancy it go filling up the void
Above my mote-self it devours, or what
Proves—wrath, immensity wreaks on nothingness.
925 Just how I felt once, couching through the dark,
Hard by Vittiano; young I was, and gay,
And wanting to trap fieldfares: first a spark
Tipped a bent, as a mere dew-globule might
Any stiff grass-stalk on the meadow,—this
930 Grew fiercer, flamed out full, and proved the sun.
What do I want with proverbs, precepts here?
Away with man! What shall I say to God?

---

pretence   910| MS:plays *P1869:*plays,   911| MS:peacock-tail
*P1869:*peacock-tail,   912| MS:You laugh *P1869:*Are laughed
913| MS:horn-blind,—but <> forth *P1869:*horn-blind: but <> forth—
914| MS:prove the lynx *P1869:*prove a lynx   915| MS:That looks the stone wall
through and through,—read hearts! *P1869:*And look the heart, that stone-wall, through
and through!   916-17| MS:§ no ¶ § *P1869:*§ ¶ §   917| MS:Yes, in the next § last
three words crossed out and replaced above by § presently . . what *1889a:*presently . . .
what   918| MS:me *P1869:*me,   920-22| MS:dread eye § crossed out and
replaced by § orb/ I fancy may go <> the sky § crossed out and replaced by § void
*P1869:*orb;/ I fancy it go *1872:*orb/ As the eye of God, since such an eye there glares:/I
924| MS:Immensity may do for § last two words crossed out and replaced above by two
words § wreak on *P1869:*Immensity please to wreak *CP1869:*Immensity please wreak
*1872:*Proves wrath, immensity wreaks *1889a:*Proves—wrath   925| MS:Just so I <>
dark *P1869:*dark, *1872:*Just how I   926| MS:by Vittiano, young and gay § last two
words crossed out § *P1869:*by Vittiano; young   927| MS:And watched § crossed out
and replaced above by § wanting to catch § crossed out and replaced above by two words §
trap the § crossed out § feldfares; first *P1869:*fieldfares: first   928| MS:bent, like
§ crossed out and replaced above by § as <> dew globule *P1869:*dew-globule
931| MS:§ squeezed between lines 930-32 §   932| MS:with you. What *P1869:*with

This, if I find the tongue and keep the mind—
"Do Thou wipe out the being of me, and smear
935　This soul from off Thy white of things, I blot!
I am one huge and sheer mistake,—whose fault?
Not mine at least, who did not make myself!"
Someone declares my wife excused me so!
Perhaps she knew what argument to use.
940　Grind your teeth, Cardinal: Abate, writhe!
What else am I to cry out in my rage,
Unable to repent one particle
O' the past? Oh, how I wish some cold wise man
Would dig beneath the surface which you scrape,
945　Deal with the depths, pronounce on my desert
Groundedly! I want simple sober sense,
That asks, before it finishes with a dog,
Who taught the dog that trick you hang him for?
You both persist to call that act a crime,
950　Which sense would call . . . yes, I maintain it, Sirs, . . .
A blunder! At the worst, I stood in doubt
On cross-road, took one path of many paths:
It leads to the red thing, we all see now,
But nobody saw at first: one primrose-patch
955　In bank, one singing-bird in bush, the less,
Had warned me from such wayfare: let me prove!

---

man! What　　　934–36| MS:Do Thou § last two words added in margin § Wipe < > me,
and § added above line § smear § slash indicating end of line § this § altered to § This soul
§ indication that line continues on next line § From off the white of things, it blots,— § line
936 crowded into small space at end of 935 § I am one huge and sheer mistake,—whose fault?
P1869:"Do < > wipe < > / < > soul from off Thy white of things, I blot!/ I
937–40| MS:mine, at < > / Gnash your < > Cardinal, contort your brow,—　P1869:mine at
< > / Some one said that my wife excused me so!/ Perhaps she knew what argument to
use:/Grind your < > Cardinal, Abate, writhe!　CP1869:/ Someone declares my < > / < >
use./ Grind　1889a:/ / / < > teeth, Cardinal: Abate　　　941|　MS:rage　P1869:rage,
946|　MS:Groundedly,—I　CP1869:Groundedly! I　　　947|　MS:That says § crossed out
and replaced above by § asks　　　949|　MS:crime　CP1869:crime,　　　950|　MS:He would
call . . yes, I do assure you, Sirs, . . CP1869:Sense would　1889a:Which sense would call
. . . yes, I maintain it, Sirs, . . .　　　951|　MS:blunder,—at　P1869:blunder! At
952|　MS:cross road < > paths,—　P1869:paths:—　CP1869:paths:　1869:cross-road
954|　MS:nobody at first saw one primrose　1872:saw: one　1889a:nobody saw at first: one
primrose-patch　　　955|　MS:The less in § altered to § In bank or § over illegible word §
singing-bird in bush, § marks indicate the less to be placed at end of line §　P1869:less,
CP1869:bank, one　　　956|　MS:To warn of the § last two words crossed out and replaced
above by § from wayfarer § altered to § wayfare < > prove you that!　1872:Had warned me

Put me back to the cross-road, start afresh!
Advise me when I take the first false step!
Give me my wife: how should I use my wife,
960   Love her or hate her? Prompt my action now!
There she is, there she stands alive and pale,
The thirteen-years'-old child, with milk for blood,
Pompilia Comparini, as at first,
Which first is only four brief years ago!
965   I stand too in the little ground-floor room
O' the father's house at Via Vittoria: see!
Her so-called mother,—one arm round the waist
O' the child to keep her from the toys, let fall
At wonder I can live yet look so grim,—
970   Ushers her in, with deprecating wave
Of the other,—and she fronts me loose at last,
Held only by the mother's finger-tip.
Struck dumb,—for she was white enough before!—
She eyes me with those frightened balls of black,
975   As heifer—the old simile comes pat—
Eyes tremblingly the altar and the priest.
The amazed look, all one insuppressive prayer,—
Might she but breathe, set free as heretofore,
Have this cup leave her lips unblistered, bear
980   Any cross anywhither anyhow,
So but alone, so but apart from me!

---

from such wayfare, let me prove! *1889a:*wayfare: let   957| MS:afresh,—
*P1869:*afresh!—   *CP1869:*afresh!   959| MS:I have a wife <> use this wife, *P1869:*Give
me my wife <> use my wife,   961| MS:she stands, there she is alive *1872:*she is, there
she stands alive   964| MS:ago. *P1869:*ago!   965| MS:ground floor
room, *P1869:*ground-floor room   966| MS:At Via Vittoria, of the father's house: see—
§ transposed to read § Of the father's house at Via Vittoria: see—   *P1869:*O' the <>
see!   967| MS:mother, one *P1869:*mother,—one   968–70| MS:Of the <> toys let
fall,/ Ushers her in with *P1869:*O' the <> toys—let fall,/ At the wonder I can live yet look
so grim,—/ Ushers her in, with *CP1869:*/ At wonder <> / Ushers *1872:*toys, let fall
971| MS:other,—there she <> loose, at large, *1872:*other,—and she <> loose at last,
972| MS:finger-tip: *P1869:*finger-tip— *1872:*finger-tip.   973| MS:dumb—for <>
before— *P1869:*dumb, for <> before! *1889a:*dumb,—for <> before!—
974| MS:black— *P1869:*black *CP1869:*black,   975| MS:pat *P1869:*pat—
976| MS:priest— *P1869:*priest: *1872:*priest.   977| MS:look all <> prayer
*P1869:*look, all <> prayer,—   978| MS:but be set *1889a:*but breathe, set
980| MS:anyhow *P1869:*anyhow,   981| MS:Only alone, only apart *P1869:*So but

You are touched? So am I, quite otherwise,
If 'tis with pity. I resent my wrong,
Being a man: I only show man's soul
985 Through man's flesh: she sees mine, it strikes her thus!
Is that attractive? To a youth perhaps—
Calf-creature, one-part boy to three-parts girl,
To whom it is a flattering novelty
That he, men use to motion from their path,
990 Can thus impose, thus terrify in turn
A chit whose terror shall be changed apace
To bliss unbearable when grace and glow,
Prowess and pride descend the throne and touch
Esther in all that pretty tremble, cured
995 By the dove o' the sceptre! But myself am old,
O' the wane at least, in all things: what do you say
To her who frankly thus confirms my doubt?
I am past the prime, I scare the woman-world,
Done-with that way: you like this piece of news?
1000 A little saucy rose-bud minx can strike
Death-damp into the breast of doughty king
Though 'twere French Louis,—soul I understand,—
Saying, by gesture of repugnance, just
"Sire, you are regal, puissant and so forth,
1005 But—young you have been, are not, nor will be!"
In vain the mother nods, winks, bustles up,
"Count, girls incline to mature worth like you!
As for Pompilia, what's flesh, fish, or fowl

---

alone, so but apart   982| MS:touched,—so am I, but § crossed out and replaced above
by § quite   P1869:touched? So   983| MS:pity: I   P1869:pity. I   984| MS:man: we
only   1872:man: I only   985| MS:flesh, she <> thus: CP1869:thus!   1872:flesh: she
986| MS:perhaps   P1869:perhaps—   987| MS:Calf-creature three parts girl to one part
boy: § transposed to § Calf-creature one part boy to three parts girl   P1869:Calf-creature,
one-part boy to three-parts girl,   992| MS:when, grace   1889a:when grace
995| MS:on the sceptre: but   P1869:o' the sceptre! But   996| MS:On <> least in
P1869:O' <> least, in   997| MS:doubt,   P1869:doubt?   998| MS:past the § over
illegible word §   999| MS:Done with   CP1869:Done-with   1000| MS:Sweet sir,
§ last two words and comma crossed out § a § altered to § A <> saucy rose-bud § added
above line §   1003| MS:by the gesture   CP1869:by gesture   1005| MS:But young—
you <> be."   P1869:But—young <> be!"   1006| MS:up   1889a:up,
1008| MS:for Pompilia, show § crossed out and replaced above by § what's <> fish or

199

To one who apprehends no difference,
1010 And would accept you even were you old
As you are . . . youngish by her father's side?
Trim but your beard a little, thin your bush
Of eyebrow; and for presence, portliness,
And decent gravity, you beat a boy!"
1015 Deceive yourself one minute, if you may,
In presence of the child that so loves age,
Whose neck writhes, cords itself against your kiss,
Whose hand you wring stark, rigid with despair!
Well, I resent this; I am young in soul,
1020 Nor old in body,—thews and sinews here,—
Though the vile surface be not smooth as once,—
Far beyond that first wheelwork which went wrong
Through the untempered iron ere 'twas proof:
I am the wrought man worth ten times the crude,
1025 Would woman see what this declines to see,
Declines to say "I see,"—the officious word
That makes the thing, pricks on the soul to shoot
New fire into the half-used cinder, flesh!
Therefore 'tis she begins with wronging me,
1030 Who cannot but begin with hating her.
Our marriage follows: there she stands again!
Why do I laugh? Why, in the very gripe
O' the jaws of death's gigantic skull, do I

*1889a:*fish, or   1011| MS:are . . youngish <> side,   *P1869:*side?   *1889a:*are . . .
youngish   1013| MS:eyebrow, and <> portliness   *P1869:*eyebrow; and
*1889a:*portliness,   1014| MS:gravity you   *P1869:*gravity, you   1015| MS:Deceive
you for a second if you may   *CP1869:*second, if you may,   *1889a:*Deceive yourself one
minute, if   1016| MS:of Pompilia that loves age   *P1869:*of the child that so loves age,
1018| MS:Whose hand you wring § last four words added in margin § Stark § altered to §
stark <> despair. at what shall § last three words crossed out §   *P1869:*despair!
1022| MS:With ten times § three words crossed out and replaced above by two words § Far
beyond the old § crossed out and replaced above by § first wheelwork that went
*1872:*beyond that <> wheelwork which went   1024| MS:am the steel man § last three
words added above line § <> the man I was § replaced above by § used before § last five
words crossed out and replaced above by word, comma and dash § crude,—   *1889a:*the
wrought man <> crude,   1025| MS:If a woman saw what   *P1869:*Would woman see
what   1026| MS:say " 'Tis there," the   *P1869:*say "I see,"—the   1028| MS:cinder
§ over illegible word § , flesh.   *CP1869:*flesh!   1031| MS:there we stand   *1872:*there she
stands   1033| MS:Of <> skull does he § last two words crossed out and replaced above

Grin back his grin, make sport of my own pangs?
1035 Why from each clashing of his molars, ground
To make the devil bread from out my grist,
Leaps out a spark of mirth, a hellish toy?
Take notice we are lovers in a church,
Waiting the sacrament to make us one
1040 And happy! Just as bid, she bears herself,
Comes and kneels, rises, speaks, is silent,—goes:
So have I brought my horse, by word and blow,
To stand stock-still and front the fire he dreads.
How can I other than remember this,
1045 Resent the very obedience? Gain thereby?
Yes, I do gain my end and have my will,—
Thanks to whom? When the mother speaks the word,
She obeys it—even to enduring me!
There had been compensation in revolt—
1050 Revolt's to quell: but martyrdom rehearsed,
But predetermined saintship for the sake
O' the mother?—"Go!" thought I, "we meet again!"
Pass the next weeks of dumb contented death,
She lives,—wakes up, installed in house and home,
1055 Is mine, mine all day-long, all night-long mine.
Good folk begin at me with open mouth
"Now, at least, reconcile the child to life!
Study and make her love . . . that is, endure
The . . . hem! the . . . all of you though somewhat old,

by two words § do I   *P1869:*O'   *1872:*skull, do   1034| MS:So I § last two words crossed
out § grin § altered to § Grin   1035| MS:from each § added above line §
1038| MS:church   *CP1869:*church,   1041| MS:Comes and sits, § last three words and
comma added in margin § Rises   *P1869:*sits, rises   *CP1869:*and kneels, rises
1043| MS:stock still   *P1869:*stock-still   1047| MS:word   *P1869:*word,
1048| MS:obeys—even to supporting me!   *P1869:*obeys it—even to enduring me!
1050| MS:Left me to   *P1869:*Revolt's to   1052| MS:Of the mother!—"Go   *P1869:*O'
the mother?—"Go   1054| MS:She lives,— § word, comma and dash added above line §
<> up, is § comma and word crossed out § installed   *P1869:*up, installed
1055| MS:day long <> night long mine   *P1869:*mine.   *CP1869:*day-long <> night-long
1056| MS:folks   *1889a:*folk   1057| MS:life,   *CP1869:*life!   1058| MS:love
. . that   *1889a:*love . . . that   1059| MS:The . . hem! the . . all <> old

1060 Till it amount to something, in her eye,
As good as love, better a thousand times,—
Since nature helps the woman in such strait,
Makes passiveness her pleasure: failing which,
What if you give up boy-and-girl-fools'-play
1065 And go on to wise friendship all at once?
Those boys and girls kiss themselves cold, you know,
Toy themselves tired and slink aside full soon
To friendship, as they name satiety:
Thither go you and wait their coming!" Thanks,
1070 Considerate advisers,—but, fair play!
Had you and I, friends, started fair at first,
We, keeping fair, might reach it, neck by neck,
This blessed goal, whenever fate so please:
But why am I to miss the daisied mile
1075 The course begins with, why obtain the dust
Of the end precisely at the starting-point?
Why quaff life's cup blown free of all the beads,
The bright red froth wherein our beard should steep
Before our mouth essay the black o' the wine?
1080 Foolish, the love-fit? Let me prove it such
Like you, before like you I puff things clear!
"The best's to come, no rapture but content!
Not love's first glory but a sober glow,
Not a spontaneous outburst in pure boon,
1085 So much as, gained by patience, care and toil,
Proper appreciation and esteem!"
Go preach that to your nephews, not to me
Who, tired i' the midway of my life, would stop
And take my first refreshment, pluck a rose:

*P1869:*old, *1889a:*The . . . hem! the . . . all   1064| MS:boys'-and girls'-fool's play
*P1869:*boys' and girls' fools'-play   *1872:*boy and girl   *1889a:*boy-and-girl-fools'-play
1068| MS:satiety, *P1869:*satiety: 1069| MS:And there go *P1869:*Thither go
1071| MS:Had she and I but started <> first, *CP1869:*Had you and *1889a:*and I, friends,
started <> first § emended to § first, § see Editorial Notes §   1077| MS:beads
*P1869:*beads,   1078| MS:That bright <> our § over perhaps *his* § *P1869:*The bright
1082| MS:content— *P1869:*content!   1083| MS:Not the first *1889a:*Not love's first
1084| MS:Nor a <> boon *P1869:*boon, *1889a:*Not a   1085–87| MS:as gained <>
toil,—/ Go <> nephew *P1869:*as, gained <> toil!"/ Go <> nephew *CP1869:*nephews
*1872:*as gained <> toil,/ Proper appreciation and esteem!"/ Go *1889a:*as, gained
1088| MS:in *P1869:*i'   1089| MS:refreshment in a *1889a:*refreshment, pluck a

1090   What's this coarse woolly hip, worn smooth of leaf,
      You counsel I go plant in garden-plot,
      Water with tears, manure with sweat and blood,
      In confidence the seed shall germinate
      And, for its very best, some far-off day,
1095   Grow big, and blow me out a dog-rose bell?
      Why must your nephews begin breathing spice
      O' the hundred-petalled Provence prodigy?
      Nay, more and worse,—would such my root bear rose—
      Prove really flower and favourite, not the kind
1100   That's queen, but those three leaves that make one cup
      And hold the hedge-bird's breakfast,—then indeed
      The prize though poor would pay the care and toil!
      Respect we Nature that makes least as most,
      Marvellous in the minim! But this bud,
1105   Bit through and burned black by the tempter's tooth,
      This bloom whose best grace was the slug outside
      And the wasp inside its bosom,—call you "rose"?
      Claim no immunity from a weed's fate
      For the horrible present! What you call my wife
1110   I call a nullity in female shape,
      Vapid disgust, soon to be pungent plague,
      When mixed with, made confusion and a curse
      By two abominable nondescripts,
      That father and that mother: think you see
1115   The dreadful bronze our boast, we Aretines,
      The Etruscan monster, the three-headed thing,

1090| MS:hip without a § last two words crossed out and replaced above by three words §
worn smooth of leaf *P1869:*hip, worn <> leaf,   1091| MS:garden-pot
*P1869:*garden-pot, *1889a:*garden-plot,   1094| MS:§ crowded between 1093-95 § And for
<> far off *P1869:*And, for <> far-off   1095| MS:Grow, greaten, blow <> bell—
*P1869:*Grow great in, blow <> bell? *CP1869:*Grow big, and blow   1096| MS:nephew
only § crossed out and replaced above by § begin breathe the spice *CP1869:*nephews begin
breathing spice   1097| MS:Of *P1869:*O'   1099| MS:Really the flower and favorite
*P1869:*Prove really flower and favourite   1102| MS:toil—*P1869:*toil!   1103| MS:we
nature *P1869:*we Nature   1104| MS:this frowzy bud, *P1869:*this bud,
1106| MS:bloom § added above line § <> was in § crossed out §   1107| MS:bosom, call
no rose, *P1869:*bosom,—call you "rose?" *1889a:*rose"?   1109| MS:present! What they
gave f § last two words and fragment crossed out and replaced above by three words § you
call my   1111| MS:disgust, made § crossed out and replaced above by dash and four
words § —soon to be a pungent and a § last two words crossed out § *P1869:*be pungent
1113| MS:nondescripts *P1869:*nondescripts,   1116| MS:monster and three headed

Bellerophon's foe! How name you the whole beast?
You choose to name the body from one head,
That of the simple kid which droops the eye,
¹¹²⁰ Hangs the neck and dies tenderly enough:
I rather see the griesly lion belch
Flame out i' the midst, the serpent writhe her rings,
Grafted into the common stock for tail,
And name the brute, Chimæra which I slew!
¹¹²⁵ How was there ever more to be—(concede
My wife's insipid harmless nullity)—
Dissociation from that pair of plagues—
That mother with her cunning and her cant—
The eyes with first their twinkle of conceit,
¹¹³⁰ Then, dropped to earth in mock-demureness,—now,
The smile self-satisfied from ear to ear,
Now, the prim pursed-up mouth's protruded lips,
With deferential duck, slow swing of head,
Tempting the sudden fist of man too much,—
¹¹³⁵ That owl-like screw of lid and rock of ruff!
As for the father,—Cardinal, you know,
The kind of idiot!—such are rife in Rome,
But they wear velvet commonly; good fools,
At the end of life, to furnish forth young folk
¹¹⁴⁰ Who grin and bear with imbecility:
Since the stalled ass, the joker, sheds from jaw
Corn, in the joke, for those who laugh or starve.

---

thing *P1869:*monster, the three-headed thing,   ¹¹¹⁷| MS:Bellerophon § altered to §
Bellerophon's slew § crossed out and replaced above by § foe: how *P1869:*foe! How
¹¹¹⁸| MS:chose < > head *P1869:*choose < > head,   ¹¹¹⁹| MS:eyes *P1869:*eye,
¹¹²⁰| MS:the head and *P1869:*the neck and   ¹¹²²| MS:midst, and where § last two
words crossed out § the   ¹¹²⁴| MS:brute, Chimæra < > slew. *P1869:*brute, Chimæra,
which I slew! *1889a:*brute, Chimæra which   ¹¹²⁵| MS:be . . concede *P1869:*be—
(concede   ¹¹²⁶| MS:nullity . . *P1869:*nullity)—   ¹¹³⁰| MS:Then the § crossed
out and replaced above by § dropped < > now *P1869:*Then, dropped < > now,
¹¹³²| MS:Now the < > lips *P1869:*Now, the < > lips,   ¹¹³³| MS:head,—
*P1869:*head,   ¹¹³⁴| MS:much, *CP1869:*much,—   ¹¹³⁶| MS:know *P1869:*know,
¹¹³⁷| MS:idiot,—rife are such in *CP1869:*idiot!—rife *1872:*idot § obvious printer's error §
!—such are rife in *1889a:*idiot   ¹¹³⁸| MS:commonly, rich fools *P1869:*commonly,
such fools, *1872:*commonly; good fools,   ¹¹³⁹| MS:life, fit to help poor young
*P1869:*life, can furnish forth young *1872:*life, to furnish   ¹¹⁴⁰| MS:imbecility
*P1869:*imbecility, *1872:*imbecility: ¹¹⁴¹| MS:Since § over illegible erasure § < >
sheds thereby § crossed out and replaced above by § from   ¹¹⁴²| MS:laugh and starve:

But what say we to the same solemn beast
Wagging his ears and wishful of our pat,
1145 When turned, with holes in hide and bones laid bare,
To forage for himself i' the waste o' the world,
Sir Dignity i' the dumps? Pat him? We drub
Self-knowledge, rather, into frowzy pate,
Teach Pietro to get trappings or go hang!
1150 Fancy this quondam oracle in vogue
At Via Vittoria, this personified
Authority when time was,—Pantaloon
Flaunting his tom-fool tawdry just the same
As if Ash-Wednesday were mid-Carnival!
1155 That's the extreme and unforgiveable
Of sins, as I account such. Have you stooped
For your own ends to bestialize yourself
By flattery of a fellow of this stamp?
The ends obtained or else shown out of reach,
1160 He goes on, takes the flattery for pure truth,—
"You love, and honour me, of course: what next?"
What, but the trifle of the stabbing, friend?—
Which taught you how one worships when the shrine
Has lost the relic that we bent before.
1165 Angry! And how could I be otherwise?
'Tis plain: this pair of old pretentious fools
Meant to fool me: it happens, I fooled them.
Why could not these who sought to buy and sell
Me,—when they found themselves were bought and sold,

---

*P1869:*laugh or starve: *1872:*starve. ¹¹⁴⁴| MS:pat *CP1869:*pat, ¹¹⁴⁵| MS:with
hide in holes and *1872:*with holes in hide and ¹¹⁴⁷| MS:the Dumps! Pat *P1869:*the
dumps? Pat ¹¹⁴⁹| MS:And § in margin § Teach § altered to § teach the Pietro to go
trapped or hang. *P1869:*to get trapped or hang! *CP1869:*Teach Pietro to get trappings or
go hang! ¹¹⁵²| MS:was,—this Pantaloon *P1869:*was,—Pantaloon
¹¹⁵³| MS:Flaunting § over illegible fragment § < > just § written over illegible word,
perhaps *all* § ¹¹⁵⁴| MS:if Ash wednesday *P1869:*if Ash-Wednesday
¹¹⁵⁵| MS:Thats *P1869:*That's ¹¹⁵⁶| MS:sins as < > such; have *CP1869:*sins, as < >
such. Have ¹¹⁵⁹| MS:obtained, or else clear out *P1869:*else shown out
*1889a:*obtained or ¹¹⁶¹| MS:love and *1872:*love, and ¹¹⁶²| MS:What but < >
friend, *P1869:*What, but < > friend?— ¹¹⁶³| MS:That taught *CP1869:*Which
taught ¹¹⁶⁵| MS:Angry? And *1872:*Angry! And ¹¹⁶⁹| MS:sold *P1869:*sold,

¹¹⁷⁰ Make up their mind to the proved rule of right,
Be chattel and not chapman any more?
Miscalculation has its consequence;
But when the shepherd crooks a sheep-like thing
And meaning to get wool, dislodges fleece
¹¹⁷⁵ And finds the veritable wolf beneath,
(How that staunch image serves at every turn!)
Does he, by way of being politic,
Pluck the first whisker grimly visible?
Or rather grow in a trice all gratitude,
¹¹⁸⁰ Protest this sort-of-what-one-might-name sheep
Beats the old other curly-coated kind,
And shall share board and bed, if so it deign,
With its discoverer, like a royal ram?
Ay, thus, with chattering teeth and knocking knees,
¹¹⁸⁵ Would wisdom treat the adventure! these, forsooth,
Tried whisker-plucking, and so found what trap
The whisker kept perdue, two rows of teeth—
Sharp, as too late the prying fingers felt.
What would you have? The fools transgress, the fools
¹¹⁹⁰ Forthwith receive appropriate punishment:
They first insult me, I return the blow,
There follows noise enough: four hubbub months,
Now hue and cry, now whimpering and wail—
A perfect goose-yard cackle of complaint
¹¹⁹⁵ Because I do not gild the geese their oats,—
I have enough of noise, ope wicket wide,
Sweep out the couple to go whine elsewhere,
Frightened a little, hurt in no respect,
And am just taking thought to breathe again,
¹²⁰⁰ Taste the sweet sudden silence all about,
When, there they raise it, the old noise I know,

---

^{1170|} MS:right *P1869:*right, ^{1174|} MS:to pluck § crossed out and replaced above by §
get ^{1176|} MS:(How still § crossed out § that staunch § added above line §
^{1178|} MS:visible?— *1872:*visible? ^{1184|} MS:thus with <> knees *P1869:*thus, with
<> knees, ^{1185|} MS:adventure: these *1872:*adventure! these ^{1188|} MS:as the
prying fingers felt too late. § transposed to § as too late the prying fingers felt.
^{1192|} MS:four hubbub § added above line § ^{1194|} MS:gooseyard *P1869:*goose-yard
^{1195|} MS:Because I did § crossed out and replaced above by § do ^{1196|} MS:oped
§ altered to § ope <> wide *CP1869:*wide, ^{1199|} MS:And am § written over illegible
word § <> breathe once more, *P1869:*breathe again, ^{1201|} MS:they are at it <>

At Rome i' the distance! "What, begun once more?
Whine on, wail ever, 'tis the loser's right!"
But eh, what sort of voice grows on the wind?
1205 Triumph it sounds and no complaint at all!
And triumph it is. My boast was premature:
The creatures, I turned forth, clapped wing and crew
Fighting-cock-fashion,—they had filched a pearl
From dung-heap, and might boast with cause enough!
1210 I was defrauded of all bargained for:
You know, the Pope knows, not a soul but knows
My dowry was derision, my gain—muck,
My wife, (the Church declared my flesh and blood)
The nameless bastard of a common whore:
1215 My old name turned henceforth to . . . shall I say
"He that received the ordure in his face"?
And they who planned this wrong, performed this wrong,
And then revealed this wrong to the wide world,—
Rounded myself in the ears with my own wrong,—
1220 Why, these were (note hell's lucky malice, now!)
These were just they who, they alone, could act
And publish and proclaim their infamy,
Secure that men would in a breath believe
Compassionate and pardon them,—for why?
1225 They plainly were too stupid to invent,
Too simple to distinguish wrong from right,—
Inconscious agents they, the silly-sooth,

---

know *P1869:*know, *1872:*they raise it   1202| MS:in < > begun again? *P1869:*begun
once more? *CP1869:*i'   1203| MS:losers' right!" § quotation marks crossed out §
*P1869:*loser's right!"   1206| MS:it was! My *P1869:*it is! My *1872:*is. My
1207| MS:creatures I < > forth clapped *P1869:*creatures, I < > forth, clapped
1209| MS:From the dung heap < > boast before the w § last two words and fragment crossed
out and replaced above by three words and period § with cause enough. *P1869:*From dung-
heap < > enough!   1210| MS:for,— *1872:*for: 1211| MS:soul disputes
*P1869:*soul but knows   1213| MS:wife, the < > blood, *P1869:*wife, (the < > blood,)
*CP1869:*blood)   1215| MS:to . . shall *1889a:*to . . . shall   1216| MS:face"?
*P1869:*face?" § emended to § face"? see Editorial Notes §   1220| MS:were . . note < >
now! . . *1872:*were (note < > now!)   1221| MS:they, and they *1872:*they who, they
1222| MS:publish in this wise their infamy *CP1869:*infamy, *1872:*publish and proclaim
their   1227| MS:Mere passive § last two words crossed out and replaced above by §

Of heaven's retributive justice on the strong
Proud cunning violent oppressor—me!
1230 Follow them to their fate and help your best,
You Rome, Arezzo, foes called friends of me,
They gave the good long laugh to, at my cost!
Defray your share o' the cost, since you partook
The entertainment! Do!—assured the while,
1235 That not one stab, I dealt to right and left,
But went the deeper for a fancy—this—
That each might do me two-fold service, find
A friend's face at the bottom of each wound,
And scratch its smirk a little!
                                            Panciatichi!
1240 There's a report at Florence,—is it true?—
That when your relative the Cardinal
Built, only the other day, that barrack-bulk,
The palace in Via Larga, someone picked
From out the street a saucy quip enough
1245 That fell there from its day's flight through the town,
About the flat front and the windows wide
And bulging heap of cornice,—hitched the joke
Into a sonnet, signed his name thereto,
And forthwith pinned on post the pleasantry:
1250 For which he's at the galleys, rowing now
Up to his waist in water,—just because
Panciatic and *lymphatic* rhymed so pat!
I hope, Sir, those who passed this joke on me
Were not unduly punished? What say you,

Inconscious   1231| MS:foes § written over illegible erasure § < > of mine,   1889a:of
me,   1232| MS:to at   1872:to, at   1233| MS:of the cost since   P1869:o'   1872:cost,
since   1234| MS:entertainment—Do! assured the while   P1869:entertainment!
Do!— assured the while,   1235| MS:stab that I < > left   P1869:stab,
I < > left,   1239| MS:little. § ¶ § Panciatichi!   P1869:little! § ¶ § Panciatichi!
1242| MS:barrack-bulk   P1869:barrack-bulk,   1245| MS:days   P1869:day's
1247| MS:And ugly heap   1872:And bulgeing heap   1889a:bulging   1248| MS:thereto
P1869:thereto,   1249| MS:pleasantry,   P1869:pleasantry.   1872:pleasantry:
1250| MS:gallies § altered to § galleys   1252| MS:Panciatic and lymphatic < > pat:
P1869:Panciatic and lymphatic   1872:pat!   1254| MS:you   P1869:you,

208

Prince of the Church, my patron? Nay, indeed,
I shall not dare insult your wits so much
As think this problem difficult to solve.
This Pietro and Violante then, I say,
These two ambiguous insects, changing name
1260 And nature with the season's warmth or chill,—
Now, grovelled, grubbing toiling moiling ants,
A very synonym of thrift and peace,—
Anon, with lusty June to prick their heart,
Soared i' the air, winged flies for more offence,
1265 Circled me, buzzed me deaf and stung me blind,
And stunk me dead with fetor in the face
Until I stopped the nuisance: there's my crime!
Pity I did not suffer them subside
Into some further shape and final form
1270 Of execrable life? My masters, no!
I, by one blow, wisely cut short at once
Them and their transformations of disgust,
In the snug little Villa out of hand.
"Grant me confession, give bare time for that!"—
1275 Shouted the sinner till his mouth was stopped.
His life confessed!—that was enough for me,
Who came to see that he did penance. 'S death!
Here's a coil raised, a pother and for what?
Because strength, being provoked by weakness, fought
1280 And conquered,—the world never heard the like!
Pah, how I spend my breath on them, as if
'Twas their fate troubled me, too hard to range

1255| MS:my Patron? No indeed! *P1869:*patron? Nay, indeed! *1872:*indeed,
1257| MS:solve! *1889a:*solve.   1258| MS:and his Violante, then,   *P1869:*and Violante,
then, I say,   *1872:*and Violante then   1259| MS:Were two <> insects changing
*P1869:*These two <> insects, changing   1260| MS:chill,   *P1869:*chill,—
1261| MS:grovelling § altered to § grovelled <> ants   *P1869:*ants,   1262| MS:very
metaphor § crossed out and replaced above by § synonym   1265| MS:me, § followed by
illegible erasure §   1271| MS:blow wisely   *P1869:*blow, wisely   1272| MS:disgust
*1872:*disgust,   1274| MS:confession, the bare <> that!"   *P1869:*confession, give bare
<> that!"—   1275| MS:stopped: *P1869:*stopped.   1276| MS:I had not waited
§ last four words crossed out and replaced above by three words and colon § His life
confessed: that <> me   *P1869:*confessed!—that <> me,   1282| MS:me, was hard

Among the right and fit and proper things!

Ay, but Pompilia,—I await your word,—
¹²⁸⁵ She, unimpeached of crime, unimplicate
In folly, one of alien blood to these
I punish, why extend my claim, exact
Her portion of the penalty? Yes, friends,
I go too fast: the orator's at fault:
¹²⁹⁰ Yes, ere I lay her, with your leave, by them
As she was laid at San Lorenzo late,
I ought to step back, lead you by degrees,
Recounting at each step some fresh offence,
Up to the red bed,—never fear, I will!
¹²⁹⁵ Gaze at her, where I place her, to begin,
Confound me with her gentleness and worth!
The horrible pair have fled and left her now,
She has her husband for her sole concern:
His wife, the woman fashioned for his help,
¹³⁰⁰ Flesh of his flesh, bone of his bone, the bride
To groom as is the Church and Spouse to Christ:
There she stands in his presence: "Thy desire
Shall be to the husband, o'er thee shall he rule!"
—"Pompilia, who declare that you love God,
¹³⁰⁵ You know who said that: then, desire my love,
Yield me contentment and be ruled aright!"
She sits up, she lies down, she comes and goes,
Kneels at the couch-side, overleans the sill
O' the window, cold and pale and mute as stone,
¹³¹⁰ Strong as stone also. "Well, are they not fled?
Am I not left, am I not one for all?
Speak a word, drop a tear, detach a glance,

---

*P1869:*me, too hard   ¹²⁹²| MS:lead her by   *1872:*lead you by   ¹²⁹⁵| MS:her where
you place her to begin   *P1869:*her, where <> her, to begin,   *1872:*where I place
¹²⁹⁶| MS:worth: *P1869:*worth!   ¹²⁹⁸| MS:concern,   *1872:*concern:
¹³⁰¹| MS:To the groom <> Church, the Spouse   *P1869:*the Church and
Spouse   *CP1869:*To groom   *1889a:*and Spouse to Christ: ¹³⁰²| MS:presence,— "Thy
§ written over illegible word, perhaps *her* §   *1872:*presence: "Thy   ^{1303–5}| MS:rule"/
You   *P1869:*rule!"/—"Pompilia, who declare that you love God,/ You
¹³⁰⁶| MS:aright!   *P1869:*aright!"   ¹³⁰⁹| MS:Of   *P1869:*O'   ¹³¹⁰| MS:also: well,

Bless me or curse me of your own accord!
Is it the ceiling only wants your soul,
¹³¹⁵ Is worth your eyes?" And then the eyes descend,
And do look at me. Is it at the meal?
"Speak!" she obeys, "Be silent!" she obeys,
Counting the minutes till I cry "Depart,"
As brood-bird when you saunter past her eggs.
¹³²⁰ Departs she? just the same through door and wall
I see the same stone strength of white despair.
And all this will be never otherwise!
Before, the parents' presence lent her life:
She could play off her sex's armoury,
¹³²⁵ Entreat, reproach, be female to my male,
Try all the shrieking doubles of the hare,
Go clamour to the Commissary, bid
The Archbishop hold my hands and stop my tongue,
And yield fair sport so: but the tactics change,
¹³³⁰ The hare stands stock-still to enrage the hound!
Since that day when she learned she was no child
Of those she thought her parents,—that their trick
Had tricked me whom she thought sole trickster late,—
Why, I suppose she said within herself
¹³³⁵ "Then, no more struggle for my parents' sake!
And, for my own sake, why needs struggle be?"
But is there no third party to the pact?
What of her husband's relish or dislike
For this new game of giving up the game,
¹³⁴⁰ This worst offence of not offending more?

---

are not they fled? *P1869:*also. "Well *CP1869:*are they not fled? ¹³¹⁵| MS:eyes? And
<> descend *P1869:*eyes?" And *1872:*descend, ¹³¹⁶| MS:me: Is *P1869:*me. Is
¹³¹⁷| MS:obeys, "be *P1869:*obeys, "Be ¹³¹⁸| MS:till I bid depart, *P1869:*till I cry
"Depart," ¹³¹⁹| MS:As the partridge § crossed out and replaced above by § brood-bird
<> eggs: *P1869:*eggs. *CP1869:*As brood-bird ¹³²⁰| MS:"Go then!"—why, all §
crossed out and replaced above by § just *P1869:*Departed, just *1889a:*Departs she? just
¹³²⁴| MS:sexes' *P1869:*sex's ¹³²⁵| MS:Intreat *1889a:*Entreat ¹³²⁹| MS:change
*P1869:*change, ¹³³⁰| MS:hound. *P1869:*hound! ¹³³²| MS:parents,—that their
§ last two words added above line § trick of theirs § last two words crossed out §
¹³³³| MS:Tricking § crossed out and replaced above by two words § Had tricked me whom
§ added above line § she supposed § crossed out and replaced above by § thought
¹³³⁵| MS:sake, *1872:*sake! ¹³³⁸| MS:husband's liking § crossed out and replaced

I'll not believe but instinct wrought in this,
Set her on to conceive and execute
The preferable plague: how sure they probe—
These jades, the sensitivest soft of man!
1345 The long black hair was wound now in a wisp,
Crowned sorrow better than the wild web late:
No more soiled dress, 'tis trimness triumphs now,
For how should malice go with negligence?
The frayed silk looked the fresher for her spite!
1350 There was an end to springing out of bed,
Praying me, with face buried on my feet,
Be hindered of my pastime,—so an end
To my rejoinder, "What, on the ground at last?
Vanquished in fight, a supplicant for life?
1355 What if I raise you? 'Ware the casting down
When next you fight me!" Then, she lay there, mine:
Now, mine she is if I please wring her neck,—
A moment of disquiet, working eyes,
Protruding tongue, a long sigh, then no more,—
1360 As if one killed the horse one could not ride!
Had I enjoined "Cut off the hair!"—why, snap
The scissors, and at once a yard or so
Had fluttered in black serpents to the floor:
But till I did enjoin it, how she combs,
1365 Uncurls and draws out to the complete length,
Plaits, places the insulting rope on head
To be an eyesore past dishevelment!
Is all done? Then sit still again and stare!
I advise—no one think to bear that look
1370 Of steady wrong, endured as steadily

---

above by § relish or § over illegible erasure §   1343| MS:plague . . . how well § crossed
out and replaced above by § sure they probe   CP1869:probe,—   1872:plague: how
1889a:probe—   1345| MS:wisp,—   1872:wisp,   1347| MS:dress, a triumph day by
day,   P1869:dress, 'tis trimness triumphs now,   1350| MS:bed   P1869:bed,
1355| MS:Why, then I'll § last three words crossed out and replaced above by three words §
What if I   1356| MS:me!" Then she lay there mine.   P1869:me!" Then she lay there,
mine: 1869:me!" Then, she   1357| MS:neck,   P1869:neck,—   1359| MS:more—
1872:more,—   1361| MS:hair!" why   P1869:hair!"—why   1365| MS:length
P1869:length,   1370| MS:wrong endured as steadily   P1869:wrong, endured as steadily,

—Through what sustainment of deluding hope?
Who is the friend i' the background that notes all?
Who may come presently and close accounts?
This self-possession to the uttermost,
1375   How does it differ in aught, save degree,
From the terrible patience of God?
                   "All which just means,
She did not love you!" Again the word is launched
And the fact fronts me! What, you try the wards
With the true key and the dead lock flies ope?
1380   No, it sticks fast and leaves you fumbling still!
You have some fifty servants, Cardinal,—
Which of them loves you? Which subordinate
But makes parade of such officiousness
That,—if there's no love prompts it,—love, the sham,
1385   Does twice the service done by love, the true?
God bless us liars, where's one touch of truth
In what we tell the world, or world tells us,
Of how we love each other? All the same,
We calculate on word and deed, nor err,—
1390   Bid such a man do such a loving act,
Sure of effect and negligent of cause,
Just as we bid a horse, with cluck of tongue,
Stretch his legs arch-wise, crouch his saddled back
To foot-reach of the stirrup—all for love,
1395   And some for memory of the smart of switch
On the inside of the foreleg—what care we?
Yet where's the bond obliges horse to man

*1889a:*steadily   1371| MS:Through   *P1869:*—Through   1372| MS:in   *P1869:*i'
1374| MS:uttermost   *P1869:*uttermost,   1375| MS:aught save degree   *P1869:*aught,
save degree,   1377| MS:you!" Now the   *P1869:*you!" Again the   1378| MS:me:
now you   *P1869:*me! What, you   1379| MS:ope!   *P1869:*ope?   1384| MS:That if
<> it, love the truth § crossed out and replaced by § sham   *P1869:*That,—if <> it,—
love, the sham,   1385| MS:love the true.   *P1869:*love, the   DC,BrU:true?   *1889:*true?
1387| MS:world, the world   *P1869:*world, or world   1388| MS:we like each <> same
*P1869:*same,   *1872:*we love each   1389| MS:err,   *P1869:*err,—   1390| MS:do such
an § crossed out and replaced above by two words § a loving   1392| MS:as you bid a
horse with <> tongue   *P1869:*as we bid a horse, with <> tongue,   1395| MS:Or
§ added in margin § And § erased §   *P1869:*And some   1396| MS:care you?   *P1869:*care

Like that which binds fast wife to husband? God
Laid down the law: gave man the brawny arm
1400 And ball of fist—woman the beardless cheek
And proper place to suffer in the side:
Since it is he can strike, let her obey!
Can she feel no love? Let her show the more,
Sham the worse, damn herself praiseworthily!
1405 Who's that soprano, Rome went mad about
Last week while I lay rotting in my straw?
The very jailer gossiped in his praise—
How,—dressed up like Armida, though a man;
And painted to look pretty, though a fright,—
1410 He still made love so that the ladies swooned,
Being an eunuch. "Ah, Rinaldo mine!
But to breathe by thee while Jove slays us both!"
All the poor bloodless creature never felt,
Si, do, re, mi, fa, squeak and squall—for what?
1415 Two gold zecchines the evening. Here's my slave,
Whose body and soul depend upon my nod,
Can't falter out the first note in the scale
For her life! Why blame me if I take the life?
All women cannot give men love, forsooth!
1420 No, nor all pullets lay the henwife eggs—
Whereat she bids them remedy the fault,
Brood on a chalk-ball: soon the nest is stocked—
Otherwise, to the plucking and the spit!
This wife of mine was of another mood—
1425 Would not begin the lie that ends with truth,
Nor feign the love that brings real love about:
Wherefore I judged, sentenced and punished her.

---

we?   1403| MS:love, let   P1869:love? Let   1404| MS:her-self praiseworthily.
P1869:herself praiseworthily!   1405| MS:soprano Rome   1872:soprano, Rome
1409| MS:pretty though a fright   P1869:pretty, though a fright,—   1412| MS:both!"
1889a:both! § emended to § both!" § see Editorial Notes §   1413| MS:felt   CP1869:felt,
1414| MS:Si, do, re, mi, fa <> what   P1869:what?   1872:Si, do, re, mi, fa
1415| MS:evening! Here's my wife,   P1869:my slave,   1872:evening. Here's
1417| MS:faulter   P1869:falter   1419| MS:love, it seems § last two words crossed out
and replaced above by § forsooth: P1869:forsooth!   1427| MS:her.   1889a:her

214

But why particularize, defend the deed?
Say that I hated her for no one cause
¹⁴³⁰ Beyond my pleasure so to do,—what then?
Just on as much incitement acts the world,
All of you! Look and like! You favour one,
Browbeat another, leave alone a third,—
Why should you master natural caprice?
¹⁴³⁵ Pure nature! Try: plant elm by ash in file;
Both unexceptionable trees enough,
They ought to overlean each other, pair
At top, and arch across the avenue
The whole path to the pleasaunce: do they so—
¹⁴⁴⁰ Or loathe, lie off abhorrent each from each?
Lay the fault elsewhere: since we must have faults,
Mine shall have been,—seeing there's ill in the end
Come of my course,—that I fare somehow worse
For the way I took: my fault . . . as God's my judge,
¹⁴⁴⁵ I see not where my fault lies, that's the truth!
I ought . . . oh, ought in my own interest
Have let the whole adventure go untried,
This chance by marriage: or else, trying it,
Ought to have turned it to account, some one
¹⁴⁵⁰ O' the hundred otherwises? Ay, my friend,
Easy to say, easy to do: step right
Now you've stepped left and stumbled on the thing,
—The red thing! Doubt I any more than you
That practice makes man perfect? Give again
¹⁴⁵⁵ The chance,—same marriage and no other wife,

DC,BrU: her. *1889:*her.   ¹⁴³²| MS:one, *1889a:*one DC,BrU:one, *1889:*one,
¹⁴³³| MS:Browbeat *P1869:*Brow-beat *1889a:*Browbeat   ¹⁴³⁵| MS:nature! Try—
§ word and dash added above line § Plant § altered to § plant *1872:*nature! Try: plant
*1889a:*nature Try DC,BrU:nature! Try *1889:*nature! Try   ¹⁴³⁸| MS:top and
*1872:*top, and   ¹⁴⁴¹| MS:elsewhere, since < > faults: *1872:*elsewhere: since < > faults,
¹⁴⁴⁴| MS:took,—my < > judge *P1869:*fault . . . . as *1872:*judge, *1889a:*took: my fault
. . . as   ¹⁴⁴⁵| MS:where the fault *1872:*where my fault   ¹⁴⁴⁶| MS:ought . . oh
*1889a:*ought . . . oh   ¹⁴⁴⁸| MS:marriage,—or *1889a:*marriage: or
¹⁴⁴⁹| MS:account some *1872:*account, some   ¹⁴⁵⁰| MS:Of < > otherwises. Ay
*P1869:*O' *CP1869:*otherwises! Ay *1869:*otherwises? Ay   ¹⁴⁵¹| MS:do,—step
*1872:*do: step   ¹⁴⁵³| MS:The red thing: doubt *P1869:*—The red thing! Doubt

215

Be sure I'll edify you! That's because
I'm practised, grown fit guide for Guido's self.
You proffered guidance,—I know, none so well,—
You laid down law and rolled decorum out,
1460   From pulpit-corner on the gospel-side,—
Wanted to make your great experience mine,
Save me the personal search and pains so: thanks!
Take your word on life's use? When I take his—
The muzzled ox that treadeth out the corn,
1465   Gone blind in padding round and round one path,—
As to the taste of green grass in the field!
What do you know o' the world that's trodden flat
And salted sterile with your daily dung,
Leavened into a lump of loathsomeness?
1470   Take your opinion of the modes of life,
The aims of life, life's triumph or defeat,
How to feel, how to scheme, and how to do
Or else leave undone? You preached long and loud
On high-days, "Take our doctrine upon trust!
1475   Into the mill-house with you! Grind our corn,
Relish our chaff, and let the green grass grow!"
I tried chaff, found I famished on such fare,
So made this mad rush at the mill-house-door,
Buried my head up to the ears in dew,
1480   Browsed on the best: for which you brain me, Sirs!
Be it so. I conceived of life that way,
And still declare—life, without absolute use
Of the actual sweet therein, is death, not life.
Give me,—pay down,—not promise, which is air,—
1485   Something that's out of life and better still,
Make sure reward, make certain punishment,

---

¹⁴⁵⁶| MS:you: that's *P1869:*you! That's   ¹⁴⁵⁷| MS:self: *P1869:*self.
¹⁴⁶⁰| MS:From the pulpit-corner *P1869:*From pulpit-corner   ¹⁴⁶²| MS:Save § over
illegible erasure §   ¹⁴⁶⁴| MS:The muzzled § added above line §   ¹⁴⁶⁵| MS:path,
*P1869:*path,—   ¹⁴⁶⁶| MS:field. *P1869:*field!   ¹⁴⁶⁷| MS:of *P1869:*o'
¹⁴⁷²| MS:scheme and *1889a:*scheme, and   ¹⁴⁷³| MS:undone? You shall § written over
illegible word, perhaps *will* § lesson me— *P1869:*undone? You preached long and loud
¹⁴⁷⁸| MS:made one mad <> millhouse door *P1869:*made this mad <> mill-house-door,
¹⁴⁸⁰| MS:Browzed <> best, for *1872:*best: for *1889a:*Browsed   ¹⁴⁸¹| MS:so! I
*1872:*so. I   ¹⁴⁸²| MS:still maintain § crossed out and replaced above by § declare life
without *P1869:*declare—life, without   ¹⁴⁸³| MS:therein is *P1869:*therein, is
¹⁴⁸⁴| MS:down not *P1869:*down,—not   ¹⁴⁸⁶| MS:Secure reward *P1869:*Make sure

Entice me, scare me,—I'll forgo this life;
Otherwise, no!—the less that words, mere wind,
Would cheat me of some minutes while they plague,
1490 Baulk fulness of revenge here,—blame yourselves
For this eruption of the pent-up soul
You prisoned first and played with afterward!
"Deny myself" meant simply pleasure you,
The sacred and superior, save the mark!
1495 You,—whose stupidity and insolence
I must defer to, soothe at every turn,—
Whose swine-like snuffling greed and grunting lust
I had to wink at or help gratify,—
While the same passions,—dared they perk in me,
1500 Me, the immeasurably marked, by God,
Master of the whole world of such as you,—
I, boast such passions? 'Twas "Suppress them straight!
Or stay, we'll pick and choose before destroy.
Here's wrath in you, a serviceable sword,—
1505 Beat it into a ploughshare! What's this long
Lance-like ambition? Forge a pruning-hook,
May be of service when our vines grow tall!
But—sword use swordwise, spear thrust out as spear?
Anathema! Suppression is the word!"
1510 My nature, when the outrage was too gross,
Widened itself an outlet over-wide
By way of answer, sought its own relief

---

reward   1487| MS:scare me, I forego   P1869:scare me,—I'll forego   1889a:forgo
1488| MS:less for words   P1869:less that words   1489| MS:Which
cheat us of some minutes all the while.   P1869:Would cheat me of some
minutes while they plague.   1889a:plague,   1490| MS:The fulness <>
blame such words   P1869:blame yourselves   1889a:Baulk fulness   1491| MS:pent-up
self   P1869:pent-up soul   1492| MS:They prisoned <> afterward—
P1869:You prisoned <> afterward!   1498| MS:I must § crossed out and replaced above
by § have to   CP1869:I had to   1499| MS:passions . . dare   P1869:passions,—dare
CP1869:dared   1500| MS:marked by God   P1869:marked, by God,   1502| MS:I, to
boast passions   P1869:I, boast such passions   1503| MS:stay, best pick <> destroy
§ over discard § :   P1869:stay, we'll pick   1872:destroy.   1504| MS:you,—a   1872:you,
a   1505| MS:ploughshare: what's   P1869:ploughshare! What's
1506| MS:pruning-hook   P1869:pruning-hook,   1507| MS:Shall be <> when the vines
grow tall.   P1869:May be <> when our vines grow tall!   1508| MS:But sword used
<> as spear,   P1869:But—sword <> as spear?   1889a:use   1512| MS:answer, sought

With more of fire and brimstone than you wished.
All your own doing: preachers, blame yourselves!

1515 'Tis I preach while the hour-glass runs and runs!
God keep me patient! All I say just means—
My wife proved, whether by her fault or mine,—
That's immaterial,—a true stumbling-block
I' the way of me her husband. I but plied
1520 The hatchet yourselves use to clear a path,
Was politic, played the game you warrant wins,
Plucked at law's robe a-rustle through the courts,
Bowed down to kiss divinity's buckled shoe
Cushioned i' the church: efforts all wide the aim!
1525 Procedures to no purpose! Then flashed truth.
The letter kills, the spirit keeps alive
In law and gospel: there be nods and winks
Instruct a wise man to assist himself
In certain matters, nor seek aid at all.
1530 "Ask money of me,"—quoth the clownish saw,—
"And take my purse! But,—speaking with respect,—
Need you a solace for the troubled nose?
Let everybody wipe his own himself!"
Sirs, tell me free and fair! Had things gone well
1535 At the wayside inn: had I surprised asleep
The runaways, as was so probable,
And pinned them each to other partridge-wise,
Through back and breast to breast and back, then bade
Bystanders witness if the spit, my sword,
1540 Were loaded with unlawful game for once—
Would you have interposed to damp the glow

---

*P1869:*answer?—sought   *1872:*answer, sought   1513| MS:than was wished:
*P1869:*than you wished?   *1872:*wished.   1515| MS:I <> while here's the hourglass
P1869:'Tis I <> while the   *1872:*hour-glass   1516| MS:means   *P1869:*means—
1517| MS:mine   *P1869:*mine,—   1519| MS:In the <> husband: I   *P1869:*I' the
*1872:*husband. I   1522| MS:a rustle   *P1869:*a-rustle   1524| MS:in <> aim,
*P1869:*i' <> aim!   1525| MS:purpose. Then quoth I,   *P1869:*purpose! Then flashed
truth!   *1889a:*truth.   1526| MS:"The letter kills, the letter keeps   *P1869:*The letter
kills, the spirit keeps   1529| MS:matters nor <> all: *P1869:*all.   *1872:*matters, nor
1530| MS:me,"—says the   *P1869:*me,"—quoth the   1531| MS:purse; but, speaking with

Applauding me on every husband's cheek?
Would you have checked the cry "A judgment, see!
A warning, note! Be henceforth chaste, ye wives,
1545 Nor stray beyond your proper precinct, priests!"
If you had, then your house against itself
Divides, nor stands your kingdom any more.
Oh why, why was it not ordained just so?
Why fell not things out so nor otherwise?
1550 Ask that particular devil whose task it is
To trip the all-but-at perfection,—slur
The line of the painter just where paint leaves off
And life begins,—put ice into the ode
O' the poet while he cries "Next stanza—fire!"
1555 Inscribe all human effort with one word,
Artistry's haunting curse, the Incomplete!
Being incomplete, my act escaped success.
Easy to blame now! Every fool can swear
To hole in net that held and slipped the fish.
1560 But, treat my act with fair unjaundiced eye,
What was there wanting to a masterpiece
Except the luck that lies beyond a man?
My way with the woman, now proved grossly wrong,
Just missed of being gravely grandly right
1565 And making mouths laugh on the other side.
Do, for the poor obstructed artist's sake,
Go with him over that spoiled work once more!
Take only its first flower, the ended act

---

respect, _P1869:_purse! But,—speaking with respect,— ¹⁵⁴⁶| MS:you did, then
_P1869:_you had, then ¹⁵⁴⁸| MS:Oh, why, why _1889a:_Oh why, why
¹⁵⁵¹| MS:perfection,—slur § word and punctuation written over illegible erasure §
¹⁵⁵²| MS:of _P1869:_o' _1889:_of ¹⁵⁵³| MS:puts _1889a:_put ¹⁵⁵⁴| MS:Of <>
"next verse and § last two words crossed out and replaced above by one word and dash §
stanza— _P1869:_O' <> "Next ¹⁵⁵⁵| MS:Inscribes _1889a:_Inscribe ¹⁵⁵⁶| MS:§
illegible erasure § artistry's § altered to § Artistry's ¹⁵⁵⁷| MS:incomplete the act
<> success, _P1869:_incomplete, the <> success. _1889a:_incomplete, my act
¹⁵⁵⁸| MS:now: every _P1869:_now! Every ¹⁵⁵⁹| MS:fish: _P1869:_fish. ¹⁵⁶⁰| MS:But
treat <> eye _P1869:_But, treat <> eye, ¹⁵⁶¹| MS:What seems there _P1869:_What was
there ¹⁵⁶⁵| MS:making critics laugh o' _1872:_on _1889a:_making mouths laugh
¹⁵⁶⁶| MS:sake _P1869:_sake, ¹⁵⁶⁷| MS:more. _P1869:_more! ¹⁵⁶⁸| MS:flower,

Now in the dusty pod, dry and defunct!
1570 I march to the Villa, and my men with me,
That evening, and we reach the door and stand.
I say . . . no, it shoots through me lightning-like
While I pause, breathe, my hand upon the latch,
"Let me forebode! Thus far, too much success:
1575 I want the natural failure—find it where?
Which thread will have to break and leave a loop
I' the meshy combination, my brain's loom
Wove this long while, and now next minute tests?
Of three that are to catch, two should go free,
1580 One must: all three surprised,—impossible!
Beside, I seek three and may chance on six,—
This neighbour, t'other gossip,—the babe's birth
Brings such to fireside, and folks give them wine,—
'Tis late: but when I break in presently
1585 One will be found outlingering the rest
For promise of a posset,—one whose shout
Would raise the dead down in the catacombs,
Much more the city-watch that goes its round.
When did I ever turn adroitly up
1590 To sun some brick embedded in the soil,
And with one blow crush all three scorpions there?
Or Pietro or Violante shambles off—
It cannot be but I surprise my wife—
If only she is stopped and stamped on, good!
1595 That shall suffice: more is improbable.
Now I may knock!" And this once for my sake

---

that ended   *P1869:*flower, the ended   1570| MS:the Villa and the men with me
*P1869:*the Villa, and my men with me,   1571| MS:the gate § crossed out and replaced
above by § door   1572| MS:say . . no   *1889a:*say . . . no   1574| MS:forbode: too
much success thus far: § transposed to § forbode: thus far: too much success   *P1869:*forbode!
Thus far, too much success: *CP1869:*forebode   1577| MS:In   *P1869:*I'
1578| MS:while and now the minute   *P1869:*now next minute   *1872:*while, and
1580| MS:surprised, impossible!   *CP1869:*surprised,—impossible!   1581| MS:Beside I
<> six   *P1869:*six,—   *CP1869:*Beside, I   1583| MS:fireside and   *1872:*fireside, and
1587| MS:catacombs   *P1869:*catacombs,   1588| MS:city watch   *P1869:*city-watch
1590| MS:soil   *CP1869:*soil,   1592| MS:or Violante § *V* written over illegible letter §
1594–96| MS:And, so but she <> good!/Now I will § crossed out and replaced above by §
may   *P1869:*If only she <> good!/That shall suffice: more is improbable./Now

220

The impossible was effected: I called king,
Queen and knave in a sequence, and cards came,
All three, three only! So, I had my way,
1600 Did my deed: so, unbrokenly lay bare
Each tænia that had sucked me dry of juice,
At last outside me, not an inch of ring
Left now to writhe about and root itself
I' the heart all powerless for revenge! Henceforth
1605 I might thrive: these were drawn and dead and damned.
Oh Cardinal, the deep long sigh you heave
When the load's off you, ringing as it runs
All the way down the serpent-stair to hell!
No doubt the fine delirium flustered me,
1610 Turned my brain with the influx of success
As if the sole need now were to wave wand
And find doors fly wide,—wish and have my will,—
The rest o' the scheme would care for itself: escape?
Easy enough were that, and poor beside!
1615 It all but proved so,—ought to quite have proved,
Since, half the chances had sufficed, set free
Anyone, with his senses at command,
From thrice the danger of my flight. But, drunk,
Redundantly triumphant,—some reverse
1620 Was sure to follow! There's no other way
Accounts for such prompt perfect failure then
And there on the instant. Any day o' the week,
A ducat slid discreetly into palm
O' the mute post-master, while you whisper him—
1625 How you the Count and certain four your knaves,

1598| MS:came. *P1869:*came, 1599| MS:only: so I *P1869:*only! So, I
1601| MS:Each § over illegible erasure § 1603| MS:Was § crossed out § left § altered to §
Left within § crossed out and replaced above by § now 1604| MS:In *P1869:*I'
1605| MS:might die: these were drawn, and dead, and damned! *P1869:*might thrive: these
were drawn and dead and damned. 1613| MS:of <> escape? *CP1869:*o'
*1889a:*escape § emended to § escape? § see Editorial Notes § 1615| MS:to so have
proved *P1869:*to quite have proved, 1616| MS:Since half *P1869:*Since, half
1617| MS:Anyone with <> command *P1869:*Anyone, with <> command,
1618| MS:of the flight: but drunk, *P1869:*of my flight. But, drunk, 1620| MS:follow:
there's *P1869:*follow! There's 1621| MS:for such § added above line §
1622| MS:instant: any <> week *P1869:*instant. Any <> week, 1624| MS:Of the
post-master <> him *P1869:*O' the mute post-master <> him— 1625| MS:knaves

Have just been mauling who was malapert,
Suspect the kindred may prove troublesome,
Therefore, want horses in a hurry,—that
And nothing more secures you any day
1630 The pick o' the stable! Yet I try the trick,
Double the bribe, call myself Duke for Count,
And say the dead man only was a Jew,
And for my pains find I am dealing just
With the one scrupulous fellow in all Rome—
1635 Just this immaculate official stares,
Sees I want hat on head and sword in sheath,
Am splashed with other sort of wet than wine,
Shrugs shoulder, puts my hand by, gold and all,
Stands on the strictness of the rule o' the road!
1640 "Where's the Permission?" Where's the wretched rag
With the due seal and sign of Rome's Police,
To be had for asking, half-an-hour ago?
"Gone? Get another, or no horses hence!"
He dares not stop me, we five glare too grim,
1645 But hinders,—hacks and hamstrings sure enough,
Gives me some twenty miles of miry road
More to march in the middle of that night
Whereof the rough beginning taxed the strength
O' the youngsters, much more mine, both soul and flesh,
1650 Who had to think as well as act: dead-beat,
We gave in ere we reached the boundary
And safe spot out of this irrational Rome,—
Where, on dismounting from our steeds next day,
We had snapped our fingers at you, safe and sound,

---

*P1869:*knaves,   1626| MS:Having been <> malapert   *P1869:*Have just been <>
malapert,   1627| MS:Suspect his kindred may be troublesome   *P1869:*Suspect the
kindred may prove troublesome,   1628| MS:And so want   *P1869:*Therefore, want
1630| MS:of   *P1869:*o'   1631| MS:for Count   *P1869:*for Count,   1633| MS:And
find, for once, that § last two words crossed out and replaced above by two words § my pains
§ marks indicate *find* to be placed after *pains* §   *P1869:*And for <> find I
1636| MS:Sees I have no hat on head nor sword in sheath   *P1869:*sheath,   *1869:*Sees I want
hat on head and sword   1637| MS:And cloak with   *P1869:*Am splashed with
1639| MS:road   *P1869:*road!   1642| MS:asking half an hour   *P1869:*asking,
half-an-hour   1644| MS:He don't dare stop   *P1869:*He dares not stop
1649| MS:Of <> mine, such as you see,   *P1869:*O'   *1889a:*mine, both soul and flesh,
1650| MS:dead-beat   *P1869:*dead-beat,   1651| MS:boundary,   *P1869:*boundary
1652| MS:The safe <> Rome,   *P1869:*And safe <> Rome,—   1654| MS:you safe

¹⁶⁵⁵ Tuscans once more in blessed Tuscany,
Where laws make wise allowance, understand
Civilized life and do its champions right!
Witness the sentence of the Rota there,
Arezzo uttered, the Granduke confirmed,
¹⁶⁶⁰ One week before I acted on its hint,—
Giving friend Guillichini, for his love,
The galleys, and my wife your saint, Rome's saint,—
Rome manufactures saints enough to know,—
Seclusion at the Stinche for her life.
¹⁶⁶⁵ All this, that all but was, might all have been,
Yet was not! baulked by just a scrupulous knave
Whose palm was horn through handling horses' hoofs
And could not close upon my proffered gold!
What say you to the spite of fortune? Well,
¹⁶⁷⁰ The worst's in store: thus hindered, haled this way
To Rome again by hangdogs, whom find I
Here, still to fight with, but my pale frail wife?
—Riddled with wounds by one not like to waste
The blows he dealt,—knowing anatomy,—
¹⁶⁷⁵ (I think I told you) bound to pick and choose
The vital parts! 'Twas learning all in vain!
She too must shimmer through the gloom o' the grave,
Come and confront me—not at judgment-seat
Where I could twist her soul, as erst her flesh,
¹⁶⁸⁰ And turn her truth into a lie,—but there,
O' the death-bed, with God's hand between us both,
Striking me dumb, and helping her to speak,
Tell her own story her own way, and turn

---

*P1869:*you, safe   ¹⁶⁵⁶| MS:Where the laws make allowance   *1889a:*Where laws make
wise allowance   ¹⁶⁵⁷| MS:right—   *P1869:*right!   ¹⁶⁵⁹| MS:uttered and the Duke
confirmed   *P1869:*uttered, the Granduke confirmed,   ¹⁶⁶¹| MS:friend Guillichini for
his love   *P1869:*friend Guillichini, for his love,   ¹⁶⁶²| MS:gallies < > Rome's saint
*P1869:*galleys < > Rome's saint,—   ¹⁶⁶³| MS:That manufactures < > know,
*P1869:*Rome manufactures < > know,—   ¹⁶⁶⁴| MS:life: *P1869:*life.
¹⁶⁶⁵| MS:been   *P1869:*been,   ¹⁶⁶⁶| MS:And was not—baulked   *P1869:*Yet was not!
baulked   ¹⁶⁷²| MS:Is still < > with but   *P1869:*Here, still < > with, but
¹⁶⁷⁴| MS:anatomy,   *P1869:*anatomy,—   ¹⁶⁷⁵| MS:I think < > you,—who could § last
two words crossed out and replaced above by two words § one to   *P1869:*(I think < > you)
one   *1889a:*you) bound to   ¹⁶⁷⁶| MS:parts: twas learning all § added above line § in
pure wa § last word and fragment crossed out and replaced above by § vain.   *P1869:*parts!
'Twas < > vain!   ¹⁶⁷⁷| MS:grave   *P1869:*grave,   ¹⁶⁷⁸⁻⁸³| MS:me at the judgment

My plausibility to nothingness!
1685 Four whole days did Pompilia keep alive,
With the best surgery of Rome agape
At the miracle,—this cut, the other slash,
And yet the life refusing to dislodge,
Four whole extravagant impossible days,
1690 Till she had time to finish and persuade
Every man, every woman, every child
In Rome, of what she would: the selfsame she
Who, but a year ago, had wrung her hands,
Reddened her eyes and beat her breasts, rehearsed
1695 The whole game at Arezzo, nor availed
Thereby to move one heart or raise one hand!
When destiny intends you cards like these,
What good of skill and preconcerted play?
Had she been found dead, as I left her dead,
1700 I should have told a tale brooked no reply:
You scarcely will suppose me found at fault
With that advantage! "What brings me to Rome?
Necessity to claim and take my wife:
Better, to claim and take my new-born babe,—
1705 Strong in paternity a fortnight old,
When 'tis at strongest: warily I work,
Knowing the machinations of my foe;
I have companionship and use the night:
I seek my wife and child,—I find—no child

---

seat/Tell   *P1869:*me—not at the judgment-seat/ Where I could twist her soul, as erst her
flesh,/And turn her truth into a lie,—but there,/O' the death-bed, with God's hand between
us both,/Striking me dumb, and helping her to speak,/Tell   *CP1869:*at judgment-seat
1684| MS:nothingness: *P1869:*nothingness!   1685| MS:alive *P1869:*alive,
1687| MS:cut the *P1869:*cut, the   1688| MS:dislodge *P1869:*dislodge,
1689| MS:days *P1869:*days,   1690| MS:has *P1869:*had   1692| MS:In Rome of
*1872:*In Rome, of   1695| MS:at Arezzo nor *P1869:*at Arezzo, nor   1697| MS:these
*P1869:*these,   1698| *1872:*pre-concerted *1889a:*preconcerted   1699| MS:dead as
<> dead *P1869:*dead, as <> dead,   1702| MS:advantage: why I come § last three
words crossed out and replaced above by three words § what brings me *P1869:*advantage!
"What   1704| MS:newborn babe *P1869:*new-born babe,—   1705| MS:old
*P1869:*old,   1706| MS:work *P1869:*work,   1707| MS:of the § crossed out and
replaced above by § my foe, *P1869:*foe;   1708| MS:night. *P1869:*night:
1709| MS:find the priest § last two words crossed out and replaced above by two words and

1710 But wife, in the embraces of that priest
Who caused her to elope from me. These two,
Backed by the pander-pair who watch the while,
Spring on me like so many tiger-cats,
Glad of the chance to end the intruder. I—
1715 What should I do but stand on my defence,
Strike right, strike left, strike thick and threefold, slay,
Not all—because the coward priest escapes.
Last, I escape, in fear of evil tongues,
And having had my taste of Roman law."
1720 What's disputable, refutable here?—
Save by just this one ghost-thing half on earth,
Half out of it,—as if she held God's hand
While she leant back and looked her last at me,
Forgiving me (here monks begin to weep)
1725 Oh, from her very soul, commending mine
To heavenly mercies which are infinite,—
While fixing fast my head beneath your knife!
'Tis fate not fortune. All is of a piece!
When was it chance informed me of my youths?
1730 My rustic four o' the family, soft swains,
What sweet surprise had they in store for me,
Those of my very household,—what did Law
Twist with her rack-and-cord-contrivance late
From out their bones and marrow? What but this—
1735 Had no one of these several stumbling-blocks
Stopped me, they yet were cherishing a scheme,
All of their honest country homespun wit,
To quietly next day at crow of cock

---

dash § no child— *P1869:*find—no child   1710| MS:My wife *P1869:*But wife
1711| MS:me. The pair § last two words crossed out and replaced above by two words §
These two,   1716| MS:slay *P1869:*slay,   1718| MS:Last I escape in <> tongues
*P1869:*Last, I escape, in <> tongues,   1720| MS:here *P1869:*here?—
1721| MS:earth *P1869:*earth,   1723| MS:leans <> looks <> me *P1869:*me,
*CP1869:*leant <> looked   1724| MS:me . . here <> weep . . *P1869:*me (here <>
weep)   1726| MS:infinite *P1869:*infinite,—   1728| MS:fortune! All
*1889a:*fortune. All   1729-31| MS:What was it you informed <> my friends?/What
*P1869:*my youths?/My rustic four o' the family, soft swains,/What   1872:When was it
chance informed   1735| MS:Had not one *P1869:*Had no one   1737| MS:All of
§ added above § their own § crossed out §   1738| MS:quietly, next day § over *morn* §

Cut my own throat too, for their own behoof,
1740 Seeing I had forgot to clear accounts
O' the instant, nowise slackened speed for that,—
And somehow never might find memory,
Once safe back in Arezzo, where things change,
And a court-lord needs mind no country lout.
1745 Well, being the arch-offender, I die last,—
May, ere my head falls, have my eyesight free,
Nor miss them dangling high on either hand,
Like scarecrows in a hemp-field, for their pains!

And then my Trial,—'tis my Trial that bites
1750 Like a corrosive, so the cards are packed,
Dice loaded, and my life-stake tricked away!
Look at my lawyers, lacked they grace of law,
Latin or logic? Were not they fools to the height,
Fools to the depth, fools to the level between,
1755 O' the foolishness set to decide the case?
They feign, they flatter; nowise does it skill,
Everything goes against me: deal each judge
His dole of flattery and feigning,—why,
He turns and tries and snuffs and savours it,
1760 As some old fly the sugar-grain, your gift;
Then eyes your thumb and finger, brushes clean
The absurd old head of him, and whisks away,
Leaving your thumb and finger dirty. Faugh!

And finally, after this long-drawn range
1765 Of affront and failure, failure and affront,—

<> cock, *P1869:*quietly next *1889a:*cock   1739| MS:my own § added above § <>
too for *P1869:*too, for   1741| MS:On <> that, *P1869:*O' <> that,—
1742| MS:memory *P1869:*memory,   1744| MS:needs fear § crossed out and replaced
above by § mind   1745| MS:arch-offender I die last, *P1869:*arch-offender, I die last,—
1746| MS:And ere <> falls have *P1869:*May, ere <> falls, have   1747| MS:miss § over
illegible fragment §   1748| MS:hempfield for their pains *P1869:*hemp-field, for their
pains!   1750| MS:Like any corrosive, the *P1869:*Like a corrosive, so the
1751| MS:away. *P1869:*away!   1754| MS:between *P1869:*between,   1755| MS:Of
*P1869:*O'   1756| MS:flatter, nowise *P1869:*flatter; nowise   1757| MS:All § crossed
out and replaced above by § Everything   1759| MS:it *P1869:*it,   1760| MS:As an
old <> sugar-grain your gift, *P1869:*sugar-grain, your gift; *1872:*As some old
1762| MS:away *P1869:*away,   1765| MS:and failure, failure and affront,

This path, 'twixt crosses leading to a skull,
Paced by me barefoot, bloodied by my palms
From the entry to the end,—there's light at length,
A cranny of escape: appeal may be
1770 To the old man, to the father, to the Pope,
For a little life—from one whose life is spent,
A little pity—from pity's source and seat,
A little indulgence to rank, privilege,
From one who is the thing personified,
1775 Rank, privilege, indulgence, grown beyond
Earth's bearing, even, ask Jansenius else!
Still the same answer, still no other tune
From the cicala perched at the tree-top
Than crickets noisy round the root: 'tis "Die!"
1780 Bids Law—"Be damned!" adds Gospel,—nay,
No word so frank,—'tis rather, "Save yourself!"
The Pope subjoins—"Confess and be absolved!
So shall my credit countervail your shame,
And the world see I have not lost the knack
1785 Of trying all the spirits: yours, my son,
Wants but a fiery washing to emerge
In clarity! Come, cleanse you, ease the ache
Of these old bones, refresh our bowels, boy!"
Do I mistake your mission from the Pope?
1790 Then, bear his Holiness the mind of me!

---

*P1869:*affront, failure, failure and affront,— *1889a:*affront and failure, failure
1766| MS:path twixt <> skull *P1869:*path, twixt <> skull, *1872:*'twixt
1769| MS:escape,—appeal *1872:*escape: appeal 1770| MS:man, to our father, to this
Pope *P1869:*man, to the father, to the Pope, 1773| MS:rank and privilege
*P1869:*rank, privilege, 1774| MS:For one *P1869:*From one 1775| MS:privilege
and indulgence grown *P1869:*privilege, indulgence, grown 1776| MS:bearing even
*P1869:*bearing, even 1777| MS:still no § written over illegible erasure §
1779| MS:And crickets <> root,—tis "Die"— *P1869:*Than crickets <> 'tis "Die!"
*1889a:*root: 'tis 1780| MS:Quoth Law <> damned!" quoth Gospel *P1869:*Bids Law
<> damned!" adds Gospel 1781| MS:tis <> yourself"— *P1869:*'tis <> yourself!"
1782| MS:confess *P1869:*subjoins—"Confess 1783| MS:shame *P1869:*shame,
1784| MS:see we have *P1869:*see I have 1785| MS:spirits,—yours, we know,
*P1869:*yours, my son, *1872:*spirits: yours 1787| MS:clarity: come *CP1869:*clarity!
Come 1788-90| MS:bowels, Son!"/Then, Cardinal § crossed out § bear him § crossed
out and replaced above by two words § his Holiness <> me: *P1869:*bowels, boy!"/Do I

227

I do get strength from being thrust to wall,
Successively wrenched from pillar and from post
By this tenacious hate of fortune, hate
Of all things in, under, and above earth.
1795 Warfare, begun this mean unmanly mode,
Does best to end so,—gives earth spectacle
Of a brave fighter who succumbs to odds
That turn defeat to victory. Stab, I fold
My mantle round me! Rome approves my act:
1800 Applauds the blow which costs me life but keeps
My honour spotless: Rome would praise no more
Had I fallen, say, some fifteen years ago,
Helping Vienna when our Aretines
Flocked to Duke Charles and fought Turk Mustafa;
1805 Nor would you two be trembling o'er my corpse
With all this exquisite solicitude.
Why is it that I make such suit to live?
The popular sympathy that's round me now
Would break like bubble that o'er-domes a fly:
1810 Solid enough while he lies quiet there,
But let him want the air and ply the wing,
Why, it breaks and bespatters him, what else?
Cardinal, if the Pope had pardoned me,
And I walked out of prison through the crowd,
1815 It would not be your arm I should dare press!
Then, if I got safe to my place again,
How sad and sapless were the years to come!

---

mistake your mission from the Pope?/Then <> me! 1792| MS:From § altered to §
from post and from § added above line § pillar wrenched successively § altered to §
Successively § transposed to § Successively wrenched from pillar and from post
1793| MS:fortune, say § crossed out § 1794| MS:Hate § crossed out § of § altered to § Of
all § added above line § 1795| MS:Warfare begun <> mode P1869:Warfare, begun
<> mode, 1796| MS:give the spectacle P1869:gives earth spectacle
1798| MS:victory: come, I P1869:victory. Stab, I 1799| MS:me! Rome applauds
§ crossed out and replaced above by § approves 1801| MS:spotless: Rome had done
§ last two words crossed out and replaced above by two words § would praise
1803| MS:when those § crossed out and replaced above by § our 1809| MS:like foam
ball § last two words crossed out and replaced above by § bubble <> fly— 1889a:fly:
1810| MS:Pretty enough 1889a:Solid enough 1815| MS:would not § added above
line § <> dare hold! P1869:dare press! 1816| MS:again,— CP1869:again,
1817| MS:'Tis doubtful § last two words crossed out and replaced above by three words §

228

I go my old ways and find things grown grey;
You priests leer at me, old friends look askance,
1820 The mob's in love, I'll wager, to a man,
With my poor young good beauteous murdered wife:
For hearts require instruction how to beat,
And eyes, on warrant of the story, wax
Wanton at portraiture in white and black
1825 Of dead Pompilia gracing ballad-sheet,
Which eyes, lived she unmurdered and unsung,
Would never turn though she paced street as bare
As the mad penitent ladies do in France.
My brothers quietly would edge me out
1830 Of use and management of things called mine;
Do I command? "You stretched command before!"
Show anger? "Anger little helped you once!"
Advise? "How managed you affairs of old?"
My very mother, all the while they gird,
1835 Turns eye up, gives confirmatory groan;
For unsuccess, explain it how you will,
Disqualifies you, makes you doubt yourself,
—Much more, is found decisive by your friends.
Beside, am I not fifty years of age?
1840 What new leap would a life take, checked like mine
I' the spring at outset? Where's my second chance?
Ay, but the babe . . . I had forgot my son,
My heir! Now for a burst of gratitude!
There's some appropriate service to intone,
1845 Some *gaudeamus* and thanksgiving-psalm!
Old, I renew my youth in him, and poor
Possess a treasure,—is not that the phrase?

How sad and < > come,— *P1869:*come!   1818| MS:find all § crossed out and replaced
above by § things < > grey— *P1869:*grey;   1819| MS:askance,— *P1869:*askance;
*1889a:*askance DC,BrU:askance, *1889:*askance,   1820| MS:man *P1869:*man,
1826| MS:Who, had she died unmurdered *P1869:*Which, had *1872:*Which eyes, lived she
unmurdered   1831| MS:before"! *P1869:*before!" *1889a:*before! DC,BrU:before!"
*1889:*before!"   1833| MS:old?"— *P1869:*old?"   1835| MS:Giving, belike, the
confirmatory groan,— *P1869:*Turns eye up, gives confirmatory *1872:*groan;
1836| MS:will *P1869:*will,   1838| MS:Much *P1869:*—Much   1840| MS:take,
baulked like *P1869:*take, checked   1841| MS:In *P1869:*I'   1842| MS:babe . . I
*1889a:*babe . . . I   1845| MS:gaudeamus and thanksgiving psalm! *P1869:gaudeamus*

Only I must wait patient twenty years—
Nourishing all the while, as father ought,
1850   The excrescence with my daily blood of life.
Does it respond to hope, such sacrifice,—
Grows the wen plump while I myself grow lean?
Why, here's my son and heir in evidence,
Who stronger, wiser, handsomer than I
1855   By fifty years, relieves me of each load,—
Tames my hot horse, carries my heavy gun,
Courts my coy mistress,—has his apt advice
On house-economy, expenditure,
And what not. All which good gifts and great growth
1860   Because of my decline, he brings to bear
On Guido, but half apprehensive how
He cumbers earth, crosses the brisk young Count,
Who civilly would thrust him from the scene.
Contrariwise, does the blood-offering fail?
1865   There's an ineptitude, one blank the more
Added to earth in semblance of my child?
Then, this has been a costly piece of work,
My life exchanged for his!—why he, not I,
Enjoy the world, if no more grace accrue?
1870   Dwarf me, what giant have you made of him?
I do not dread the disobedient son:
I know how to suppress rebellion there,

---

and thanksgiving-psalm!   1851| MS:hope, this sacrifice,   P1869:hope, such sacrifice,—
1857| MS:his word to say § last three words crossed out and replaced above by two words §
apt advice   1858| MS:house economy, § word and comma added above line §
P1869:house-economy   1859| MS:not? All these § crossed out and replaced above by §
which good gifts over § crossed out and replaced above by two words § and much growth
P1869:gifts and great growth   DC,BrU:not. All   1889:not. All   1860| MS:Through
§ crossed out and replaced above by two words § Because of <> he justly § added above line;
crossed out § brings forthwith § crossed out §   1861| MS:On Guido, only half-aware
§ last two words crossed out and replaced above by two words § hardly apprehensive how
shamefully § crossed out §   P1869:On Guido, but half apprehensive   1862| MS:earth,
makes wait § last two words crossed out and replaced above by § crosses   1863| MS:Fit
civilly to thrust   P1869:Who civilly would thrust   1865| MS:There's one § altered to
this § ineptitude, and § altered to § one   P1869:There's an ineptitude   1866| MS:in
fashion § crossed out and replaced above by § semblance of my son § crossed out and
replaced above by § child?   1867| MS:Why, this   P1869:Then, this
1868| MS:his,—why   P1869:his!—why   1871| MS:son—   1889a:son:

Being not quite the fool my father was.
But grant the medium measure of a man,
¹⁸⁷⁵ The usual compromise 'twixt fool and sage,
—You know—the tolerably-obstinate,
The not-so-much-perverse but you may train,
The true son-servant that, when parent bids
"Go work, son, in my vineyard!" makes reply
¹⁸⁸⁰ "I go, Sir!"—Why, what profit in your son
Beyond the drudges you might subsidize,
Have the same work from, at a paul the head?
Look at those four young precious olive-plants
Reared at Vittiano,—not on flesh and blood,
¹⁸⁸⁵ These twenty years, but black bread and sour wine!
I bade them put forth tender branch, hook, hold,
And hurt three enemies I had in Rome:
They did my hest as unreluctantly,
At promise of a dollar, as a son
¹⁸⁹⁰ Adjured by mumping memories of the past.
No, nothing repays youth expended so—
Youth, I say, who am young still: grant but leave
To live my life out, to the last I'd live
And die conceding age no right of youth!
¹⁸⁹⁵ It is the will runs the renewing nerve
Through flaccid flesh that faints before the time.
Therefore no sort of use for son have I—
Sick, not of life's feast but of steps to climb

---

^{1875|} MS:The § added in margin § Usual § altered to § usual compromise between
§ crossed out and replaced above by § 'twixt   ^{1876|} MS:tolerably obstinate,
*P1869:*tolerably-obstinate,   ^{1877|} MS:not so much perverse <> may guide § crossed out
and replaced above by § train,   *P1869:*not-so-much-perverse   ^{1879|} MS:work, Son
*P1869:*work, son   ^{1881|} MS:subsidize *P1869:*subsidize,   ^{1882|} MS:To do the same
work   *P1869:*Have the same work from at   *1872:*from, at   ^{1883|} MS:young fellows,
olive plants   *P1869:*young previous olive-plants   *CP1869:*precious   ^{1884|} MS:blood
*P1869:*blood,   ^{1885|} MS:wine,—   *P1869:*wine!   ^{1886|} MS:bade put
forth the tender branch and hook   *P1869:*bade them put forth tender branch, and
*1889a:*branch, hook, hold,   ^{1887|} MS:And hang three   *P1869:*And hurt
three   ^{1888|} MS:unreluctantly   *P1869:*unreluctantly,   ^{1889|} MS:as my son
*P1869:*as a son   ^{1890|} MS:by all sweet memories   *1869:*by mumping memories <>
past!   *1889a:*past.   ^{1892|} MS:still,—give but   *1872:*still: give   *1889a:*still: grant but
^{1893|} MS:I live <> last I live   *P1869:*To live <> last I'd live   ^{1894|} MS:youth;
*1869:*youth!   ^{1896|} *P1869:*flesh, would faint   *1872:*flesh that faints   ^{1898|} MS:life's

To the house where life prepares her feast,—of means
1900 To the end: for make the end attainable
Without the means,—my relish were like yours.
A man may have an appetite enough
For a whole dish of robins ready cooked,
And yet lack courage to face sleet, pad snow,
1905 And snare sufficiently for supper.

                                              Thus
The time's arrived when, ancient Roman-like,
I am bound to fall on my own sword: why not
Say—Tuscan-like, more ancient, better still?
Will you hear truth can do no harm nor good?
1910 I think I never was at any time
A Christian, as you nickname all the world,
Me among others; truce to nonsense now!
Name me, a primitive religionist—
As should the aboriginary be
1915 I boast myself, Etruscan, Aretine,
One sprung,—your frigid Virgil's fieriest word,—
From fauns and nymphs, trunks and the heart of oak,
With,—for a visible divinity,—
The portent of a Jove Ægiochus
1920 Descried 'mid clouds, lightning and thunder, couched
On topmost crag of your Capitoline:
'Tis in the Seventh Æneid,—what, the Eighth?
Right,—thanks, Abate,—though the Christian's dumb,

---

feast § added above line § but of the weary way § last two words crossed out and replaced
above by three words § steps to climb *P1869:*of steps   1899| MS:her banquet,—means
*P1869:*her feast,—of means   1900| MS:end,—and make *P1869:*end: for make
1901–3| MS:mean < > were as keen/As for a dish < > cooked— *P1869:*means < > were like
yours./A man may have an appetite enough/For a whole dish < > cooked,
1904| MS:Though of no mind to face sleet and pad snow *P1869:*And yet lack courage to
face sleet, pad snow,   1905| MS:To snare sufficiency of mornings. Thus *P1869:*And
snare sufficiently for supper. § ¶ § Thus   1906| MS:ancient-Roman-like, *P1869:*ancient
Roman-like,   1907| MS:sword,—why *1889a:*sword: why   1908| MS:Die § added
in margin § Tuscan-like, which is older § last three words crossed out and replaced above by
two words § more ancient *P1869:*Say—Tuscan-like   1912| MS:now: *P1869:*now!
1913| MS:me a < > religionist *P1869:*me, a < > religionist—   1918| MS:divinity
*P1869:*divinity,—   1920| MS:mid *P1869:*'mid   1921| MS:On the top crag < >
Capitoline— *P1869:*On topmost crag *1889a:*your Capitoline: 1923| MS:dumb

The Latinist's vivacious in you yet!
1925 I know my grandsire had our tapestry
Marked with the motto,'neath a certain shield,
Whereto his grandson presently will give gules
To vary azure. First we fight for faiths,
But get to shake hands at the last of all:
1930 Mine's your faith too,—in Jove Ægiochus!
Nor do Greek gods, that serve as supplement,
Jar with the simpler scheme, if understood.
We want such intermediary race
To make communication possible;
1935 The real thing were too lofty, we too low,
Midway hang these: we feel their use so plain
In linking height to depth, that we doff hat
And put no question nor pry narrowly
Into the nature hid behind the names.
1940 We grudge no rite the fancy may demand;
But never, more than needs, invent, refine,
Improve upon requirement, idly wise
Beyond the letter, teaching gods their trade,
Which is to teach us: we'll obey when taught.
1945 Why should we do our duty past the need?
When the sky darkens, Jove is wroth,—say prayer!
When the sun shines and Jove is glad,—sing psalm!
But wherefore pass prescription and devise
Blood-offering for sweat-service, lend the rod

---

*P1869:*dumb,   1926| MS:shield *1872:*shield,   1927| MS:His <> give some gules
*1889a:*Whereto his <> give gules   1928| MS:vary argent. First *P1869:*vary azure. First
1930| MS:in Jove ᵉgiochus; *P1869:*in Jove ᵉgiochus!   1931| MS:Nor the Greek Gods
*P1869:*Nor do Greek *CP1869:*gods   1932| MS:understood— *P1869:*understood.
1934| MS:possible,— *P1869:*possible;   1936| MS:these; we *P1869:*these: we
1937| MS:depth, we doff our hat *P1869:*depth, that we doff hat   1938| MS:And put
§ over perhaps *ask* § no questions *P1869:*question   1939| MS:natures *P1869:*nature
1940| MS:may require § crossed out and replaced above by § demand— *P1869:*demand;
1941| MS:But do not, more <> refine *P1869:*But never, more <> refine,
1942| MS:idly § over erasure §   1944| MS:us: we obey *P1869:*us: we'll obey
1945| MS:should I § crossed out and replaced above by § we do my § crossed out and replaced
above by § our <> the due? *1889a:*the need?   1946| MS:say § over erasure § prayer.
*P1869:*prayer!   1947| MS:shines, sing psalm, for § crossed out and replaced above by §
and Jove is glad! § transposed to § When the sun shines, and Jove is glad, sing psalm!

233

A pungency through pickle of our own?
Learned Abate,—no one teaches you
What Venus means and who's Apollo here!
I spare you, Cardinal,—but, though you wince,
You know me, I know you, and both know that!
1955 So, if Apollo bids us fast, we fast:
But where does Venus order we stop sense
When Master Pietro rhymes a pleasantry?
Give alms prescribed on Friday: but, hold hand
Because your foe lies prostrate,—where's the word
1960 Explicit in the book debars revenge?
The rationale of your scheme is just
"Pay toll here, there pursue your pleasure free!"
So do you turn to use the medium-powers,
Mars and Minerva, Bacchus and the rest,
1965 And so are saved propitiating—whom?
What all-good, all-wise and all-potent Jove
Vexed by the very sins in man, himself
Made life's necessity when man he made?
Irrational bunglers! So, the living truth
1970 Revealed to strike Pan dead, ducks low at last,
Prays leave to hold its own and live good days
Provided it go masque grotesquely, called
Christian not Pagan. Oh, you purged the sky
Of all gods save the One, the great and good,

---

*P1869:*shines and <> glad,—sing   1950| MS:A novel smart § last two words crossed
out and replaced above by § pungency <> of your own? *P1869:*of our own?
1951| MS:Learned Abate, no *P1869:*Learned Abate,—no   1952| MS:here: *P1869:*here!
1953| MS:you, Cardinal,—enough, you wince: *P1869:*you, Cardinal,—but, though you
wince,   1954| MS:that. *P1869:*that!   1955| MS:So if <> bids me fast, I fast:
*P1869:*So, if <> bids us fast, we fast: 1956| MS:order I stop *P1869:*order we stop
1958| MS:Give the poor alms on Friday,—but hold *P1869:*Give alms prescribed on <>
but, hold *1889a:*on Friday: but   1959| MS:When there your *P1869:*Because your
1960| MS:book prevents revenge? *P1869:*book debars revenge?   1963–65| MS:use your
medium-powers/And <> propitiating—what? *P1869:*use the medium-powers,/Mars and
Minerva, Bacchus and the rest,/And *1872:*/ / <> propitiating—whom?   1966| MS:all
good, all wise and all potent Jove *1872:*all-good, all-wise and
all-potent   1968| MS:Made man's § altered to § life's <> made. *P1869:*he made?
1969| MS:bunglers! what, the *P1869:*bunglers! So, the   1971| MS:Prays that he hold
his own *P1869:*that it hold its own *CP1869:*Prays leave to hold   1972| MS:Provided
he go *P1869:*Provided it go   1973| MS:not Pagan? Oh *1872:*not Pagan. Oh

¹⁹⁷⁵ Clapped hands and triumphed! But the change came fast:
The inexorable need in man for life—
(Life, you may mulct and minish to a grain
Out of the lump, so that the grain but live)
Laughed at your substituting death for life,
¹⁹⁸⁰ And bade you do your worst: which worst was done
In just that age styled primitive and pure
When Saint this, Saint that, dutifully starved,
Froze, fought with beasts, was beaten and abused
And finally ridded of his flesh by fire:
¹⁹⁸⁵ He kept life-long unspotted from the world!
Next age, how goes the game, what mortal gives
His life and emulates Saint that, Saint this?
Men mutter, make excuse or mutiny,
In fine are minded all to leave the new,
¹⁹⁹⁰ Stick to the old,—enjoy old liberty,
No prejudice in enjoyment, if you please,
To the new profession: sin o' the sly, henceforth!
The law stands though the letter kills: what then?
The spirit saves as unmistakeably.
¹⁹⁹⁵ Omniscience sees, Omnipotence could stop,
Omnibenevolence pardons: it must be,

---

^{1975|} MS:change is come, § last two words and comma crossed out and replaced above by
two words and colon § came fast: ^{1977|} MS:Life you *P1869:*Life,—you *1872:*(Life,
you   ^{1978|} MS:so the grain left but live— *P1869:*live,— *1872:*live) *1889a:*so that the
grain but   ^{1979|} MS:life *P1869:*life,   ^{1980|} MS:worst,—which *1869:*worst:
which   ^{1981|} MS:In that age styled the primitive *P1869:*—Pass that *1872:*In just
that age styled primitive   ^{1984|} MS:rid <> fire, *P1869:*ridded *1889a:*fire:
^{1985|} MS:Kept all the while unspotted *P1869:*Keeping the *CP1869:*world!— *1872:*He
kept life-long unspotted *1889a:*world!   ^{1986|} MS:Good: but next <> game, who gives
*1872:*Next <> game, what mortal gives   ^{1987|} MS:that and this? *1872:*that, Saint
this?   ^{1988|} MS:They haggle, mutter who knows what excuse? *P1869:*They mutiny,
mutter *1872:*Men mutter, make excuse, or mutiny, *1889a:*excuse or   ^{1989|} MS:fine
make up their minds to <> new *P1869:*new, *1872:*fine are minded all to
^{1990|} MS:enjoy the liberty, *P1869:*enjoy old liberty,   ^{1991|} MS:prejudice,
all the same, if so it please, *1872:*prejudice in enjoyment, if you please,
^{1992|} MS:the late profession <> henceforth,— *P1869:*the new profession <> henceforth.
*1869:*henceforth!   ^{1993|} MS:Let the law stand: the letter kills, what *1872:*The law
stands though the letter kills: what   ^{1995|} MS:omnipotence *P1869:*sees, Omnipotence
^{1996|} MS:All mercifulness pardons,—it *P1869:*All-mercifulness *1872:*Omnibenevolence

Frown law its fiercest, there's a wink somewhere!

Such was the logic in this head of mine:
I, like the rest, wrote "poison" on my bread,
2000 But broke and ate:—said "Those that use the sword
Shall perish by the same;" then stabbed my foe.
I stand on solid earth, not empty air:
Dislodge me, let your Pope's crook hale me hence!
Not he, nor you! And I so pity both,
2005 I'll make the true charge you want wit to make:
"Count Guido, who reveal our mystery,
And trace all issues to the love of life:
We having life to love and guard, like you,
Why did you put us upon self-defence?
2010 You well knew what prompt pass-word would appease
The sentry's ire when folk infringed his bounds,
And yet kept mouth shut: do you wonder then
If, in mere decency, he shot you dead?
He can't have people play such pranks as yours
2015 Beneath his nose at noonday: you disdained
To give him an excuse before the world
By crying 'I break rule to save our camp!'
Under the old rule, such offence were death;

---

pardons: it ¹⁹⁹⁷| MS:somewhere. *1872:*somewhere! ¹⁹⁹⁷⁻⁹⁸| MS:§ no ¶ §
P1869:§ ¶ § ¹⁹⁹⁸| MS:mine,— *P1869:*mine: ¹⁹⁹⁹| MS:bread *P1869:*bread;
*1872:*bread, ²⁰⁰⁰| MS:ate, said "those *P1869:*ate:—said *1889a:*said "Those
²⁰⁰¹| MS:same,' then *P1869:*same," then *CP1869:*same;" then ²⁰⁰²| MS:Stand
therefore on the solid <> not air— *P1869:*I stand on solid <> not empty air—
*CP1869:*air: ²⁰⁰³| MS:your logic pluck § last two words crossed out and replaced
above by three words § Pope's crook hale ²⁰⁰⁴| MS:And welcome § last two words
crossed out and replaced above by four words, comma and exclamation point § Not he, nor
you! <> both *P1869:*both, ²⁰⁰⁵| MS:the speech you *1872:*the true charge you
²⁰⁰⁶| MS:"Count Guido, you have bared § last three words crossed out and replaced above
by two words § who reveal ²⁰⁰⁷| MS:You bring all issues from the <> life:
*P1869:*You trace all issues to the *1872:*And trace *1889a:*life. § emended to § life: § see
Editorial Notes § ²⁰⁰⁸| MS:what's the pass-word *P1869:*well knew what prompt
pass-word ²⁰¹¹| MS:when you § crossed out and replaced above by § folk infringe
*1889a:*infringed ²⁰¹²| MS:yet keep silence,—where's the § last three words crossed out
and replaced above by four words § mouth shut—do you *P1869:*yet kept mouth
*CP1869:*shut: do ²⁰¹³| MS:he shoots you *P1869:*he shot you ²⁰¹⁴| MS:people
play § over erasure § <> you *1889a:*yours ²⁰¹⁵| MS:noonday, who disdain
*1889a:*noonday: you disdained ²⁰¹⁶| MS:world, *1889a:*world ²⁰¹⁷| MS:crying

236

And you had heard the Pontifex pronounce
2020 'Since you slay foe and violate the form,
Slaying turns murder, which were sacrifice
Had you, while, say, law-suiting foe to death,
But raised an altar to the Unknown God
Or else the Genius of the Vatican.'
2025 Why then this pother?—all because the Pope,
Doing his duty, cried 'A foreigner,
You scandalize the natives: here at Rome
Romano vivitur more: wise men, here,
Put the Church foward and efface themselves.
2030 The fit defence had been,—you stamped on wheat,
Intending all the time to trample tares,—
Were fain extirpate, then, the heretic,
You now find, in your haste was slain a fool:
Nor Pietro, nor Violante, nor your wife
2035 Meant to breed up your babe a Molinist!
Whence you are duly contrite. Not one word
Of all this wisdom did you urge: which slip
Death must atone for.' "
                              So, let death atone!
So ends mistake, so end mistakers!—end
2040 Perhaps to recommence,—how should I know?
Only, be sure, no punishment, no pain

"I do this to < > Camp." *P1869:*crying 'I break rule to < > camp!'   2019| MS:Just so
had you heard Pontifex   *P1869:*And so   *1872:*And you had heard the Pontifex
2020| MS:"Here you < > and want the proper form: *P1869:*'Since you < > and violate the
form,   2021-23| MS:That is now murder which < > / Had you raised altar   *P1869:*That
turns to murder, which < > / Had you, while, say, law-suiting him to death,/But raised an
altar   *1872:*Slaying turns murder < > / < > law-suiting foe to < > / /
2025| MS:pother all < > Pope   *P1869:*pother?—all   *1872:*the Pope,   2026| MS:duty,
cries "You foreigner   *P1869:*cries 'A foreigner,   *1872:*cried   2027| MS:Scandalize
natives wantonly: at   *P1869:*You scandalize the natives: here at   2028| MS:wise men
here   *P1869:*wise men, here,   2029| MS:themselves: *P1869:*themselves.
2030| MS:Had it been hard to urge, you < > wheat   *P1869:*The fit defense had been, —you
< > wheat,   2031| MS:to root out tares,—   *P1869:*to trample tares,—
2032| MS:fain to extirpate the heretic   *CP1869:*fain extirpate, then, the heretic,
2033| MS:And now find, in your haste you slew a   *1872:*You now < > haste was slain a
2035| MS:a Molinist—   *P1869:*a Molinist!   2036-38| MS:contrite. 'Tis this slip/Death
< > for!" § ¶ § So let   *P1869:*contrite. Not one word/Of all this wisdom did you urge!—
which slip/Death < > for!' " § ¶ § So, let   *1872:*/ < > urge: which
2039| MS:mistakers!—End   *CP1869:*mistakers!—end   2041| MS:Only be sure no < >

Childish, preposterous, impossible,
But some such fate as Ovid could foresee,—
Byblis in fluvium, let the weak soul end
2045 In water, *sed Lycaon in lupum,* but
The strong become a wolf for evermore!
Change that Pompilia to a puny stream
Fit to reflect the daisies on its bank!
Let me turn wolf, be whole, and sate, for once,—
2050 Wallow in what is now a wolfishness
Coerced too much by the humanity
That's half of me as well! Grow out of man,
Glut the wolf-nature,—what remains but grow
Into the man again, be man indeed
2055 And all man? Do I ring the changes right?
Deformed, transformed, reformed, informed, conformed!
The honest instinct, pent and crossed through life,
Let surge by death into a visible flow
Of rapture: as the strangled thread of flame
2060 Painfully winds, annoying and annoyed,
Malignant and maligned, thro' stone and ore,
Till earth exclude the stranger: vented once,
It finds full play, is recognized a-top
Some mountain as no such abnormal birth,
2065 Fire for the mount, not streamlet for the vale!
Ay, of the water was that wife of mine—
Be it for good, be it for ill, no run
O' the red thread through that insignificance!
Again, how she is at me with those eyes!

---

pains   *P1869:*Only, be sure, no < > pain   2042| MS:impossible,—
*CP1869:*impossible,   2043| MS:such end as   *P1869:*such fate as
2044-47| MS:Byblis in fluvium, Lycaon in lupum—ay—/Change   *P1869:Byblis in fluvium,*
let the weak soul end/In water, *sed Lycaon in lupum,* but/The strong become a wolf for
evermore!/Change   2048| MS:bank,—   *P1869:*bank!   2049| MS:sate for
*P1869:*sate, for   2050| MS:now the wolfishness   *P1869:*now a wolfishness
2051| MS:Coërced through life § last two words crossed out and replaced above by two
words § too much by this humanity   *P1869:*Coërced < > by the humanity
2052| MS:well: grow   *P1869:*well! Grow   2055| MS:man; do   *P1869:*man? Do
2056| MS:conformed: *P1869:*conformed!   2061| MS:thro' earth § crossed out and
replaced above by § stone   2062| MS:Till angry § added above line § earth < > the
creature: vented   *P1869:*Till earth < > stranger: vented   2064| MS:birth.   *1889a:*birth
*DC,BrU:*birth, *1889:*birth,   2065| MS:mount, the streamlet   *DC,BrU:*mount, not
streamlet   *1889:*mount, not streamlet   2068| MS:Of   *P1869:*O'   2069| MS:Again,

2070 Away with the empty stare! Be holy still,
And stupid ever! Occupy your patch
Of private snow that's somewhere in what world
May now be growing icy round your head,
And aguish at your foot-print,—freeze not me,
2075 Dare follow not another step I take,
Not with so much as those detested eyes,
No, though they follow but to pray me pause
On the incline, earth's edge that's next to hell!
None of your abnegation of revenge!
2080 Fly at me frank, tug while I tear again!
There's God, go tell Him, testify your worst!
Not she! There was no touch in her of hate:
And it would prove her hell, if I reached mine!
To know I suffered, would still sadden her,
2085 Do what the angels might to make amends!
Therefore there's either no such place as hell,
Or thence shall I be thrust forth, for her sake,
And thereby undergo three hells, not one—
I who, with outlet for escape to heaven,
2090 Would tarry if such flight allowed my foe
To raise his head, relieved of that firm foot
Had pinned him to the fiery pavement else!
So am I made, "who did not make myself:"
(How dared she rob my own lip of the word?)
2095 Beware me in what other world may be!—
Pompilia, who have brought me to this pass!
All I know here, will I say there, and go

---

§ word and comma added in margin § How § altered to § how she is ever § last two words
crossed out and replaced above by § is < > eyes— *CP1869:*eyes!   ²⁰⁷¹| MS:ever:
occupy *P1869:*ever! Occupy   ²⁰⁷²⁻⁷⁴| MS:Of April snow < > / Is aguish *P1869:*Of
private snow < > / May now be growing icy round your head,/And aguish
²⁰⁷⁸| MS:incline, the § crossed out and replaced above by § earth's < > Hell! *P1869:*hell!
²⁰⁸⁰| MS:Fly at me § last two words added above line §   ²⁰⁸¹| MS:tell and testify
*P1869:*tell Him, testify   ²⁰⁸³| MS:mine,— *P1869:*mine!— *CP1869:*mine!
²⁰⁸⁴| MS:her *P1869:*her,   ²⁰⁸⁵| MS:amends— *P1869:*amends!   ²⁰⁸⁷| MS:shall I
have respite for her sake *P1869:*shall I be thrust forth, for her sake,   ²⁰⁹²| MS:Late
pinned < > pavement there. *P1869:*Had pinned < > pavement else!
²⁰⁹³⁻⁹⁷| MS:made, who < > myself:/ < > be!/ All *P1869:*made, "who < > myself:"/(How
dared she rob my own lip of the word?)/ < > be!—/Pompilia, who have brought me to this

Beyond the saying with the deed. Some use
There cannot but be for a mood like mine,
2100 Implacable, persistent in revenge.
She maundered "All is over and at end:
I go my own road, go you where God will!
Forgive you? I forget you!" There's the saint
That takes your taste, you other kind of men!
2105 How you had loved her! Guido wanted skill
To value such a woman at her worth!
Properly the instructed criticize
"What's here, you simpleton have tossed to take
Its chance i' the gutter? This a daub, indeed?
2110 Why, 'tis a Rafael that you kicked to rags!"
Perhaps so: some prefer the pure design:
Give me my gorge of colour, glut of gold
In a glory round the Virgin made for me!
Titian's the man, not Monk Angelico
2115 Who traces you some timid chalky ghost
That turns the church into a charnel: ay,
Just such a pencil might depict my wife!
She,—since she, also, would not change herself,—
Why could not she come in some heart-shaped cloud,
2120 Rainbowed about with riches, royalty
Rimming her round, as round the tintless lawn
Guardingly runs the selvage cloth of gold?

---

pass!/All   2099| MS:mine CP1869:mine,   2101| MS:She would say "All
P1869:She maundered "All   2102| MS:will: P1869:will!   2105| MS:her! 'Tis I
§ crossed out and replaced above by § myself wanted § altered to § want   P1869:her! Guido
wanted   2106| MS:worth,— P1869:worth!   2107| MS:Myself, § over illegible
word § you the P1869:Properly the   2108| MS:here, the § crossed out and replaced
above by § you <> has § corrected to § have   2109| MS:It's <> in the gutter? That he
calls a § last four words crossed out and replaced above by two words § Dirty indeed daub
§ transposed to § daub indeed? P1869:Its <> i' the gutter? This a daub, indeed?
2110| MS:a Rafael this has § crossed out and replaced above by § you kicked § altered to §
kick P1869:a Rafael that you kicked   2111| MS:design P1869:design:
2115| MS:some tintless chalky P1869:some timid chalky   2117-19| MS:pencil should
§ crossed out and replaced above by § might <> /Why <> cloud P1869:wife!/She,—since
she, also, would not change herself,—/Why <> cloud,   2121| MS:Rimmed her, as runs
a selvage cloth of gold, § line crossed out and replaced above by § Rimming her round, as
round the feeble lawn P1869:the tintless lawn   2122| MS:Guardingly § added in
margin § Runs for a guard § last three words crossed out § P1869:runs

240

I would have left the faint fine gauze untouched,
Needle-worked over with its lily and rose,
2125 Let her bleach unmolested in the midst,
Chill that selected solitary spot
Of quietude she pleased to think was life.
Purity, pallor grace the lawn no doubt
When there's the costly bordure to unthread
2130 And make again an ingot: but what's grace
When you want meat and drink and clothes and fire?
A tale comes to my mind that's apposite—
Possibly true, probably false, a truth
Such as all truths we live by, Cardinal!
2135 'Tis said, a certain ancestor of mine
Followed—whoever was the potentate,
To Paynimrie, and in some battle, broke
Through more than due allowance of the foe,
And, risking much his own life, saved the lord's.
2140 Battered and bruised, the Emperor scrambles up,
Rubs his eyes and looks round and sees my sire,
Picks a furze-sprig from out his hauberk-joint,
(Token how near the ground went majesty)
And says "Take this, and if thou get safe home,
2145 Plant the same in thy garden-ground to grow:
Run thence an hour in a straight line, and stop:

2123-25| MS:fine vow alone § crossed out and replaced above by § untouched,/Let her stand
unmolested in P1869:fine gauze untouched,/Needle-worked over with its lily and rose,/Let
her bleach unmolested   2126| MS:Keep that P1869:Chill that   2127| MS:life:
1889a:life.   2129| MS:there's the § crossed out and replaced above by one word § beside
bordure one unthreads P1869:there's the costly bordure to unthread   2130| MS:makes
P1869:make   2136| MS:Followed whoever <> potentate P1869:Followed —whoever
<> potentate,   2138| MS:foe 1872:foe,   2139| MS:And saved the lord's life,
risking much his own. P1869:And, risking much his own life, saved the lord's.
2140| MS:bruised the P1869:bruised, the   2142| MS:Then § crossed out § Picks
2143| MS:(Witness § crossed out and replaced above by § Token how near § added above
line § the ground was majesty) P1869:ground went majesty)   2144| MS:says, "Take
<> and if <> home again, P1869:says "Take <> and, if <> home, 1872:this, and if
2145| MS:garden ground P1869:garden-ground   2146| MS:stop, P1869:stop:

Describe a circle round (for central point)
The furze aforesaid, reaching every way
The length of that hour's run: I give it thee,—
2150   The central point, to build a castle there,
The space circumjacent, for fit demesne,
The whole to be thy children's heritage,—
Whom, for thy sake, bid thou wear furze on cap!"
Those are my arms: we turned the furze a tree
2155   To show more, and the greyhound tied thereto,
Straining to start, means swift and greedy both;
He stands upon a triple mount of gold—
By Jove, then, he's escaping from true gold
And trying to arrive at empty air!
2160   Aha! the fancy never crossed my mind!
My father used to tell me, and subjoin
"As for the castle, that took wings and flew:
The broad lands,—why, to traverse them to-day
Scarce tasks my gouty feet, and in my prime
2165   I doubt not I could stand and spit so far:
But for the furze, boy, fear no lack of that,
So long as fortune leaves one field to grub!
Wherefore, hurra for furze and loyalty!"
What may I mean, where may the lesson lurk?
2170   "Do not bestow on man, by way of gift,
Furze without land for framework,—vaunt no grace
Of purity, no furze-sprig of a wife,
To me, i' the thick of battle for my bread,
Without some better dowry,—gold will do!"

2147| MS:round, for <> point,   *P1869:*round (for <> point)   2151| MS:With
§ crossed out § The surrounding § crossed out and replaced above by § circumjacent space
for *P1869:*space, for   *1872:*The space circumjacent, for   2153-61| MS:for my sake <> /
My *P1869:*cap!"/Those are my arms: we turned the furze a tree/To show more, and the
greyhound tied thereto,/Straining to start, means swift and greedy both,/He stands upon a
triple mount of gold—/By Jove, then, he's escaping from true gold/And trying to arrive at
empty air!/Aha! the fancy never crossed my mind!/My   *CP1869:*/ / / <> both;   *1872:*for
thy sake   2164| MS:Would task <> feet, though in   *1872:*Scarce tasks <> feet, and in
2166| MS:that *CP1869:*that,   2167| MS:grub, *P1869:*grub!   2168| MS:Wherefore
hurra *1872:*Wherefore, hurra   2169| MS:What do § crossed out and replaced above
by § may   2170| MS:man by <> gift   *1872:*man, by <> gift,   2171| MS:without
some substantial framework,—grace   *1872:*without land for framework, —vaunt no grace
2172| MS:purity, a furze-sprig   *1872:*purity, no furze-sprig   2174| MS:dowry,—house

²¹⁷⁵ No better gift than sordid muck? Yes, Sirs!
Many more gifts much better. Give them me!
O those Olimpias bold, those Biancas brave,
That brought a husband power worth Ormuz' wealth!
Cried "Thou being mine, why, what but thine am I?
²¹⁸⁰ Be thou to me law, right, wrong, heaven and hell!
Let us blend souls, blent, thou in me, to bid
Two bodies work one pleasure! What are these
Called king, priest, father, mother, stranger, friend?
They fret thee or they frustrate? Give the word—
²¹⁸⁵ Be certain they shall frustrate nothing more!
And who is this young florid foolishness
That holds thy fortune in his pigmy clutch,
—Being a prince and potency, forsooth!—
He hesitates to let the trifle go?
²¹⁹⁰ Let me but seal up eye, sing ear to sleep
Sounder than Samson,—pounce thou on the prize
Shall slip from off my breast, and down couch-side,
And on to floor, and far as my lord's feet—
Where he stands in the shadow with the knife,
²¹⁹⁵ Waiting to see what Delilah dares do!
Is the youth fair? What is a man to me
Who am thy call-bird? Twist his neck—my dupe's,—
Then take the breast shall turn a breast indeed!"
Such women are there; and they marry whom?
²²⁰⁰ Why, when a man has gone and hanged himself

---

and land!" *1872:*dowry,—gold will do!"   ^{2175-76|} MS:§ written in a single line,
separated by a slash, squeezed in between 2174-77 § No other gift than sordid muck? Yes,
Sir!/ <> more and much   *1872:*No better gift <> / <> more gifts much   *1889a:*muck?
Yes, Sirs!/   ^{2177|} MS:those Olimpias bold § added above line § <> brave
*P1869:*brave,   ^{2178|} MS:husband wills worth Ormuz   *P1869:*will <> Ormuz'
*1872:*husband power worth   ^{2179|} MS:why what, am I, but thine? § transposed to §
what but thine am I?   *CP1869:*why, what   ^{2181|} MS:souls, be thou in me to
*1872:*souls, blent, thou in me, to   ^{2183|} MS:king and § crossed out § priest, called
§ crossed out and replaced above by two words § father, mother, stranger or called § last two
words crossed out §   *P1869:*king, priest   ^{2188|} MS:—Being § dash added in margin §
^{2189|} MS:And hesitates   *1889a:*He hesitates   ^{2192|} MS:breasts <> couch-side
*P1869:*breast   *1889a:*couch-side,   ^{2194|} MS:the sword   *1872:*sword,   *1889a:*the knife,
^{2195|} MS:do: *P1869:*do!   ^{2197|} MS:neck,—my dupe,—   *P1869:*neck—my dupe's,—
^{2198|} MS:breasts <> turn to breasts   *P1869:*breast <> turn a breast

Because of what he calls a wicked wife,—
See, if the very turpitude bemoaned
Prove not mere excellence the fool ignores!
His monster is perfection,—Circe, sent
2205 Straight from the sun, with wand the idiot blames
As not an honest distaff to spin wool!
O thou Lucrezia, is it long to wait
Yonder where all the gloom is in a glow
With thy suspected presence?—virgin yet,
2210 Virtuous again, in face of what's to teach—
Sin unimagined, unimaginable,—
I come to claim my bride,—thy Borgia's self
Not half the burning bridegroom I shall be!
Cardinal, take away your crucifix!
2215 Abate, leave my lips alone,—they bite!
Vainly you try to change what should not change,
And shall not. I have bared, you bathe my heart—
It grows the stonier for your saving dew!
You steep the substance, you would lubricate,
2220 In waters that but touch to petrify!

You too are petrifactions of a kind:
Move not a muscle that shows mercy. Rave
Another twelve hours, every word were waste!
I thought you would not slay impenitence,

2201| MS:Because he had, he says, § last four words and commas crossed out and replaced
above by four words § of what he calls a worthless § crossed out and replaced above by §
wicked   2202| MS:if this monster that he howls about § last six words crossed out and
replaced above by six words § the turpitude he makes his moan   *P1869:*turpitude, he <>
moan,   *1872:*the very turpitude bemoaned,   *1889a:*bemoaned   2203| MS:Be not <>
ignores,—   *P1869:*ignores!   *1872:*Prove not   2204| MS:perfection, Circe sent
*CP1869:*perfection, Circe, sent   *1872:*perfection,—Circe   2205| MS:with rod the
*1872:*with wand the   2209| MS:presence,—virgin   *P1869:*presence?—virgin
2210| MS:again in <> what shall § crossed out and replaced above by § must be—
*P1869:*what's to teach—   *1872:*again, in   2212| MS:My bride I come to claim
§ transposed to § I come to claim my bride thy   *P1869:*bride,—thy   2213| MS:burning
Bridegroom   *P1869:*bridegroom   2215| MS:alone, they   *1872:*alone,—they
2216| MS:'Tis no use trying to change, what   *P1869:*'Tis vain you try to   *1872:*Vainly you
<> change what   2217| MS:And cannot. I have bared the heart, you steep § crossed out
and replaced above by § bathe—   *P1869:*bared, you bathe my heart—   *1889a:*And shall not.
I   2222| MS:mercy,—rave   *P1869:*mercy; rave   *1889a:*mercy. Rave
2223| MS:word's in waste.   *P1869:*word were waste!   2224| MS:impenitence,—

244

²²²⁵ But teased, from men you slew, contrition first,—
I thought you had a conscience. Cardinal,
You know I am wronged!—wronged, say, and wronged, maintain.
Was this strict inquisition made for blood
When first you showed us scarlet on your back,
²²³⁰ Called to the College? Your straightforward way
To your legitimate end,—I think it passed
Over a scantling of heads brained, hearts broke,
Lives trodden into dust! How otherwise?
Such was the way o' the world, and so you walked.
²²³⁵ Does memory haunt your pillow? Not a whit.
God wills you never pace your garden-path,
One appetizing hour ere dinner-time,
But your intrusion there treads out of life
A universe of happy innocent things:
²²⁴⁰ Feel you remorse about that damsel-fly
Which buzzed so near your mouth and flapped your face?
You blotted it from being at a blow:
It was a fly, you were a man, and more,
Lord of created things, so took your course.
²²⁴⁵ Manliness, mind,—these are things fit to save,
Fit to brush fly from: why, because I take
My course, must needs the Pope kill me?—kill you!
You! for this instrument, he throws away,
Is strong to serve a master, and were yours
²²⁵⁰ To have and hold and get much good from out!

---

*1872:*impenitence, ²²²⁵| MS:Teazed first contrition from the man you slew,—
*1872:*But teazed, from men you slew, contrition first,— *1889a:*teased ²²²⁷| MS:and
wronged maintain. *1872:*and wronged, maintain. ²²²⁸| MS:Was there § crossed out §
this strict § added above line § ²²²⁹| MS:us red upon your *P1869:*us scarlet on your
²²³⁰| MS:the College? That straightforward *1872:*the College? Your straightforward
²²³¹| MS:To that legitimate *1872:*To your legitimate ²²³³| MS:dust,—how
*1872:*dust!—how *1889a:*dust! How ²²³⁴| MS:Such is the way of <> walk: *P1869:*o'
*1872:*Such was the <> walked: *1889a:*walked. ²²³⁶| MS:garden-path
*1872:*garden-path, ²²³⁷| MS:dinner-time *1872:*dinner-time, ²²³⁹| MS:An
universe *1872:*A universe ²²⁴¹| MS:face, *1872:*face? ²²⁴²| MS:blow?
*1872:*blow: ²²⁴⁶| MS:To brush the fly <> why because *P1869:*Fit to brush fly <>
why, because ²²⁴⁷| MS:me? Kill you? *P1869:*you!— *CP1869:*me?—kill you!
²²⁴⁸| MS:Because this instrument he <> away *1872:*You! for this instrument, he <>
away, ²²⁴⁹| MS:master: it were *1872:*master, and were ²²⁵⁰| MS:get such good

The Pope who dooms me needs must die next year;
I'll tell you how the chances are supposed
For his successor: first the Chamberlain,
Old San Cesario,—Colloredo, next,—
2255   Then, one, two, three, four, I refuse to name;
After these, comes Altieri; then come you—
Seventh on the list you come, unless . . . ha, ha,
How can a dead hand give a friend a lift?
Are you the person to despise the help
2260   O' the head shall drop in pannier presently?
So a child seesaws on or kicks away
The fulcrum-stone that's all the sage requires
To fit his lever to and move the world.
Cardinal, I adjure you in God's name,
2265   Save my life, fall at the Pope's feet, set forth
Things your own fashion, not in words like these
Made for a sense like yours who apprehend!
Translate into the Court-conventional
"Count Guido must not die, is innocent!
2270   Fair, be assured! But what an he were foul,
Blood-drenched and murder-crusted head to foot?
Spare one whose death insults the Emperor,
Nay, outrages the Louis you so love!
He has friends who will avenge him; enemies
2275   Who will hate God now with impunity,
Missing the old coercive: would you send

---

*1872:*get much good   2251| *P1869:*me, needs   *1889a:*me needs   2253| MS:the Chamberlain—   *CP1869:*the Chamberlain,   2255| MS:name,   *1872:*name;   2256| MS:these, Altieri,—then   *P1869:*these, comes Altieri; then   2257| MS:you are, unless . . ha, ha,   *1872:*you come, unless   *1889a:*unless . . . ha, ha,   2258| MS:dead hand § over *man* §   2260| MS:Of < > panier   *P1869:*O' < > pannier   2261-62| MS:§ two lines, separated by slash, written on one line § child seesaws on or § last three words added above line § < > /The leverage § crossed out and replaced above by § fulcrum-stone   2263| MS:Wherewith the sages pry § added above; last four words crossed out and replaced above by three words § To fit his lever with and § last two words added above line § moves § altered to § move   *P1869:*lever to and   2264| MS:name *P1869:*name,   2268| MS:court-conventional   *1889a:*the Court-conventional   2269| MS:innocent,   *P1869:*innocent!   2272| MS:Save one   *P1869:*Spare one   2273| MS:And outrages   *1872:*Nay, outrages   2274| MS:him,—enemies   *P1869:*him; enemies   2275| MS:Who hate the church now with impunity   *1872:*Who will hate God now with impunity,   2276| MS:coercive: there you   *P1869:*coercive: would you

A soul straight to perdition, dying frank
An atheist?" Go and say this, for God's sake!
—Why, you don't think I hope you'll say one word?
2280 Neither shall I persuade you from your stand
Nor you persuade me from my station: take
Your crucifix away, I tell you twice!

Come, I am tired of silence! Pause enough!
You have prayed: I have gone inside my soul
2285 And shut its door behind me: 'tis your torch
Makes the place dark: the darkness let alone
Grows tolerable twilight: one may grope
And get to guess at length and breadth and depth.
What is this fact I feel persuaded of—
2290 This something like a foothold in the sea,
Although Saint Peter's bark scuds, billow-borne,
Leaves me to founder where it flung me first?
Spite of your splashing, I am high and dry!
God takes his own part in each thing He made;
2295 Made for a reason, He conserves his work,
Gives each its proper instinct of defence.
My lamblike wife could neither bark nor bite,
She bleated, bleated, till for pity pure
The village roused up, ran with pole and prong
2300 To the rescue, and behold the wolf's at bay!
Shall he try bleating?—or take turn or two,
Since the wolf owns some kinship with the fox,
And, failing to escape the foe by craft,

2278| MS:atheist!" Go *P1869:*atheist?" Go   2279| MS:—Why § dash added in margin §
2280| MS:Neither shall § added above line § < > stand § slash § —nor you § two words and
dash crossed out §   2281| MS:Nor you persuade § three words added in margin, above
line § Me < > station — take it from my mouth § last four words crossed out § *P1869:*me
*CP1869:*station: take   2282| MS:crucifix away, § word and comma added above §
2286| MS:dark,—the *1872:*dark: the   2287| MS:twilight,—one *1872:*twilight: one
2289| MS:of *P1869:*of—   2292| MS:Bidding § crossed out and replaced above by §
Leaves me to § added above §   2294| MS:he *1889a:*thing He   2295| MS:he
*1889a:*reason, He   2298| MS:'till for pity's § altered to § pity sake § crossed out § pure,
*P1869:*till *1889a:*pure   2299| MS:roused it, ran with staff § crossed out and replaced
above by § pole *1889a:*roused up, ran   2300| MS:wolf *P1869:*wolf's
2302| MS:owns to kinship *1889a:*owns some kinship   2303| MS:And failing < > by

Give up attempt, die fighting quietly?
2305 The last bad blow that strikes fire in at eye
And on to brain, and so out, life and all,
How can it but be cheated of a pang
If, fighting quietly, the jaws enjoy
One re-embrace in mid back-bone they break,
2310 After their weary work thro' the foe's flesh?
That's the wolf-nature. Don't mistake my trope!
A Cardinal so qualmish? Eminence,
My fight is figurative, blows i' the air,
Brain-war with powers and principalities,
2315 Spirit-bravado, no real fisticuffs!
I shall not presently, when the knock comes,
Cling to this bench nor claw the hangman's face,
No, trust me! I conceive worse lots than mine.
Whether it be, the old contagious fit
2320 And plague o' the prison have surprised me too,
The appropriate drunkenness of the death-hour
Crept on my sense, kind work o' the wine and myrrh,—
I know not,—I begin to taste my strength,
Careless, gay even. What's the worth of life?
2325 The Pope's dead now, my murderous old man,
For Tozzi told me so: and you, forsooth—
Why, you don't think, Abate, do your best,
You'll live a year more with that hacking cough
And blotch of crimson where the cheek's a pit?
2330 Tozzi has got you also down in book!
Cardinal, only seventh of seventy near,
Is not one called Albano in the lot?
Go eat your heart, you'll never be a Pope!

---

these, *1872:*And, failing *1889a:*by craft, 2305| MS:The last § added above §
2308| MS:While, fighting *1872:*If, fighting 2309| MS:Their re-embrace <> backbone
<> break *P1869:*back-bone <> break, *1872:*One re-embrace 2310| MS:flesh.
*P1869:*flesh? 2312| MS:The Cardinal is qualmish *1872:*A Cardinal so qualmish
2315| MS:fisticuffs: *P1869:*fisticuffs! 2317| MS:nor flea the *P1869:*nor flee the
*1872:*nor claw the 2319| MS:be the *1872:*be, the 2320| MS:of *P1869:*o'
2322| MS:sense, the work <> myrrh, *P1869:*Creep <> myrrh,— *1872:*Crept <> sense,
kind work 2324| MS:even: what's *1872:*even. What's 2325| MS:pope is dead, my
*P1869:*The Pope *1872:*The Pope's dead now, my 2328| MS:live three years
*CP1869:*live a year 2330| MS:book. *1872:*book! 2331-33| MS:seventy two,/Go

Inform me, is it true you left your love,
2335   A Pucci, for promotion in the church?
She's more than in the church,—in the churchyard!
Plautilla Pucci, your affianced bride,
Has dust now in the eyes that held the love,—
And Martinez, suppose they make you Pope,
2340   Stops that with *veto*,—so, enjoy yourself!
I see you all reel to the rock, you waves—
Some forthright, some describe a sinuous track,
Some, crested brilliantly, with heads above,
Some in a strangled swirl sunk who knows how,
2345   But all bound whither the main-current sets,
Rockward, an end in foam for all of you!
What if I be o'ertaken, pushed to the front
By all you crowding smoother souls behind,
And reach, a minute sooner than was meant,
2350   The boundary whereon I break to mist?
Go to! the smoothest safest of you all,
Most perfect and compact wave in my train,
Spite of the blue tranquillity above,
Spite of the breadth before of lapsing peace
2355   Where broods the halcyon and the fish leaps free,
Will presently begin to feel the prick
At lazy heart, the push at torpid brain,
Will rock vertiginously in turn, and reel,

---

*P1869:*seventy near,/Is not one called Albano in the lot?/Go   ²³³⁴| MS:me if 'tis true
*P1869:*me, is it true   ²³³⁶| MS:churchyard; *P1869:*churchyard!
²³³⁷| MS:Plautilla Pucci your <> bride *P1869:*Plautilla Pucci, your <> bride,
²³³⁸| MS:eyes, that *P1869:*eyes that   ²³⁴⁰| MS:veto,—so enjoy *P1869:*veto,—so,
enjoy   ²³⁴³| MS:Some crested, brilliantly with *1872:*Some, crested brilliantly, with
²³⁴⁶| MS:you. *P1869:*you!   ²³⁴⁷| MS:It happens I am oertaken *P1869:*What if I am
o'ertaken *1872:*be   ²³⁴⁸| MS:By you, the crowd of smoother *P1869:*By all you
crowding smoother   ²³⁵⁰| MS:boundary, whereon <> mist. *P1869:*mist?
*1872:*boundary whereon   ²³⁵¹| MS:of my train § last two words crossed out and
replaced above by two words § you all,   ²³⁵²| MS:compact wave § added above line §
²³⁵⁴| MS:Spite of the § last two words added above § breadth of lapsing § added
above § peacefulness § altered to § peace before *P1869:*breadth before of <> peace
*1872:*peace, *1889a:*peace   ²³⁵⁵| MS:halcyon, and *P1869:*halcyon and
²³⁵⁸| MS:Vertiginously rock in turn and reel *P1869:*Will rock vertiginously in turn,

And, emulative, rush to death like me.
2360 Later or sooner by a minute then,
So much for the untimeliness of death!
And, as regards the manner that offends,
The rude and rough, I count the same for gain.
Be the act harsh and quick! Undoubtedly
2365 The soul's condensed and, twice itself, expands
To burst thro' life, by alternation due,
Into the other state whate'er it prove.
You never know what life means till you die:
Even throughout life, 'tis death that makes life live,
2370 Gives it whatever the significance.
For see, on your own ground and argument,
Suppose life had no death to fear, how find
A possibility of nobleness
In man, prevented daring any more?
2375 What's love, what's faith without a worst to dread?
Lack-lustre jewelry! but faith and love
With death behind them bidding do or die—
Put such a foil at back, the sparkle's born!
From out myself how the strange colours come!
2380 Is there a new rule in another world?
Be sure I shall resign myself: as here
I recognized no law I could not see,
There, what I see, I shall acknowledge too:
On earth I never took the Pope for God,
2385 In heaven I shall scarce take God for the Pope.
Unmanned, remanned: I hold it probable—
With something changeless at the heart of me
To know me by, some nucleus that's myself:
Accretions did it wrong? Away with them—

and reel,   2359| MS:me: 1872:me.   2361| MS:death,— 1872:death!
2362| MS:as his § crossed out and replaced above by two words § regards the
2363| MS:gain— 1872:gain.   2366| MS:To § added in margin § Bursts § altered to §
Burst right § crossed out § < > life, in alternation P1869:burst 1889a:life, by alternation
2369| MS:Even through life P1869:through our life CP1869:Even throughout life
2374| MS:man prevented CP1869:man, prevented   2375| MS:without the § crossed out
and replaced above by § a   2376| MS:jewelry; but 1872:jewelry! but
2386| MS:Unmanned, remade: I CP1869:Unmade, remade 1869:Unmanned, remade

²³⁹⁰ You soon shall see the use of fire!

                                  Till when,
All that was, is; and must forever be.
Nor is it in me to unhate my hates,—
I use up my last strength to strike once more
Old Pietro in the wine-house-gossip-face,
²³⁹⁵ To trample underfoot the whine and wile
Of beast Violante,—and I grow one gorge
To loathingly reject Pompilia's pale
Poison my hasty hunger took for food.
A strong tree wants no wreaths about its trunk,
²⁴⁰⁰ No cloying cups, no sickly sweet of scent,
But sustenance at root, a bucketful.
How else lived that Athenian who died so,
Drinking hot bull's blood, fit for men like me?
I lived and died a man, and take man's chance,
²⁴⁰⁵ Honest and bold: right will be done to such.

Who are these you have let descend my stair?
Ha, their accursed psalm! Lights at the sill!
Is it "Open" they dare bid you? Treachery!
Sirs, have I spoken one word all this while
²⁴¹⁰ Out of the world of words I had to say?
Not one word! All was folly—I laughed and mocked!

1872: Unmanned, remanned: I   ^{2390|}   MS:fire,—till when   *P1869:* fire! § ¶ § Till when,
^{2391|}   MS:is, and <> be—   *P1869:* is; and <> be.   ^{2394|}   MS:wine-house-gossip face,
P1869: wine-house-gossip-face,   ^{2395|}   MS:trample out of life § last three words crossed
out and replaced above by one word § underfoot   ^{2396|}   MS:Of § in margin § That
Violante   *P1869:* that   *1872:* Of beast Violante   ^{2399|}   MS:wreathes <> trunk
P1869: wreaths <> trunk,   ^{2400|}   MS:of stars,   *P1869:* of scent,
^{2401|}   MS:bucket-ful—   *P1869:* bucketful.   ^{2402|}   MS:How § over erasure § <> so
P1869: so,   ^{2403|}   MS:bull's-blood   *1872:* bull's blood   ^{2405|}   MS:done the bold.
§ last two words crossed out and replaced above by two words and colon § to such:
P1869: to such.   ^{2405-6|}   MS:§ no ¶ §   *P1869:* § ¶ §   ^{2406|}   MS:Whom are <> let
ascend the § crossed out and replaced above by § my   *P1869:* let descend my   *1869:* Who are
^{2407|}   MS:the door! § exclamation point altered to § sill   *P1869:* the sill!
^{2408|}   MS:"open" <> you? § next two words and comma crossed out; first word *God* §
Treachery!   *P1869:* it "Open"   ^{2409|}   MS:Judge § crossed out and replaced above by
word and comma § Sirs,   ^{2410-11|}   MS:§ written on one line §   ^{2410|}   MS:Out of the
world § last four words in margin § Of words a world § last two words crossed out and
replaced above by two words § I had   *P1869:* of words   ^{2411|}   MS:Not one word,—all

Sirs, my first true word, all truth and no lie,
Is—save me notwithstanding! Life is all!
I was just stark mad,—let the madman live

2415   Pressed by as many chains as you please pile!
Don't open! Hold me from them! I am yours,
I am the Granduke's—no, I am the Pope's!
Abate,—Cardinal,—Christ,—Maria,—God, . . .
Pompilia, will you let them murder me?

was folly— § last six words, comma and dashes added above § I <> mocked   *P1869:*word!
All <> mocked!   2412| MS:Cardinal § crossed out and replaced above by § Sirs <>
true § inserted above § word all <> lie *P1869:*word, all <> lie,   2413| MS:all—
*P1869:*all!   2414| MS:mad, let *P1869:*mad,—let   2415| MS:Under § crossed
out and replaced above by two words § Pressed by <> you can pile! *P1869:*you
please pile!   2416| MS:open—hold <> them, I *P1869:*open! Hold <> them! I
2417-18| MS:§ written on one line, with slash between lines §   2417| MS:I am the
Granduke's—no, I Am § last seven words written in margin § The Pope's! *P1869:*am
the   2418| MS:Abate, § word and comma above illegible erasure § Cardinal,—
Abate,— § word crossed out and dashes erased, replaced above by two words and commas §
Christ, Maria, God,— *P1869:*Abate,—Cardinal,—Christ,—Maria,—God, . . .

XII

THE BOOK AND THE RING

Here were the end, had anything an end:
Thus, lit and launched, up and up roared and soared
A rocket, till the key o' the vault was reached
And wide heaven held, a breathless minute-space,
5   In brilliant usurpature: thus caught spark,
Rushed to the height, and hung at full of fame
Over men's upturned faces, ghastly thence,
Our glaring Guido: now decline must be.
In its explosion, you have seen his act,
10   By my power—may-be, judged it by your own,—
Or composite as good orbs prove, or crammed
With worse ingredients than the Wormwood Star.
The act, over and ended, falls and fades:
What was once seen, grows what is now described,
15   Then talked of, told about, a tinge the less
In every fresh transmission; till it melts,
Trickles in silent orange or wan grey
Across our memory, dies and leaves all dark,
And presently we find the stars again.
20   Follow the main streaks, meditate the mode
Of brightness, how it hastes to blend with black!

After that February Twenty-Two,
Since our salvation, Sixteen-Ninety-Eight,
Of all reports that were, or may have been,
25   Concerning those the day killed or let live,
Four I count only. Take the first that comes.
A letter from a stranger, man of rank,
Venetian visitor at Rome,—who knows,
On what pretence of busy idleness?

3| MS:reached, DC:BrU:reached *1889:*reached   6| MS:height and *P1869:*height,
and   7| MS:mens' *P1869:*men's   9| MS:act *P1869:*act,
21| MS:brightness—how *P1869:*brightness, how   22| MS:that February Twenty
Two, *P1869:*that February Twenty-Two,   23| MS:salvation Sixteen Ninety Eight,
*P1869:*salvation Sixteen-Ninety-Eight,   28| MS:Venitian *P1869:*Venetian

30   Thus he begins on evening of that day.

———————

"Here are we at our end of Carnival;
Prodigious gaiety and monstrous mirth,
And constant shift of entertaining show:
With influx, from each quarter of the globe,
35   Of strangers nowise wishful to be last
I' the struggle for a good place presently
When that befalls fate cannot long defer.
The old Pope totters on the verge o' the grave:
You see, Malpichi understood far more
40   Than Tozzi how to treat the ailments: age,
No question, renders these inveterate.
Cardinal Spada, actual Minister,
Is possible Pope; I wager on his head,
Since those four entertainments of his niece
45   Which set all Rome a-stare: Pope probably—
Though Colloredo has his backers too,
And San Cesario makes one doubt at times:
Altieri will be Chamberlain at most.

"A week ago the sun was warm like May,
50   And the old man took daily exercise
Along the river-side; he loves to see
That Custom-house he built upon the bank,
For, Naples born, his tastes are maritime:
But yesterday he had to keep in-doors
55   Because of the outrageous rain that fell.
On such days the good soul has fainting-fits,
Or lies in stupor, scarcely makes believe

31| MS:of Carnival: *P1869:*of Carnival;   33| MS:show—   *P1869:*show:
34| MS:influx from <> globe   *P1869:*influx, from <> globe,   37| MS:befalls—fate
*P1869:*befalls, fate   *1889a:*befalls fate   40| MS:ailments—age,   *P1869:*ailments: age,
41| MS:renders now inveterate.   *P1869:*renders these inveterate.   42| MS:actual
minister,   *P1869:*actual Minister,   46| MS:Though Coloredo   *P1869:*Though
Colloredo   48–49| MS:§ no ¶ §   *P1869:*§ ¶ §   52| MS:That Customhouse
*P1869:*That Custom-house   53| MS:For, Naples-born   *1889a:*For, Naples born

Of minding business, fumbles at his beads.
They say, the trust that keeps his heart alive
60 Is that, by lasting till December next,
He may hold Jubilee a second time,
And, twice in one reign, ope the Holy Doors.
By the way, somebody responsible
Assures me that the King of France has writ
65 Fresh orders: Fénelon will be condemned:
The Cardinal makes a wry face enough,
Having a love for the delinquent: still,
He's the ambassador, must press the point.
Have you a wager too, dependent here?

70 "Now, from such matters to divert awhile,
Hear of to-day's event which crowns the week,
Casts all the other wagers into shade.
Tell Dandolo I owe him fifty drops
Of heart's blood in the shape of gold zecchines!
75 The Pope has done his worst: I have to pay
For the execution of the Count, by Jove!
Two days since, I reported him as safe,
Re-echoing the conviction of all Rome:
Who could suspect its one deaf ear—the Pope's?
80 But prejudices grow insuperable,
And that old enmity to Austria, that
Passion for France and France's pageant-king
(Of which, why pause to multiply the proofs
Now scandalously rife in Europe's mouth?)
85 These fairly got the better in our man
Of justice, prudence, and *esprit de corps*,
And he persisted in the butchery.
Also, 'tis said that in his latest walk
To that Dogana-by-the-Bank he built,

58| MS:beads; *P1869:*beads.   65| MS:orders: Fenelon *1889a:*orders: Fénelon
68| MS:the Ambassador *P1869:*the ambassador   69| MS:too dependent *1872:*too,
dependent   70| MS:§ marginal note that new ¶ begins §   74| MS:hearts' < >
zecchines: *P1869:*heart's < > zecchines!   75| MS:worst,—I *P1869:*worst: I
79| MS:suspect the one *1872:*suspect its one   85| MS:in the man *1889a:*in our man
89| MS:that Dogana-by-the-Bank, he *1889a:*that Dogana-by-the-Bank he

90   The crowd,—he suffers question, unrebuked,—
Asked, 'Whether murder was a privilege
Only reserved for nobles like the Count?'
And he was ever mindful of the mob.
Martinez, the Cæsarian Minister,
95   —Who used his best endeavours to spare blood,
And strongly pleaded for the life 'of one,'
Urged he, 'I may have dined at table with!'—
He will not soon forget the Pope's rebuff,
—Feels the slight sensibly, I promise you!
100   And but for the dissuasion of two eyes
That make with him foul weather or fine day,
He had abstained, nor graced the spectacle:
As it was, barely would he condescend
Look forth from the *palchetto* where he sat
105   Under the Pincian: we shall hear of this.
The substituting, too, the People's Square
For the out-o'-the-way old quarter by the Bridge,
Was meant as a conciliatory sop
To the mob; it gave one holiday the more.
110   But the French Embassy might unfurl flag,—
Still the good luck of France to fling a foe!
Cardinal Bouillon triumphs properly.
Palchetti were erected in the Place,
And houses, at the edge of the Three Streets,
115   Let their front windows at six dollars each:
Anguisciola, that patron of the arts,
Hired one; our Envoy Contarini too.

"Now for the thing; no sooner the decree
Gone forth,—'tis four-and-twenty hours ago,—

91| MS:Asked 'whether < > privelege   *P1869:*Asked, 'Whether < > privilege
95| MS:blood   *P1869:*blood,   96| MS:one'   *P1869:*one,'   97| MS:Urged § over
illegible erasure § < > he 'I   *P1869:*he, 'I   99| MS:Feels   *P1869:*—
Feels   105| MS:this!   *1889a:*this.   112| MS:properly!   *1889a:*properly.
113| MS:Palchetti   *P1869:*Palchetti   114| MS:houses at   *P1869:*houses, at
115| MS:at six § over illegible erasure § dollars   117-18| MS:§ no ¶ §   *P1869:*§ ¶ §
1889a:§ no ¶ §   *1889:*§ no ¶ ; emended to restore ¶ ; see Editorial Notes §   118| MS:the
Count; no   *P1869:*the thing; no   119| MS:four and twenty   *P1869:*four-and-twenty

¹²⁰   Than Acciaiuoli and Panciatichi,
       Old friends, indeed compatriots of the man,
       Being pitched on as the couple properest
       To intimate the sentence yesternight,
       Were closeted ere cock-crow with the Count.
¹²⁵   They both report their efforts to dispose
       The unhappy nobleman for ending well,
       Despite the natural sense of injury,
       Were crowned at last with a complete success.
       And when the Company of Death arrived
¹³⁰   At twenty-hours,—the way they reckon here,—
       We say, at sunset, after dinner-time,—
       The Count was led down, hoisted up on car,
       Last of the five, as heinousest, you know:
       Yet they allowed one whole car to each man.
¹³⁵   His intrepidity, nay, nonchalance,
       As up he stood and down he sat himself,
       Struck admiration into those who saw.
       Then the procession started, took the way
       From the New Prisons by the Pilgrim's Street,
¹⁴⁰   The street of the Governo, Pasquin's Street,
       (Where was stuck up, 'mid other epigrams,
       A quatrain . . . but of all that, presently!)
       The Place Navona, the Pantheon's Place,
       Place of the Column, last the Corso's length,
¹⁴⁵   And so debouched thence at Mannaia's foot
       I' the Place o' the People. As is evident,
       (Despite the malice,—plainly meant, I fear,
       By this abrupt change of locality,—

---

^{120|} MS:Acciaioli *1889a:*Acciaiuoli   ^{121|} MS:the Count, *P1869:*the man,
^{122|} MS:Were pitched *P1869:*Being pitched   ^{124|} MS:And closeted *P1869:*Were
closeted   ^{127|} MS:injury, § last word over illegible erasure §   ^{128|} MS:success:
*1872:*success.   ^{130|} MS:twenty-hours, the way they count time § last two words crossed
out and replaced above by § reckon here, *P1869:*twenty-hours,—the < > here,—
^{131|} MS:say, past § crossed out and replaced above by § at < > after-dinner-time,
*P1869:*after dinner-time,—   ^{133|} MS:know, *P1869:*know: ^{134|} MS:(Yet < >
man.) *P1869:*Yet < > man.   ^{135|} MS:nonchalance *P1869:*nonchalance,
^{140|} MS:The Street < > Street *P1869:*The street < > Street,   ^{141|} *P1869:*up, 'mid
*1872:*up, mid § emended to § 'mid § see Editorial Notes §   ^{142|} MS:quatrain . . but
*1889a:*quatrain . . . but   ^{145|} MS:at § followed by word illegibly crossed out §
^{146–50|} MS:evident,/ We *P1869:*evident,/ (Despite the malice,—plainly meant, I fear,/ By

The Square's no such bad place to head and hang)
150 We had the titillation as we sat
Assembled, (quality in conclave, ha?)
Of, minute after minute, some report
How the slow show was winding on its way.
Now did a car run over, kill a man,
155 Just opposite a pork-shop numbered Twelve:
And bitter were the outcries of the mob
Against the Pope: for, but that he forbids
The Lottery, why, Twelve were Tern Quatern!
Now did a beggar by Saint Agnes, lame
160 From his youth up, recover use of leg,
Through prayer of Guido as he glanced that way:
So that the crowd near crammed his hat with coin.
Thus was kept up excitement to the last,
—Not an abrupt out-bolting, as of yore,
165 From Castle, over Bridge and on to block,
And so all ended ere you well could wink!

"To mount the scaffold-steps, Guido was last
Here also, as atrociousest in crime.
We hardly noticed how the peasants died,
170 They dangled somehow soon to right and left,
And we remained all ears and eyes, could give
Ourselves to Guido undividedly,
As he harangued the multitude beneath.
He begged forgiveness on the part of God,

this abrupt change of locality,—/ The Square's no such bad place to head and hang)/
We   152| MS:minute, each report P1869:minute, some report   153| MS:Of
how the show <> way: P1869:How the slow show <> way. 1889a:way
DC:way? BrU:way. 1889:way.   155| MS:Twelve— P1869:Twelve:
156| MS:the crowd P1869:the mob   158| MS:The Lottery, why twelve § altered to
§ Twelve <> Quatern: P1869:The Lottery, why, twelve <> Quatern! 1872:Twelve
159| MS:by Saint Agnes', lame § over illegible word § P1869:by Saint Agnes
161| MS:way,— P1869:way: 162| MS:coin: P1869:coin.   164| MS:out-bolting,
§ followed by illegible erasure §   165| MS:block P1869:block,   166-67| MS:§ no
¶ § P1869:§ ¶ §   167| MS:Guido was last to mount the scaffold-steps 1872:To mount
the scaffold-steps, Guido was last   168| MS:There also <> crime: P1869:Here also
<> crime.   173| MS:he addressed § crossed out and replaced above by § harangued
174| MS:Entreated pardon § last two words crossed out and replaced above by three words §

175 And fair construction of his act from men,
　　Whose suffrage he entreated for his soul,
　　Suggesting that we should forthwith repeat
　　A *Pater* and an *Ave,* with the hymn
　　Salve Regina Cœli, for his sake.
180 Which said, he turned to the confessor, crossed
　　And reconciled himself, with decency,
　　Oft glancing at Saint Mary's opposite,
　　Where they possess, and showed in shrine to-day,
　　The blessed *Umbilicus* of our Lord,
185 (A relic 'tis believed no other church
　　In Rome can boast of)—then rose up, as brisk
　　Knelt down again, bent head, adapted neck,
　　And, with the name of Jesus on his lips,
　　Received the fatal blow.

　　　　　　　　　　　　"The headsman showed
190 The head to the populace. Must I avouch
　　We strangers own to disappointment here?
　　Report pronounced him fully six feet high,
　　Youngish, considering his fifty years,
　　And, if not handsome, dignified at least.
195 Indeed, it was no face to please a wife!
　　His friends say, this was caused by the costume:
　　He wore the dress he did the murder in,
　　That is, a *just-a-corps* of russet serge,
　　Black camisole, coarse cloak of baracan
200 (So they style here the garb of goat's-hair cloth)
　　White hat and cotton cap beneath, poor Count,

He begged forgiveness <> God　*P1869:*God,　　　175| 　MS:men　*P1869:*men,
178| 　MS:an Ave　*P1869:*an *Ave*　　　180| 　MS:the Confessor there　*P1869:*the confessor,
crossed　　　182| 　MS:§ crowded between lines 181-83 § opposite　*1889a:*opposite,
183-85| 　MS:Then knelt down, bent head and adapted neck, § entire line crossed out § Where
<> possess the *Umbilicum* of our Lord,/ (A relic　*P1869:*possess, and showed in shrine
to-day,/ The blessed *Umbilicus* of our Lord,/ (A relic　　　188| 　MS:lips　*P1869:*lips,
189| 　MS:blow: the　*P1869:*blow. § ¶ § The　　　193| 　MS:Youngish considering
*P1869:*Youngish, considering　　　194-96| 　MS:least./ His　*P1869:*least./ Indeed, it was no
face to please a wife!/ His　　　198| 　MS:is a　*P1869:*is, a　　　200| 　MS:goats-hair
*P1869:*goat's-hair　　　201| 　MS:poor Count,　*1889a:*poor Count § emended to § Count,

Preservative against the evening dews
During the journey from Arezzo. Well,
So died the man, and so his end was peace;
205 Whence many a moral were to meditate.
Spada,—you may bet Dandolo,—is Pope!
Now for the quatrain!"

No, friend, this will do!
You've sputtered into sparks. What streak comes next?
A letter: Don Giacinto Arcangeli,
210 Doctor and Proctor, him I made you mark
Buckle to business in his study late,
The virtuous sire, the valiant for the truth,
Acquaints his correspondent,—Florentine,
By name Cencini, advocate as well,
215 *Socius* and brother-in-the-devil to match,—
A friend of Franceschini, anyhow,
And knit up with the bowels of the case,—
Acquaints him, (in this paper that I touch)
How their joint effort to obtain reprieve
220 For Guido had so nearly nicked the nine
And ninety and one over,—folk would say
At Tarocs,—or succeeded,—in our phrase.
To this Cencini's care I owe the Book,
The yellow thing I take and toss once more,—
225 How will it be, my four-years'-intimate,
When thou and I part company anon?—
'Twas he, the "whole position of the case,"

§ see Editorial Notes §   203-8| MS:Well,/ Spada, you <> Dandolo, is Pope./ <>
Quatrain!" § note that ¶ begins here after inserted line § No <> do,/ You've P1869:Well,/
So died the man, and so his end was peace;/ Whence many a moral were to meditate./
Spada,—you <> Dandolo,—is Pope!/ <> quatrain!" § ¶ § No <> do!/ You've
208-28| § vertical line in margin indicating continued quotation mark, crossed out §
209| MS:letter of Don P1869:letter: Don   210| MS:you hear P1869:you mark
211| MS:late. P1869:late,   215| MS:match, P1869:match,—   218| MS:him,—in
<> touch,— P1869:him, (in <> touch)   221| MS:over, he would say,
P1869:over,—he 1889a:over,—folk would say   222| MS:At Tarocs, or succeeded, in
P1869:At Tarocs,—or succeeded,—in   223| MS:the book P1869:the Book,
224| MS:more 1872:more,—   225| MS:—How 1872:How   227| MS:the whole

Pleading and summary, were put before;
Discreetly in my Book he bound them all,
230　Adding some three epistles to the point.
Here is the first of these, part fresh as penned,
The sand, that dried the ink, not rubbed away,
Though penned the day whereof it tells the deed:
Part—extant just as plainly, you know where,
235　Whence came the other stuff, went, you know how,
To make the Ring that's all but round and done.

———————

"Late they arrived, too late, egregious Sir,
Those same justificative points you urge
Might benefit His Blessed Memory
240　Count Guido Franceschini now with God:
Since the Court,—to state things succinctly,—styled
The Congregation of the Governor,
Having resolved on Tuesday last our cause
I' the guilty sense, with death for punishment,
245　Spite of all pleas by me deducible
In favour of said Blessed Memory,—
I, with expenditure of pains enough,
Obtained a respite, leave to claim and prove
Exemption from the law's award,—alleged
250　The power and privilege o' the Clericate:
To which effect a courier was despatched.
But ere an answer from Arezzo came,
The Holiness of our Lord the Pope (prepare!)
Judging it inexpedient to postpone
255　The execution of such sentence passed,
Saw fit, by his particular cheirograph,

<> case,　*P1869:*the "whole <> case,"　228| 　MS:summary were <> before,
*P1869:*summary, were <> before;　229| 　MS:in a book　*P1869:*in my Book
232| 　MS:sand that <> ink not　*P1869:*sand, that <> ink, not　236| 　MS:the ring
*1889a:*the Ring　237| 　MS:§ marginal note that new ¶ begins §　239| 　MS:benefit
His § over illegible word, perhaps *the* §　243| 　MS:our Cause　*P1869:*our cause
246| 　MS:said Blessed Memory　*P1869:*said Blessed Memory,—　256| 　MS:chirograph,

To derogate, dispense with privilege,
And wink at any hurt accruing thence
To Mother Church through damage of her son:
260 Also, to overpass and set aside
That other plea on score of tender age,
Put forth by me to do Pasquini good,
One of the four in trouble with our friend.
So that all five, to-day, have suffered death
265 With no distinction save in dying,—he,
Decollate by mere due of privilege,
The rest hanged decently and in order. Thus
Came the Count to his end of gallant man,
Defunct in faith and exemplarity:
270 Nor shall the shield of his great House lose shine
Thereby, nor its blue banner blush to red.
This, too, should yield sustainment to our hearts—
He had commiseration and respect
In his decease from universal Rome,
275 *Quantum est hominum venustiorum,*
The nice and cultivated everywhere:
Though, in respect of me his advocate,
Needs must I groan o'er my debility,
Attribute the untoward event o' the strife
280 To nothing but my own crass ignorance
Which failed to set the valid reasons forth,
Find fit excuse: such is the fate of war!
May God compensate us the direful blow
By future blessings on his family,
285 Whereof I lowly beg the next commands;
—Whereto, as humbly, I confirm myself . . ."

And so forth,—follow name and place and date.

---

*1889a:*cheirograph,   259| MS:son; *1872:*son: 261| MS:age *P1869:*age,
263| MS:friend: *P1869:*friend.   266| MS:Decollated by way of privilege
*P1869:*privilege, *1872:*Decollate by mere due of   270| MS:shine, *1872:*shine
271| MS:Nor its < > red thereby. *1872:*Thereby, nor its < > red.   277| MS:respect to
me *P1869:*respect of me   279| MS:event of things *P1869:*event o' the strife
282| MS:The fit *P1869:*Find fit   283| *1872:*blow, *1889a:*blow   284| MS:family
*1889a:*family,   286-89| MS:myself . . . / (And < > date:/ Then § crossed out § On the

On next leaf—

    "Hactenus senioribus!

There, old fox, show the clients t'other side
290 And keep this corner sacred, I beseech!
You and your pleas and proofs were what folk call
Pisan assistance, aid that comes too late,
Saves a man dead as nail in post of door.
Had I but time and space for narrative!
295 What was the good of twenty Clericates
When Somebody's thick headpiece once was bent
On seeing Guido's drop into the bag?
How these old men like giving youth a push!
So much the better: next push goes to him,
300 And a new Pope begins the century.
Much good I get by my superb defence!
But argument is solid and subsists,
While obstinacy and ineptitude
Accompany the owner to his tomb—
305 What do I care how soon? Beside, folk see!
Rome will have relished heartily the show,
Yet understood the motives, never fear,
Which caused the indecent change o' the People's Place
To the People's Playground,—stigmatize the spite
310 Which in a trice precipitated things!
As oft the moribund will give a kick
To show they are not absolutely dead,
So feebleness i' the socket shoots its last,
A spirt of violence for energy!

315   "But thou, Cencini, brother of my breast,
    O fox whose home is 'mid the tender grape,

---

next leaf—) <> / There   *P1869:*myself . . . "/ § ¶ § And <> / On next leaf— <> /
There   *1872:*/ <> date.   290| MS:sacred I   *P1869:*sacred, I   291| MS:what folks
call   *1889a:*what folk call   295| MS:twenty clericates   *P1869:*twenty Clericates
296| MS:When <> thick § inserted above § headpiece was § crossed out § once fairly
§ crossed out and replaced above by § was   299| MS:him   *P1869:*him,
304| MS:tomb;   *1889a:*tomb—   305| MS:folks see: *P1869:*see!   *1889a:*folk
309| MS:the People's playground,—whence the spite had birth   *P1869:*the People's
Playground,—stigmatize the spite   310| MS:That in   *P1869:*Which in
314-15| MS:§ no ¶ §   *P1869:*§ ¶ §   *1889a:*§ no ¶ §   *1889:*§ no ¶ § ; emended to restore ¶ ; see
Editorial Notes §   316| MS:fox, whose <> mid   *P1869:*'mid   *1889a:*fox whose

Whose couch in Tuscany by Themis' throne,
Subject to no such . . . best I shut my mouth
Or only open it again to say,
320 This pother and confusion fairly laid,
My hands are empty and my satchel lank.
Now then for both the Matrimonial Cause
And the Case of Gomez! Serve them hot and hot!

"Reliqua differamus in crastinum!
325 The impatient estafette cracks whip outside:
Still, though the earth should swallow him who swears
And me who make the mischief, in must slip—
My boy, your godson, fat-chaps Hyacinth,
Enjoyed the sight while Papa plodded here.
330 I promised him, the rogue, a month ago,
The day his birthday was, of all the days,
That if I failed to save Count Guido's head,
Cinuccio should at least go see it chopped
From trunk—'So, latinize your thanks!' quoth I.
335 'That I prefer, *hoc malim,*' raps me out
The rogue: you notice the subjunctive? Ah!
Accordingly he sat there, bold in box,
Proud as the Pope behind the peacock-fans:
Whereon a certain lady-patroness
340 For whom I manage things (my boy in front,
Her Marquis sat the third in evidence;
Boys have no eyes nor ears save for the show)
'This time, Cintino,' was her sportive word,
When whiz and thump went axe and mowed lay man,
345 And folk could fall to the suspended chat,
'This time, you see, Bottini rules the roast,

318| MS:such . . . but I   *1889a:*such . . . best I   321| MS:lank; § erased and replaced
by § .   323| MS:the case   *1889a:*the Case   323-24| MS:§ no ¶ §   *P1869:*§ ¶ §
327| MS:slip   *1872:*slip—   328| MS:—My   *1872:*My   333| MS:Cintino § *tino*
crossed out and replaced above by *uccio* §   334| MS:trunk—so latinize <> thanks,
quoth I: *P1869:*trunk—'So, latinize <> thanks!' quoth I: *1872:*quoth I   *1889a:*thanks!
§ emended to § thanks!' § see Editorial Notes § quoth I.   335| MS:That § over illegible
erasure §   340| MS:whom I stretch a point § last three words crossed out and replaced
above by two words § manage things   341| MS:The Marquis <> evidence,   *P1869:*Her
Marquis <> evidence;   343| MS:time, Cintino § over illegible name ending §
345| MS:folks   *1889a:*folk   346| MS:time, you see, § last two words and comma

264

Nor can Papa with all his eloquence
Be reckoned on to help as heretofore!'
Whereat Cinone pouts; then, sparkishly—
350 'Papa knew better than aggrieve his Pope,
And baulk him of his grudge against our Count,
Else he'd have argued-off Bottini's' . . what?
'His nose,'—the rogue! well parried of the boy!
He's long since out of Cæsar (eight years old)
355 And as for tripping in Eutropius . . . well,
Reason the more that we strain every nerve
To do him justice, mould a model-mouth,
A Bartolus-cum-Baldo for next age:
For that I purse the pieces, work the brain,
360 And want both Gomez and the marriage-case,
Success with which shall plaster aught of pate
That's broken in me by Bottini's flail,
And bruise his own, belike, that wags and brags.
Adverti supplico humiliter
365 *Quod* don't the fungus see, the fop divine
That one hand drives two horses, left and right?
With this rein did I rescue from the ditch
The fortune of our Franceschini, keep
Unsplashed the credit of a noble House,
370 And set the fashionable cause at Rome
A-prancing till bystanders shouted ' 'ware!'
The other rein's judicious management
Suffered old Somebody to keep the pace,
Hobblingly play the roadster: who but he
375 Had his opinion, was not led by the nose
In leash of quibbles strung to look like law!
You'll soon see,—when I go to pay devoir
And compliment him on confuting me,—
If, by a back-swing of the pendulum,

---

inserted above § Bottini, § erased §   348| MS:on for § erased and replaced by § to
353| MS:rogue: well   *P1869:*rogue! well   355| MS:in Eutropius . . Well,
*P1869:*well,   *1889a:*in Eutropius . . . well,   365| MS:*Quod,* don't   *1889a:Quod* don't
368| MS:of your Franceschini   *P1869:*of our Franceschini   370| MS:cause of Rome
*1872:*cause at Rome   376| MS:In a leash   *P1869:*In leash   379| MS:pendulum

Grace be not, thick and threefold, consequent.
       'I must decide as I see proper, Don!
       I'm Pope, I have my inward lights for guide.
       Had learning been the matter in dispute,
       Could eloquence avail to gainsay fact,
385   Yours were the victory, be comforted!'
       Cinuzzo will be gainer by it all.
       Quick then with Gomez, hot and hot next case!"

       ————————

       Follows, a letter, takes the other side.
       Tall blue-eyed Fisc whose head is capped with cloud,
390   Doctor Bottini,—to no matter who,
       Writes on the Monday two days afterward.
       Now shall the honest championship of right,
       Crowned with success, enjoy at last, unblamed,
       Moderate triumph! Now shall eloquence
395   Poured forth in fancied floods for virtue's sake,
       (The print is sorrowfully dyked and dammed,
       But shows where fain the unbridled force would flow,
       Finding a channel)—now shall this refresh
       The thirsty donor with a drop or two!
400   Here has been truth at issue with a lie:
       Let who gained truth the day have handsome pride
       In his own prowess! Eh? What ails the man?

       ————————

       "Well, it is over, ends as I foresaw:
       Easily proved, Pompilia's innocence!
405   Catch them entrusting Guido's guilt to me

---

*P1869:*pendulum,   ³⁸⁰| *P1869:*consequent! *1889a:*consequent.   ³⁸²| MS:Being
Pope, I *P1869:*The Pope, I *1889a:*I'm Pope, I   ³⁸⁸| MS:letter—takes <> side
*P1869:*letter, takes <> side.   ³⁹⁰| MS:whom, § altered to § who,   ³⁹²| MS:the
confidence in § last two words crossed out and replaced above by three words § honest
championship of   ³⁹⁴| MS:triumph: now *P1869:*triumph! Now
³⁹⁶| MS:dammed *P1869:*dammed,   ³⁹⁷| MS:fain, without § crossed out and replaced
above by two words § the unbridled *P1869:*fain the   ⁴⁰²| MS:prowess. Eh? What
*P1869:*prowess! Eh? *1889a:*prowess! Eh! What § emended to § Eh? § see Editorial Notes §
⁴⁰³⁻⁷| MS:foresaw:/ <> entrusting Guido's cause to me!/ I *P1869:*foresaw:/ Easily proved,

Who had, as usual, the plain truth to plead.
I always knew the clearness of the stream
Would show the fish so thoroughly, child might prong
The clumsy monster: with no mud to splash,
410 Small credit to lynx-eye and lightning-spear!
This Guido,—(much sport he contrived to make,
Who at first twist, preamble of the cord,
Turned white, told all, like the poltroon he was!)—
Finished, as you expect, a penitent,
415 Fully confessed his crime, and made amends,
And, edifying Rome last Saturday,
Died like a saint, poor devil! That's the man
The gods still give to my antagonist:
Imagine how Arcangeli claps wing
420 And crows! 'Such formidable facts to face,
So naked to attack, my client here,
And yet I kept a month the Fisc at bay,
And in the end had foiled him of the prize
By this arch-stroke, this plea of privilege,
425 But that the Pope must gratify his whim,
Put in his word, poor old man,—let it pass!'
—Such is the cue to which all Rome responds.
What with the plain truth given me to uphold,
And, should I let truth slip, the Pope at hand
430 To pick up, steady her on legs again,
My office turns a pleasantry indeed!
Not that the burly boaster did one jot
O' the little was to do—young Spreti's work!
But for him,—mannikin and dandiprat,
435 Mere candle-end and inch of cleverness
Stuck on Arcangeli's save-all,—but for him

Pompilia's innocence!/ Catch <> Guido's guilt to me!/ I had, as usual, the plain truth to
plead./ I   *1889a:*/ / <> to me/ Who had <> / I   408| MS:so plain, a child   *P1869:*so
thoroughly, child   410| MS:What Where § last two words crossed out and replaced above
by two words § Small credit   411| MS:sport was he fit to § last four words crossed out
and replaced above by three words § he contrived to   413| MS:white and told—like
*P1869:*white, told all, like   415| MS:crime, made all amends,   *P1869:*crime, and made
amends,   418| MS:antagonist—   *P1869:*antagonist: 419| MS:wing,   *1889a:*wing
426| MS:word—poor   *P1869:*word, poor   427| MS:responds: *P1869:*responds.
428| MS:to def § crossed out §   435| MS:The candle-end   *P1869:*Mere candle-end

The spruce young Spreti, what is bad were worse!

"I looked that Rome should have the natural gird
At advocate with case that proves itself;
440 I knew Arcangeli would grin and brag:
But what say you to one impertinence
Might move a stone? That monk, you are to know,
That barefoot Augustinian whose report
O' the dying woman's words did detriment
445 To my best points it took the freshness from,
—That meddler preached to purpose yesterday
At San Lorenzo as a winding-up
O' the show which proved a treasure to the church.
Out comes his sermon smoking from the press:
450 Its text—'Let God be true, and every man
A liar'—and its application, this
The longest-winded of the paragraphs,
I straight unstitch, tear out and treat you with:
'Tis piping hot and posts through Rome to-day.
455 Remember it, as I engage to do!"

———————

"But if you rather be disposed to see
In the result of the long trial here,—
This dealing doom to guilt and doling praise
To innocency,—any proof that truth
460 May look for vindication from the world,
Much will you have misread the signs, I say.
God, who seems acquiescent in the main
With those who add 'So will he ever sleep'—

438| MS:§ note that new ¶ begins §   439–41| MS:itself;/ But   P1869:itself;/ I knew
Arcangeli would grin and brag:/ But   442| MS:a man? That   1872:a stoic? That
1889a:a stone? That   445| MS:best speech § crossed out and replaced above by § points
it skimmed § crossed out and replaced above by § took   446| MS:—This meddler
P1869:—That meddler   448| MS:shows have proved   P1869:shows, have   1872:show
which proved   449| MS:comes the sermon   P1869:comes his sermon
450| MS:His § crossed out § Its   451| P1869:this,   1889a:this
452| MS:paragraphs   P1869:paragraphs,   454| MS:through Rome by this.
P1869:through Rome to-day.   455| MS:do!   1889:do! § emended to § do!" § see
Editorial Notes §   456| MS:But if   1889:But if § emended to § "But § see Editorial
Notes §   457| MS:long Trial   P1869:trial   463| MS:add "And so will ever be"—

Flutters their foolishness from time to time,
465 Puts forth His right-hand recognizably;
Even as, to fools who deem He needs must right
Wrong on the instant, as if earth were heaven,
He wakes remonstrance—'Passive, Lord, how long?'
Because Pompilia's purity prevails,
470 Conclude you, all truth triumphs in the end?
So might those old inhabitants of the ark,
Witnessing haply their dove's safe return,
Pronounce there was no danger, all the while
O' the deluge, to the creature's counterparts,
475 Aught that beat wing i' the world, was white or soft,—
And that the lark, the thrush, the culver too,
Might equally have traversed air, found earth,
And brought back olive-branch in unharmed bill.
Methinks I hear the Patriarch's warning voice—
480 'Though this one breast, by miracle, return,
No wave rolls by, in all the waste, but bears
Within it some dead dove-like thing as dear,
Beauty made blank and harmlessness destroyed!'
How many chaste and noble sister-fames
485 Wanted the extricating hand, so lie
Strangled, for one Pompilia proud above
The welter, plucked from the world's calumny,
Stupidity, simplicity,—who cares?

"Romans! An elder race possessed your land

P1869:add 'So will He ever sleep'—   1872:Will those who add 'So will he   1889a:With those
464| MS:§ first word illegibly crossed out § Flutters that foolishness   P1869:Flutters their
foolishness   465| MS:his   P1869:forth His   1872:forth His   1889a:forth His
466| MS:deem He   1872:he   1889a:deem He   468| MS:remonstrance: "passive <>
long?"   P1869:remonstrance—'Passive <> long?'   469| MS:purity is plain,
P1869:purity prevails,   470| MS:you truth must triumph in   P1869:you, all truth
triumphs in   472| MS:haply the dove's   P1869:haply their dove's
473| MS:danger all   1889a:danger, all   474| MS:deluge to   P1869:deluge, to
475| MS:white and soft,—   P1869:white or soft,—   476| MS:thrush,
the nightingale,   P1869:thrush, the culver too,   480| MS:breast
return by miracle,   P1869:breast, by miracle, return,   485| MS:hand,
and lie   1889a:hand, so lie   488–89| MS:§ no ¶ §   P1869:§ ¶ §
1889a:§ no ¶ §   1889:§ no ¶ ; emended to restore ¶ ; see Editorial Notes §
489| MS:Romans, § altered to § ! The elder race, possessed   P1869:Romans! An elder race

269

490 Long ago, and a false faith lingered still,
As shades do, though the morning-star be out.
Doubtless some pagan of the twilight-day
Has often pointed to a cavern-mouth
Obnoxious to beholders, hard by Rome,
495 And said,—nor he a bad man, no, nor fool,
Only a man born blind like all his mates,—
'Here skulk in safety, lurk, defying law,
The devotees to execrable creed,
Adoring—with what culture . . . Jove, avert
500 Thy vengeance from us worshippers of thee! . . .
What rites obscene—their idol-god, an Ass!'
So went the word forth, so acceptance found,
So century re-echoed century,
Cursed the accursed,—and so, from sire to son,
505 You Romans cried 'The offscourings of our race
Corrupt within the depths there: fitly fiends
Perform a temple-service o'er the dead:
Child, gather garment round thee, pass nor pry!'
Thus groaned your generations: till the time
510 Grew ripe, and lightning had revealed, belike,—
Thro' crevice peeped into by curious fear,—
Some object even fear could recognize

---

possessed   490| MS:ago, while the false   *P1869:*ago, and a false   491| MS:do,
though < > out: *P1869:*out.   *1889a:*do though § emended to § do, though § see Editorial
Notes §   492| MS:Doubtless, some < > twilight-day,   *P1869:*twilight-day
*1872:*Doubtless some   493| MS:cavern's mouth   *P1869:*cavern-mouth
*1889a:*cavern-mouth   495| MS:no nor fool,—   *P1869:*no, nor   *1889a:*fool,
496| MS:man and blind   *P1869:*man, so, blind   *1889a:*man born blind
497| MS:'Here skulked § altered to § skulk in safety, died § crossed out and replaced
above by § lurked § altered to § lurk   498| MS:devotees of § crossed out §
499| MS:Adorers—with < > culture . . Jove   *P1869:*Adoring—with < > culture . . .
Jove   500| MS:thee! . .   *1889a:*thee! . . .   501| MS:obscene their idol-god—an
Ass!   *P1869:*obscene—their idol-god, an Ass!'   *1872:*idol-god an   *1889a:*idol-god, an
503| MS:century   *P1869:*century,   504| MS:accursed,—so   *P1869:*accursed,—and so
505| *1872:*race,   *1889a:*race   506| MS:fitly, fiends   *1889a*fitly fiends
507| MS:Perform there § crossed out and replaced above by § a temple service
*P1869:*temple-service   509| MS:So groaned   *1889a:*Thus groaned
510| MS:ripe,—and lightning hath revealed,—belike,   *P1869:*ripe, and < > revealed,
belike,—   *1889a:*had   512| MS:even you could   *P1869:*even fear could

270

I' the place of spectres; on the illumined wall,
To-wit, some nook, tradition talks about,
515 Narrow and short, a corpse's length, no more:
And by it, in the due receptacle,
The little rude brown lamp of earthenware,
The cruse, was meant for flowers but now held blood,
The rough-scratched palm-branch, and the legend left
520 *Pro Christo.* Then the mystery lay clear:
The abhorred one was a martyr all the time,
Heaven's saint whereof earth was not worthy. What?
Do you continue in the old belief?
Where blackness bides unbroke, must devils brood?
525 Is it so certain not another cell
O' the myriad that make up the catacomb
Contains some saint a second flash would show?
Will you ascend into the light of day
And, having recognized a martyr's shrine,
530 Go join the votaries that gape around
Each vulgar god that awes the market-place?
Are these the objects of your praising? See!
In the outstretched right hand of Apollo, there,
Lies screened a scorpion: housed amid the folds
535 Of Juno's mantle lurks a centipede!

513| MS:of shadows—on *P1869:*of spectres; on   515| MS:more, *P1869:*more:
518| MS:flowers, that held the blood, *P1869:*flowers, but held *1889a:*flowers but now
held blood,   520| MS:*Pro Christo*: then the mystery lay § over *was* § clear.
P1869:Pro Christo. Then <> clear: 521| MS:abhorred ones § altered to § one were
the § last two words crossed out and replaced above by two words § was a martyrs § altered
to § martyr <> while § crossed out and replaced above by § time,   522| MS:The
§ crossed out and replaced above by § a saints § *s* erased § <> worthy. Well? § crossed
out and replaced above by § What? *P1869:*A saint *1889a:*Heaven's saint
523| MS:belief— *P1869:*belief?   524| MS:unbroke must devils be? *P1869:*unbroke,
must *1889a:*devils brood?   525| MS:The certainty that not *P1869:*Is it so certain,
not *1889a:*certain not   526| MS:catacomb, *1889a:*catacomb   527| MS:show
*P1869:*show?   530| MS:Go the § crossed out §   531| MS:Each vulgar
§ inserted above § god that triumphs in § last two words written above an
illegibly crossed out word, and then crossed out § awes § inserted above §
532| MS:Be these <> praising? § next word illegibly crossed out, perhaps
Probe § See! *1872:*Are these   533| MS:outstretched hand of the § inserted above §
Apollo *P1869:*outstretched right hand of Apollo   534| MS:Is hidden § last two words
crossed out and replaced above by two words § Is screened *1889a:*Lies screened
535| MS:mantle, lo a cockatrice! *P1869:*mantle, lo, a *1889a:*mantle lurks a centipede!

Each statue of a god were fitlier styled
Demon and devil. Glorify no brass
That shines like burnished gold in noonday glare,
For fools! Be otherwise instructed, you!
540   And preferably ponder, ere ye judge,
Each incident of this strange human play
Privily acted on a theatre
That seemed secure from every gaze but God's,—
Till, of a sudden, earthquake laid wall low
545   And let the world perceive wild work inside
And how, in petrifaction of surprise,
The actors stood,—raised arm and planted foot,—
Mouth as it made, eye as it evidenced,
Despairing shriek, triumphant hate,—transfixed,
550   Both he who takes and she who yields the life.

"As ye become spectators of this scene,
Watch obscuration of a pearl-pure fame
By vapoury films, enwoven circumstance,
—A soul made weak by its pathetic want
555   Of just the first apprenticeship to sin
Which thenceforth makes the sinning soul secure
From all foes save itself, soul's truliest foe,—
Since egg turned snake needs fear no serpentry,—

537| MS:devil: glorify   *P1869:*devil. Glorify   538| MS:That shines like § last two
words inserted above § burnishes § altered to § burnished like § crossed out §
539| MS:Say fools: be   *P1869:*For fools! Be   540| MS:ye pass   *P1869:*ye pass,
*1889a:*ye judge,   542| *P1869:*theatre,   *1889a:*theatre   543| MS:Was deemed secure
*1889a:*That seemed secure   544| MS:Whereof a sudden earthquake lays wall
*P1869:*Till, of a sudden, earthquake   *1889a:*earthquake laid wall   545| MS:And
lets < > world see the wild < > inside,   *1889a:*And let < > world perceive wild
< > inside   547| MS:stand < > foot,   *P1869:*foot,—   *1889a:*stood
548| MS:Mouth as it made, § last four words and comma inserted above §
Eye § altered to § eye   549| MS:triumphant hate, § over illegible
erasure § transfixed   *P1869:*hate,—transfixed,   550| MS:life,—   *P1869:*life.
550–51| MS:§ no ¶ §   *P1869:*§ ¶ §   551| MS:scene—   *1889a:*scene,   552| MS:a
fame pearl-pure   *1889a:*a pearl-pure fame   553| MS:In vapoury films, of § crossed
out § enwoven   *1889a:*By vapoury   555| *P1869:*sin,   *1889a:*sin
556| MS:Would thenceforth make the   *1889a:*Which thenceforth makes the
557| MS:itself, that's truest foe,—   *P1869:*that's truliest foe,—   *1889a:*itself, souls' truliest
§ emended to § soul's § see Editorial Notes §   558| MS:Egg that turns snake

As ye behold this web of circumstance
560 Deepen the more for every thrill and throe,
Convulsive effort to disperse the films
And disenmesh the fame o' the martyr,—mark
How all those means, the unfriended one pursues,
To keep the treasure trusted to her breast,
565 Each struggle in the flight from death to life,
How all, by procuration of the powers
Of darkness, are transformed,—no single ray,
Shot forth to show and save the inmost star,
But, passed as through hell's prism, proceeding black
570 To the world that hates white: as ye watch, I say,
Till dusk and such defacement grow eclipse
By,—marvellous perversity of man!—
The inadequacy and inaptitude
Of that self-same machine, that very law
575 Man vaunts, devised to dissipate the gloom,
Rescue the drowning orb from calumny,
—Hear law, appointed to defend the just,
Submit, for best defence, that wickedness
Was bred of flesh and innate with the bone
580 Borne by Pompilia's spirit for a space,
And no mere chance fault, passionate and brief:
Finally, when ye find,—after this touch
Of man's protection which intends to mar
The last pin-point of light and damn the disc,—
585 One wave of the hand of God amid the worlds
Bid vapour vanish, darkness flee away,
And let the vexed star culminate in peace

---

*P1869:*For egg turned snake   *1889a:*Since egg   563| MS:means the <> pursued
*P1869:*means, the <> pursues,   564| MS:breast—   *P1869:*breast,   565| MS:life—
*P1869:*life,   567| MS:darkness were transformed   *P1869:*darkness, are transformed
568| MS:star   *P1869:*star,   569| MS:proceeded   *P1869:*proceeding
570| MS:watched   *P1869:*watch   571| MS:grew   *P1869:*grow   572| MS:man,—
*P1869:*man!—   576| MS:orb of innocence;— § last two words, semi-colon and dash
crossed out and replaced above by two words § from calumny   *P1869:*calumny,
577| MS:—And law   *P1869:*—Hear law   578| MS:Submitted for defence that
*P1869:*Submit, for best defence, that   579-81| MS:bred of § over illegible erasure § <>
bone / And   *P1869:*bone/ Borne by Pompilia's spirit for a space,/ And   582| MS:Last
§ crossed out and replaced above by § Finally, when <> this happy § crossed out §
585| MS:world   *P1869:*worlds   587| MS:And leave the   *1889a:*And let the

Approachable no more by earthly mist—
What I call God's hand,—you, perhaps,—mere chance
590 Of the true instinct of an old good man
Who happens to hate darkness and love light,—
In whom too was the eye that saw, not dim,
The natural force to do the thing he saw,
Nowise abated,—both by miracle,—
595 All this well pondered,—I demand assent
To the enunciation of my text
In face of one proof more that 'God is true
And every man a liar'—that who trusts
To human testimony for a fact
600 Gets this sole fact—himself is proved a fool;
Man's speech being false, if but by consequence
That only strength is true: while man is weak,
And, since truth seems reserved for heaven not earth,
Plagued here by earth's prerogative of lies,
605 Should learn to love and long for what, one day,
Approved by life's probation, he may speak.

"For me, the weary and worn, who haply prompt
To mirth or pity, as I move the mood,—
A friar who glides unnoticed to the grave,
610 With these bare feet, coarse robe and rope-girt waist,—
I have long since renounced your world, ye know:
Yet what forbids I weigh the prize forgone,
The wordly worth? I dare, as I were dead,

589| MS:hand; and the world,—this chance P1869:hand,—you, perhaps,—this
1889a:perhaps,—mere chance   592| MS:eye, that <> dim P1869:eye that <> dim,
593| MS:saw P1869:saw,   595| MS:pondered,—why refuse assent P1869:pondered,—
I demand assent   597| MS:that God is P1869:that 'God is   598| MS:liar—that
P1869:liar'—that   600| MS:fool, P1869:fool;   602| MS:true, while P1869:true;
while 1872:true! while 1889a:true: while   603-7| MS:earth,/ Learns to love now
what he may speak one day. / For <> and the worn, who prompt P1869:earth,/ Should
learn to love what <> / § ¶ § For 1872:earth,/ Plagued here by earth's prerogative of lies,/
Now learns to love and long for what, one day,/ Approved by life's probation, he may
speak./ § ¶ § For 1889a:earth,/ / Should learn <> / / § ¶ § For <> and worn, who haply
prompt   608-11| MS:pity as may move the mood/ Bare feet, coarse <> waist of mine,/
<> know, P1869:pity, as I move the mood,—/ A friar who glide unnoticed to the grave,/
<> mine,—/ <> know: 1872:/ <> glides <> grave,/ With these bare <> waist,—/ I
612-14| MS:Yet weigh the worth of worldly prize put by § last two words crossed out §

Disinterestedly judge this and that
615 Good ye account good: but God tries the heart.
Still, if you question me of my content
At having put each human pleasure by,
I answer, at the urgency of truth:
As this world seems, I dare not say I know
620 —Apart from Christ's assurance which decides—
Whether I have not failed to taste much joy.
For many a doubt will fain perturb my choice—
Many a dream of life spent otherwise—
How human love, in varied shapes, might work
625 As glory, or as rapture, or as grace:
How conversancy with the books that teach,
The arts that help,—how, to grow good and great,
Rather than simply good, and bring thereby
Goodness to breathe and live, nor, born i' the brain,
630 Die there,—how these and many another gift
Of life are precious though abjured by me.
But, for one prize, best meed of mightiest man,
Arch-object of ambition,—earthly praise,
Repute o' the world, the flourish of loud trump,
635 The softer social fluting,—Oh, for these,
—No, my friends! Fame,—that bubble which, world-wide
Each blows and bids his neighbour lend a breath,
That so he haply may behold thereon

---

foregone;/ Disinterestedly pronounce on this   *P1869:*foregone,/ Disinterestedly judge this
*1872:*Yet what forbids I weigh the prize forgone,/ The worldly worth? I dare, as I were
dead,/ /   615| MS:good: But   *P1869:*but   617| MS:put the human   *P1869:*put
each human   618| MS:truth,   *1872:*truth: 619| MS:'As   *P1869:*As
621| MS:joy: *P1869:*joy.   622–25| MS:a dream would fain < > choice—/ How
love, in those the varied shapes, might show/ As   *1872:*a doubt would < > choice—/
Many a dream of life spent otherwise—/ How human love, in varied shapes, might work/
As   *1889a:*doubt will fain   626| MS:And conversancy   *P1869:*How conversancy
627| MS:help,—that to grow great, in fine,   *P1869:*help,—how, to   *1872:*to grow good and
great,   630| MS:there: all these   *P1869:*there,—how these   631| MS:May well be
precious   *1872:*Of life are precious   632| MS:But for < > of mighty man,   *P1869:*But,
for < > of mightiest man,   634–38| MS:of fame's trump,/ < > friends! for that < > /
Each § in margin § Ye § crossed out § blow § altered to § blows and bid § altered to § bids
you § crossed out and replaced above by § his < > lend the § over *his* § breath,   *P1869:*of
loud trump,/ The softer social fluting,—Oh, for these,/ < > friends! Fame,—that < > / < >

One more enlarged distorted false fool's-face,
640 Until some glassy nothing grown as big
Send by a touch the imperishable to suds,—
No, in renouncing fame, my loss was light,
Choosing obscurity, my chance was well!"

"Didst ever touch such ampollosity
645 As the monk's own bubble, let alone its spite?
What's his speech for, but just the fame he flouts?
How he dares reprehend both high and low,
Nor stoops to turn the sentence 'God is true
And every man a liar—save the Pope
650 Happily reigning—my respects to him!'
And so round off the period. Molinism
Simple and pure! To what pitch get we next?
I find that, for first pleasant consequence,
Gomez, who had intended to appeal
655 From the absurd decision of the Court,
Declines, though plain enough his privilege,
To call on help from lawyers any more—
Resolves earth's liars may possess the world

----

lend a breath,/ That   642| MS:fame, the loss   1872:fame, my loss
643| MS:obscurity, I have not erred § last four words crossed out and replaced above by four
words § the chance was well!   P1869:well!"   1872:obscurity, my chance
644| MS:Didst   1889:Didst § emended to § "Didst § see Editorial Notes §
645-49| MS:the man's § followed by word illegibly crossed out § fool's-speech, let <> / He
might have coined period § last two words crossed out and replaced above by three words §
turned the sentence <> / And   P1869:man's own bubble, let <> / What's his speech for,
but just the fame he flouts—/ How he dares reprehend both high and low?/Else
had he turned the sentence "God § emended to § 'God § see Editorial Notes § <> /
And   1872:/ <> flouts?/ <> low,/ Nor stoops to turn the <> / And   1889a:the
monk's own   650| MS:him!"   P1869:him!" § emended to § him!' § see Editorial
Notes §   651| MS:And § crossed out § —So rounded   P1869:—So,
rounded   1872:rounding   1889a:And so round   652| MS:pure—to this § crossed out
and replaced above by § what   P1869:pure! To   656| MS:though plainly § altered to §
plain on § crossed out and replaced above by § enough his § followed by word illegibly
crossed out, possibly injustice §   657| MS:To have to do with § last four words crossed
out and replaced above by four words § call on help from   658| MS:Resolves the liars
may persuade § crossed out and replaced above by § harangue the world,   P1869:liars may
possess   1889a:Resolves earth's liars <> world,   DC,BrU:world   1889:world

Till God have had sufficiency of both:
660 So may I whistle for my job and fee!

"But, for this virulent and rabid monk,—
If law be an inadequate machine,
And advocacy, froth and impotence,
We shall soon see, my blatant brother! That's
665 Exactly what I hope to show your sort!
For, by a veritable piece of luck,
The providence, you monks round period with,
All may be gloriously retrieved. Perpend!

"That Monastery of the Convertites
670 Whereto the Court consigned Pompilia first,
—Observe, if convertite, why, sinner then,
Or what's the pertinency of award?—
And whither she was late returned to die,
—Still in their jurisdiction, mark again!—
675 That thrifty Sisterhood, for perquisite,
Claims every piece whereof may die possessed
Each sinner in the circuit of its walls.
Now, this Pompilia seeing that, by death
O' the couple, all their wealth devolved on her,
680 Straight utilized the respite ere decease,
By regular conveyance of the goods
She thought her own, to will and to devise,—
Gave all to friends, Tighetti and the like,
In trust for him she held her son and heir,
685 Gaetano,—trust which ends with infancy:

659| MS:both,— *P1869:*both: 660-61| MS:§ no ¶ § *P1869:*§ ¶ §
661| MS:virurent *P1869:*virulent   663| MS:advocates—superfluous impotence,
*P1869:*advocacy, so much impotence, *1872:*advocacy, froth and impotence,
664| MS:brother! There's *P1869:*brother! That's   665| MS:sort— *P1869:*sort!
667| MS:The providence you *P1869:*True providence, you *1872:*The providence
668-69| MS:§ no ¶ § *P1869:*§ ¶ § *1872:*§ no ¶ § *1889:*§ no ¶ ; emended to restore ¶ ; see
Editorial Notes §   671| MS:then *P1869:*then,   672| MS:Or where the *1872:*Or
what's the   678| MS:this Pompilia, seeing that by *1872:*this Pompilia seeing that, by
680| MS:Had utilized < > decease *P1869:*Straight utilized *1872:*decease,   681| MS:of
all good *P1869:*of the goods   682| MS:devise *P1869:*devise,—   683| MS:To
certain friends < > the rest, *P1869:*Gave all to friends < > the like,   684| MS:for
whom she *P1869:*for him she   685| MS:trust to end with *1889a:*trust which ends

277

So willing and devising, since assured
The justice of the Court would presently
Confirm her in her rights and exculpate,
Re-integrate and rehabilitate—
690 Place her as, through my pleading, now she stands.
But here's the capital mistake: the Court
Found Guido guilty,—but pronounced no word
About the innocency of his wife:
I grounded charge on broader base, I hope!
695 No matter whether wife be true or false,
The husband must not push aside the law,
And punish of a sudden: that's the point:
Gather from out my speech the contrary!
It follows that Pompilia, unrelieved
700 By formal sentence from imputed fault,
Remains unfit to have and to dispose
Of property which law provides shall lapse.
Wherefore the Monastery claims its due:
And whose, pray, whose the office, but the Fisc's?
705 Who but I institute procedure next
Against the person of dishonest life,
Pompilia whom last week I sainted so?
I it is teach the monk what scripture means,
And that the tongue should prove a two-edged sword,
710 No axe sharp one side, blunt the other way,
Like what amused the town at Guido's cost!
Astræa redux! I've a second chance

---

with   686| MS:Willing, devising, as assured, no doubt,   *P1869:*So willing and devising, since assured   687| MS:The pending § crossed out and replaced above by § justice   688| MS:rights as exculpate,   *P1869:*rights and exculpate,
689–91| MS:rehabilitate—/ § illegible word § as, thro' my endeavour, now <> / But *P1869:*rehabilitate—/ Station as, through my pleading, now <> / But   *1872:/* Place her as <> / But   694| MS:I warily § crossed out and replaced above by § grounded
696| MS:The § over perhaps *her* § <> not put by with his hands § last five words crossed out and replaced below by four words § push aside the law,   697| MS:point— *P1869:*point! *1889a:*point: 702| MS:property, such fault provides <> lapse: *P1869:*property, which law provides   *1889a:*property which <> lapse.   703| MS:due— *P1869:*due.   *1889a:*due: 704| MS:pray,—whose <> Fisc's,   *P1869:*pray, whose <> Fisc's?   705| MS:now   *P1869:*next   707| MS:Pompilia, whom   *1889a:*Pompilia whom   708| MS:I'll, § altered to § I, it is, teach   *1889a:*I it is teach   709| MS:should be a   *P1869:*should prove a   712| MS:Astræa redux, I've   *P1869:Astræa redux!* I've

278

Before the self-same Court o' the Governor
Who soon shall see volte-face and chop, change sides.
715 Accordingly, I charge you on your life,
Send me with all despatch the judgment late
O' the Florence Rota Court, confirmative
O' the prior judgment at Arezzo, clenched
Again by the Granducal signature,
720 Wherein Pompilia is convicted, doomed,
And only destined to escape through flight
The proper punishment. Send me the piece,—
I'll work it! And this foul-mouthed friar shall find
His Noah's-dove that brought the olive back
725 Turn into quite the other sooty scout,
The raven, Noah first put forth the ark,
Which never came back but ate carcasses!
No adequate machinery in law?
No power of life and death i' the learned tongue?
730 Methinks I am already at my speech,
Startle the world with 'Thou, Pompilia, thus?
How is the fine gold of the Temple dim!'
And so forth. But the courier bids me close,
And clip away one joke that runs through Rome,
735 Side by side with the sermon which I send.
How like the heartlessness of the old hunks
Arcangeli! His Count is hardly cold,
The client whom his blunders sacrificed,

714| MS:sides! *1889a:*sides.   · 716| MS:the sentence § crossed out and replaced above
by § judgment   717| MS:the Florence Rota and § crossed out and replaced above by §
Court, confirmative   719| MS:the Ganduke's signature and seal— *P1869:*the
Granducal signature,   722| MS:the piece,— *1872:*the peace,— *1889a:*the piece,—
724| MS:back, *1889a:*back   725| MS:Is turned into the *1872:*Turn into quite
the   726| MS:raven Noah first of all put *P1869:*raven, Noah *1889a:*first put
727| MS:That never <> back, but *P1869:*And never *1872:*Which never *1889a:*back but
728-30| MS:law?/ Methinks *P1869:*law?/ No power of life and death i' the learned tongue?/
Methinks   731| MS:Start § altered to § Startle the exordium § crossed out and replaced
above by two words § world with "Thou *1889:*"Thou § emended to § 'Thou § see Editorial
Notes §   732| MS:dim," *P1869:*dim!" § emended to § dim!' § see Editorial Notes §
733-48| MS:close./ § ¶ § Alack *P1869:*§ adds lines 734-47 §   733| MS:close.
*P1869:*close,   735| *P1869:*send— *1872:*send.   738| MS:His client *1872:*The

When somebody must needs describe the scene—
740 How the procession ended at the church
That boasts the famous relic: quoth our brute,
'Why, that's just Martial's phrase for "make an end"—
Ad umbilicum sic perventum est!'
The callous dog,—let who will cut off head,
745 He cuts a joke and cares no more than so!
I think my speech shall modify his mirth.
'How is the fine gold dim!'—but send the piece!"

Alack, Bottini, what is my next word
But death to all that hope? The Instrument
750 Is plain before me, print that ends my Book
With the definitive verdict of the Court,
Dated September, six months afterward,
(Such trouble and so long the old Pope gave!)
"In restitution of the perfect fame
755 Of dead Pompilia, *quondam* Guido's wife,
And warrant to her representative
Domenico Tighetti, barred hereby,
While doing duty in his guardianship,
From all molesting, all disquietude,
760 Each perturbation and vexation brought
Or threatened to be brought against the heir
By the Most Venerable Convent called
Saint Mary Magdalen o' the Convertites
I' the Corso."
              Justice done a second time!

client   742| *P1869:*"Why, that's < > 'make an end'— § emended to § 'Why, that's < >
"make an end"— § see Editorial Notes §   743| *P1869:est!*" § emended to § *est!*' § see
Editorial Notes §   745| *P1869:*joke, and *1889a:*joke and   746| *P1869:*mirth:
*1889a:*mirth.   747| *P1869:*"How < > dim!" < > piece! § emended to § 'How < > dim'
< > piece!" § see Editorial Notes §   751| MS:definitive jud § crossed out § < > Court
*P1869:*the Court,   752| MS:afterward *P1869:*afterward,   753| MS:long, the
*1889a:*long the   757| MS:thereby, *P1869:*hereby,   761| MS:the same *P1869:*the
heir   764| MS:the Corso." § note that new ¶ begins § Justice < > time— *P1869:*time!

765   Well judged, Marc Antony, *Locum-tenens*
    O' the Governor, a Venturini too!
    For which I save thy name,—last of the list!

    Next year but one, completing his nine years
    Of rule in Rome, died Innocent my Pope
770   —By some account, on his accession-day.
    If he thought doubt would do the next age good,
    'Tis pity he died unapprised what birth
    His reign may boast of, be remembered by—
    Terrible Pope, too, of a kind,—Voltaire.

775   And so an end of all i' the story. Strain
    Never so much my eyes, I miss the mark
    If lived or died that Gaetano, child
    Of Guido and Pompilia: only find,
    Immediately upon his father's death,
780   A record, in the annals of the town—
    That Porzia, sister of our Guido, moved
    The Priors of Arezzo and their head
    Its Gonfalonier to give loyally
    A public attestation of the right
785   O' the Franceschini to all reverence—
    Apparently because of the incident
    O' the murder,—there's no mention made o' the crime,
    But what else could have caused such urgency

765| MS:Locumtenens *P1869:Locum-tenens*   766| MS:the Governor, and Venturini
*P1869:*the Governor, a Venturini   767| MS:name: last <> list. *P1869:*name,—last
<> list!   767-68| MS:§ note that new ¶ begins §   770| MS:accounts <> accession
day. *P1869:*account <> accession-day.   773| MS:boast and be *P1869:*boast of, be
774| MS:Terribe *1869:*Terrible   774-75| MS:§ marginal note that ¶ begins §
776| MS:miss aught marks *P1869:*miss the mark   777| MS:There lived <> that
Gaetano-child *P1869:*that Gaetano, child *1872:*If lived   778| MS:find *P1869:*find,
779| MS:death *P1869:*death,   780| MS:record in <> town *1872:*record, in <>
town—   781| MS:our worthy *P1869:*our Guido   784| MS:attestation to the
*1872:*attestation of the   785| MS:to men's reverence— *1872:*to all reverence—
787| MS:of that, *P1869:*of crime, *1872:*o' the crime,   788-93| MS:else caused <>
urgency to cure/ The common people § last two words crossed out and replaced above by
three words and commas § mob, just then, of their § crossed out and replaced above by §
chronic qualms so prompt § last two words crossed out and *qualms* altered to §
qualmishness?/ To § crossed out and replaced above by four words § Do not folks ever
swallow <> report so it § last two words crossed out § / That brings <> betters?—Bane/

To cure the mob, just then, of greediness
790 For scandal, love of lying vanity,
And appetite to swallow crude reports
That bring annoyance to their betters?—bane
Which, here, was promptly met by antidote.
I like and shall translate the eloquence
795 Of nearly the worst Latin ever writ:
"Since antique time whereof the memory
Holds the beginning, to this present hour,
The Franceschini ever shone, and shine
Still i' the primary rank, supreme amid
800 The lustres of Arezzo, proud to own
In this great family, the flag-bearer,
Guide of her steps and guardian against foe,—
As in the first beginning, so to-day!"
There, would you disbelieve the annalist,
805 Go rather by the babble of a bard?
I thought, Arezzo, thou hadst fitter souls,
Petrarch,—nay, Buonarroti at a pinch,
To do thee credit as *vexillifer!*
Was it mere mirth the Patavinian meant,
810 Making thee out, in his veracious page,
Founded by Janus of the Double Face?

Well, proving of such perfect parentage,
Our Gaetano, born of love and hate,

Which *P1869:*/ < > chronic greediness/ For scandal, love of lying vanity,/ And appetite to swallow < > reports/ That bring < > / Which *1872:*else could have caused < > urgency/ To cure the < > of greediness/ / / < > bane/ Which   794| MS:I have § crossed out § read and shall repeat you word for word § last five words crossed out and replaced above by three words § translate the eloquence *P1869:*I like and   797| MS:Reserves § crossed out and replaced above by two words § Holds the   798| MS:shine, *1889a:*shine
799| MS:I' the < > supreme their lustre mid *P1869:*Still i' the < > supreme amid   800| MS:The lights of our Arezzo *P1869:*the lustres of Arezzo   801| MS:family—her flag-bearer, *1872:*family, the flag-bearer,   803| MS:to-day! *P1869:*to-day!"
804| MS:disbelieve stern History, *1872:*disbelieve the annalist,   805-10| MS:Trust rather to the < > bard?/ Ah, City, was it mirth that Livius § last two words crossed out and replaced above by two words § the Paduan meant/ Making *P1869:*bard?/ I thought, Arezzo, thou hadst fitter souls,/ Petrarch,—nay, Buonarroti at a pinch,/ To do thee credit as *vexillifer!*/ Was it mere mirth the Patavinian meant,/ Making *1872:*Go rather by the < > / / / / /   811-12| MS:§ no ¶ § *P1869:*§ ¶ §   812-15| MS:of this perfect parentage,/

282

Did the babe live or die? I fain would find!
815 What were his fancies if he grew a man?
Was he proud,—a true scion of the stock
Which bore the blazon, shall make bright my page—
Shield, Azure, on a Triple Mountain, Or,
A Palm-tree, Proper, whereunto is tied
820 A Greyhound, Rampant, striving in the slips?
Or did he love his mother, the base-born,
And fight i' the ranks, unnoticed by the world?

Such, then, the final state o' the story. So
Did the Star Wormwood in a blazing fall
825 Frighten awhile the waters and lie lost.
So did this old woe fade from memory:
Till after, in the fulness of the days,
I needs must find an ember yet unquenched,
And, breathing, blow the spark to flame. It lives,
830 If precious be the soul of man to man.

So, British Public, who may like me yet,
(Marry and amen!) learn one lesson hence
Of many which whatever lives should teach:
This lesson, that our human speech is naught,
835 Our human testimony false, our fame
And human estimation words and wind.

Did <> die?—one fain would know:/ What   *P1869:*of such perfect parentage,/ Our
Gaetano, born of love and hate,/ Did <> would find!/ What   *1872:*/ / <> die?—I fain
<> / What   *1889a:*/ / <> die? I <> / What   816| MS:true chip § crossed out and
replaced above by § scion of the old block,— § last two words crossed out and replaced above
by § stock,—   *1872:*stock   817| MS:Of bearing blason, still makes <> my book—
*P1869:*blason, shall make <> Book—   *1872:*Which bore the blazon <> my page—
818–20| MS:§ *a, t, m, p, p, g* and *r* altered to capitals in next seven words § Azure <> Triple
Mountain <> / <> Palm-tree, Proper <> / <> Greyhound, Rampant
821| MS:low-born   *P1869:*base-born,   822| MS:And get to her, unnoticed   *P1869:*And
fight i' the ranks, unnoticed   823| MS:Such were the final flash o'   *P1869:*Such, then,
the final state o'   825| MS:lost: *1889a:*lost.   826| MS:memory,   *1872:*memory.
*1889a:*memory: 828| MS:unquenched,   *1872:*unquench'd,   *1889a:*unquenched,
831| MS:§ marginal note that new ¶ begins § yet   *P1869:*yet,   832| MS:(Marry, and
P1869:(Marry and   833| MS:Of the § crossed out § many whatsoever § last word crossed
out and replaced above by two words § anything that lives   *P1869:*many which whatever
lives   834| MS:This one, that our best human   *P1869:*This lesson, that our human
835| MS:false—and, oh   *P1869:*false, our fame   836| MS:Our human estimate, our

Why take the artistic way to prove so much?
Because, it is the glory and good of Art,
That Art remains the one way possible
840 Of speaking truth, to mouths like mine at least.
How look a brother in the face and say
"Thy right is wrong, eyes hast thou yet art blind,
Thine ears are stuffed and stopped, despite their length:
And, oh, the foolishness thou countest faith!"
845 Say this as silverly as tongue can troll—
The anger of the man may be endured,
The shrug, the disappointed eyes of him
Are not so bad to bear—but here's the plague
That all this trouble comes of telling truth,
850 Which truth, by when it reaches him, looks false,
Seems to be just the thing it would supplant,
Nor recognizable by whom it left:
While falsehood would have done the work of truth.
But Art,—wherein man nowise speaks to men,
855 Only to mankind,—Art may tell a truth
Obliquely, do the thing shall breed the thought,
Nor wrong the thought, missing the mediate word.
So may you paint your picture, twice show truth,
Beyond mere imagery on the wall,—
860 So, note by note, bring music from your mind,
Deeper than ever e'en Beethoven dived,—

fame, how false! *P1869:*And human estimation words and wind.   837| MS:to tell so
*P1869:*to prove so   838| MS:Because,—it < > art § altered to § Art,—   *P1869:*Because,
it < > Art,   839| MS:Art still remains   *P1869:*That Art remains   840| MS:mine,
at least: *P1869:*mine at least.   843| MS:stopped, for all their length,   *P1869:*stopped,
despite their length,   *1872:*length: 844| MS:And what a foolishness   *P1869:*And, oh,
the foolishness   845-47| MS:troll—/ The shrug   *P1869:*troll—/ The anger of the man
may be endured,/ The   848-53| MS:Were not < > the bane/ That truth < > /
supplant,/ While falsehood comes in aid of truth that fails.   *P1869:*Are not < > the plague/
That all this trouble comes of telling truth,/ Which truth < > / / Nor recognizable by
whom it left—/ < > falsehood would have done the work of truth.   *1872:*/ / / / < > left:/ /
854| MS:men   *P1869:*men,   856| MS:thing that breeds the thought.   *P1869:*thing
shall breed the thought,   857| MS:thought, by the § last two words crossed out and
replaced above by two words § missing the immediate   *P1869:*the mediate
858| MS:picture and show truth   *P1869:*picture, twice show truth,   859| MS:Beyond
that imagery   *P1869:*Beyond mere imagery   860| MS:Or, note < > your soul § crossed
out § mind   *P1869:*So, note < > mind,   861| MS:ever the Andante dived § over
illegible erasure §   *P1869:*dived,—   *1889a:*ever e'en Beethoven dived,—

284

So write a book shall mean beyond the facts,
Suffice the eye and save the soul beside.

And save the soul! If this intent save mine,—
865   If the rough ore be rounded to a ring,
Render all duty which good ring should do,
And, failing grace, succeed in guardianship,—
Might mine but lie outside thine, Lyric Love,
Thy rare gold ring of verse (the poet praised)
870   Linking our England to his Italy!

862-64| MS:mean, beyond the facts,/ And save your soul. If <> mine,   *P1869:/* Suffice the
eye and save the soul beside./ § ¶ § And save the soul! If <> mine,—   *1889a:*mean beyond
<> / / § no ¶ § /   *1889:/ /* § no ¶ ; emended to restore ¶ ; see Editorial Notes § /
866-68| MS:And serve as symbol, as good <> / May it go outside thine, § followed by
illegible erasure § O Lyric   *P1869:*Render all duty which good <> / And, failing grace,
succeed in guardianship,—/ Might mine but lie outside thine, Lyric   869| MS:Thy
ring of verse, rare gold,—her § partially blotted out § poet praised,—   *P1869:*Thy rare gold
ring of verse (the poet praised)   870| MS:to their Italy?   *P1869:*to his Italy!

THE RING AND THE BOOK, Books 9-12

Emendations to the Text

The following emendations have been made to the 1888-89 text:

9. *Juris Doctor Johannes-Baptista Bottinius*

9.427: The 1888-89 edition omits the required quotation marks at the end of the line. The MS-1872 quotation marks are restored.

9.437: MS-1872 *Yet* became *Yea* in 1888-89, thereby losing the irony of Bottini's defense, yet accusation of Pompilia's coquetry toward her "friend,/ Yet stranger," Caponsacchi. The MS-1872 reading *Yet* is restored.

9.1511: The 1888-89 edition omits the required single quotation mark after *years:*, though the space for it remains. The MS-1872 quotation mark is restored.

10. *The Pope*

10.371: The 1888-89 edition has only a single quotation mark at the end of the line; the required quotation marks present in MS-1872 are restored.

10.734: The P1869-1872 comma after *beside* became a period in 1888-89. The line is part of a description of *Greed* beginning 10.733, within a larger categorization of *Craft*, *Greed* and *Violence* (10.730-47), and both sense and syntax in the passage require a comma rather than a period after *beside*. The line contains one correction in both DC and BrU, but, curiously, not this one (see Variants). The 1869-72 reading is restored.

10.983: The 1888-89 edition omits the object of the preposition *under* required by the parallel construction *who art under . . . / As I am under God* in this and the following line; the same expression occurs at 10.1450. It is frequently the case in B's revision that the contraction of a preposition to a single vowel (*i'* for *in*, *o'* for *of*, etc.) reduces the metrical weight of the preposition, eliding it into the beat of the next word. That elision appears to have been the purpose here, but in making the revision the word *me* which occasioned it was lost. Syntax, sense and rhythm all argue the restoration of the MS-1872 reading *under me*, and the revision has been made.

10.945: The hyphen in the compound noun *birthright-badge*, present in 1869, was lost in 1872 and never restored. The hyphen was probably lost because the line was broken in the middle of the word and *birthright* came at the outer edge of the line of type. The 1869 reading *birthright-badge* is restored.

10.1877: The 1888-89 reading *that* destroys the contrast obviously intended between the following word *reason*, and *finer sense* in the line above. The MS-1872 reading *than* is restored.

10.2074: The 1872-1889 reading *make* is inconsistent with the verb tenses in the passage, which develops an ironic forecast of the Pope's imminent death (beginning 10.2053) and the demoralizing consequences of his supposed hypocrisy and injustice in sentencing Guido and the accomplices to death. The irony depends on rhetorically treating all the deaths as a fait accompli, and the past tense of the verb is important to this irony. Since both sense and grammatical consistency in the passage require the past tense, the MS-1869 reading *made* is restored.

11. *Guido*

11.599: The 1888-89 edition omits the required question mark at the end of the line. The MS-1872 question mark after *disbelieve* is restored.

11.619: MS-1872 *make* became *made* in the 1888-89 edition. Both consistency with the other verbs in the passage and the tone of Guido's ironic hypothesis require the present tense; the MS-1872 reading is restored.

11.827: The 1888-89 edition omits the apostrophe in *wolf's*, though the space for it remains. The MS-1872 apostrophe is restored.

11.1071: The 1888-89 edition omits the comma at the end of the line required by the subordinate clause. The MS-1872 comma is restored.

11.1216: The question mark applies to the clause beginning *shall I say* in line 1215, while the quotation marks refer only to line 1216. MS has the correct punctuation *"?*, but MS was misread by compositors of P1869 and the error was never corrected. The 1888-89 edition has been emended to restore the MS reading *face"?*

11.1412: The 1888-89 edition omits the required quotation marks at the end of the line. The MS-1872 quotation marks are restored.

11.1613: The 1888-89 edition omits the required question mark at the end of the line. The MS-1872 question mark after *escape* is restored.

11.2007: The MS-1872 colon at the end of the line, required by syntax, appears as a period in 1888-89. The MS-1872 colon is restored.

12. *The Book and the Ring*

A note on punctuation:
The problem of omitted and inconsistent quotation marks in copy text of Book 12 began with MS and persisted throughout all printed editions. The problem was compounded by Smith, Elder's practice of repeating

quotation marks at the beginning of every line of all quotations. The multiple narrators of Book 12 and the complex quotes-within-quotes in this book apparently led B to employ very freely and loosely a shorthand that he used more precisely elsewhere in the MS of *The Ring and the Book*, a line drawn down the left margin from quotation marks at the top of the page; the indication appears first at 12.31. A still simpler notation appears in the margin at 12.403 (where Bottini's letter begins), *Quotes to end*. After this point in MS there is no attempt to indicate which end is meant nor where it is, nor to discriminate quotes-within-quotes by single quotation marks. In the monk's sermon (12.456-643), for instance, both single and double quotes appear on the same page of MS for quotes-within-quotes. These indications suggest that B did not regard the structure of the quotations as confusing, nor did he wish the punctuation of the quotations to become needlessly complex. In short, the most practical and straightforward method of discriminating the various narrators and speakers was apparently his intention. We have therefore treated the monk's sermon as if it were the sermon itself, and punctuated it independently, not as a quote within a quote, despite the fact that it is inserted into Bottini's letter. We have emended the copy text to add punctuation at the beginning and at the end of quotations at the lines below, for the specific reasons indicated.

12.455: Quotation marks added at the end of the line where Bottini's letter breaks off.

12.456: Quotation marks indicating new speaker added at the beginning of the line where the monk's sermon begins.

12.644: Quotation marks added at the beginning of the line where Bottini's letter resumes.

12.747: Quotation marks added at the end of the line where Bottini's letter ends.

We have emended the punctuation of quotes-within-quotes from double to single quotation marks in the following lines:

12.648-50
12.731-32
12.742-43
12.747

We have emended the punctuation of the quote-within-quote from single to double quotation marks at 12.742.

12.141: The apostrophe in the contraction *'mid*, present in the 1869 edition, is missing in all subsequent editions. The 1869 apostrophe is restored.

12.201: The punctuation at the end of the line, present MS-1872, is only faintly visible in 1888-89, probably because of type damage. The comma is restored.

12.334: The quotation mark at the end of the quotation, present 1869-72, is missing in the 1888-89 edition. The quotation mark after *thanks!* is restored.

12.402: The MS-1872 question mark after *Eh* became an exclamation point in 1888-89. Idomatic usage and the sense of the line, which is a cue to the whining tone of Bottini's letter to follow, suggest that the loss of the question mark was an error; the MS-1872 question mark is restored.

12.491: The subordinate clause beginning *though* was set off by a comma MS-1872, but the comma is missing in 1888-89. The comma may have been set and subsequently lost through type damage, since the space for it remains in 1889. The MS-1872 comma is restored.

12.557: The 1888-89 revision *souls'*, of MS-1872 *that's*, was almost certainly intended to be singular, *soul's*, which is consistent with the referent *itself* and with *soul* in the line above. B's script is characteristically ambiguous about the placement of apostrophes, and the error was probably a misreading of a lost handwritten revision. The 1888-89 *souls'* is emended to *soul's*.

B indicated divisions in discourse by line spacing rather than by indentation. During the printing history of *The Ring and the Book* paragraph divisions were occasionally lost when they happened to occur between pages. We have restored all of B's paragraphs. These form a separate class of emendations to the 1888-89 text. Paragraphing is restored at:

9.211-12	9.714-15	10.1424-25	12.488-89
9.237-38	9.880-81	10.1784-85	12.668-69
9.288-89	9.1495-96	10.1948-49	12.863-64
9.605-6	10.380-81	12.117-18	
9.637-38	10.960-61	12.314-15	

The paragraph is also restored at 9.372-73, where confusion resulting from the addition of lines 371-72 between MS and P1869 led first to displacement of the paragraph marked in MS at line 373, to line 371 in P1869, and subsequently to its loss in 1869-1889. In accordance with B's twice asserted intention, in MS and CP1869, the paragraph is restored at 9.372-73.

A note on variants:

Since the publication of Volumes VII and VIII, further light has been shed on the publishing history of the poem and on the set of 1872 sheets with revisions in B's hand which are among the proofs in the Beinecke Library at Yale. Michael Meredith ("A Botched Job: Publication of *The Ring and the Book*," *SIB* 15 [1988], 41-50) has convincingly identified the provenance of these sheets in his reconstruction of the different stages of revision of the poem for the 1872 edition, some revisions being made as late as 1883, he argues, but still bearing an 1872 title-page. Several small mysteries of the printing history of *The Ring and the Book* are accounted for by Meredith's reconstruction, including the missing Book 2 in the revised sheets and the fact that the documents remained outside the descent of the text. The line of descent of the text is accurately recorded in the variants in this edition, but as Meredith makes clear, the role of invention, necessity and circumstance in that line was almost as influential as within the poem itself.

Book 9, Juris Doctor Johannes-Baptista Bottinius

2] *If . . . speech* See Vol. VII, *Sources.*

4] *blow* Bloom.

5] *wildings . . . parterre* Wild plants in a cultivated ornamental garden.

13] *louts him low* Bows obsequiously.

19] *nutritive of arts* A reference to the Roman tradition of patronage to art.

27] *A-journeying to Egypt* For the flight of Joseph and Mary to Egypt to protect the infant Jesus from Herod's wrath, see Matthew 2:13-16. The flight was a favorite subject for medieval painters.

29-33] *painter . . . Molinist* Bottini implies an analogy between the flight of the Holy Family into Egypt and the flight of Caponsacchi and Pompilia to Rome, then with an irony typical of his defense, he suggests his willingness to martyr Pompilia in his artful argument. Bodies of infidel casualties in Holy Wars are useful (*assistant*) in studying anatomy, says Bottini. The irony that the artist's models for the Holy Family in flight from Herod's tyranny are victims of Christian oppressors is not lost on him. *girding loin* and *lighting lamp*: "Let your loins be girded about, and your lights burning" (Luke 12:35). *Molinist*: see 1.303-13n.

35-40] *To . . . foot* Reminiscent of the method of Leonardo da Vinci as preserved in his notebooks.

44-45] *flax-polled . . . Joseph* White headed old man (*sire*). Joseph was usually represented in art as aged, though there is no Biblical authority for this.

50] *be . . . me* Perhaps the sense here is, "May I find the words to bring this figure (i.e. Pompilia) to life on paper" (as the painter does on his).

53] *Marmoreal . . . uberous* Marblelike, sculptured . . . swelling, full of milk. *Uberous* is used of animals and suggests Bottini's condescension to Pompilia—by analogy to Mary—and perhaps also the asexuality B attributes to him; see 1.1188-98 and 8.234-36 and n.

56] *stumped* The lines of the picture are shaded by an artist's instrument called a *stump*, which is used to blend lines drawn by pencil or crayon or chalk.

61] *unpanniered and elate* Relieved of his load of baskets and thus happy.

63] *clouted . . . scrip* Shoes patched or reinforced with metal or nails . . . a bag or wallet carried by travellers or beggars. Both *clout* and *scrip* are humble articles. Cf. Milton's "dull swain . . . with his clouted shoon" (*Comus* 635) and Jesus' instructions to the disciples going forth to preach, "Take nothing for your journey, neither staves, nor scrip" (Luke 9:3).

65] *jot nor tittle* A *jot* is the smallest portion. A *tittle* is a small diacritical mark. Jesus promised in the Sermon on the Mount, "Till heaven and earth pass, one jot or one tittle shall in no wise pass from the law, till all be fulfilled" (Matt. 5:18). Jesus' reference is to the laws of Moses. By his analogy between painting and law, Bottini casts himself as law giver (Moses).

74] *Thy . . . oils* See 9.27.

84] *conceit* Fanciful image.

86-107] *Rather . . . false* Bottini's description of the artistic process has strong similarities with B's. See 1.451-72. The analogy with law is expedient, in that it allows Bottini to question circumstantial evidence. *E pluribus unum:* One from many.

97] *chyme* Food after digestion.

105] *stole . . . clout* Cape-like wrap such as Mary is represented as wearing in many paintings . . . rag, diaper.

106-7] *spirit-birth . . . false* The painting figure and Bottini's case come together and both are associated with the improbable miracle of the virgin birth.

109] *eximious* Another Latinism, meaning literally "select, distinguished," but having in English ironic overtones (OED).

112] *Capena* Entry gate for the Appian Way, the ancient Roman road from Capua in the N to Rome.

114-17] *Florentine . . . Ferri* Michelangelo, Raphael, Pietro of Cortona, and Ciro Ferri, who died 1689. See 5.486-87n.

119] *exordium . . . ear* The rhetorical term for the introduction to an oration is the *exordium*. *Phoebus*, or Apollo, god of poetry, is mentioned in Virgil, *Eclogues* 6.3-4 and in Milton's "Lycidas": "Phoebus . . . touched my trembling ears" (77).

121] *Ciro's* See 5.486-87n.

123-26] *Family . . . babe* St. Anne, not mentioned in the Bible, is known as the mother of the Virgin Mary and here stands for Violante; Pietro must be the father of Mary (a figure not identified in Bible or legend), and Pompilia is the Virgin Mary. Joseph is missing in the picture.

132] *a month* See *Chronology.*

136] *Herod . . . innocents* Herod the Great, tetrarch of Jerusalem, out of fear because of the reported birth of a Messiah ordered all young children slaughtered. See Matthew 2:1-18.

143] *rack* An instrument of torture on which a body is stretched until its limbs are pulled out of joint. See also 1.971-72n. and 5.12-13n.

144] *lyrist* Horace.

145-47] *Lene . . . duro* Horace likens torture to wine in that both loosen the tongue. "You apply gentle compulsion to an intellect . . . usually dull" (*Odes* 3.21, 13-14).

148] *full . . . o'er* But hardly with goodness and mercy. "Thou preparest a table before me in the presence of mine enemies: thou annointest my head with oil; my cup runneth over. Surely goodness and mercy shall follow me all the days of my life (Ps. 23:5-6).

170-73] *Phryne . . . drapery* The beautiful Greek courtesan *Phryne* was a model, it was said, for Praxiteles' Cnidian Venus and other representations of the goddess. The story is told of her that when on trial for a capital offense she bared her breast and was acquitted. *Doing away with drapery*, Bottini will reveal his client to be, if not guiltless, yet understandably tempted and tempting.

177-79] *What . . . Lucretia* See 8.1660-66n.

181-82] *antiquity . . . infallible* The reference to *antiquity, infallible*, and *innocence* are a play on words suggested by the dogma of Papal Infallibility. See 5.1344n.

186] *Phrynean* See 9.170n.

187] *Lucretia's . . . Tarquin's* See 8.1660-66n.

188] *thistles . . . figs* "For of thorns men do not gather figs, nor of a bramble bush gather they grapes" (Luke 6:44)..

189] *oblique* Misdirected, unjust.

190-209] *A . . . last* Mock epic introduction. Contrast with 1.1382-1408.

203] *opaline* The changeable opal was associated with inconstancy and bad luck; Bottini's symbolism is ambiguous.

206] *lapidary* Worker in gems.

213-14] *Sermocinando . . . clepsydram* "Let me not declaim beyond the clepsydram with my discoursing." A clepsydram was a water glass for measuring time, or by extension, a period of time so measured.

215] *hour-glass* Since Bottini's speech was never delivered aloud (see *Sources*), it is curious that he measures its length by an *hour-glass*. Yet Arcangeli also used an hour-glass; see 8.59 and 8.1427 and nn.

216] *Flaccus . . . plunge* As Horace prompts in *Ars Poetica*, 148. Homer, he says, "always hastens to the issue and hurries his readers into the heart of the story, just as if they were familiar with it."

218] *arrest your love* Catch your attention; win your approval.

224] *O' . . . sex* Satan "first attacked the mind of the weaker sex," said Bottini in OYB,E 211.

234-35] *Hebe-slips . . . foot* Daughter of Jupiter and Juno, goddess of youth and cupbearer to the gods, *Hebe* lost her office as cupbearer (according to one version of the story) through a slip and fall while in attendance on the gods.

236] *wiselier wink* Throughout his presentation Bottini insists that he proposes to prove Guido guilty, not to prove Pompilia innocent. The burden of proof of adultery, he contends, lay solely with the Advocate of the Poor. His effort to be "objective" makes him all too willing to acknowledge some natural feminine "frisking" on Pompilia's part.

237] *dear* Costly.

238] *Hymen* The god of marriage.

239-40] *Discedunt . . . amor* "Loves now depart . . . Let love remain."

245] *foodful glebe* Productive land.

248-49] *cohabita . . . ducere* "She was barred from leading a freer life." The phrasing is from Arcangeli's opening argument (OYB,E 11).

250-53] *heifer . . . yoke* A *heifer* is a young cow which has not calved; the term is used figuratively for a wife. A *hind* is a rustic, a male farm laborer. *natural law:* the law as it is observed in animals, and by extension as a wife should behave toward her husband. *Yoke* has double meaning: the yoke of marriage and the yoke of bondage.

262-65] *Importunate . . . ire* Precisely the charges Guido brought against her.

269-81] *mind . . . new* Throughout this passage there are echoes of 2 Corinthians 5:17 and Revelation 21:4-5: "Therefore if any man be in Christ, he is a new creature: old things are passed away; behold, all things are become new." "And God shall wipe away all tears from their eyes; and there shall be no more death, neither sorrow, nor crying, neither shall there be any more pain: for the former things are passed away. And he that sat upon the throne said, Behold, I make all things new."

280] *Partake . . . bower* Initially Pompilia had refused to consummate the marriage. See 7.715 ff.

283-85] *Novorum . . . ordo* "Of new things the order is being born!" (Virgil [the *Mantuan*], *Eclogues* 4.5-7).

285-88] *Every . . . Canticles* To *confer* is to compare. A *canticle* is a liturgical song from the Bible. The passage here referred to is Song of Solomon 2:11-14. "For, lo, the winter is past, the rain is over and gone; The flowers appear on the earth. . . . "

290] *suppression . . . end* See 9.280n.

297-300] *lady . . . true* This charge against Pompilia is not found in the record. *feminity:* femininity.

301] *choice* Favor.

304] *donative* A noun meaning "gift, donation."

306] *escapes* Transgressions, peccadillos (OED).

307] *prepense* Premeditated.

312] *olent* Giving off a fragrance.

314] *One chalice* A perverse reference to the common cup of the Holy Eucharist.

317] *advertise* Inform.

339-41] *Constans . . . away* "Constant in lightness"ˆ(Ovid, *Tristia* 5.8.18). Bottini makes *levity* carry the triple sense of "lightness" (as in the Latin original, where the reference is to Fate); "object of humor" (including the joke Bottini is making now), and "levite" (deacon; see 1.260-62n.). *Bears the bell* also has triple significance: B took the title "Bells and Pomegranates" (1845) from their Biblical association with "Pleasure and Profit, the Gay and the Grave . . . " (RB-EBB, ed. Kintner, 1.241 [Oct. 18, 1845]). "To bear the bell" is proverbial for "to be the best," and of course Caponsacchi bore away the belle as well.

345-47] *Trust . . . delectum* "Believe him not from the criminal mob chosen for you" (Horace, *Odes* 2.4.17-18).

349] *phoenix* The very summation.

351-53] *precept . . . blemish* A reference to the laws laid down in Leviticus 21:21, "No man that hath a blemish of the seed of Aaron the priest shall come nigh to offer the offerings of the Lord made by fire: he hath a blemish; he shall not come nigh to offer the bread of his God."

353-54] *lest . . . flesh* "Lest the mind be reflected unclearly (*uncandid*) through the obstructing (*thwarting*) flesh."

355-65] *Was . . . well* A conflation of three passages of scripture. The description of David comes from 1 Samuel 16:12. David first encountered Abigail when she came to mediate between him and her "churlish and misbehaved" husband, Nabal, who had insulted David and his men. When she told Nabal of what she had done, he became ill and died ten days later, smote by the Lord (1 Sam. 25:1-38). David did not dance before Abigail but before the Ark of God, which he had brought into the city of David (2 Sam. 6:14-16).

367] *Heu . . . fides* "Also the antique faith." Virgil, *Aeneid* 6.878.

370] *Discover* Uncover.

371-72] *Pope . . . simile* See 10.485-93 and 10.1435-45 for *sea-side similes*.

377-81] *Truly . . . fine* Pompilia so stated in her deposition. See OYB,E 92.

393] *Comacchian* The vale of Comaccio, N of Ravenna, was known for its large eels.

396] *fasting bearable* Church discipline prohibited the eating of meat on Fridays and fast days and seasons, such as the Lenten season now in course, but permitted fish, a category which would include eels.

399] *Lernaean snake* The fabled nine-headed monster which haunted the marshes of Lerna by Argos. Hercules slew him as one of the twelve labors imposed as punishment on him by Eurystheus.

402] *lunes* Irrational acts.

403] *Insanit homo* "The man is insane." Horace, *Satires* 2.7.17.

417] *lose his soul* "For what is a man profited, if he shall gain the whole world, and lose his own soul?" (Matt. 16:26).

424-31] *And . . . shield* See 9.225-27n.

432-41] *Alike . . . folly* While denying that Pompilia was guilty of adultery, Bottini does say, "Although Pompilia's love for the latter [Caponsacchi] was merely pretended for the purpose of winning him . . . " (OYB,E 184).

446] *Allow . . . hers* "Although they seem amatory, yet they were ordained to the purpose of alluring this same Caponsacchi, in order that he might flee with her. . . . Inasmuch as the end is permissable the means are so considered" (OYB,E 182).

451-54] *move . . . speech* In the prologue to *Satires*, *Persius* the Latin poet (34-62 A.D.) says that just as the stomach (*maw*)—that is, necessity—can make the parrot, the *pie* (magpie) and the *crow* speak like a man, so hunger can spur a man to poetry. The argument that Pompilia was driven by necessity to learn how to write is adapted from Bottini in OYB,E 180. *Concave*: "the vault of heaven" (OED).

457] *one letter* The letter written by Pompilia to her parents from Castelnuovo was certainly her own. See OYB,E 160.

462] *She . . . love-letters* An addition by B to the record; Bottini did not concede this in OYB.

463] *Negatas voces* "Skill at speaking the words denied." See 9.451-54n.

465] *lies i'* Shares.

466] *Forged . . . all* It is impossible that Guido forged the "one." See 9.457n.

473] *candid* Unblemished.

511] *muckworms* Worms or grubs that live in muck; figuratively, money grubbers.

513] *generous* Unselfish, with ironic overtones.

515] *Samson . . . snare* Samson, because of his love for Delilah, revealed to her the secret of his strength and she betrayed him to his enemies. The story is told in Judges 16:15-21.

520-24]   *Quia . . . else* See OYB,E 184.

526-27]   *Venus . . . Moschi* Moschus, *Idyls* 1.3-5, of which B provides a paraphrase in the lines following.

534]   *for example-sake* "Now all these things happened unto them for ensamples: and they were written for our admonition" (1 Cor. 10:11).

538]   *Myrtillus, Amaryllis* Names commonly given to lovers in pastoral verse, and used in the letters allegedly written by Caponsacchi and Pompilia.

545-47]   *Ulysses . . . garb* Ulysses, in the guise of a beggar, slipped into the Trojan camp, slew many of the Trojans, and returned to tell his own army about the enemy and their plans. See *Odyssey* 4.245-61.

548]   *clout* Beggar's rags.

549]   *clack dish* A lidded wooden dish carried and clacked by beggars.

561]   *perdue* Concealed.

563]   *Molinist* See 1.303-13n.

566-68]   *Judith's . . . lust* Judith was the beautiful young Jewess who by seductive wiles attracted the Assyrian general Holophernes and then, having lured him into a drunken state, cut off his head. Thus she inspired the Israelites to a great military victory over the Assyrians. See Judith 13.

570-71]   *faulchion . . . dish* A falchion (the usual spelling) is a sword. Holophernes' head was carried in a net concealed in a food bag, not on a dish. It was John the Baptist whose head was presented to Herod on a dish (Matt. 14:68). The confusion of John the Baptist and Holophernes suggests the substitution of Salome for Judith; Bottini's defense again betrays his ambivalence about Pompilia.

574-79]   *wax . . . Icarus* Icarus attempted to reach heaven using wings attached to his body with wax, but when he came too close to the sun, the wax melted, the wings dropped, and he fell to earth.

593]   *still . . . heretics* By the seventeenth century the worst of the Inquisition was over. Heresy remained a continuing concern of the Church, however. In 1689, Innocent XII himself condemned Fénelon's writings. See 12.65n., 12.66-67n.

594]   *Give . . . Gath* The gigantic Philistine warrior *Gath* challenged the army of Israel with these words: "Choose you a man from you and let him come down to me. If he be able to fight with me, and to kill me, then will we be your servants: But if I prevail against him and kill him, then shall ye be our servants and serve us" (1 Sam. 17:8-9). The giant was killed by the young David with his sling shot.

598]   *dragon . . . George* See 1.579n.

602-3]   *Saint Paul . . . presence* "For his letters, say they, are weighty and powerful; but his bodily presence is weak" (2 Cor. 10:10). He is depicted as *puny* also in the apocryphal "Acts of Paul and Tecla."

605] *true . . . oak* It was popularly believed that the *oak* was especially susceptible to being struck by lightning.

613] *inapprehensive* Imperceptive, unaware.

614] *premiss* Premise.

615] *bear . . . bush* From Shakespeare's "A Midsummer Night's Dream" 5.1.21-22: "Or in the night, imagining some fear, / How easy is a bush supposed a bear!"

622] *Helen's nepenthe* After the Trojan war when Odysseus's son Telemachus was seeking his father, he visited Helen, now reunited with Menelaus in Greece. To assuage Telemachus' grief and anxiety, Helen gave him an Egyptian drug called *Nepenthe* (*Odyssey* 4.220-21).

632] *apparition* Appearance (here, real).

634] *former speech* A reference to Bottini's first argument in OYB; see *Sources*.

641] *Suis . . . militat* "Who goeth a warfare any time at his own charges? (1 Cor. 9:7).

648-50] *Money . . . store* The list is in the records; see OYB, E 184.

652-53] *With . . . queen* Pygmalion, King of Tyre, murdered his sister Dido's rich husband and took his wealth. The husband's ghost revealed to Dido both the perpetrator of the crime and the place where he had hidden the treasure. She secured it and decamped, later founding Carthage and becoming its queen. The story is told by Virgil in the *Aeneid* 1.348-64.

669] *bale* Trouble, disaster.

676] *Sororia . . . oscula* "At least sisterly kisses" (Ovid, *Metamorphoses* 4.334, 9.537). The real Bottini did not admit the kissing, but many of the other arguments about the subject here were adapted from OYB,E 185.

680-82] *driver . . . Governor* See 6.1668n. That Borsi's evidence was given after some weeks or months of prison (he was not acquitted until December, nine months after the flight, though he may have been released earlier), may indicate pressure from the authorities in Arezzo that he depose in Guido's behalf.

687] *full tale* The complete sum.

692] *first argument* See *Sources*.

708-9] *nectar . . . imbue* "The sweet lips that Venus had imbued with the quintessence of her own nectar" (Horace, *Odes* 1.13.15-16).

722] *Molinist* See 1.303-13n.

723-24] *built . . . her* Jesus said to Peter, "And I say also unto thee, that thou art Peter, and upon this rock I will build my church: and the gates of hell shall not prevail against it" (Matt. 16:18).

729] *Spirit . . . weak* So Jesus said to the sleeping disciples who were too weary to watch while he prayed in the Garden of Gethsemane (Matt. 26:41).

742-43] *Ut . . . perii* Virgil, *Eclogues* 8.41 The translation is accurate but not the tone.

755-63] *Archimedes . . . innocence* Livy, *Ab Urbe Condita Libri* 25.31.9. Actually Archimedes was "intent upon the figures which he had traced in the dust." He is said to have been so absorbed in a problem that he did not know that Syracuse had been attacked. He was killed without realizing that there was danger. The analogy between the death of the sage and the death of innocence is a masterpiece of double entendre and innuendo. As Altick and Loucks say, the passage "must be the most audacious sexual scene in Victorian literature. Only a poet confident of his reputation for unintelligibility would have dared print such lines" (Richard D. Altick and James F. Loucks, *Browning's Roman Murder Story* [Chicago: University of Chicago Press, 1968], 180).

776-77] *Non . . . Debemus* "We ought not always to hold the same language, but we ought always to aim at the same end" (Cicero, *Epistulae ad Familiares* 1.9.21).

778] *Lie . . . bids* The contrast between the old and new law is reminiscent of Jesus' interpretation of the law in Matthew 5:20-48.

787] *greatest . . . womanhood* A play on the Pharisees' question to Jesus: "Master, which is the greatest commandment in the law?" (Matt. 22:36)].

789] *impudence* The opposite of modesty; shamelessness.

797-99] *Hold . . . veil* The *Medici* Venus in the Ufizzi in Florence, which is a copy of an original by Praxiteles, shields her nakedness with both hands.

803-5] *epistle . . . Violante* See 2.678n.

817] *pose* I.e., the Medicean pose of 9.797-98.

820] *repugnant* Resisting.

826-29] *Nero . . . write* Nero, called upon to sign a death sentence when he was about seventeen, is said to have wished that he could not write.

832] *O . . . mendacious* Horace, *Odes* 3.11.35-36.

835] *Beware . . . unsuccess* I.e., don't confuse guilt and failure.

838-39] *Troy . . . stood* In the war between the Greeks and the Trojans, the Trojans were eventually defeated not by superior valor but by guile.

844] *assist* Are present.

845] *succeeds* Follows.

846] *moonstruck* Demented.

851]   *cubiculum* Bedroom.

854]   *Good . . . sleep* Literally, *commerce* means communication; the line refers to the belief that God often communicated with man through angels. *Commerce* may also carry the contrary notion of sexual intercourse between devils, incubi, and their human victims. Thus, again, Bottini compromises Pompilia while professing to defend her.

861-62]   *Vulcan . . . net* See 3.1444-49n.

866]   *Demodocus . . . song* Demodocus was the minstrel in the *Odyssey* whose song tells the story Bottini has just repeated. It was widely thought in the nineteenth century that the passage was spurious, therefore *nugatory*, worthless.

870]   *pickthank* One who curries favor; in this case, one who sensationalizes in order to gain popular favor.

878]   *desecrated brow* A reference to the cuckold's horns.

880]   *Tacitus* Roman historian c.55-c.120. There is a pun on "silence" (Altick).

883-86]   *bare . . . Thalassian-pure* The lines are a series of broad jokes on the expression "the naked truth." Thalassian means "pertaining to the sea," and *Thalassian-pure* may refer back to the Aphrodite (Venus) of 9.798, whose name means "foam-born" and who according to legend arose from the foam of the sea. Bottini thus represents Pompilia naked as an innocent new-born—or naked as an adultress.

887]   *catches . . . sword* See 2.1023n.

890-91]   *Crowned . . . obedience* "A virtuous woman is a crown to her husband." See 5.580-81n.

917]   *Drew . . . life* See 2.1023n.

925]   *awaiting . . . stone* To the crowd about to stone the woman caught in adultery, Jesus said, "He that is without sin among you, let him first cast a stone at her" (John 8:7).

931-33]   *Magdalen . . . gardener* Magdalen mistook the risen Jesus to be the *gardener* (John 20:15).

961-73]   *Hesione . . . trick* King Laomedon attempted to defraud the builders of the wall around Troy, and as punishment for his breach of faith the city was threatened with destruction by a sea monster. As a propitiatory offering the king left his daughter *Hesione* on a rock to be devoured by the beast. She was rescued by Hercules, *Alcmena's son.*

963]   *vest* Clothing, covering.

974]   *Nimis incongrue* OYB,E 110.

975]   *Sententiam . . . contrariam* "I hold the contrary opinion" (OYB,E 188).

977-80]   *Jove . . . Aethiop* Achilles begged his mother Thetis to persuade Zeus (*Jove*) to mediate his quarrel with Agamemnon, but Thetis informed him that Zeus was banqueting with the Ethiopian king and would be unavilable for twelve days (Homer, *Iliad* 1.351-427).

980-88] *Hercules . . . fate* Hercules slew his friend Iphitus and for punishment was exiled for a year to serve as slave to *Omphale*, queen of Lydia. She put him to doing woman's work. According to one version of the legend, Hercules fell in love with her and served her willingly. He did eventually stir himself, however, to kill the monster orc. See 9.961-73n.

985-86] *Governor . . . Archbishop* See 3.965-66n.

990-92] *anti-Fabius . . . restuit* Fabian tactics, from the policies advocated by Fabius Maximus, an opponent of Hannibal in the Second Punic War, are strategic delays designed to keep the opponent off balance. The Latin, "Who by not delaying restored the thing," is an adaptation of Cicero, *de Seneca* 4.10; there was no negative in the original.

996] *ranged* Positioned as spectators.

999] *gripe* Old spelling for "grip."

1009] *Quid vetat* From a line in Horace's *Satires* 1.1.24-25: "Why shouldn't one tell the truth in jest?"

1011] *recreate* Entertain, distract.

1013] *apologue* Moral tale.

1015] *Tradition . . . scripture* The beginnings of Christianity and its spread over the western world preceded the authorized canon of the New Testament.

1020-21] *lying . . . Yeschu* Psalm 31:6, "I have hated them that regard lying vanities." *Sepher Toldoth Yeschu* (*The Book of the Generation of Jesus*), is an apocryphal account from a Jewish point of view of some of the events in the New Testament.

1025] *schismatic* Molinist? See 1.303-13n.

1039] *Molinism* See 1.303-13n.

1063] *proud . . . mine* At Jesus' right hand in his coming kingdom. See Matthew 20:20-21.

1065] *Loved Disciple* "When Jesus [from the cross] saw his mother, and the disciple standing by, whom he loved, he saith unto his mother, Woman behold thy son!" (John 19:26).

1068] *Vicar and Vice-gerent* The words are close in meaning: representative of God.

1069] *keys . . . hell* Jesus said to Peter: "Thou art Peter, and upon this rock I will build my church, and the gates of hell shall not prevail against it. And I will give unto thee the keys of the kingdom of heaven: and whatsoever thou shalt bind on earth shall be bound in heaven: and whatsoever thou shalt loose on earth shall be loosed in heaven" (Matt. 17:18-19).

1077-78] *And . . . all* At the Last Supper, Jesus washed the disciples' feet, a task ordinarily that of servants, and said: "If I then, your Lord and Master have washed your feet, ye also ought to wash one another's feet" (John 13:14).

1093] *give . . . poor* When Mary annointed Jesus' feet with costly ointment, Judas asked, "Why was not this ointment sold for three hundred pence and given to the poor? This he said not that he cared for the poor; But because he was a thief" (John 12:3-6).

1098] *Merry-thought* Wish Bone.

1100-1101] *Thucydides . . . laughed* Greek historian and model in his careful documentation and historical method for later historians, c.464-c.402 B.C. A medieval scholar writing in the margins of Thucydides' *History of the Peloponnesian Wars* said, "Here the lion smiles." The passage is not humorous and the comment may refer to the historian's presumed pride in the polish of his work, not to its comedy (Cook). But the point of the reference is Bottini's apology for his relish in his own extended humorous relief. He makes the obscure and forced allusion to Thucydides in order to associate himself with the exemplary methods and seriousness of the classical author, in contrast to the historian of the farcical story just concluded, that "foolish Jew / Pretending to write Christian history" (9.1033-34).

1107] *Nor . . . vain* St. Paul admonishes everyone to be subject to the "higher powers" since all power derives from God. "For he is the minister of God to thee for good. But if thou do that which is evil be afraid; for he beareth not the sword in vain" (Rom. 13:1,4).

1109] *oil . . . wine* In the parable, the Good Samaritan went to the aid of the man who was beaten and robbed, and "bound up his wounds, pouring in oil and wine . . . and took care of him" (Luke 10:34).

1114] *barley-bread* Jesus fed the multitude with five barley loaves. See John 6:7-11.

1127-28] *Sophocles . . . throned* "Justice declared from of old, sits with Zeus in the might of the eternal laws" (*Oedipus at Colonus* 1832).

1140] *pother . . . cocked* See 9.377-81n.

1149] *light* Happily, readily.

1157] *Twelve enthroned* "And Jesus said unto them, verily I say unto you, that ye which have followed me, in the regeneration when the Son of man shall sit in the throne of his glory, ye also shall sit upon twelve thrones, judging the twelve tribes of Israel" (Matt. 19:28). See also Luke 22:30.

1159] *impossible . . . come* Jesus said, "it must needs be that offenses come; but woe to that man by whom the offence cometh!" (Matt. 18:7).

1160] *leet-day* The day on which the court sits. A somewhat quaint foreview of heaven.

1164] *Put . . . ear* When one of the disciples, attempting to defend Jesus at the time of his arrest, cut off the ear of a servant amidst the arresting party, Jesus demanded, "Put up again thy sword into his place; for all they that take the sword shall perish with the sword" (Matt. 26:51-52).

1175] *toys* Innocent flirtations.

1177] *curt* Short.

1185-86] *range . . . pound* Open fields for grazing . . . enclosure for retaining domestic animals. The reference is to Pompilia's relegation to the monastery.

1187] *ashes, dust* Symbols of penitence.

1188] *mollitious* Voluptuous, sensuous.

1195] *wicked . . . sonnet-book* Pietro Aretino (1492-1557) wrote ribald verse that was widely read and much admired.

1198] *wire-shirt . . . discipline* References to the hair shirt (rough hair was likened to wire, as in "wire-haired terrier") and twisted or braided cord used as a whip by religious ascetics and penitents who believed that punishing the flesh was a necessary part of religious discipline.

1201] *since . . . miss* Law's abundant reserves are not diminished by use.

1203] *holy house* See 2.1189-90n.

1206-7] *Being . . . matter* Jesus commanded the leper whom he had healed to tell no one. "But he went out, and began to publish it much, and to blaze abroad the matter, insomuch as Jesus could no more openly enter into the city" (Mark 1:45).

1209-11] *Bethesda . . . physician* "Now there is at Jerusalem by the sheep market a pool, which is called in the Hebrew tongue, Bethesda, having five porches. In these lay a great multitude of impotent folk, of blind, halt, withered, waiting for the moving of the water" (Luke 5:2-3). "They that be whole need not a physician, but they that are sick" (Matt. 2:12).

1216] *prison's style* I.e. *Domus pro carcere*, "house arrest." See 2.1333n.

1218] *Redeunt . . . regna* "The Golden Age returns" (Virgil, *Eclogues* 4.6). See also 10.776-77 and n.

1218] *Six . . . slip* A mistake. See 2.1314 and *Chronology*.

1223] *pots* A mistaken translation of Psalm 18:13. KJV reads, "Though ye have lien among the pots, ye shall be as the wings of a dove covered with silver, and feathers with yellow gold." All modern versions substitute "sheepfolds" for *pots*.

1224] *mued* Molted.

1231] *preoccupy* Occupy in advance.

1232] *Darnel* Weed-grass.

1233] *Infelix . . . horridus* "Unfruitful darnel, prickly thistle." Inaccurately quoted from Virgil's *Georgics* 1.154, 151-52.

1239] *Interdum* Now and then.

1259] *Tozzi* Malpighi's (or Malpichi's) successor as physician to the Pope. See 7.419n; 11.2326, 2330; 12.40.

1267, 1272, 1273] *intercourse / broached / discuss* All puns in the course of Bottini's heavily suggestive account of Caponsacchi's motives for the journey. All can be taken either as terms for conversation or for sex; *discuss* had a colloquial sense of "consume" (OED). See 9.755-63 and n. for a still more outrageous innuendo.

1274] *use* Custom.

1276] *colocynth* A cathartic made from the bitter seed of the *colocynth*, an Asian fruit of the gourd family.

1288-89] *Lebanon . . . beloved* "My nose is as the tower of Lebanon which looks toward Damascus" (Song of Sol. 1:4).

1290] *Forsan . . . olim* The complete quote is, *forsan et haec olim meminisse iuvabit*: "Someday perhaps remembering even this will be a pleasure" (Virgil, *Aeneid* 1.3).

1297] *hap . . . unconscious* Luck . . . unsuspecting.

1302] *palm* Of victory; the expression goes back to the gladiatorial contests, when victors received a palm tree branch.

1309] *apple . . . eye* "He kept him as the apple of his eye" (Deut. 32:10).

1310-14] *crown . . . child* The *sage* remains unidentified. In substance, however, the passage is reminiscent of Proverbs 17:6: "Children's children are the crown of old men; and the glory of children are their fathers." *summum bonum*: highest good.

1316-18] *filius . . . doubt* A legal expression: "He is the son according to the marriage contract." See 5.1462n., 2016. The *text twits* (rebukes) the doubter.

1319] *faith . . . world* "When the Son of man cometh, shall he find faith upon the earth?" (Luke 18:8).

1322] *bandied* Tossed from side to side.

1323-25] *Cujum . . . Aegonis* "Whose is this flock?" . . . "Meliboeus'?" . . . "Nay, Aegon's." Loosely quoted from Virgil, *Eclogues* 3.1-2.

1328-31] *To . . . marriage* Pompilia said in her deposition that about a year after the consummation of her marriage the Franceschini turned against her because she had borne no child. See OYB,E 91.

1335-46] *Like . . . horse* Until the middle of the seventeenth century naturalists, following Aristotle, universally accepted spontaneous generation in at least the lower forms of life. It was not until the middle of the nineteenth century that the idea was totally discredited. Bottini's first example refers to the story of Aristaeus' bees as recorded (*memorized*) by Virgil (*Maro*). *Aristaeus' bees* were destroyed as a punishment but restored to him in the carcass of one of the four bulls and four cows which he sacrificed to atone for his offense (*Georgics* 4.554-68); *bowels*: viscera. Another superstition was that horsehair soaked in *water* (or dung) would produce a *snake*; thus the snake is the *spontaneous product of the horse* through its horsehair. Bottini's defense once again slides into incrimination as he implies that Pompilia has borne a snake.

1349] *our conception* Guido's "spontaneous" conception, and Bottini's ingenious idea.

1350] *Is . . . City-arms* Many Tuscan cities had animals as emblems on their flags. In *Casa Guidi Windows* EBB describes several of these, including the one on which "Arezzo's steed pranced clear from bridle-hold" (1.509).

1352-56] *Cur . . . viro* "Why should I / Without a mate despair of becoming / a mother ? And of giving birth provided I'm / pure and haven't touched a man?" (Ovid, *Fasti* 5.241-42) A *distich* is a couplet.

1357] *prodigy* Miracle (of spontaneous generation).

1361] *Gaetano* See 7.100-104n.

1364-65] *exult . . . song* With the reminder "Thy maker is thy husband," the prophet Isaiah exhorts the barren to rejoice, "For ye shall go out with joy and be led forth with peace; the mountains and the hills shall break forth before you in singing" (Isa. 55:12).

1366-67] *Incipe . . . patrem* Virgil, *Eclogues* 4.60. The translation is exact.

1368-71] *Nor . . . Cognoscendo* "And do not doubtful hesitate, father, in recognizing your child." Spoken by Juno to Jupiter at the birth of Minerva from Jupiter's head.

1373-77] *devil . . . first* "When the unclean spirit is gone out of a man, he walketh through dry places, seeking rest, and findeth none. Then he saith, I will return into my house from whence I came out; and when he is come, he findeth it empty, swept, and garnished. Then goeth he, and taketh with himself seven other spirits more wicked than himself, and they enter in and dwell there: and the last state of that man is worse than the first" (Matt. 12:43-45). The passage is about a demon going out of and then returning to an unbelieving, unsaved man. The swept and garnished (*decorated*) house in the Bible is the temporarily reformed man; in the poem it is also the house of the Comparini. Guido summoned four, of course, not seven.

1382-83] *simile . . . dam* "He [Diomede] went storming up the plain like a winter swollen river in spate that scatters the dikes in the running current, / one that the strong-compacted dikes can contain no longer, / neither the mounded banks of the blossoming vineyards hold it / rising suddenly as Zeus' rain makes heavy the water and many lovely works of the young men crumble beneath it" (Homer, *Iliad* 9.87-92).

1389] *effigies* Latin for effigy, likeness.

1393] *offuscated* Darkened.

1397] *What's . . . Bacchus* The earliest Greek dramas were in honor of Dionysus, or Bacchus. As the form developed chants were introduced on other subjects, and the audience would protest, *What's this to Bacchus?* Bottini twits Arcangeli's one-track epicure's mind.

1399-1400] *Poor . . . pauperes* "Blessed are the poor" (Matt. 5:3). But not when the present Advocate of the Poor is in charge of their livelihood, says Bottini.

1411] *simulated death* The Second Anonymous Pamphlet, OYB,E 225.

1416] *full confession* OYB,E 57-61.

1419-25] *Oh . . . tale* Bottini admits the variance of his and Pompilia's versions, but denies that the unpleadable confession of innocence has any bearing on his more plausible argument. The syntax is complex and elliptical but not ungrammatical. The first *as* (1420) means "for example," while the second *as* (1425) introduces a conditional clause and means "as if."

1433] *Adamic flesh* Fallen humanity.

1436] *That with this* Bottini's presentation with Pompilia's statement.

1449] *art's . . . short* Hippocrates, *Aphorisms*, quoted by Seneca in *De Brevitate Vitae* 1.1.

1450] *compass* Within bounds.

1456] *so circumstanced* Under these circumstances.

1479] *Who . . . sin* The argument here is that the means (Pompilia's possibly false confession) justified the ends (Guido's punishment and repentence).

1484] *Triarii* The backup soldiers of the third rank, the older men in the Roman army, who were called upon in time of crisis.

1486-88] *she . . . sense* The argument is expressed in the First Anonymous Pamphlet, OYB,E 156. If Pompilia confessed her "true" guilt privately before her public protestation of innocence, she was absolved and therefore technically innocent afterwards. The real Bottini argued that the public confession was true.

1489] *Molinist* See 1.303-13n.

1496] *Solvuntur . . . go* "Is the account paid?" (i.e., Is the case settled?) A variation on "Solventur risu tabulae," "The case will be dismissed with laughter." Horace, *Satires* 2.1.86.

1507-11] *Decretum . . . years* See 6.1980-90n.

1516] *misapprehensiveness* Misunderstanding.

1517-31] *Titulus . . . find* The *Titulus* is the description of the crime or charge, in this case "Romana Homicidiorum" or "Roman (case) of Homicides." The argument is from Bottini's address, OYB,E 175.

1533] *tense . . . bids* "Apollo sometimes rouses the silent lyric muse, neither does he always bend his bow" (Horace, *Odes* 2.10.13-20). Apollo (*Phoebus*) is god of the sun, thus like Law a bringer of light.

1535-45] *draught . . . crime* B found the illustration of the argument in the Second Anonymous Pamphlet, OYB, E 223. The ivy was sacred to Bacchus and from early times, a bough hung over a door meant that wine was sold there.

1552] *Law's . . . help* Bottini returns to the imagery of the opening of his argument, this time not the holy family of 9.23, but Law as the mother of truth (9.1515, 1559) and the son (Bottini) who crowns her through his efforts (9.1556).

1553] *tenax proposito* "Tenacious of my purpose" (loosely quoted from Horace, *Odes* 3.3.1).

1559] *eliminate* To draw out.

1562] *panegyric of Isocrates* The Athenian orator and rhetorician (436-338 B.C.) whose famous *panegyric* urged an invasion of Persia. It was said that the orator took more time advising the invasion than Alexander took to conquer Asia.

1568] *priest for auditory* The Roman Rota; see *Sources*.

Book 10, The Pope

1] *Ahasuerus* Biblical king of Persia, identified with the well-known Xerxes, who reigned 486-465 B.C. B refers to the following passage in Esther 6:1: "On that night could not the king sleep, and he commanded to bring the book of record of the chronicles; and they were read before the king." The king read in the records that a plot against his life had been discovered by the Jew Mordecai. Mordecai at the time was in fear of his life from his enemy Haman, who had built a gallows on which he hoped to have Mordecai hanged but on which he himself was executed by the King's orders. The reference to *Ahasuerus* is thus appropriate both to the Pope's habit of daily reading and to the question presently preoccupying him, whether or not to sentence Guido.

2] *seven years* Pope Innocent XII held office beginning in 1691; he is speaking in February, 1698.

3-11] *History . . . Peter* The particular history has not been identified. B does refer to Sigebert of Gembloux (c. 1030-1115), historian and hagiographer, as one of his sources. The Apostle *Peter*, for whom St. Peter's Church is named, was known as the founder of the Church; *Alexander* VIII was the Pope's immediate predecessor, in office 1689-91. A collection of biographies of the Popes called *Liber Pontificalis* was first compiled in the sixth century and maintained through the fifteenth century. It extends back to St. Peter and comprises many different authors, which approximates the Pope's description. It was reprinted in Paris 1886-92; it is possible that B had heard mention of its preparation.

9] *making . . . end* "Of making many books there is no end" (Eccl. 12:12).

13] *how . . . Pope* On the question of judgment and Papal infallibility, see 5.1344n.

20] *His . . . Vicar* In the Roman Catholic Church, the Pope is regarded as Christ's representative on earth. The Title *Vicar* of Christ was given to him as early as the eighth century.

22-23] *page . . . cyst* A reference to the record of a Pope's deeds that is customarily placed in his casket (*cyst*).

25] *Formosus* Innocent describes one of the most sensational episodes in the annals of the history of the popes, perhaps because as a noted reformer of church abuses himself he is particularly aware of their history. *Formosus* was first made Cardinal Bishop of Porto in Spain, and then served as Pope 891-96 during the height of two centuries of turmoil and corruption in the Roman Catholic church. His posthumous trial by the pope who succeeded him is one of the wonders included in Nathaniel Wanley's *Wonders of the Little World*, a favorite childhood book of B's where he doubtless first became acquainted with the incident.

26] *Sigebert* See 10.3-11n.

32] *Stephen* Pope 896-97. He was as B says "Seventh of the name," although he is generally recognized as Stephen VI since an earlier Stephen was elected to the office but died before he was consecrated. His brief and violent reign ended in his own imprisonment and strangulation.

39] *embalmed* Cook cites Story as authority on the date after which Popes were embalmed (1513). Thus the body was in a worse state than Innocent describes.

40] *buried . . . Vatican* About 150, or more than half the number of Popes, are buried in the Vatican.

43-44] *pontific chair* The body was robed in papal vestments and seated on the papal throne, both symbolic of the office of Christ's vicar.

45-49] *Stephen . . . Church* Canon law contains the rules of the Church for her organization, government and administration. Canons designed to curb ambition and forbidding the translation or promotion of bishops were used against Formosus at one point in his career, later overridden, then posthumously invoked against him in the manner the Pope describes—only to be subsequently overridden again. Since Stephen had been a bishop too (see 10.59-61), and ordained by Formosus, it was in the interest of his own legitimation to declare Formosus and all his offices void, thus removing the objection to his own papal authority, though this does not appear to have been his only motive.

50] *Deacon* See 1.260-62n.

62] *Synod* A representative body of the Church charged with determining doctrine and discipline.

68] *Christ's Vicar* See 10.20n.

85] *three fingers* The three middle fingers used in blessing are symbolic of the Trinity.

89] *Fish* The initial letters of the Greek words for Jesus Christ, Son of God, Savior, make up the Greek word for *fish*. The *fish* very early became the symbol for Christ and for Christianity.

91-92] *Pope . . . Fisher's-signet* The Pope is the representative of Christ, whose symbol is the fish; he also is the successor to St. Peter, the Fisherman, to whom Jesus said, "Follow me, and I will make you fisher of men" (Matt. 4:19). The Pope's signet ring depicts St. Peter fishing from a boat.

100] *Wot . . . thus* Do you suppose Herod crucified Jesus because Jesus offended him in the same way Formosus offended you? The satirical comparison likens Jesus' carrying the cross to Calvary and Formosus' corpose being trailed from street to street (10.94).

103] *captive . . . strangled* See 10.32n.

104] *Romanus* Became Pope in 897 and served less than four months.

107] *Theodore* Was Pope in 898.

108] *synod* See 10.62n.

113] *Jonas* The name is a variant of Jonah, who was swallowed by a large fish and discharged after three days; his story is found in the Book of Jonah.

116] *embalmer's spice* See 10.39n.

121] *Luitprand* A tenth century historian and Bishop of Cremona. B assumes, contrary to contemporary opinion, that he wrote *Liber Pontificalis.*

128-31] *John . . . Ravenna* John was Pope 898-900. He moved the synod meeting to Ravenna because of the disturbances in Rome.

133] *Eude . . . France* Odo, Count of Paris, who became King of the Western Franks in 888.

134] *anathematize* B uses the word in its general sense of strong disapproval, not in reference to the ceremony accompanying a formal anathematization.

136] *Auxilius* Early tenth century priest who strongly defended Formosus and argued for the validity of his ordination in *Defensionem Sacrae Ordinationis Papae Formosi Libellus* (*Defense of the Sacred Ordination of the Libeled Pope Formosus*).

140] *Marinus* Pope 882-84, Marinus restored Formosus to his see as Bishop of Porto after Formosus' earlier deposition and excommunication in 876.

141] *Sergius* Sergius III, the third Pope after John. He reigned 904-11.

150] *infallible* See 10.13; 5.1344n.

154-56] *Fear . . . hell* "And fear not them which kill the body, but are not able to kill the soul; but rather fear him which is able to destroy both soul and body in hell (Matt. 10:28).

159] *Vice-gerent* See 9.1068n.

163] *twilight . . . work* "I must work the work of him who sent me, while it is day: The night cometh, when no man can" (John 9:4).

164] *His staff* The papal staff is one of the symbols of the office.

165-66] *my . . . sorrow* "The days of our years are three score ten: and if by reason of strength they be four score years, yet is their strength labour and sorrow; for it is soon cut off, and we fly away" (Ps. 90:10). The Pope was actually 82 at the time.

168] *Pope for Christ* See 10.20n.

169] *man's assize* Civil court.

179-80] *exceeded . . . license* "My spirit will not always strive with man" (Gen. 6:3).

180-81] *Adam's . . . die* "God hath said, Ye shall not eat of it, neither shall ye touch it, lest ye die. And the serpent said unto the woman, Ye shall not surely die" (Gen. 3:3-4).

182-83] *All . . . grace* "All have sinned, and cometh short of the glory of God; being justified fully by his grace" (Rom. 3:23-24).

199] *passion . . . bear* Christ's *passion* on the cross is an association of the word here; more immediately, *passion* denotes the suffering that the Pope not only bears responsibility for in regard to Guido, but must also bear himself in his imminent death.

215] *figure* Representation.

219-20] *chief . . . lie* Guido's *excuse* for the murders was that he had been duped from the beginning, with the final *excuse* of calling out Caponsacchi's name at the Comparini's door to test Pompilia. Arcangeli's *lie* was his use of the cause of honor as the major supporting argument for the defense.

222] *start subterfuge* Expose deceit, take it by surprise; from a hunting idiom, as in "start a hare." Arcangeli's defense set Guido's murder up as a direct and honest, honorable retaliation against deceit.

223-24] *torture's . . . brutal* See 1.971-72n.

227] *rede* Interpretation. OED credits B with using *rede* in this sense.

235] *Irresolute* The fault most historians have found with Innocent XII.

249] *Breathe* Lance.

268] *changed* Exchanged.

281] *arrased* Curtained.

292-96] *sagacious . . . Virgil* Emanuel Swedenborg (1688-1772) is surely the reference of the passage, although in fact he was only ten years old at the time the Pope is speaking. The writings of Swedenborg were the authority and guide in the nineteenth-century vogue for spiritualism; Swedenborgians believed in a spirit world and practiced clairvoyance. EBB was a fervent believer in spiritualism and it was a major point of disagreement between the Bs. According to Mrs. Orr, B "remained subject, for many years, to gusts of uncontrollable emotion, which would sweep over him whenever the question of 'spirits' or 'spiritualism' was revived" (Orr, *Life*, 217). *Sagacious* suggests the intense, paranormal powers of perception claimed by spiritualists, and *figures* means, as so often in B's work, "symbols," or the material figure for the transcendent spiritual reality. The references to prediction by means of chance, either by casting lots or by random selection of passages from *Virgil* (see 5.401n.), strongly suggest B's feeling that Victorian spiritualism was simply ancient superstition masquerading in a fashionable guise. The whole passage is another example of B's identification with the Pope, and his consequent imperviousness to anachronism or other such unhistorical liberties. For discussion and examples of spiritualism and spiritualists, including Swedenborg, see Irvine and Honan, 304-9. On the related topic of Mesmerism see also 1.722-52n. and notes to the poem "Mesmerism," Vol. V, 373-74.

308] *house-magistrate* Head of the house.

318] *twice . . . seven-times-ten* See 10.165n.

321] *cark* Archaic for "distress."

327] *posset* A hot drink made of curdled milk with ale or wine.

329] *smoking flax* "A bruised reed shall he not break and the smoking flax shall he not quench" (Isa. 42:5). The Pope, in contrast, sees human life as a *smoking flax* subject to being quenched by the most trivial and unexpected circumstance.

340] *Since . . . judged* "For the tree is known by his fruit" (Matt. 12:33).

350] *curse* "And unto Adam he said . . . cursed is the ground for thy sake; in sorrow shalt thou eat of it all the days of thy life" (Gen. 3:17).

372] *filthy . . . coil* "But we are all as an unclean thing, and our righteousnesses are as filthy rags" (Isa. 54:6). *coil*: noisy dispute.

375] *He . . . Truth* "I am the way, the truth, and the life" (John 14:6). "In the beginning was the Word . . . and the Word was made flesh and dwelt among us" (John 1:1,14).

382-83] *Antonio . . . self* The Pope addresses his former self by his real name. The passage which follows, particularly the extended comparison of Guido to the soldier crab (10.485-509) is appropriate to the Neopolitan birthplace of the Pope.

385-86] *I' . . . lands* He served in various capacities in Urbino, Malta, Perugia, Florence, Poland, and Germany. In 1681 he became a Cardinal, and then Bishop of Faenza, Legate of Bologna, and Archbishop of Naples before being elected Pope.

386] *legate-rule* A legate was the special representative of the Pope to whom the power of the Holy See was entrusted.

392] *old . . . world* Here *old* has the sense of former, earlier.

393] *inquisitive* Eager for knowledge.

397] *Wise . . . world* "For the children of this world are in their generation wiser than the children of light" (Luke 16:8).

398] *reprobate* Condemned. Since the Pope, who has power to "bind and loose" (see 5.1344n.) is speaking, the word may carry its theological meaning of being lost in sin and beyond redemption.

415] *Straitened* Restricted, hindered.

416] *cirque* Arena.

417] *penfold for probation* A *penfold* is a pen or fold for confining animals; *probation*: trial, testing.

419] *monition* Admonition.

425] *miss . . . march* Mistakenly overstep the natural course.

434-35] *Man . . . God* "We beseech you brethren, and exhort you, by the Lord Jesus, that as ye have received of us how ye ought to walk and please God . . . " (1 Thess. 4:1).

435-42] *He . . . bruise* See 1.260-62n.

436] *man's obedience* The rule of obedience required when he accepted orders in the Church.

440-41] *Professed . . . sinned* See 1.257n.

442] *frocked* Clothed in the clerical robes, i.e., invested with a clerical office.

448] *portentous* Omnious.

450] *pale* Protected sphere of governance.

451] *Abate . . . Girolamo* See 1.547n.

465] *sunscreen . . . ombrifuge* Protection against sun, wind and rain.

470] *sacristan* Keeper of the sacristy, a place in the church where sacred vessels and vestments are kept.

471-74] *Shall . . . company* A reference to the miracle of the multiplication of the loaves and fishes, recorded in all four gospels, with the added suggestion that Judas was by nature a thief. It is reminiscent also of John 12:6: "This he [Judas] said, not that he cared for the poor; but because he was a thief, and had the bag, and bare what was put therein." *Attent with fifties* (a large number) *in a company* is an echo of Luke's account of the story: "Make them sit down by fifties in a company" (Luke 9:14).

485] *ambiguous fish* The hermit crab (soldier crab) often inhabits the shell of other sea creatures which he can discard at will. He also can shed his own shell, as all crabs can.

489] *Armour* Reminiscent of Paul's admonition: "Put on the whole armour of God, that ye may be able to stand against the wiles of the devil" (Eph. 6:11).

492] *affiliate* A legal term meaning "to fix the paternity of a child, to ascribe a child to its putative father." Guido was almost a priest, a son of the Church.

494-95] *Does . . . deep* No. The rhetorical questions deflate both Guido's conceit and society's imperviousness to it, by scaling the one against the plan of the universe, and by weighing the other as a law of custom equal in force to the laws of nature. The Pope's search for the roots of the murder are everywhere deeper and broader than a probe into its immediate circumstances or specific agent.

496] *mew* A place of confinement, or, more appropriate here, of hiding.

498] *sand-fly and slush-worm* Pests, parasites; *slush* means waste, garbage.

502-4] *filthy . . . carrion-prey* Scavenger sea life.

509] *soldier-crab* See 10.485n.

513] *armour* See 10.489n.

530] *Or . . . or* Either . . . or.

531] *remark* Notice.

539] *all to instigate* I.e., all directed to *instigate*, to spur on some evil action, without declaring so.

542-43] *All . . . murder* "The love of money is the root of all evil" (1 Tim. 6:10).

549-51] *toad . . . victims* It was thought that toads secrete a poison that silenced a victim. See also 5.1382n.

556] *Edged . . . month* Forced to leave, actually in four months; see *Chronology*.

566] *painted* Imagined.

567-69] *crown . . . marriage* See 9.890-91n.

578] *gor-crow* Carrion crow.

588] *draws . . . crime* Approaches the highly detailed, elaborate crime.

595] *thought . . . deed* Phrase from the General Confession, *Book of Common Prayer*.

600] *gripe* Old spelling for "grip."

618] *Campagne* Countryside.

634-35] *frenzy-stung . . . anywhere* Io, daughter of a river-god, beloved by Zeus, was hated by jealous Hera. She was changed into a heifer, either by Hera out of spite, or, some accounts say, by Zeus in order to protect her. Hera in retaliation sent a gadfly to pursue her. Maddened, Io wandered frenzied over the world seeking relief.

636] *should front* Happen to meet.

640] *pluck . . . hand* "And I give unto them eternal life; and they shall never perish, neither shall any man pluck them out of my hand" (John 10:28).

652] *other Aretine* See 9.1195 and n.

661-62] *star / Fought* "They fought from heaven, the stars in their courses fought against Sisera" (Judges 5:20).

668] *holy ground* In presence of the burning bush, Moses was commanded: "Draw not nigh hither: Put off thy shoes from off thy feet, for the place whereon thou standeth is holy ground" (Ex. 3:5).

670] *Satan . . . lightning* Jesus said, "I beheld Satan as lightning fall from heaven" (Luke 10:18), recalling, perhaps, the Old Testament verse, "How art thou fallen from heaven, O Lucifer" (Isa. 14:12).

677] *ermine-like* The ermine has white fur in winter, except for its black tail.

684-85] *thorn . . . rose* A reversal of the popular proverb.

689] *preconcerts* Contrives beforehand.

693] *armed . . . teeth* According to the record, Guido was either unarmed (OYB,E 148), or armed only with a traveling sword (OYB,E 122).

705-6] *Probation . . . purge* Guido was given a chance, a test (*Probation*) to repent and be saved, if he could have opened himself to (*could he know*) the mercy of confession and repentance, the *fiery purge* which lasts only a *minute* compared to the eternal reward. Cf. 2 Cor. 4:17, "For our light affliction, which is but for a moment, worketh for us a far more exceeding and eternal weight of glory."

708]　*heaped . . . head* "If thine enemy be hungry, give him bread to eat; and if he be thirsty, give him water to drink: for thou shalt heap coals of fire upon his head" (Prov. 25:22).

710]　*Eliminate* Eliminated.

711]　*saved . . . fire* "If a man's work shall be burned, he shall suffer loss: But he himself shall be saved; yet as by fire" (1 Cor. 3:15).

712]　*go softly* "I shall go softly all my years in the bitterness of my soul" (Isa. 38:15).

715]　*deigns* Stoops to (Obs.).

721]　*luring owl* See 3.338n.

730]　*complot* Plot together, conspire (arch.).

740]　*Murder . . . knife* See 2.146n. and 8.1151-56n.

747-48]　*dove's . . . olive* When the dove, released from the Ark, returned with an olive leaf in her bill, Noah knew that the flood waters had abated (Gen. 8:6-11).

756-59]　*My . . . wife* Had he murdered Pompilia before the birth of his son, he would not have received the proceeds of the usufruct. See also 3.1539-45; 4.1096-99.

760]　*determined on* Depended on.

776-77]　*gold . . . ruled* The Golden Age when Saturn ruled the world was characterized by pastoral simplicity. It was followed by steady decline through the silver and bronze heroic ages to the leaden, the present. The Pope mocks the equation of virtue and rustic life. See also 9.1218n.

778-79]　*clown . . . clownship* In the archaic sense of a rustic, and also in the modern sense of a fool.

785-86]　*On . . . will* The song of the angels announcing the birth of Jesus. Luke 2:14.

797]　*bring . . . death* "Then when lust hath conceived, it bringeth forth sin: and sin, when it is finished, bringeth forth death" (James 1:15).

811]　*hebetude* Dullness.

816]　*warrant* See 3.1621n.

821]　*resident . . . years* A mistake. See 2.302n.

828]　*reach . . . frontier* Had they reached the Tuscan border they would no longer have been subject to Roman authority.

830-32]　*judgment . . . Granduke* Guido brought a charge of adultery and theft against Pompilia in Arezzo. She was found guilty and sentenced to life imprisonment, a verdict confirmed by the Court in Florence on 24 December 1697, two months before the Pope rejected Guido's appeal. See OYB,E 5-7. That verdict branding her an adultress permitted

Guido to murder her with impunity so far as the Tuscan Court was concerned. See also 4.1501-5.

842] *blood-flustered* Drunk with blood. See also 11.1609, 1618 and nn.

844] *permissible* I.e., allowed by their exhausted but desperate state; they went twenty mi.

847] *swine . . . him* "The devils besought him saying, If thou cast us out, suffer us to go away into the herd of swine. And he said to them, Go. And when they were cast out, they went into the herd of swine: and behold, the whole herd of swine ran violently down the steep place into the sea, and plunged in the waters" (Matt. 8:31-32).

862] *Had* Would have.

863-64] *Thither . . . see* In Hell, where Guido, if he confesses before the execution, will not go. Guido was executed on 22 February. The real Pope denied his appeal on the 20th.

871] *mage* Magician, worker of black magic.

877] *Abate* See 1.547n., 2.289n.

879-80] *yellow . . . craft* The color *yellow* is the symbolic color of guile or betrayal; Judas wears *yellow* in medieval paintings. Paul is *twice Guido* because in his hypocrisy he is twice as dangerous. *Twice* replaces the misleading *This* in the first edition; see variants. In 10.903-5, as the worst of the three, Girolamo is blue as the hottest flames of hell are blue, and the word is used in this context to symbolize lust. Pompilia accused Girolamo of trying to seduce her. Paul's *yellow* seems to be like Guido's red, one of the colors of fire; Guido's red is also symbolic of violence. In 10.907, the mother of the three is associated with the color gray and with smoke rather than fire. She has grown old and although still of hell she only smolders.

881-83] *copier . . . temple-porch* In function and in name Paolo is only *copier* of the two great apostles. The *temple-porch* is the court of the Temple in Jerusalem. Peter taught and healed there. To one lame beggar he said, "Silver and gold I have none, but such as I have I give thee"—and he healed him (Acts 3:6).

885] *trims . . . lamp* Eph. 6:14.

889-91] *Paul . . . time* See 3.1533-34n.

893] *Girolamo* See 1.547n., 2.289n.

899] *simple quality* Undisguised evil.

903-7] *lust . . . smoke* See 10.879-80n.

924] *unwholesome . . . breath* Of Rome, where Guido has been.

933] *glebe* Field.

960] *exceed . . . year* An error. Minority was claimed for only two of the accomplices. According to the law at the time that meant that they were under twenty-five.

968] *Civility* Courtesy due from one titled gentleman to another.

968-83] *Marzi-Medici . . . Archbishop* The Governor of Arezzo was Vincenzo Marzi-Medici and the Granduke of Tuscany was Cosimo III of the Medici family, but despite their common name it does not appear that they were kinsmen. See 3.965-66n.

971] *rushlight-end* A makeshift candle made by dipping the absorbent pith of a rush in grease.

985-87] *Shepherd's . . . reach* The sign of office of a bishop was a shepher's crook, symbolizing his duty under Christ, the Good Shepherd (John 10:11, 21:17).

988] *hireling . . . flee* The hireling who fled in the face of danger and not the good shepherd who cared for the sheep. See John 10:1-14.

991] *heat . . . sevenfold* Angered because Shadrach, Meshach and Abednego would not worship his golden calf, Nebuchadnezzar commanded that the furnace be heated "seven times more than it was wont to be heated," and that the rebels be thrown into it (Dan. 3:9-30). The three were miraculously delivered from the flames unharmed.

1001-5] *whiteness . . . garb* "And to her was granted that she should be arrayed in fine linen, clean and white: for the fine linen is the righteousness of saints" (Rev. 19:8).

1006] *new . . . vesture* The "immortal nakedness" of 6.956; see 6.951-58n.

1006-8] *Armed . . . angel* The statue of the Archangel Michael, leader of the celestial armies, on the Castel St. Angelo near St. Peter's. The statue was erected in gratitude for Michael's supposed preservation of Rome from a raging pestilence. The statue by Rafaello da Montelup erected in 1535 which the Pope refers to has been moved to a courtyard. The statue atop St. Angelo's in B's time is by Verschaffelt and it is *armed and crowned.*

1010-11] *sword . . . shield* The language is suggestive of Ephesians 6:14-17. See 10.489n.

1017] *Memorized* Memorialized.

1019] *plucking fiend* Perhaps an echo of John 10:38, "And I give unto them eternal life; and they shall never perish, neither shall any man pluck them out of my hand."

1020-21] *new . . . known* "To him that overcometh will I give to eat of the hidden manna, and I will give him a white stone and in the stone a new name is written, which no man knoweth saving him that receiveth it" (Rev. 4:8).

1023] *If . . . praise* "if there be any virtue, and if there be any praise, think on these things" (Phil. 4:8).

1033-34] *fat . . . eye* "Those that be planted in the house of the Lord shall flourish in the courts of our God. They shall bring forth fruit in old age; they shall be fat [R.V. 'full of sap') and flourishing" (Psa. 92:13-14).

1036-38] *seed . . . enemy* "A sower went out to sow his seed: and as he sowed, some fell by the wayside; and it was trodden down, and the fowls of the air devoured it" (Luke 8:5).

1049] *meaner miserable* Servants.

1050] *hests, eked out* Biddings, added to.

1053] *trump . . . service* "For the Lord himself shall descend from heaven with a shout, with the voice of the archangel, and with the trump of God: and the dead in Christ shall arise first." (1 Thess. 4:16).

1064-67] *standing . . . law* That a wife obey her husband. See 5.580-81n.

1065-66] *novel . . . requirement* Of her unborn child.

1069] *fools call Nature* "The fool hath said in his heart, There is no God" (Psa. 14:1).

1078] *own sword* See 2.1023n.

1080-87] *Him . . . servant* The language and imagery of the passage contrast the visible providence represented by Caponsacchi with the inner prompting of emotion (*motion*) felt by Pompilia. Caponsacchi was more prone to *scruple* and less *true to touch*—*touch* implying both "hint" and reference to the finger of God—because he had not been through the long apprenticeship of obedience that Pompilia had served, described above 10.1044-55. The image of the finger of God for truth or faith occurs often in B's poetry; cf. "Abt Vogler" 49-50 for an open reference, and the lines describing the discovery of OYB at 1.39-40: "a Hand, / Always above my shoulder, pushed me once," for another, less obvious one. Like the *good and faithful servant* of Matthew 25:23, Pompilia's judgment was authentic in that her experienced ear recognized a higher authority: "His lord said to him, Well done, good and faithful servant; thou hast been faithful over a few things, I will make thee ruler of many things."

1092-94] *other . . . degree* The comparison of *other* is to the *rose* symbolic of the Virgin Mary, to Pompilia. The Golden *Rose* was a spray of roses made of gold and containing a small vial into which balsam and musk were poured, the whole symbolizing God and his grace. *grave*: engrave, sculpt. The *rose* was awarded to kings or other leaders who had contributed some important service to the Church. It was blessed on the fourth Sunday of Lent, not long after the date of the Pope's monologue.

1098-1108] *leviathan . . . mouth* See 5.1497-98n., 8.1717-21n. Here the references include Job 41:12,21, 24, 26, 32: "I will not conceal . . . his comely proportion . . . His breath kindleth coals, and a flame goeth out of his mouth . . . His heart is as firm as a stone; yea, as hard as a piece of the nether millstone . . . The sword of him that layeth at him cannot hold. . . . He maketh a path to shine after him; one would think the deep to be hoary."

1103] *deep to deep* "Deep calleth unto deep at the noise of thy water-spouts: all thy waves and thy billows are gone over me" (Ps. 42:7).

1112-17] *idol . . . gratitude* The Church initially destroyed or defaced pagan statuary but later reinterpreted them in light of Christian teaching and sometimes used them in their efforts to convert the pagans. The Pope emphasizes the secondary nature of Caponsacchi's role all through this description; cf. "in its degree" above 10.1094.

1118] *sweet savour* "Walk in love, as Christ also hath loved us, and hath given himself for us an offering and a sacrifice to God for a sweet smelling savour" (Eph. 5:2).

1119] *Nard* Spikenard, an aromatic herb.

1134-35] *moan . . . beasts* Reference to the martyrdom of early Christians in the Roman arena.

1137] *pale* See 10.450n.

1138] *mid-cirque* Middle ring or circle.

1141] *laws . . . pudicity* The pronoun "which," often elided in B's style, is apparently understood after *laws*, which is unrevised MS is not possessive; see variants. *Pudicity*: modesty.

1143-45] *tax . . . cloud* The tax (*mulct*) on foolish youth is paid by wiser manhood through loss of trust.

1158-61] *White-cinct . . . coat* The *white* belt, *red* stockings, and the insignia are part of the attire symbolic of the office of a cardinal. The Pope fancies that *red* symbolizes unhesitating willingness (*unchariness*) to shed blood.

1162] *bewraying* Betraying.

1164] *thought . . . deed* From the general confession, Book of Common Prayer.

1168] *strait* Difficult time.

1181] *master . . . foot* One of several images of Caponsacchi as a conquering Saint George. See 1.579n.

1183] *Lead . . . temptation* An ironic application of the phrase from the Lord's Prayer (Matt. 6:13).

1186] *Reluctant dragons* Reminiscent of Horace's *reluctantes dracones* (*Odes* 4.4.11), and of the legend of Saint George; see 1.579n.

1189] *deserve* Serve (OED).

1192] *standing . . . ranged* Deployed in strict formation by rank. An image of the stultifying effects of inflexible church teaching and discipline.

1201] *irregular . . . boundary* Both the unconventional leap over the pale at 10.1137 and a break in the ranks of the stiff clergy of 10.1192.

1206] *Deserve . . . spasm* See 10.1189n. Serve, justify the urgent im-

pulse (*spasm*—the leap of 10.1137) which initiated the new life of dedica-
tion. *Initiatory spasm* may carry also the more general sense of the suffer-
ing which came of original sin; see 6.951-58n.

1208-20] *you . . . death* The pronouns *you, they* both refer to the
Comparini, the shift in point of view meant perhaps to suggest their
representative and typical, median qualities. The historical present
tense throughout the passage also invokes the persistence of the pattern.

1228] *Challenge . . . purging* Dare, invite destruction.

1240] *lynx-gift* Not the large wild cat known as a *lynx*, but a fabulous
beast with extraordinary sight capable of seeing in the dark or even
through solids.

1242] *decayed intelligence* See also 8.1442n.; 12.56-58n., 295n.

1252] *mount* Amount.

1253] *conglobed* Formed into a round mass.

1256] *recognize* Receive the testimony or confession of.

1260] *Perk and pry* Recover liveliness, inquire into (OED)..

1264] *due wage* "The labourer is worthy of his reward" (1 Tim. 5:18).

1265] *gyves* A shackle for the legs.

1266] *Pay . . . misprision* Punish misunderstanding.

1275] *signs* Sun, moon.

1279] *darkness . . . felt* "The Lord said to Moses, Stretch out thine
arm toward heaven, that there may be darkness over the land of Egypt,
even darkness which may be felt" (Ex. 10:21).

1283-84] *truth . . . Remembered* A suggestion of the Platonic doc-
trine of "recollections" developed in the *Phaedo*.

1297-98] *near . . . end* See 10.165n.

1330] *new philosophy* The *new philosophy* was the Copernican helio-
centric theory of the universe, which was published in 1543 and was
generally regarded as a threat to faith in the divine order. Copernicus'
book was placed on the Catholic Index of prohibited works in 1616, and
Donne's famous lines are a reference to the effect of Copernican thought:
"The new philosophy calls all in doubt / The element of fire is quite put
out; / The sun is lost, and th'earth, and no man's wit / Can well direct
him where to look for it . . . 'Tis all in pieces, all coherence gone; / All
just supply, and all relation" ("The First Anniversary" 205-8, 213-14).
The Pope's positive reading of the new philosophy is unusual, and an
indication of the original and modern cast of his thinking.

1331-33] *This . . . swarm* The Copernican discovery that the earth is
not the stationary center of the cosmos.

1334] *transcendent act* The word *transcendent* when used of the deity
signifies His being "above and distinct from the universe" (OED), as in
"operation outside this our sphere" at 10.1339 below. Here the *tran-*

scendent act is the Incarnation, the direct evidence of the *transcendent* love.

1337] *thing I am* The Vicar of Christ. See 10.20n.

1342] *take Thy place* I.e., the place You assigned to me, and Your place as Your deputy on earth (10.20, 1328-29).

1243-44] *tale . . . mouth* The New Testament, and also, from the ambiguous phrasing reminiscent of Half-Rome and Other Half-Rome's gossip, the controversial story of *The Ring and the Book*. In its allusiveness the Pope's monologue has at times an anagogic structure similar to the Bible's; in the sufferings and vision of Caponsacchi and Pompilia the Pope finds a microcosm of earthly probation and a proof of the fundamental love of God.

1346] *discept* Differ.

1355-64] *cause . . . limit* An equilateral *triangle* is symbolic of the Trinity. The Pope argues that it is possible to deduce two of the attributes of God, *strength* and *intelligence*, from His *work i' the world*. Until the present case, however, there was no equal power of *love* observable, but only an *isoscele*, a triangle with two equal sides and an unequal or *deficient* base. "Isosceles" is the usual spelling; OED cites B's use as a variant.

1369] *Feel . . . stands* "Now faith is the substance of things hoped for, the evidence of things not seen" (Heb. 11:1).

1372-73] *all . . . pain* No man pays so dearly as did God in Christ.

1379] *I . . . Gods* "I have said, Ye are gods: and all of you are children of the most High" (Ps. 82:6). "Jesus answered them, Is it not written in your law, I said, Ye are gods?" (John 10:34).

1380-83] *pain . . . revealed* The reference of *this* is to *pleasure* (the love inductively arrived at in 10.1374); the reference of *other* is to *pain*, the "dread machinery of sin and sorrow" of 10.1370-71.

1396] *fret* Roughness.

1398] *choppy . . . law* Chapped, by chemical action.

1402] *God's . . . bare* By knowledge of God's power through the agency of chemistry, or by direct observance.

1403-9] *Nor . . . world* See 1343-44 and n. Similarly, *tale* here can be both the miracles and the mysteries of the Bible, and the notorious discrepancies of the various versions of the story of *The Ring and the Book*, especially the night spent at Castelnuovo, all *dubious in the transmitting*. Rationalist interpretations of the Bible by the Higher Criticism questioning the Bible's historical truth were concurrent with the writing of *The Ring and the Book* and doubtless influenced B to make the controversy between rationalism and faith central to the Pope's monologue, skirting the anachronism to which his close identification with the Pope makes him vulnerable by merely invoking, not naming, the influence. For background on the Higher Criticism see Vol. V, 341. Close to the date of *The Ring and the Book* were *Renan's Life of Jesus* (1863) and Strauss's *New Life of Jesus* (1864), both of which questioned the divinity of the man called Jesus, the point on which B's thinking and the Higher Criticism were most divided. See W. O. Raymond, "Browning and the Higher Criticism," in *The Infinite Moment and Other Essays in Robert Browning* (Toronto, 1950), 32-44. The Pope argues that some ambiguity is essential to the development of the moral sense. Conflating the tale and man's earthly progress, he says that *transmitting* the meaning of the tale is like persisting in the moral passage of life: both are dependant on confronting *riddles*, rendering *obstacle flat*; if truth were readily apparent, where would the moral sense get its exercise?

1411] *probatively* By trial.

1428-29] *subordinate . . . present* The difference between the two points of view is prepared in 10.1411-17.

1431-34] *Life . . . goal* The doctrine of incompletion regarded theologically.

1436] *pearl* "Again the kingdom is like unto a merchant man, seeking goodly pearls: Who when he had found one pearl of great price, went and sold all he had and bought it" (Matt. 13:45).

1438-39] *certain . . . contemptuous* The higher critics. See 10.1403-9n.

1444-45] *whelks . . . Mud-worms* A *whelk* is a mollusc found on the shore when the tide recedes; a *mud-worm* is a worm that lives in mud, also a term used figuratively to express contempt.

1448] *robes . . . world* "Pure religion and undefiled before God and the Father is this, To visit the fatherless and widows in their affliction, and to keep himself unspotted from the world" (James 1:27).

1449] *Aretine Archbishop* See 3.965-66n.

1456] *heady* Impetuous.

1467] *barefoot monk* See 3.1013n.

1471] *cuticle* Skin.

1477] *dared . . . ark* See 1.192n.

1480] *I . . . promise* To write a letter for her to her parents.

1483-84] *If . . . wonder* In the parable, the foolish virgins failed to secure sufficient oil for their lamps and were therefore unprepared to meet the bridegroom when he appeared (Matt. 25:1-13).

1486] *mystic . . . Bridegroom* The mystic Spouse is the Church, and Christ is the Bridegroom. "Let us be glad and rejoice, and give honor to him: for the marriage of the Lamb is come, and his wife has made herself ready" (Rev. 9:7). But in this case the Spouse, like the foolish virgins, was unready.

1489] *weighed . . . wanting* Daniel interpreted the prophetic handwriting on the wall as a sentence of doom against Belshazzar, last king of the Neo-Babylonian Empire: "Thou art weighed in the balance and art found wanting" (Dan. 5:27). Soon thereafter his kingdom fell.

1494] *Monastery . . . Convertites* See 2.1189-90n.

1511] *pretends to* Claims.

1513] *Fisc's advice* The case on behalf of the convertites was actually filed by Gambi, who assisted Bottini in the prosecution of Guido and the defense of Pompilia. See OYB,E 253.

1515] *one saint* Mary Magdalen.

1517] *infant-heir to cheat* The heir was not the infant son but one Domenico Tighetti.

1521] *Soldiers . . . coat* Because the coat "was without seam, woven from the top throughout," the soldiers who were dividing Jesus' clothes after his crucifixion said, "let us not rend it, but cast lots for it, whose it shall be" (John 19:23-24).

1524] *woof of price* Valuable cloth, the coat without seams.

1532] *terror* Both fear and holy awe at the tangible evidence of God. The words *terror* and *terrible* are frequently associated with God in the Bible; cf. "Knowing therefore the terror of the Lord" (2 Cor. 5:11), and "Let them praise thy great and terrible name; for it is holy" (Ps. 99:3).

1541] *Impassible* Insensitive.

1544] *advent . . . star* The star of Bethlehem at Christ's birth (Matt. 2:2) was *authoritative* because the birth of Christ bore witness to God's love.

1549] *uncommissioned meteors* In contrast to "authoritative star" above 10.1544. Caponsacchi acted not on the inadequate law and rule of church authority, but on his own unauthorized initiative.

1561] *Panoply* Suit of armor.

1562-65] *loins . . . God* Eph. 6:14-17. See also 10:489 and n.

1575] *or* Either.

1576] *boots* Is the value of.

1580] *publicans the same* It is not enough, Jesus said, to love those who love you. "Do not the Publicans the same?" (Matt. 6:46) You must love your enemies.

1584-99] *Five . . . difference* The dispute between the missionary Jesuits and the Pope's Vicar Apostolic in China, Bishop Maigrot, arose over which Chinese word should be used to designate the Christian God, the *politic* Jesuits having long fostered a policy of tolerance and compromise between Christians and Chinese. In 1693 (*five years since*) the Bishop condemned the term allowed by the Jesuits because he thought it inconsistent with the teachings of the Church. The Pope apparently considered the matter of minor importance. He did not respond to pressing appeals to intervene. Later, in 1704, *Tournon* was sent by Innocent XII's successor to enforce the stricter usage, but *Tournon* was not a cardinal at this time. Tournon was not successful and a sharp decline in Christian converts in China dates from this period. The Bishop resided in the province of Fo-kien, not *To-kein*; the MS spelling is ambiguous and may be *F*, but in any case was not corrected in any printed edition.

1584] *rounds . . . ear* See 4.597n.

1613] *justify its price* The price of man's salvation, death on the cross.

1614-15] *adept . . . Work* A fully initiated, highly skilled member of the mystical Rosicrucian Order whose *Great Work* was to discover the infinite in the finite. They sought the philosopher's stone that would transmute base metal into gold.

1645] *comports* Provides.

1649] *first . . . new* "And he that sat upon the throne said, Behold, I make all things new. . . . I am Alpha and Omega, the beginning and the end" (Rev. 21:5-6).

1662] *pleads some bard* Euripides (c. 479-4096), to whom B was especially attracted. On 19 September 1864 B wrote to Isa Blagden from Biarritz that he was "having a great read at Euripides—the only book that I brought with me" (*Dearest Isa: Robert Browning's Letters to Isabella Blagden*, ed. Edward C. McAleer [Austin, 1951], 193). Euripides is the imagined speaker in lines 1664-1784.

1669] *engine hoists* See 4.15-16n.

1672] *Machinist* Zeus, the "Deus ex machina." Many of Euripides' plays end with the unexpected appearance of a god who is lowered onto the stage by means of a mechanism. Such action, while appearing irrational to man, may be perfectly rational to the god.

1677] *long . . . birth* See 10.1662 and n.

1686] *warrant* Authorization by higher authority.

1692] *Know . . . mean* Motto engraved on the Temple at Delphi; and a favorite maxim of Greek philosophy.

1695-96] *born . . . law* Since salvation was impossible for him.

1701] *Third . . . Two* The third is Euripides. The other two are his predecessors, Aeschylus and Sophocles. *surprised*: Euripides scorned the old traditions and was considered a rebel in his time.

1704] *one . . . circumstance* He was born before the coming of Christ.

1705-8] *Adopted . . . years* B seems to have Paul's words to the Romans (2:14-15) in mind: "For when the Gentiles, which have not the law, do by nature the things contained in the law, these, having not the law, are a law unto themselves: Which shew the work of the law written in their hearts, their consciences also bearing witness, and their thoughts the meanwhile accusing or excusing one another." Thus the Pope discerns in Euripides, born too soon to be a believer, the spirit of the Christ. B's own thoughts are more precisely expressed in the translation of The New English Bible: "When Gentiles who do not possess the law carry out its precepts by the light of nature, then, although they have no law, they are their own law, for they display the effects of the law inscribed on their hearts."

1712-14]   *Paul . . . come* When Paul was arrested on charges brought against him by the Jews, he pled his case before Felix, the Roman procurator of Judea (52-60). In response to Felix's questions he spoke: "As he reasoned of righteousness, temperance, and judgment to come, Felix trembled, and answered, Go thy way for this time: when I have a more convenient season, I will call for thee" (Acts 24:25).

1715]   *strong style* His stylus or pen; also, his bold manner of writing.

1716]   *branding brow* A Possible reference to Cain and his mark. Euripides attacked concepts of the gods which he considered unworthy of the Divine, and consequently, was accused of atheism by his critics. Ironically, the mark of Cain was less a condemnation than a means of protection: "And the Lord set a mark upon Cain, lest any finding him should kill him" (Gen. 4:15).

1720]   *duty . . . doctrine* Paul's faith in the revelation of God in Christ.

1724]   *Galileo's tube* Galileo (1564-1642) was condemned by the Inquisition and his works remained on the Index until 1835. Nevertheless, B's Pope is interested in his telescope or *tube*, as it was often called.

1739]   *one revealment* The Incarnate Christ.

1750]   *prints* Makes footprints on.

1753]   *nature* The name given to the mystery above, 10.1730.

1756]   *tenebrific* Darkened.

1776]   *descrying* Discerning.

1780-81]   *strong . . . staff* See 10.1715n. The figure of the *style* as a *staff* invokes the Pope's office and reinforces his kinship with Euripides.

1782]   *pricked* Chosen, found.

1783]   *slush* Waste, muck; see 10.498n.

1786]   *Paul . . . Seneca* St. Jerome pronounced *Seneca* (Roman philosopher, dramatist and tutor to Emperor Nero) a Christian, a judgment based upon forged letters alleged to have been exchanged between him and St. *Paul.*

1791-94] *Assured . . . new* The final destruction of the world by fire is a recurring image in the New Testament. *new*: "And he that sat upon the throne, said, Behold, I make all things new" (Rev. 21:5).

1795] *rapt* Swept up into heaven.

1797-1800] *renouncing . . . hundredfold* "And Jesus answered and said, Verily I say unto you, There is no man who hast left house, or bretheren, or sisters, or father, or mother, or wife, or children, or lands for my sake, and the gospel's, but he shall receive an hundredfold now in this time . . . and in the world to come everlasting life" (Mark 10:29-30).

1802] *embalmed* "Preserved from oblivion" (OED).

1803-4] *sun . . . parts* In the land of the midnight sun where the nights are almost non-existent; cf. 10.1776. *ghastlily*: faintly, ghostlike.

1814] *Tentatives* Efforts.

1818] *Druid* The Druids were the priests who performed a religious and magical office among the Celts who inhabited ancient Gaul and Britain.

1819-20] *prism . . . true* A prism may be used to refract light rays and analyze their components (*decompose* them). The passage means "to see beyond the natural sun and the superstitious rites the real source of both, God."

1821] *last . . . first* "But many that are first shall be last and the last shall be first" (Matt. 19:30).

1827] *Nero's . . . stake* Nero (37-68), Roman emperor, was responsible for the crucifixion and burning of many Christians.

1832] *cornfield* Field of grain.

1845-47] *Unless . . . life* The eighteenth and nineteenth centuries. The eighteenth century was called the Age of Reason in contrast to the earlier Age of Faith. The nineteenth century saw an outpouring of scientific investigation that called into question the historicity and accuracy of the Bible and thus seemed to threaten the foundation of the Christian Church; see 10.1403-9n.

1852] *No . . . camp* We are no longer either infant or a camp defending ourselves against wild beasts.

1858] *old faith* Worship of pagan gods.

1860-62] *Faith . . . belie* The Pope anticipates the attack on the literal interpretation of the Bible that so disturbed the nineteenth century Church; see 10.1403-9n.

1863-68] *Molinist . . . man* The Pope's reference is a allusion to Molinist questioning of church dogma and ritual, and the sect's hypothesis of an unmediated interchange between the believer and God (see 1.303-13n.). This is one of the few passages in the poem to refer tolerantly to Molinism.

1869-70] *few . . . many* "Because strait is the gate and narrow is the way which leadeth unto life, and few there be that find it" (Matt. 7:14).

1874] *razed* Erased.

1883] *subjacent* Beneath as foundation.

1886] *lust . . . life* "For all that is in the world, the lust of the flesh and the lust of eyes, and the pride of life, is not of the Father but is of the world" (John 2:16).

1887-95] *mass . . . sink* St. Paul speaks of Gentile Christians as wild branches that have been grafted on to the olive tree that was Judaism. See Romans 11.16-24. Those of whom the Pope speaks, however, are "barren" and reminiscent of the fruitless trees that in Jesus' parable were ordered destroyed (Luke 9:6-9). The difficult passage suggests that in the new age of doubt and darkness (10.1849, 1851), although there will be a few who by habit "preserve the Christian level" (10.1873) and a rarer heroic few who "rise to the new height" (10.1869), the mass of men who are *grafted* now, in the future will *slink / Worm-like into the mud* [which] *light now lays bare* (exposes, protects them from).

1898] *antimasque . . . kibe* The burlesque interlude between parts of the more serious masque is called the *antimasque*. A *kibe* is a sore or chillblain on the heel. Cf. *Hamlet* 5.1.152-53: "The toe of the peasant comes so near the heel of the courtier, he galls his kibe."

1903] *pantaloon . . . castanet* Costume and props for the performer of the masque.

1913] *measure* Rhythm, and restraint.

1915] *prodigy* Extraordinary feat.

1919] *morrice* Morris dance. An old folk dance, popular in England especially on May Day, in which participants dressed in fancy costumes.

1922] *Augustin* Saint Augustine (354-430), early Church father, Bishop of Hippo. Like Caponsacchi he lived a worldly life before his conversion to Christianity.

1925] *Abate* See 1.547n.

1936] *Loyola* Ignatius Loyola (1491-1556), founder of the Jesuit Order in 1534. The Pope sees in him the exemplar of worldly wisdom and casuistry which he anticipates and for which the Jesuits are known popularly. He is a contrast to Augustine (see 10.1922n.).

1943] *new cause* Same as new order 10.1905 above.

1950] *last act* Of his life, and of his masque (10.1898).

1952] *Paul's sword . . . Peter's key* St. Paul was often represented in medieval art with an upraised sword in his hand. The sword was probably inspired by Ephesians 6:11-17. See 10.489n. The key is an identifying mark of St. Peter, based upon Matthew 16:18-19: "Thou art Peter. . . . And I will give unto thee the keys of the kingdom of heaven: And whatsoever thou shalt bind on earth shall be bound in heaven: and whatsoever thou shalt loose on earth shall be loosed in heaven."

1962] *barren stock* A reference to the barren twigs of 10.1891; see n.

1964] *repent . . . fruit* The plea of the dresser of the vineyard on behalf of a barren tree: "Lord, let it alone this year also, till I shall dig about it, and dung it" (Luke 13:8-9).

1969] *Remonstrants* The word had a special sense in ecclesiastical history denoting a Protestant reform sect; the Pope adapts the usage to the protest group in his own church.

1976-77] *Christ . . . place* As the Pope implies, Jesus did not say this. The Pope refers to a statement B attributes to Arcangeli that is found originally in the Second Anonymous Pamphlet (OYB,E 154-55). See 8.655-59n.

1996] *priest's immunity* See 1.257n., 1.260-62n.

2012] *Civilization is imperative* So Guido argued. See 5.2026-33.

2016] *Remonstrances* Objections based on different beliefs, a revision from the very different tone and meaning of MS-1869 *apologies*; see variants.

2023-24] *Civilization . . . Pope* In the days of the Roman Emperors, to be able to claim Roman citizenship ensured the holder all possible defense under the law. Paul protested when under threat of examination by whipping, "Is it lawful for you to scourge a man that is a Roman, and uncondemned?" (Acts 22:25) The Pope ironically heralds the return of pre-Christian Rome.

2033] *One . . . validity* "If" is understood.

2037] *coil* Noisy strife.

2042] *tenement* Structure.

2047] *life . . . socket-edge* Like a guttering candle.

2050-51] *Barabbas' . . . free* Pilate released Barabbas and condemned Jesus in response to the crowd's demands. Matt. 27:16-26.

2052] *Sabbath close* Very ironic argument. "Remember the sabbath day, to keep it holy. . . . the seventh day is the sabbath of the Lord thy God: in it thou shalt not do any work" (Ex. 20:8, 10). The Pope approached the Sabbath close of his life.

2054] *three . . . taps* A pope is pronounced dead when he fails to respond after he has been called by name and tapped three times on his forehead by the Cardinal Camerlengo.

2060] *Luthers . . . Calvins* Seventeenth century reformers regarded by the Roman Catholic Church as signs of the disintegration of Christendom.

2061] *Molinos* See 1.303-13n.

2063] *petit-maitre* Trivial, foppish.

2066] *Sanctus et Benedictus* Parts of the mass.

2074] *four lives* An error. See 10.165n., 960n.

2082-84] *Art . . . rest* When Troy was falling, the aged Priam prepared to join the battle but was restrained by Hecuba, his wife, with the words, "The hour calls not for such succor or such defenses" (Virgil, *Aeneid* 2.521-22).

2085-86] *Pope . . . bends* The two titles signify religious and temporal powers; Pope means "father."

2095] *Who . . . side* See 5.1541-42n.

2101-6] *customary . . . side* See 1.346-54n.

2123] *sad . . . state* Purgatory.

Book 11, Guido

Title / 1-2] *Guido . . . names* B took the names *Acciaiuoli* and *Panciatichi* from the Secondary Source, OYB,E 265. The two men were members of the Confraternity of Death (see 1.1303n.), charged with informing Guido of his sentence, both born in Florence and in their late sixties at the time of the execution. As members of the Confraternity of Death they would have worn "an all-enveloping black cassock and a pointed hood with narrow slits for the eyes" (Corrigan, 93, 138) designed to render them anonymous. B may not have been able to determine from OYB that they were in disguise, and at any rate it was more to his purpose here to have Guido recognize them and to have them bear witness to his own unmasking. The stripping away of aristocratic title and surname in the title of the monologue, as compared to Book 5, is indicative of Guido's lack of defense or disguise. His list of place names which follows, though it is a telling appeal to nostalgia and spirit of place as well as to family pride, emphasizes that he has lost his place and his identity in family, country, and history. The landmarks, natural scenery, and monuments mixed with references to the lineage of the two Florentines are now to Guido mere names in which he has no share and on which no claim.

3-8] *ancestor . . . rivulet* Niccolo Acciaiuoli founded the Carthusian Monastery Cortosa, which is built on a hill outside Florence where the Rivers *Greve* and *Ema* meet.

5-9]   *Greve . . . bridge* The bridge is about two mi. from the Roman
Gate of Florence.

12]   *Kingfishers* Small diving birds. They were supposed in legend to
lay their eggs on the sea shortly before the winter solstice, during which
time the sea was calm. The period was known as Halcyon (Greek for
kingfisher) Days and the phrase became proverbial for a time of peace
and happiness; Guido left his Halcyon Days behind when he took the
Roman Road, though he took it from Arezzo, not from Florence.

13]   *Cortosa* See 11.3-8n.

14]   *Senescal* The steward or master-domo in the household of a medi-
eval lord.

18]   *sink* Sewer.

24]   *ere . . . day* Guido was informed of his approaching execution at
the eighth hour or at 2 a.m. See OYB,E 265.

37]   *fee . . . good-hand* The Italian *buonamono* (good hand), a tip.

40]   *owned* Claimed, had.

45]   *subterfuge* "Device to which a person resorts in order to escape the
force of an argument" (OED).

53]   *hat and plume* Of nobility.

72]   *lawyers . . . kind* Perhaps a reference to Guido's lawyers, the
Procurator and Advocate of the Poor, or perhaps to lawyers in general.
See Jesus' response to the Pharisees, "Woe unto you, lawyers!" (Luke
11:52). See also 1.174-76n.

76]   *coyness* In the sense of "disdain."

79]   *Vicar . . . Lord* See 10.20n.

80-81]   *abrogates . . . Nullifies* Legalistic language in ironic contrast
to the stark fact of death.

96]   *pricked . . . breathe* Spurred . . . exercise briskly.

104]   *knave* Low-born country rustic.

105]   *pale* Dividing line, boundary, probably made of stone.

108]   *jauncing* Prancing.

114]   *springe* Trap.

125]   *engine* An *engine* is any contrivance which is the product of inge-
nuity. In this case, it is the new guillotine, and one of the many names by
which that instrument of death is called by Guido. See 11.212-29 and n.

132]   *lure to talk* To make a confession and perhaps, by admitting
guilt, justify the Pope's judgment. See 11.407-10.

133]   *smile* Of pardon.

137]   *tacit* Silent.

141]   *shrived* Heard his confession and absolved him of his guilt.

144]   *shrunk-shanked* Spindly. Perhaps an echo of *As You Like It*

2.7.161: "His youthful hose . . . a world too wide / For his shrunk-shank."

146] *windlestraws* Literally, dried stalks of grass. Figuratively, people weak in body and uncertain in purpose.

165] *woman's . . . man* Perhaps a reference to the making of Eve from Adam's rib (Gen. 2:21-22).

169] *Settle* Come together, become fixed, constant.

169-75] *I'm . . . her* He speaks beyond his present comprehension. See his final words when in desperation he calls on Pompilia to save him.

177] *sharp . . . tooth* Guillotine. See 11.125.

184] *Mannaia* Guillotine. See 11.212-29 and n.

186] *Mouth-of-Truth* Mask of a Triton with open mouth in the vestibule of the Church of Santa Maria in Cosmedin in Rome. It was believed that the hand of a liar would be bitten off if it were put in the mouth. The huge relief head with its grotesque expression might well give the impression of a decapitated head, perhaps the reason that Guido is reminded of the landmark.

187] *Capitol* The Temple of Jupiter on the Capitoline Hill in ancient Rome.

194] *stabled buffaloes* Herds of buffalo inhabited the countryside outside Rome.

206] *gay . . . guard* The Swiss guard is the Pope's personal guard. It was founded by Julius II (1443-1513). The elaborate and colorful costume of the Swiss guard derives from the Swiss national costume and is dominated by a bold pattern of red, yellow and black stripes. The *grim* part of the figure is the eight-foot halberd carried by the guard, a dramatic combination of spear and hachet that is to Guido like an exaggerated headsman's ax.

212-29] *There . . . with* The precision of the description suggests that B had examined a guillotine or had obtained by other means an exact knowledge of it and its history. The instrument is much older than its use in the French Revolution, when it acquired the name it is presently known by through the doctor who recommended it for its merciful efficiency. Dr. Guillotine, it is said, took his knowledge from a description of an execution in Milan in 1702, and there are engravings and other descriptions of similar instruments used in Scotland (where it was called the Maiden), and in Germany in the Middle Ages. In Italy Mannaia was used for the execution of noble criminals from the thirteenth century on. We do not know where B found his information, but we do know that from an early age he was curious about instruments of torture and death.

Alfred Domett recorded that B collected curious weapons (*The Diary of Alfred Domett*, ed. E.A. Horsman [London, 1877], 181-82), and a letter of EBB reports a visit in Paris to a collection of actual murder weapons exhibited by a famous French detective named Vidocq. Vidocq "did the honours of his museum of knives & nails and hooks that have helped great murderers to their purposes—he scarcely admits, I observe, an implement with only one attestation to its efficacy; but the one or two exceptions rather justify his latitude in their favour—thus one little sort of desert-knife [sic] did only take one life. . 'but then,' says Vidocq, 'it was the man's own mother's life, with fifty-two blows, and all for' (I think) 'Fifteen francs she had got?' " (RB-EBB, ed. Kintner, 110 [July 1, 1845]).

232] *trundles* Rolls.

241] *Discoursed* Discussed.

243] *elucubrate* Seriously, perhaps pompously, explain.

258-59] *Pope . . . Tales* This Pope could have been either Alexander VII, in office 1655-67, or Clement IX, 1667-69. B thought Guido fifty rather than his actual forty, and that he had been in Rome thirty years. Thus if he were taking a walk in the early period of his stay there, sometime after 1663, the dates of either Pope would apply. Alexander VII was known as an intellectual and patron of the arts and was said to enjoy a ribald tale. Clement IX was a poet and holds credit for creating the comic opera. The reference here may be to the *Tales* of either Boccaccio or Franco Sacchetti. See 3.1440-43 and n.; 5.557-58n.

261] *cullion* Dupe.

270-72] *Florid . . . bull* Francesco Albano (1578-1660) was a Bolognese painter. The picture referred to here, for which B makes Felice's sister the model, is in Leningrad (then St. Petersburg), which B visited in 1834; there is a copy in the Ufizzi in Florence. *Florid*: hot-blooded, lusty.

275] *I . . . deed* I.e., break the law, not kidnap a girl.

276] *lout and clout* Clod and rustic boor.

278-79] *ring . . . kerchief* Accessories of a gentleman. *Tablets*: flat ornaments such as are mentioned as offerings in Exodus 35:22, "bracelets, and earrings, and rings and tablets, all jewels of gold." (Possibly notebooks, but the context suggests value.)

283-90] *fencing-master . . . symphyses* The two top vertebrae are called *Atlas* and *Axis. Symphases* are the cartilage between bones. The interest in anatomy that B attributes to Guido was shared by himself. B's fascination with art and artists extended to drawing and modeling in clay, and he had studied anatomy in this connection. In a letter of March 1861, EBB wrote from Rome to Sarianna Browning about Robert's work in Story's studio: "As to the modeling,—well, I told you that I grudged a little the time from his own particular art. But it does not do to dishearten him about his modeling. He has given a great deal of time to anatomy with reference to the expression of form, and the clay is only the new medium which takes the place of drawing" (*Letters of EBB*, 2, 434).

291] *cant* Chant, sing.

292-97] *silver . . . losing* Here the spinal cord is the *silver cord* and the brain is the *gold bowl*. "Or ever the silver cord be loosed, or the golden bowl be broken . . . then shall the dust return to the earth as it was and the spirit shall return unto God who gave it" (Eccles. 12:6-7). Guido's puns on *loosed, lost, losing, loosing* are typical of the gallows humor he brings to his situation.

296] *Felice's ghost* See 11.189-204.

301-5] *blood . . . brain* The language is medical: *blood extravasate* is blood forced out of a vessel; *lymph suffused* is the spread of the toxic or contagious matter of a sore; the *arachnoid tunic* is the membrane covering the brain. The *sword* and *mace* (a spiked club) were the weapons of the great soldiers and friends *Roland* and *Oliver*; see 2.1485n. See also 11.283-90 above and n., for Guido's, and B's, knowledge of anatomy.

307] *engine* See 11.125n.

309] *Fagon's self* Fagon was the physician to Louis XIV.

312] *Pistoja-ware* Pistoia, Italy, was known for its fine weapons and cutlery.

317] *thrids* Slips in and out, threads.

322-27] *Peter . . . thee* A pastiche interwoven to serve his own purposes. St. Jerome tells the legend that Peter was leaving Rome during the reign of Nero when he met Christ, whom he asked, "Domine, quo vadis?" (Lord, whither goest thou?) The Lord replied, "I come to be crucified again." Whereupon Peter returned to Rome to be himself martyred. The story of Dorcas, whom Peter raised from the dead, is taken from Acts 9:36-41.

333] *mystery . . . flesh* "For the mystery of iniquity doth already work: only he who now letteth will let, until he be taken out of the way" (2 Thess. 2:7).

340] *Since . . . doom* "And it is appointed unto men once to die, but after this the judgment" (Heb. 9:27).

341] *crib* Steal.

345] *Suppose . . . me* The line was inserted between MS and P1869 (see variants), and the original revision is not in the surviving galleys. 11.343-46 in P1869 reads, "Think, Sirs, if I have done you any harm,/ And you require the natural revenge,/ Suppose, and so intend to poison me,/ —Just as you take and slip into my draught". . . . The intended word order of line 345 may have been transposed: the three words *and so intend* seem parallel with *And you require* and meant to come at the beginning of the line, while *Suppose* seems meant to be juxtaposed with the parenthetical *dash* clause in line 346. The placement of the correction in the margin or margins of an earlier proof of 1869 may have been ambiguous, and the word order of the line transposed in type setting. If there was an error, however, it was overlooked through all printed editions, an unusual circumstance in this poem.

348]   *blue* Leaden color, color of death.

349]   *overset* Archaic for "upset.".

356]   *soul . . . world* "For what shall it profit a man, if he shall gain the whole world, and lose his own soul?" (Mark 8:36; see also Matt. 16:26).

359-61]   *Christ's . . . law* A reference to Old Testament law and New Testament gospel. Jesus said, "Think not that I am come to destroy the law, or the prophets: I am not come to destroy, but to fulfil" (Matt. 5:17). *fire-new:* brand new.

362]   *Jove's . . . God* Guido argues, putting an ironic boast in the Pope's mouth, that supposed Christian justice is no better than pagan revenge.

368]   *O'erflutter . . . wings* "But unto you that fear my name shall the Sun of righteousness arise with healing in his wings" (Mal. 4:2).

377]   *nice and coy* Exacting and disdainfully aloof (arch.).

381]   *casuists* See 4.1470-75n.

394-95]   *priest . . . mine* See 1.257n., 260-62n.

400]   *crumpled* Crooked.

407-10]   *cause . . . guilty* See 11.132 and n.

425-26]   *old . . . obtuse* See 8.1442n., 12.56-58n.

431-41]   *Your . . . shag* Perverse echoes of the parable of the Good Shepherd recorded in John 10:1-18.

433]   *Damage . . . one* A thief's loss is felt the same as a guardian's, a man of thrift.

434]   *red hand* The *red hand* is proverbial for a person caught in the act, as in "caught red-handed." The line suggests that there is not much to choose between the thief (the Pope) and the wolf (Guido).

441]   *shag* Heavily matted hair.

446]   *grace* Appearance of truth.

447]   *engine* See 11.125n.

452]   *misconceive* Misrepresent.

455-56]   *Come . . . then* See 11.585n.

466]   *no . . . death* I.e., damnation.

473]   *prize* Contest.

486]   *increase* Make greater demands.

491]   *looked me low* Felled him by mere looks. See also 11.504n.

499-500] *brow . . . red* A probable reference to the mark placed on Cain by the Lord after he had slain his brother Abel: "And the Lord said unto him, Therefore whosoever slayeth Cain, vengeance shall be taken on him sevenfold. And the Lord set a mark upon Cain, lest any finding him should kill him" (Gen. 4:14). Ironically, the mark on Cain was a sign not of punishment but of protection. See also 10.1716 and n.

504] *Gorgon shield* Athene's shield upon which was the likeness of the Gorgon Medusa. Anyone who looked upon it would be turned to stone.

512-45] *I . . . thus* Perhaps B has in mind Jeremy Bentham's social theory of utilitarianism, which held that the object of man was the pursuit of happiness, that is, pleasure and the absence of pain. Bentham recognized, however, that certain restraints were necessary to prevent total license: political, social and theological. Guido here argues in favor of political restraints but rejects theological ones.

530] *reprisal* The act of seizing property by force (OED).

546] *try a fall* Wrestle.

550] *Colly my cow* A colloquial expletive of uncertain origin which is deflating here both in meaning and in its vernacular idiom; "come off it," says Guido to the argument that man's law is a reflection of the divine law.

558-59] *dead . . . ashes* Guido also anticipates the coming age of doubt of which the Pope speaks; see 10.1845ff.

563] *fabulous epoch* An epoch fond of fables, untruths.

566-67] *King . . . Mesopotamy* A legendary Ethiopian king who fell in love with and married a beggar maid. He is celebrated in poetry by both Shakespeare and Tennyson.

568] *Sacristan* See 10.470n.

569] *shrine-box* The box in which the relics of a saint are preserved.

580] *Later . . . Rome* The Pope takes so much pleasure in Guido's execution that it amounts to a doubling of Carnival from the week before Ash Wednesday to ten days into Lent. Guido was executed on 22 February; Ash Wednesday was the 12th.

581] *candle-contest* On Shrove Tuesday, the last night of Carnival, revelers carried small candles. As a final act of celebration everyone attempted to put out the others' candles. They could be relighted, and the game continued until all candles were put out.

583] *Ash* Guido makes another parallel between himself and Christ; Ash Wednesday is the beginning of Lent.

585] *moment . . . eye* "In a moment, in a twinkling of an eye, at the last trump: for the trump shall sound, and the dead shall be raised incorruptible, and we shall all be changed" (1 Cor. 15:52).

587, 595] *realize* Make real.

600] *whited tomb* One could be defiled by contact with sepulchres, so the Jews covered them with a lime wash once a year to prevent the unaware from touching them. Guido has Matthew 23:27 in mind: "For ye are like unto whited sepulchres, which indeed appear beautiful outward, but are within full of dead men's bones and of all uncleanness."

613] *gird . . . feet* At the last supper Jesus washed the disciples' feet and then commanded that they wash one another's feet as a token of Christian humility. See John 13:4-14. It is a practice performed still in many churches as part of the Maundy Thursday (the day before Good Friday) ritual.

615] *crook* Bow.

623-28] *Pope's halberdier . . . pantingly* See 11.206n. The disciplined composure of the Swiss guard makes them seem inhumanly imperturbable; Guido chooses a figure of extreme poise and extreme artificiality as a hypothetical example of what might happen if the hypocritical facade of Christianity should become suddenly real.

626] *convinced of sin* Convicted of sin. "Which of you convinceth me of sin?" Jesus asked the Pharisees (John 8:46).

633] *prize . . . world* See 11.356n.

635] *His . . . Referendary* An important Vatican official.

639] *spinal cord* See 11.292-97n.

640] *Molinism* See 1.303-13n.

641] *trundles* See 11.232n.

645] *otherwise . . . seal* I.e., what would move them to such exertions if faith is the pretense Guido thinks it is?

652] *priceless soul* See 11.356n.

656] *Referendary* See 11.635n.

664] *Which . . . world* See 11.356n.

672] *skirt* Coat-tail, hanging part of a robe or coat.

672] *round . . . ears* See 4.597n.

680] *tinkle near* The tinkle, the ringing of the bell, came during the mass at the time of the elevation to signify that the bread and wine had become the body and blood of Christ.

682] *Trebbian* An Italian wine.

694] *Gold . . . prize* "Thou puttest away all the wicked of the earth like dross" (Ps. 119:19). "Therefore, I love thy commandments above gold" (Ps. 119:127). "Take away thy dross from the silver and there shall come forth a vessel for the finer" (Prov. 25:4).

696] *a-maundering . . . mumping* To *maunder* is to walk in a dreamy or aimless way. *Mumping* means "assuming a demure, sanctimonious or miserable aspect of countenance" (OED).

727-29] *Entire . . . also* "So then because thou art lukewarm, and neither hot nor cold, I will spue thee out of my mouth" (Rev. 3:16).

732] *caudatory* A prelate's train-bearer; the word means "tail."

733] *caps* Tips his hat as a gesture of respect.

748-50] *rend . . . raves* "But the children of the kingdom [the Jews] shall be cast out into outer darkness, and there shall be weeping, and gnashing of teeth" (Matt. 8:12).

757-60] *prodigal . . . taste* The familiar story of the prodigal son is found in Luke 15:16-23.

763] *draff-box* The trough from which refuse is fed to pigs.

771-72] *bloody . . . fools* In British speech, the word *bloody* used as an expletive arose from a corruption of "God's blood," and means damned or cursed.

778] *snow in harvest* "As the cold of snow in the time of harvest so is a faithful messenger to them that sent him: (Prov. 28:13).

780] *abrupt machine* See 11.125n.

782] *chop and change* Proverbial for "to be changeable"; and literal, in Guido's case.

785] *Chap-fallen* With slack jaw.

786-87] *beareth . . . edge* "But if thou do that which is evil, be afraid; for he beareth not the sword in vain; For he is the minister of God, a revenger to execute wrath upon him who doeth evil" (Rom. 13:4).

797] *genius . . . birth* The attendant spirits or gods allotted a person at birth.

798] *compass . . . concert* Enjoy together.

798-99] *take . . . wood* I.e., take the broad way of destruction. The *irregular* way is the rule (*regular*) in the Church Guido joined. The Church's invitation is the opposite of the Biblical injunction: "Enter ye in at the strait gate: for . . . broad is the way, that leadeth to destruction, and many there be which go in thereat" (Matt. 7:14).

811] *tongues of flame* As on Pentecost: "And there appeared unto them cloven tongues as of fire" (Acts 2:3).

818-27] *renounce . . . breed* See 11.431-41n.

820] *red-crossed* Marked apart for the religious life.

834-37] *gloved . . . fears* The expression *gloved hands* is figurative for indirection, craft; having once been manipulated himself, Guido would now turn clerical sway or *popular fears* to his own benefit.

844] *Mannaia-machine* See 11.212-29 and n.

866] *martyrologist* Historian of martyrs.

867-68] *sup . . . day* Guido suggests that Saints' days are fast days, on which no flesh is eaten. Such, however, is not the case. Perhaps he is referring to the Vigil fast sometimes observed on the evening preceeding the Saint's Day.

881] *jaundiced patch* Jealous fool.

897] *March hare* The hare was said to be especially wild in March because that was his breeding time.

899] *kissed . . . blind* A kiss of an adulterous wife was believed to blind her husband to her infidelity.

902] *Crowned his head* With the horns of a cuckold.

904-6] *That's . . . was* The Vallombrosa Convent near Florence was founded by a repentant profligate who might well have appreciated such a painting as Guido describes. B himself saw the picture in 1847 when he and EBB visited the Convent. EBB was incensed by the Monks' misogyny and wrote: "The brothers attain to sanctification, among other means, by cleaning out pigsties with their bare hands, without spade or shovel; but that is uncleanliness enough—they wouldn't touch the little finger of a woman" (*Letters of EBB*, 1, 336-37). The convent was suppressed in 1866.

907-9] *But . . . through* People will believe the representation of art, but call reality pretense, artful representation.

913] *horn-blind* Unaware that his wife has been unfaithful.

914-15] *lynx . . . through* See 10.1240n.

923] *mote-self* Miniscule self.

925] *couching* Lurking.

927] *fieldfares* Thrushes.

928] *bent* Stiff coarse grass or rush.

946] *Groundedly* As he really is.

953] *red thing* See 11.212-29 and n.

975-76] *heifer . . . priest* The simile is found in the passage on the sacrifice of Iphegenia in Lucretius' *De Rerum Natura* 1.97-99.

977] *insuppressive* Irrepressible.

979-80] *cup . . . cross* In the Garden of Gethsemene Jesus prayed: "Let this cup pass from me" (Matt. 26:39).

994-95] *Esther . . . sceptre* The Jewish queen Esther appeared before her husband the Persian King Ahasuerus (Xerxes I) on behalf of the Jews who by royal edict were to be slain. As a sign of favor "the king held out to Esther the golden sceptre" (Esther 5:2).

999] *Done-with* Treated, approached.

1002] *French Louis* Louis XIV was known for his romantic exploits.

1013] *portliness* Dignity.

1020] *thews* Muscles.

1022] *wheelwork* Mechanism.

1023-24] *untempered . . . crude* Before it achieved ultimate strength or before it became tempered (*wrought*) steel.

1026] *officious* Dutiful, obliging.

1032] *gripe* Old spelling for "grip.".

1053] *weeks* More than weeks; see *Chronology*.

1058-59] *Endure . . . the* Pompilia initially refused to consummate the marriage. See 7.740-42.

1084] *pure boon* Free blessing, grace.

1095-97] *blow . . . prodigy* The dog-rose is a wild European rose with single pink blooms, not to be compared with the hundred-petalled Provence prodigy; see 5.671n.

1101] *hedge-bird's* Probably the small European warbler often found in hedges.

1114] *think* Imagine.

1115-24] *dreadful . . . slew* Bellerophon slew the monster Chimaera which Homer described (*Iliad* 6.181) as a creature that was a lion in front, a serpent behind, and a goat in the middle. A bronze statue of the Chimaera was discovered in Arezzo in 1554. Guido casts himself in the role of the dragonslayer. *griesly*: grisly.

1138] *velvet* They are more affluent.

1141-42] *Since . . . starve* The operative word is *stalled*; in contrast to Pietro, the *ass* who has no home, the ass who has a comfortable stall will always find an audience in those who come to pick up his leavings. There does not seem to be a proverbial or folk origin for the figure.

1149] *trappings* Harness.

1150] *quondam* Former.

1151] *Via Vittoria* See 1.389n.

1152] *Pantaloon* A stock character in Italian comedy, a foolish old man usually wearing loose trousers.

1153] *tawdry* Used here as a noun meaning cheap and showy. It might refer to either or both his costume or his talk.

1154] *Ash-Wednesday . . . mid-Carnival* Ash Wednesday is the solemn first day of Lent and follows the gaiety of the preceeding carnival week.

1170] *proved . . . right* Might makes Right.

1171] *chattel . . . chapman* The product bought and not the seller.

1173-75] *shepherd . . . beneath* "Beware of false prophets, which come to you in sheep's clothing, but inwardly they are ravening wolves" (Matt. 7:15). The Comparini are the shepherd here.

1182] *board and bed* The marriage state.

1187] *perdue* Concealed.

1192] *four . . . months* Actually three; see *Chronology*.

1213] *wife . . . blood* "Therefore shall a man . . . cleave unto his wife: and they shall be one flesh" (Gen. 2:24).

1219] *Rounded . . . ears* See 4.597n.

1227] *Inconscious . . . silly-sooth* Unconscious . . . gullible.

1239-43] *Panciatichi . . . Via Larga* See 11.2n. The Palazzo *Panciatichi* is located at the S end of what is now called Via Cavour.

1250] *galleys* A galley is a ship propelled by either sails or oars. They were ordinarily manned by slaves and convicts. To be sentenced to the *galleys* was a common form of punishment in the seventeenth century.

1252] *lymphatic* Uninspired, dull. People were thought to be so through an excess of the humor known as *lymph*.

1266] *fetor* Offensive smell.

1272] *transformations of disgust* Disgusting changes.

1273] *snug . . . hand* See 1.389n. *out of hand*: straight off, unhesitatingly.

1277] *'S death* An oath: "God's death."

1278] *coil* A noisy disturbance.

1285] *unimpeached* Not charged with.

1291] *San Lorenzo* See 1.866-67n.

1300] *Flesh . . . bone* "Then Adam said, This is now bone of my bone and flesh of my flesh: She shall be called woman" (Gen. 2:23).

1300-1301] *bride . . . groom* See 5.2032-33n.

1303] *husband . . . rule* See 2.251-52n., 5.579-80n.

1327-28] *Commissary . . . Archbishop* See 3.965-66n.

1345] *wisp* A twisted bunch of hay or straw.

1378-79] *wards . . . lock* The inner part of a lock cut to admit a key of the same design; a lock or padlock which opens and shuts only by means of a key.

1398-1400] *binds . . . fist* See 2.251-52n., 5.576n.

1401] *proper . . . side* Assigned function (*place*) to suffer in childbirth. "Unto the woman he said, I will greatly multiply thy sorrow and thy conception; in sorrow thou shalt bring forth children" (Gen. 3:16). *side*: loin (OED).

1408-11] *Armida . . . Rinaldo* Characters in an opera based on Tasso's *Gerusalemme Liberata*. A eunuch played the part of *Armida*.

1415] *zecchines* Coins of small value.

1422] *chalk-ball* A fake egg made of white stone.

1435-40] *plant . . . each* An old belief, not now supported, that *ash* and *elm* trees would not grow together.

1439] *pleasaunce* A pleasure ground or garden.

1453] *red thing* See 11.212-29 and n.

1460] *pulpit-corner . . . gospel-side* The *gospel side* is traditionally on the left or N side of the altar. The pulpit is ordinarily on this side also.

1463] *use* Custom, practice.

1464-66] *muzzled . . . field* Among the sundry laws laid down for the Jews was: "Thou shalt not muzzle the ox when he treadeth out the corn" (Deut. 25:4; see also 1 Cor. 9:9 and 1 Tim. 5:18). These passages advise justice to the laborer. Guido distorts the quotation and the sense, arguing that the restrained oxen have lost the ability to know what either justice or life is.

1469] *Leavened* "Corrupted by admixture" (OED).

1474] *high-days* Saints' days, festive celebrations.

1484] *promise . . . air* "I eat the air, promise crammed" (*Hamlet* 3.2.99).

1488] *words . . . wind* "Do you imagine to reprove words, and the speeches of one that is desperate, which are as wind?" (Job 6.26) "How long wilt thou speak these things? and how long shall the words of thy mouth be like a strong wind?" (Job 8.2).

1493] *Deny myself* Self-denial is a frequent demand of the Gospels; for example: "If any man would come after me, let him deny himself and take up his cross, and follow me" (Matt. 16:24).

1494, 1500] *save the mark / marked* The full phrase "God save the mark" is ironic and derisive. Guido plays on *mark* as "rank" and says that he, with no manifest or measurable superiority of standing in the clergy, was the better man.

1504-6] *wrath . . . pruning-hook* Anticiating the final triumph of Jehovah, Isaiah says a that a time will come when "They shall beat their swords into plowshares, and their spears into pruning hooks: nation shall not lift up sword against nation . . . " (Isa. 2:4).

1509] *Anathema* Strictly speaking, *anathema* is defined as complete separation from the Body of Christ, or what has been called "Major" excommunication. Here the word is used less technically: "a curse upon it."

1518-19] *stumbling-block . . . way* "Let no man put a stumbling block or an occasion to fall in his brother's way" (Rom. 14:13).

1520] *hatchet* The long-handled, spear-headed battle-ax symbolic of authority, carried in front of a dignitary in a procession.

1526] *letter . . . alive* "The letter killeth, but the spirit giveth life" (2 Cor. 3:6).

1530-33] *clownish . . . himself* "To wipe your own nose," or "to wipe your nose on your sleeve" was proverbial as early as the Greeks for taking rudimentary responsibility for oneself.

1537] *partridge-wise* Like a pair of love-birds represented breast to breast, and spitted as if for roasting in the same position.

1546-47] *house . . . kingdom* In response to his critics who had charged that he exercised demonic powers to cast out demonic powers, Jesus said, "Every kingdom divided against itself is brought to desolation, and every city or house divided against itself shall not stand" (Matt. 12:25).

1570] *Villa* See 1.389n.

1587] *catacombs* Underground rooms used for the burial of the dead in Christian Rome.

1601] *taenia* Tapeworm that in the adult stage lives as a parasite in the intestines of man and other vertebrates.

1609] *delirium flustered* See 10.842n., 11.1618-19n.

1614] *poor beside* Comparatively insignificant.

1618-19] *drunk . . . triumphant* See 11.1609; drunk with power.

1626] *malapert* Impudent.

1636] *want . . . head* According to the Secondary Source, Guido in his haste had left his *hat* at the scene of the crime (OYB,E 263).

1645] *hacks and hamstrings* Literally, cuts the hamstring tendon so as to lame the victim.

1651] *reached . . . boundary* Of Tuscany. See 3.1622n.

1658-59] *Witness . . . confirmed* See 10.830-32n.

1661] *Guillichini* It was to Guillichini that Pompilia first appealed for help in her planned flight to Rome. He excused himself on the grounds of ill health.

1664] *Stinche* Prison in Florence.

1667] *horn* Calloused.

1671] *hangdogs* Contemptible fellows.

1674-75] *knowing . . . you* See 11.283-90n.

1680] *turn . . . lie* "Who changed the truth of God into a lie and served the creature more than the creator" (Rom. 1:25). Guido ignores the introductory clause: "Professing themselves to be wise they become fools" (Rom. 1:22).

1698] *preconcerted* Premeditated.

1724-26] *Forgiving . . . infinite* OYB,E 57-59.

1725] *commending mine* Dying, Jesus cried, "Father into thy hands I commend my spirit" (Luke 23:46).

1733-39] *Twist . . . throat* See 1.971-72n., 8.1581-89n.

1745] *I die last* OYB,E 266 (The Secondary Source).

1752-55] *Look . . . case* See 1.174-75n.

1756] *skill* Archaic use of the word to mean "make a difference."

1764-68] *And . . . end* The word *crosses* is a pun referring to both the "double crosses" *failure and affront,* and to the cross of execution which he will soon suffer. The hill on which Jesus was crucified was named Golgotha, which means *skull.* The *bloody palms* refer to the nail-pierced hands of Jesus. This is another strong identification of Guido with Christ.

1776] *Jansenius* See 1.303-13n.

1785] *trying . . . spirits* "Beloved, believe not every spirit, but try the spirits whether they be of God" (1 John 4:1).

1788] *refresh . . . bowels* "Yea, brother, let me have the joy of thee in the Lord: refresh my bowels in the Lord" (Philem. 20). *Bowels* in the archaic sense refers to the inside of the body and is regarded as the source of the tender emotions. The Revised Version translates the word "heart."

1794] *in . . . earth* "Thou shalt not make unto thee any graven image, or any likeness of anything that is in heaven above, or that is in the earth beneath, or that is in the water under the earth" (Ex. 20:4).

1798-99] *Stab . . . me* Perhaps a reference to Julius Caesar, a heroic martyr in a different way from Christ. Dante placed Judas and Brutus, betrayers, in the lowest pit of hell as the supreme sinners. One had betrayed the heavenly and the other the earthly city. Again Guido makes himself a sacrificial victim.

1803-4] *Vienna . . . Mustafa* In 1683 the Turks under the Grand Vizier Kara Mustafa attacked Vienna and were routed by an allied force led by the King of Poland and his General, Charles, Duke of Lorraine. Both the victory and the leaders were much celebrated.

1823] *warrant* Strength.

1827-28] *bare . . . France* Going naked was often in Biblical times employed as a symbolic gesture by prophets and penitents. See, for example, 1 Samuel 19:24; Isaiah 20:2-4; Lamentations 4:21; Micah 1:8. B may have known of a specific event in France to which he refers.

1834] *gird* Taunt.

1839] *fifty . . . age* See 2.769n.

1845] *gaudeamus* "Let us rejoice." Guido may have in mind Psalms 103:1,5: "Bless the Lord, O my soul . . . Who satisfieth thy mouth with good things; so that thy youth is renewed like the eagle's."

1864] *blood-offering fail* See 11.1849-50. Perhaps also another identification with Christ.

1879-80] *Go . . . Sir* The son in the parable, however, said "I go, Sir, and went not" (Matt. 21:30).

1882] *paul* A minimal amount of money.

1883-84] *four . . . Vittiano* "Thy wife shall be as a fruitful vine by the side of thine house: thy children like olive plants round about thy table" (Ps. 127:3).

1889] *dollar* See 12.115n.

1890] *mumping* See 11.696n.

1894] *conceding . . . youth* Making no concessions because of age.

1907] *fall . . . sword* A manner of self-destruction preferred by the noble Roman to dishonor at the hands of an enemy.

1906-8] *ancient . . . ancient* Tuscany is the oldest part of Italy and Arezzo is the oldest town in Tuscany.

1913-17] *Name . . . oak* Guido claims to be a descendant of the Etruscans, who were the earliest inhabitants of what is now Tuscany. Arezzo boasted of being the oldest Tuscan city. Guido claims to be a primitive religionist in preference to later Christianity. *frigid Virgil*: Guido expresses a romantic view of Virgil, whose classical restraint was considered in the nineteenth century inferior to the more robust style of Homer. Nevertheless, he quotes from the eighth book (134-35) of the *Aeneid* a passage in which King Evander described to Aeneas the land that was later to become Roman as having earlier been inhabited by primitive, near-savage people engendered by nymphs and fauns and sprung (*Virgil's finest word*) from the trunks of trees or rugged oaks.

1919] *Jove Aegiocchus* The name Aegiocchus is an epithet of Zeus (*Jove*) in the *Odyssey*; it means "holder of the aegis (shield)," by means of which Jove sent thunder-bolts and storms.

1920-22] *Descried . . . Eighth* The Arcadians claimed to have seen Jove often on the Capitoline Hill shaking his shield amid thunder and lightning. See *Aeneid* 8.352-55.

1924] *vivacious* A Latinism: living.

1926-28] *motto . . . azure* There is no *motto* accompanying the Franceschini coat of arms, or *shield*. The play on words between Jove's aegis or shield (see 11.1919 and n.) and the Franceschini *shield* suggests that the motto Guido has in mind is the line describing Jove shaking his shield: "Aegida concuteret dextra nimbosque cieret" (His strong hand clashed the shield and roused the storm-clouds). See Virgil, *Aeneid* 8.354. The heraldic names for the colors red and blue are *gules* and *azure*. *Gules* symbolizes magnanimity and fortitude and is engraved perpendicularly; *azure* symbolizes loyalty and is engraved horizontally. For a full description of the coat of arms see Vol VII, 257; 11.2154-57 and 12.818-20.

1930] *Jove Aegiochus* See 11.1919n.

1933-36] *intermediary . . . these* The Greek gods "Mars and Minerva, Bacchus and the rest" (see 11.1963-64).

1949-50] *rod . . . pickle* "To have rods in pickle" means to have punishment in store. Wood soaked in brine becomes more flexible and thus a better flagellant. Or the passage may have reference to the practice of rubbing salt or salt and vinegar on a flogged man's back to make the wounds smart.

1952] *Venus . . . Apollo* In Guido's scheme *Apollo*, law, is the Pope and *Venus*, passion, himself.

1956-57] *stop . . . pleasantry* See 9.1195 and n.

1963] *medium-powers* The in-between, intercessory powers. See 1933-36 and n.

1965] *saved propitiating* Spared serving, relieved of believing in; the ambiguity of *save* is ironic.

1969] *Irrational bunglers* The gods are irrational, in contrast to the clear, skeptical "rationale" (11.1961) of the ministry.

1970] *strike Pan dead* Pan, the lustful god of flocks and herds and forests is often depicted playing a panpipe. He represents a spirit of nature which, according to Guido, Christianity had suppressed. According to legend, certain Greek sailors are said to have heard at the time of Jesus' crucifixion a voice saying "Pan is dead."

1971] *live good days* "What man is he that desireth life, and loveth many days, that he may see good" (Ps. 34:12). "For he that will love life, and see good days, let him refrain his tongue from evil" (1 Peter 8:10).

1975] *change* Reaction, counter-event.

1977] *mulct and minish* Punish and diminish.

1979-85] *substituting . . . world* Guido refers to a movement beginning in the early third century of certain devout Christians from the *world* to the seclusion of the desert. Most famous, no doubt, are St. Anthony of Egypt and St. Simeon Stylites. Anthony is generally called the first Christian monk and is remembered for his extreme asceticism, typified by his struggles with the devil under the form of wild beasts, lustful women, and brutal soldiers who sometimes beat him and left him for dead. Simeon was the first of the pillar monks and is perhaps most familiar through Tennyson's poem "Saint Simeon Stylites." These extreme ascetics represent a negation of the world that has remained an undercurrent in the Christian Church.

1985] *unspotted . . . world* "Pure religion and undefiled before God is this, to visit the fatherless and widows in their affliction, and to keep himself unspotted from the world" (James 1:17).

1989-90] *new . . . old* The *new* is Christianity exemplified in the desert ascetics; the *old* is the life-affirming spirit embodied in the mythical Pan.

1992] *profession* Pretence; the Christian masque of 11.1972-73.

1993-94] *law . . . saves* A use of scripture to serve his own purpose: "The letter killeth but the spirit giveth life" (2 Cor. 3:6).

1997] *wink* A permissive gesture, as it were, on the sly.

1999] *poison . . . bread* An oblique reference to Jesus' response to one of Satan's temptations in the wilderness, "Man shall not live by bread alone, but by every word that proceedeth out of the mouth of God" (Matt. 4:4).

2000-2001] *sword . . . foe* Another "wink" at the law.

2006] *mystery* That which is concealed to ordinary eyes, i.e. their "love of life."

2019] *pontifex* The Pope.

2023-24] *Unknown . . . Vatican* Paul said to the Athenians: "For as I passed by and beheld your devotions, I found an altar with this inscription TO THE UNKNOWN GOD. Whom ye ignorantly worship, him I declare unto you" (Acts 17:23). *Genius* has the sense of "resident spirit."

2028] *Romano vivitur more* In Rome one does as Rome does.

2030-31] *stamped . . . tares* In the parable the master refused to remove the *tares* (weeds) from his field lest he also uproot the wheat. Guido had acted less cautiously. If he had been politic, he says, and shown contrition, he might have excused his crime on the grounds of excessive zeal for the Church. See Matthew 13:24-30.

2035] *Molinist* See 1.303-13n.

2043-49] *Ovid . . . wolf* The story is told in Ovid's *Metamorphoses* 1.237-39. The ineffectual Byblis was in love with her brother, whom she pursued so tearfully that she was turned into a fountain. Lycaon, the brutal brother, was turned into a wolf. The popularity of stories such as this belonged to a later moralizing, allegorizing tradition which adapted or selected among the pagan tales of the *Metamorphoses*. Guido's allegory mocks the Christian reading of Ovid.

2051] *Coerced* Restrained.

2056] *deformed . . . conformed* An ironic echo of St. Paul's words: "And be not conformed to this world: but be ye transformed by the renewing of your mind, that ye may prove what is that good, and acceptable, and perfect will of God" (Rom. 12:2).

2073-74] *ice . . . me* Dante depicts the nethermost regions of hell as ice. See 11.1798-99n.

2079] *abnegation of revenge* See 7.1690-1705; OYB,E 57-59.

2090-92] *Would . . . else* Guido would stay in hell as long as it gave him power over Pompilia (his *foe*).

2093] *not make myself* See 7.1714.

2101] *maundered* See 11.696n.

2109] *daub* A poorly painted, worthless picture.

2110] *Rafael* A painting of the Madonna by Raphael. Cf. 6.396-402.

2114] *Titian's . . . Angelico* Guido prefers *Titian* because of his sensuous and realistic depiction of the flesh to *Angelico*, whose work is abstract and other-worldly.

2121] *lawn* A fine sheer cloth of linen or cotton.

2122] *selvage cloth* An edging or border, of wealth if Pompilia had brought it to the marriage. See 11.2129-30.

2125] *bleach* Fade out.

2137] *Paynimrie* Heathendom, particularly the Middle East during the Christian crusades.

2142] *furze-sprig . . . hauberk-joint* An evergreen shrub which grows wild all over Europe; a joining in a suit of chain mail armor.

2151] *circumjacent* The space surrounding.

2154-59] *arms . . . air* For a description of the coat of arms see Vol. VII 257 and 12.817-20.

2177] *Olimpias . . . Biancas* Passionate, unscrupulous heroines of Italian romance.

2178] *Ormuz* Diamond market on an island in the Persian Gulf.

2191-95] *Sounder . . . do* Samson revealed to the wily *Delilah* that the secret of his great strength lay in his unshaven head, whereupon she lulled him to sleep and cut his hair. His strength departed and he was delivered into the hands of his enemies (Judges 16:6-20).

2197] *call-bird* Decoy.

2199] *Such . . . whom* Both clauses are questions implying that there are no such women (except in hell; see 11.2207ff. below).

2204-5] *Circe . . . sun* The sorceress and daughter of Helios (Sun), who turned Odysseus' men into swine.

2206] *honest distaff* Literally, an instrument used in weaving. It came to signify a woman because in ancient times women spun often from morning until night. Here it refers to Penelope, Ulysses' faithful wife, who in contrast to Circe, stayed at home weaving while she waited for the return of her husband.

2207] *Lucrezia* The daughter of Pope Alexander VI and sister of Cesare Borgia, who was also, according to popular report, her lover. She did not marry and was long remembered as a passionate and treacherous woman. Guido's remark reflects a belief modified by contemporary historians.

2214-15] *Cardinal . . . alone* They are trying to get him to kiss the crucifix.

2218] *saving dew* A common image in the Old Testament of the Lord's favor, e.g., "I will be as the dew unto Israel: He shall grow as the lily, and cast forth his roots as Lebanon" (Hos. 14:5).

2228] *inquisition . . . blood* "When he maketh inquisition for blood, he remembereth them: he forgetteth not the cry of the humble" (Ps. 9:12). The Revised Version is clearer: "For he who avenges blood is mindful of them; he does not forget the cry of the afflicted."

2230]   *College* The body of the seventy cardinals was called the Sacred College.

2232]   *scantling* Few, here used ironically.

2240]   *damsel-fly* Dragon-fly.

2244]   *Lord . . . things* "And God said, let us make man in our image, after our likeness: and let them have dominion over the fish of the sea, and over the fowls of the air, and over the cattle, and over all the earth, and over every creeping thing that creepeth upon the earth" (Gen. 1:26).

2251]   *die next year* The Pope lived for another two and a half years.

2253-57]   *first . . . come* The names are historical. Guido speculates on possible successors to Innocent XII, and in 11.2332 he makes an accurate prediction.

2262-63]   *fulcrum-stone . . . world* Archimedes, the Greek mathematician (c. 287-212 B.C.) is reported to have said, "Give me a place to stand and I will move the earth."

2272-73]   *Spare . . . love* In a letter to Cencini, Gaspero del Torto writes concerning Guido's pardon, "there have not been lacking admonitions of greatest consequence, since the Ambassador of the Emperor spoke of that point on Tuesday, as he himself told me the day before yesterday; and then the matter was settled precipitately" (OYB, E 237). Acting on this suggestion B has Guido make hysterical appeals to opposed great powers of the time through the cardinal. The power struggle between France and Austria-Germany is a historical constant in European politics at this time. The Holy Roman Emperor of Austria was Leopold I. His Hapsburg relative Charles II of Spain was childless and the Pope favored an heir of Louis XIV as Charles's successor. Such an agreement would have partly reconciled tensions between France and Austria and between Catholic factions in France and Italy, but predictably, it did not occur. The opposite targets of Guido's appeal here seem meant more to emphasize his desperation than to evoke the theological and political controversies and compromises of the period.

2275-76]   *Who . . . coercive* Former hypocrites because of inducement and privilege (*coercive*) such as immunity from prosecution, will no longer pretend allegiance to the church; *with impunity* apparently means "without apology, openly." The semi-colon after *coercive* marks a break in thought.

2291]   *Saint . . . bark* The fisher-disciple St. Peter and his church are often associated with a boat or *bark*.

2307]   *it* Refers to "bad blow" 11.2305.

2314]   *powers and principalities* Terms used by New Testament writers for malignant powers through which evil works. See Ephesians 6:12, "For we wrestle not against flesh and blood, but against principalities, against powers, against the rulers of the darkness of this world, against spiritual wickedness in high places."

2322]   *wine and myrrh* The drink offered to Christ on the cross to dull his senses and alleviate pain.

2325]   *Pope's dead* As good as dead.

2326]   *Tozzi* See 9.1259n.

2330]   *down in book* To be on one's list of friends, or in this case, of prospective patients.

2331]   *seventy near* Seventy is the fixed number of the College of Cardinals when its membership is complete. At the time of this election, when a new Pope would be chosen, it was obviously not complete.

2332]   *Albano* Who would become the successor to Innocent XII.

2339]   *Martinez* The Emperor's Ambassador to Rome. See 11.2272n., 12.94n.

2340]   *Stops . . . veto* The right of the Emperor to veto a papal election was granted to Otto the Great in 963; subsequently it was not always honored, however.

2355]   *halcyon* See 11.12n.

2378]   *foil . . . sparkle's* A metallic leaf placed behind jewels to make them sparkle.

2381]   *resign* "To make surrender of [one's will or reason] in reliance upon another" (OED).

2384]   *Pope for God* See 10.20n.

2402]   *Athenian who died* Themistocles, who is thought to have committed suicide by drinking bull's blood, long thought to be a poison.

2406]   *who . . . stair* The Company of Death. See 1.1303n. B was uncertain about where in the prison Guido was incarcerated, changing MS *ascend* to *descend*; see variants.

2407]   *accursed psalm* See 1.1311-12n.

2417-19]   *Granduke's . . . me* To whom is he subject, the Granduke or the Pope? Like the opening lines of his monologue, Guido's last lines are a catalogue of names, this time signifying his desperate wish to re-enroll his own among them.

Book 12, The Book and the Ring

3]   *key* Keystone or summit.

7]   *ghastly* Ghostlike.

10] *my power* A probable reference to the ring, with its inscription *Vis Mea* (my strength, my power). See 1.1-24n.

11] *composite* Composed.

12] *Wormwood Star* The bitter herb wormwood is a symbol of divine chastizement. It is the name of the falling star that follows the breaking of the seventh seal and the sounding of the third of seven trumpets in the Book of Revelation (8:10-11). It heralds divine judgment upon the wicked.

20] *main streaks* The four accounts to be considered in the aftermath of Guido's beheading. They are: 1) a fictional letter from a Venetian gentleman (31-207); 2) a letter from Arcangeli, a paraphrase of OYB,E 235-36 (237-86) and a fictional postscript (288-387); 3) a fictional letter from Bottini (403-455, 644-747) enclosing 4) an extract from a sermon by the Augustinian friar (456-643).

38] *totters . . . grave* The Pope lived for another two and a half years.

39] *Malpichi* See 7.419n.

40] *Tozzi* See 9.1259n.

41] *inveterate* Incurable.

42-43] *Cardinal . . . head* The Venetian visitor is less prescient than Guido. See 11.2253-57n., 11.2332n.

44] *niece* The Venetian implies that the next Pope will undo the reforms of nepotism (favors to nephews—often a euphemism for bastard sons—and by extension to "nieces") accomplished by Innocent XII.

46-48] *Colloredo . . . Chamberlain* All named were possible candidates for the office of Pope. The highest ranking cardinal was the Chamberlain.

52] *Custom-house* See also 12.89n. Cook says that Innocent XII built a custom-house in the Piazza di Pietra, far from the Tiber, but that there is no record of a maritime custom-house.

56-58] *fainting-fits . . . beads* One of several disparaging remarks about the Pope's intellectual capacity. See also 8.1440-42; 10.1241-42; 12.296, 373.

61] *Jubilee . . . time* The Pope had celebrated Jubilee to mark his eightieth birthday in 1695 (see 2.532n.). Why he should celebrate another three years later is not clear.

62] *Holy Doors* See 3.566-68n.

65] *Fénelon* In 1689 Pope Innocent XII did condemn Fénelon's writing. See 6.319n.

66-67] *Cardinal . . . delinquent* Cardinal Bouillon (12.112) was the representative of Louis XIV in Rome and Dean of the College of Cardinals. He is said to have incurred the displeasure of the king for not having pushed the case against Fénelon strongly enough.

74] *zecchines* Coins of small worth.

81-82] *old . . . pageant-king* See 11.2272-73n. The *old enmity* between Austria and Italy was still fresh and keen during the Bs' stay in Italy, and EBB was as passionate a partisan of Louis Napoleon as the Pope is here of Louis XIV. Cook, Appendix VII, discusses the relationship between Innocent XII and Louis XIV at length. Their former dispute was theological and centered on the limits of papal authority and on the legitimacy of Quetist doctrine (see n. on Molinism, 1.303-13). The Pope's condemnation of Quietism in March 1699, a year after the trial, represented the truce and perhaps capitulation implied in these lines. Louis XIV is the *pageant-king* because he built Versailles (beginning in 1661) and other monuments and buildings in Paris, including the colonnade of the Louvre. For background and description of the tortured subject of nineteenth-century Italian politics and its effect on the Bs' lives (which may be the real impulse behind this passage) see Irvine and Honan 131-35, 361-65. To the Venetian, the combination of Italian-Austrian national antagonism and the Pope's recent reconciliation with Louis XIV means that the Austrian ambassador's support of Guido is the kiss of death.

89] *Dogana-by-the-Bank* See 12.52n.

94] *Martinez . . . Minister* The Austrian ambassador who tried to save Guido. See 11.2272n.

104] *palchetto* Grandstand.

105-7] *Under . . . Bridge* See 1.346-54n.

110-11] *French . . . foe* In contrast to the Austrian ambassador's sulks, the French can signal victory over their foe—not Guido, but Austria.

112] *Cardinal Bouillon* See 12.66n.

113] *palchetti* See 12.104n.

114] *edge . . . Three Streets* The three main streets running S from the Piazza are the Via del Babuino, the Corso and the Via di Ripetta; *edge* means "intersection."

115-17] *Let . . . too* See OYB,E 265.

115] *six dollars* Not the American dollar but a silver coin that circulated in several European countries before it became the standard monetary unit in the United States. The word *dollar* comes from German "thaler," a large coin current in the sixteenth century. It was worth about four shillings and six pence in 1698, a substantial unit.

116] *Anguisciola* A noted old Italian family named Aguissola corresponds to B's reference and B's spelling may be a variant of that name.

117] *Envoy Contarini* The name is not in OYB or the Secondary Source, but Contarini was the name of a Venetian envoy at the time; see Cook, Appendix VII.

119] *four-and-twenty hours ago* At 8 p.m., 21 February.

120] *Acciaiuoli and Panciatichi* The visitors were actually members of the Company of Death; see 11.1-2n.

122] *pitched* Decided.

124] *ere cock-crow* At the eighth hour (OYB,E 265) or 2 a.m..

129] *Company of Death* See 1.1303n.

130-31] *twenty-hours . . . dinner-time* 2 p.m. The statement that it was at sunset must be an error. According to OYB, E 238, the execution itself took place after dinner.

132] *led . . . car* See 11.2406n.; *car*, horse-drawn cart.

135-37] *intrepidity . . . saw* "Franceschini . . . showed more intrepidity and composure than the others, to the wonder of all" (OYB,E 265).

139] *New Prison* See 1.1276n., 2.1454n.

139-46] *From . . . People* The procession went by the "longest way" (1.1317n.) "following the most densely populated streets" (OYB,E 280).

140] *Pasquin's Street* See 6.1633n.

148] *change of locality* See 1.346-54n.

155-58] *Twelve . . . Quatern* A sum staked on three numbers was a *terno* and on four a *quaterno.* Considerable superstition attached to gambling, and the number of the shop, being a multiple of three and four, would have assured some winners. Innocent XII did prohibit the lottery system of gambling.

159] *Saint Agnes* A church along the route.

164-65] *Not . . . block* The distance was much shorter from the prison of Castel St. Angelo to the customary place of execution (as B supposed; see 1.346-54n., and 1.1276n.), than to the Piazza del Popolo.

176] *suffrage* Intercessory prayers.

178-79] *Pater . . . Ave . . . Salve Regina Coeli* Our Father; Hail (Mary); Hail Heavenly Queen. All were familiar prayers, the last to the Blessed Virgin Mary being the most popular.

182] *St. Mary's* Santa Maria del Popolo stood at the north end of the Piazza.

184] *Umbilicus* Umbilical cord.

188] *Jesus . . . lips* Guido associates himself with St. Stephen, the first Christian martyr. "And they stoned Stephen, calling upon God, and saying, Lord Jesus, receive my spirit" (Acts 7:59).

193] *fifty years* So the Secondary Source says (OYB,E 266). See, however, 1.774-76n.

197-201] *dress . . . cap* From the Secondary Source, OYB,E 266. *baracan*: usually *barracan*, a coarse water-proof cloth.

198] *just-a-corps* A tight fitting knee-length coat.

199] *camisole* Shirt.

204] *end was peace* "Mark the perfect man, and behold the upright: For the end of that man is peace" (Ps. 37:37). This is indeed the Venetian gentleman's judgment of Guido.

206] *Spada . . . Pope* Cardinal Spada, the "actual minister" of 12.42 above.

207] *quatrain* The quatrain is not supplied.

208] *streak* See 12.20n.

209] *letter* B's paraphrased version of an actual letter follows. See OYB, E 235-36; the poet adds a fictitious postscript (12.288-387).

210] *Proctor* A form of "Procurator," attorney.

212] *valiant . . . truth* The name of one of Christian's companions in Bunyan's *Pilgrim's Progress* (Altick).

215] *Socius* Colleague.

217] *bowels* The interior or vital parts. See 11.1788n.

219] *joint effort* Arcangeli sent to Cencini for the proofs of Guido's clericate, but since the Pope overruled this qualification the proofs arrived "too late" (after the execution); OYB,E 235.

220] *nicked* A technical gambling term which B explains (12.222) as meaning "succeeded."

222] *Tarocs* A game of cards which could involve fortune-telling.

223-24] *Cencini's . . . thing* Cencini was the probable compiler of the *yellow thing*, the OYB.

225] *four-years' intimate* For an account of the composition of the poem see *Composition*.

227] *whole . . . case* See 1.119-30.

234-36] *Part . . . done* B's creative imagination. See 1.452-470.

237-40] *Late . . . God* See 12.219n. *Egregious* has the archaic sense of "distinguished."

244] *sense* Direction (rare).

256] *cheirograph* Handwriting or signature. See 10.2096ff.

257] *derogate* To annul.

262] *Pasquini* See 6.1633n.

266] *Decollate . . . privilege* This is B's own interpretation of the original. The Secondary Source (see *Sources*), probably never seen by B, states that Guido was beheaded rather than hanged "rather out of respect for his being in clerical orders than for any other reason" (OYB,E 268-81).

267] *decently . . . order* "Let all things be done decently and in order" (1 Cor. 14:40).

270-71] *nor . . . red* The background of the Franceschini coat of arms was azure. See Vol. VII, 257; 11.2154-59; 12.817-20.

275] *Quantum . . . venustiorum* Catullus 3.2. Paraphrased in the following line.

288-387] *Hactenus . . . case* The Latin means "Thus far for the seniors" (clients, readers who take precedence). The postscript is entirely B's invention.

292] *Pisan assistance* A proverb deriving from the Pisan fleet's arrival too late to participate in the crucial siege of Jerusalem during the First Crusade.

296] *Somebody's . . . headpiece* See 12.56-58n.

308-9] *indecent . . . Playground* See 1.346-54n.

309] *stigmatize* Censure, blame (parallel with "will have relished" 12.306 above). Rome will enjoy the show but understand that it had little to do with Guido's guilt.

313] *socket* The base of a candle holder when a candle has burned all the way down.

316] *tender grapes* "Take us the foxes, the little foxes, that spoil the vines: for our vines have tender grapes" (Song of Sol. 2:15).

327] *Themis' throne* Goddess of justice whose *throne*, according to Arcangeli, would reside more appropriately in Tuscany than in Rome.

322-23] *both . . . hot* The lawyer Ugolinucci refers to the coming *Matrimonial Case* and the case of *Gomez* in a letter to Cencini (OYB, E 238), but according to the record Arcangeli had nothing to do with either. See 12.653-60.

324] *Reliqua . . . crastinum* Cicero, *De Re Publica* 2.44.4 "Put off the rest until tomorrow."

325] *estafette* Courier.

328] *fat-chaps Hyacinth* The son of whom Arcangeli speaks so often in Book 8.

335-36] *hoc . . . subjunctive* "That I would prefer" (rather than "That I prefer.")

338] *Proud . . . peacock-fans* Peacock fans were carried on either side of the Pope on festival occasions. They represent the virtues that adorn the saintly as the beauty of the colorful feathers adorn the peacock.

343, 349] *Cintino / Cinone* See 12.328 and 8.1-2n.

355] *Eutropius* Fourth century Roman historian.

358] *Bartolus-cum-Baldo* See 1.215-33n.

360] *Gomez . . . marriage-case* See 12.322-23n.

364-65] *Adverti . . . Quod* "I humbly beg it be noted that."

365] *fungus . . . fop* The epithets mock Bottini's youth and flashy style: *fungus*, overnight growth of no durability; *fop*, one who trusts to appearances.

366-74] *one . . . roadster* The image is Franceschini on one side of the street, on the other the Pope, and Arcangeli driving two spirited horses between them, managing to preserve both—the honor of one and

the dignity of the other—from danger or soiling. *old Somebody*: see
12.56-58n. *roadster*: pedestrian.

382] *inward . . . guide* An indirect way of accusing the Pope of
Molinism.

386] *Cinuzzo* See 12.343n.

387] *Gomez* See 12.322-23n.

388] *letter* This letter is B's invention.

391] *Monday* February 24, 1698.

410] *lynx-eye* Sharp eye. See 10.1240n.

412] *twist . . . cord* A reference to Guido's torture; see 1.971-72n.

414] *Finished . . . penitent* B took this from the Secondary Source
(OYB,E 265-66). B introduces Guido's penitence for the first time in
Book 12 and puts it in the mouths of characters governed more by self-
interest than by an objective search for truth—the Venetian, Arcangeli,
Bottini.

419-20] *claps . . . crows* The same image Arcangeli used for Bottini;
see 8.234-36 and n.

433] *Spreti's work* Arcangeli's partner in defense; see *Sources*.

434] *dandiprat* A term of contempt: dwarf, pigmy.

436] *save-all* A contrivance to hold a candle-end in a stick so that it may
burn to the end.

438] *gird* Taunt.

447] *San Lorenzo* See 2.6n.

448] *treasure . . . church* See 2.8-15.

450-51] *Let . . . liar* "Let God be true, but every man a liar" (Rom.
3:4).

456-643] This purported sermon of the Augustinian is B's invention.

468] *Lord, how long* A familiar cry in the Old Testament. For exam-
ple: "O Lord, how long shall I cry, and thou wilt not hear! even cry out
unto thee of violence, and thou wilt not save me" (Hab. 1:2).

471-78] *inhabitants . . . bill* The story is told in Genesis 8:8-11.

476] *culver* Pigeon.

491] *morning-star* Christianity.

493] *cavern-mouth* The catacombs in which Christians hid during
times of persecution.

494] *obnoxious* Liable to punishment, reprehensible.

501] *idol-god, an Ass* Pagan Rome often accused Christians of wor-
shipping an ass.

505] *offscouring . . . race* Christianity made its initial appeal espe-
cially to the lower classes and the deprived.

517-20] *lamp . . . Christo* Terracotta lamps and vessels containing blood were found in the catacombs where persecuted Christians had left them. Palm branches, scratched on the walls, were symbols of ultimate victory: "And I beheld, and, lo, a great multitude, which no man could number, of all nations, and kindreds, and people, and tongues, stood before the throne, and before the lamb, clothed with white robes, and palms in their hands" (Rev. 7:9) Many of the objects found were inscribed with the motto "Pro Christo," "For Christ."

533-35] *Apollo . . . centipede* The two statues represent light and guardianship, Apollo as god of the sun and Juno as Queen of Heaven, and the insects indicate betrayal. Certain varieties of centipedes are venemous.

537] *Demon and devil* Some Christians thought that pagan gods— Apollo and Juno, for example—were fallen angels or devils. See Milton's "Nativity Hymn."

583] *intends* Extends.

585-86] *One . . . away* "and darkness was upon the face of the deep, and the Spirit of God moved upon the face of the waters. And God said, Let there be light: and there was light" (Gen. 1:1-2).

591] *hate . . . light* "For every one that doeth evil hateth the light, neither cometh to the light, lest his deed should be reproved. But he that doeth truth cometh to the light that his deeds may be manifest, that they are wrought in God" (John 3:20-21).

597, 600, 606] *proof / proved / Approved . . . probation* The passage develops a parallel contrast between *true* and *false* and between *probation* and *proof*. In sum, *Approved by life's probation* (of falsehood) is to be *proved* by being put to *proof*; the words have the same root.

615] *God . . . heart* "I know also, my God, that thou triest the heart, and hast pleasure in uprightness" (1 Chron. 29:17).

620] *Christ's assurance* "Verily I say unto you, there is no man who hath left house, or parents, or brethren, or wife, or children, for the kingdom of God's sake, who shall not receive manifold more in this present time, and in the world to come life everlasting" (Luke 18:29-30).

625] *as grace* As for example, it had for Caponsacchi. See 6.1089.

644] *ampollosity* Included in OED as B's coinage: inflated, bubbly, insubstantial.

651] *Molinism* See 1.303-13n.

652] *pitch* Literally, the place where street or carnival hawkers set up stand.

654] *Gomez* See 12.360n.

668] *Perpend* Weigh, ponder.

669-70] *Monastery . . . first* B errs. See 2.1189-90.

673] *returned to die* See 1.1077n.

684-85]   *Tighetti . . . heir* The official document, "Instrument of Final Judgment" (OYB,E 252) declares "Domenico Tighetti as an heir beneficiary of the same Francesca Pompilia." Arcangeli, on the other hand, wrote, "But no man of sense could praise her testamentary disposition, in which she appointed as her sole heir her son, who, as I heard, was but just born and hence innocent, and who had been hidden away from his father, and which appointed as residuary legatee a stranger joined by no bond of relationship" (OYB,E 121).

693]   *innocency . . . wife* The Instrument of Final Judgment declared, "Proof is not established as regards the pretended adultery, and therefore the memory of the same Francesca Pompilia should be entirely restored" (OYB,E 254).

698]   *contrary* I.e., of innocency, 12.693 above.

699-707]   *Pompilia . . . sainted* The references are to the suit of the Convent of the Convertites for Pompilia's property after her death, and to the Fisc's role in prosecuting that claim; see *Chronology*. Though B emphasizes Bottini's duplicity in the two suits, it was actually his associate Gambi, Procurator of the Fisc, who represented the convent.

702]   *lapse* A legal term indicating the reversion of property to someone because of a failure of the original owner.

709]   *tongue . . . sword* A distortion of Hebrews 2:12, which reads, "For the word of God is quick and powerful, and sharper than any two edged sword, piercing even to the dividing asunder of joints and marrow, and is a discerner of the thoughts and intents of the heart."

710-11]   *axe . . . coast* A reference to the severe sentence of the Arezzo court and the more lenient one in Rome. See *Chronology*.

712]   *Astraea redux* See 2.1466n.

714]   *chop* He will change his position.

717]   *Florence . . . confirmative* The Sentence of the Criminal Court of Florence did pronounce as Bottini states on 15 February 1697. See OYB,E 5-7.

724]   *Noah's . . . back* See 12.471-78n.

725-27]   *sooty . . . carcasses* "And he sent forth a raven, which went forth to and fro, until the waters were dried up from off the earth" (Gen. 8:7). The rest of the sentence is Bottini's invention, based perhaps upon the fact that the raven is a scavenger related to the vulture and was considered unclean by the Jews.

732]   *How . . . dim* "How is the gold become dim! How is the most fine gold changed! The stones of this sanctuary are poured out into the top of every street" (Lam. 4:1).

734]   *clip away* Cut short. Also a pun, on top of Arcangeli's pun on "umbilicus"; see below 12.741-42.

736]   *hunks* Miserly, ungenerous person.

741]   *famous relic* See 12.184n.

743]   *Ad . . . est* Martial (c. 40-101), *Epigrammata* 4.89.1-2. "The umbilici of a book were two knobs at either end of a roller to which the parchment when filled with writing was attached. 'We have come to the umbilici' therefore means the book is finished" (Cook).

747]   *How . . . dim* see 12.732n.

747]   *send . . . piece* See 12.716-17.

749]   *Instrument* See 12.683, 693n.

752]   *Dated September* The sentence was actually rendered 19 August, 1698 (OYB,E 253).

754-64]   *In . . . Corso* A paraphrase of a portion of the original document. See 12.684-85n., 693n.

765-66]   *Marc . . . too* Judge Venturini, the Vice-governor, issued the judgment (12.754-64) in the name of the governor of Rome.

770]   *accession-day* A mistake. His accession day was 12 July 1691. He died 27 September 1700.

771]   *doubt . . . good* See 10.1849 ff.

771-74]   *doubt . . . Voltaire* Skeptic and gadfly to the church and to the ancien régime of his native France, Voltaire was born in 1694 (died 1778). He was imprisoned and exiled for his satires, and his persecution became the mark of both his *doubt* and his genius as a leading thinker of the Enlightenment.

778-85]   *Find . . . reverence* This reference to a document in the case not included in OYB indicates an early and confirmed interest in the materials of the poem, given the fact that composition did not begin until 1864 (see *Composition*). B found the book in June 1860, and his last visits to Arezzo were en route to Rome in the fall of that year, and the next spring in return to Florence. The quotation below at 12.796-803 is an accurate transcription of the original document in Arezzo.

781]   *Porzia* Guido's one sister.

783]   *Gonfalonier* Bearer of the banner (*gonfalon*) of the town; the mayor.

790]   *lying vanity* "I have hated them that regard lying vanities" (Ps. 31.6)..

792]   *bane* Deadly poison.

796-803]   *Since . . . to-day* See 12.778-85n.

804-5]   *annalist . . . bard* An annalist is a historian or record keeper, especially records of an antiquarian nature. The facetious contrast with *babble of a bard* glances at the truth-fancy theme elaborated at 1.451 ff. See also below 12.809-11 and n.

805]   *Petrarch . . . Buonarroti* The Italian lyric poet *Petrarch* was born in Arezzo in 1304, but his parents moved from the city when he was an infant. Michelangelo *Buonarroti* was born in 1475 near Chiusi, in the diocese of Arezzo, shortly before the family moved to Florence, where the child was nursed by a stonecutter's wife. As quoted by Vasari, who was from Arezzo, Michelangelo gave credit to both his early influences: "What good I have comes from the pure air of your native Arezzo, and also because I sucked in chisels and hammers with my nurse's milk" (Vasari, 4, 109).

809-11] *Patavinian . . . Face* Titus Livius (59 B.C.-A.D. 17) was born in *Patavium* (Padua) and is remembered for his exhaustive *History of Rome.* The *History* links accounts of contemporary wars and political events in the Roman Republic with the earliest myths of its founding, a combination B may have found "veracious" in a different sense than the literal, a sense more similar to his own treatment of history in *The Ring and the Book. Janus,* the god represented as having two faces, one looking back and one forward, was the god of beginnings and endings. There is no myth of the founding of Arezzo by Janus, nor does Livy mention one, and it is uncertain why B makes the connection. Janus is appropriate, on the other hand, to the final pages of a poem whose central symbol is a ring and whose theme invokes temporal circularity.

817-20] *Which . . . slips* For a full description of the coat of arms see Vol. VII 257.

824] *Star Wormwood* See 12.12n.

831] *British . . . yet* See 1.405n.

832] *Marry* An exclamation; a colloquial spelling of the name of the Virgin Mary.

842-43] *eye . . . length* "They have mouths but speak not: eyes have they, but see not: they have ears but they hear not" (Ps. 115:5-6). The ears are the ears of an ass in length—and in understanding.

845] *troll* To move nimbly, to wag.

857] *missing the mediate* "Though the intermediary words be missing." Adding alliteration to the MS reading, B also apparently reversed the original phrase "by the immediate"; see variants. The sense of the revision seems to be, "Art can tell the truth even without words, i.e. through painting and music."

866-68] *Render . . . thine* A guard-ring is one worn above another ring, expecially a wedding ring, to protect it. See 1.1-24n. for a brief history and description of the two rings referred to here. Although B wore his ring on the little finger of his right hand, in size it could easily encompass EBB's. B wrote of his wife's ring, "Can you fancy that tiny finger? Can you believe that a woman could wear such a circle as this? It is a child's" (Katharine de Kay Bronson, "Browning in Venice," *The*

Cornhill Magazine, NS 12 [1902], 152). *Guardianship* has resonances beyond the literal in the poem and in B's life: it echoes the inscription "Vis Mea" (see 12.10n.) on B's ring and the invocation that B wrote in OYB to "the Muse in her strength" (see *Composition*), and also the first real poem written by B after his marriage, "The Guardian Angel," which is about Elizabeth (see Irvine and Honan 250-60). It is perhaps significant that B has here asserted to himself the guiding, guarding function that the earlier poem conferred on EBB: the tribute to her is also a signal that "RB a poem." is complete (see *Composition*). *Lyric Love:* see 1.1383 and n.

869-70]   *The . . . Italy* On a tablet above the entrance to Casa Guidi is inscribed a tribute to EBB by the Italian poet Nicolo Tommasei in which he says she "made of her verse a golden ring linking Italy with England."